HYMNS
for
WORSHIP

HYMNS
for
WORSHIP

BETHEL PUBLISHING
COMPANY
1819 South Main
Elkhart, Indiana

Grateful acknowledgment is made to individuals and publishers who have kindly granted permission for the use of their copyrighted hymns in this volume. The compilers have attempted to ascertain the copyright status of every selection included. If there are instances where proper credit is not given, the publisher will gladly make necessary corrections in subsequent printings.

fourth printing

CONTENTS

PREFACE

Hymns for Worship is designed to serve the large community of evangelical Christians who wish to enhance their worship, public and private, through musical interpretation of the glorious truths of the Gospel. It includes selections from former centuries as well as the best hymns and Gospel songs of the present age. Its comprehensive quality provides maximum versatility in any type of service. The wide variety of material should reduce the need for additional sources to a minimum.

The primary consideration in the choice of each hymn was its potential as an aid to Christian faith and practice. Care was exercised to include songs of singable quality and with significant textual content. Editing has brought the range of tunes within the requirements for average congregational singing. Emphasis has been kept on the value of singing as a means to worship rather than as a demonstration of talent. Simplicity and sincerity, with integrity to Biblical teaching, have been regarded as guide-posts to reverence and worship.

Hymns for Worship is planned with the conviction that the type of music used will largely determine the spiritual level to which a church will attain. Accordingly, the hymnal covers a broad range of doctrinal teaching which will contribute to balanced maturity in Christian faith.

A glance at the Table of Contents will reveal the plan of *Hymns for Worship*. Selections are provided in suitable proportions in each topical category. Complete indexes, conveniently placed, make the contents readily available for many purposes. Scripture readings are provided in a wide variety of subjects and are especially arranged to afford maximum inspiration from oral reading of the Word.

Hymns for Worship is commended to individuals, families, and churches for use whenever Christians have occasion to worship in song. A reverent use of this hymnal will promote unity of faith, extend the Gospel call to the unchurched, and challenge Christians to full commitment to our Lord and Saviour Jesus Christ.

Earl D. Miller, *Editor*

Raymond G. Niesley, *Chairman*   Jesse R. Steckley
Ray M. Zercher, *Secretary*   Ray Swalm
Ralph Carpenter   Erwin W. Thomas
Emerson C. Frey   Myron L. Tweed
Franklin L. Lusk   LeRoy B. Walters
H. Royce Saltzman   Ira L. Wood
Ronald R. Sider   John E. Zercher

—Hymnal Committee

Let the word of Christ dwell in you richly in all wisdom; teaching and admonishing one another in psalms and hymns and spiritual songs, singing with grace in your hearts to the Lord.

Colossians 3:16

HYMNS for WORSHIP

O Worship the King
LYONS 10.10.11.11.

1

Sir Robert Grant, 1785-1838

J. Michael Haydn, 1737-1806

1. O wor - ship the King, all glo - rious a - bove,
2. O tell of His might, O sing of His grace,
3. Thy boun - ti - ful care what tongue can re - cite?
4. Frail chil - dren of dust, and fee - ble as frail,

O grate - ful - ly sing His power and His love;
Whose robe is the light, whose can - o - py space;
It breathes in the air, it shines in the light;
In Thee do we trust, nor find Thee to fail;

Our Shield and De - fen - der, the An - cient of Days,
His char - iots of wrath the deep thun - der - clouds form,
It streams from the hills, it de - scends to the plain.
Thy mer - cies how ten - der, how firm to the end,

Pa - vil - ioned in splen-dor, and gird - ed with praise.
And dark is His path on the wings of the storm.
And sweet-ly dis - tils in the dew and the rain.
Our Mak - er, De - fend - er, Re - deem - er, and Friend. A - men.

2 Praise the Lord, His Glories Show

LLANFAIR 7. 7. 7. 7. with Alleluias

Henry Francis Lyte, 1793-1847   Robert Williams, 1781-1821

1. Praise the Lord, His glo - ries show, Al - le - lu - ia!
2. Earth to heaven, and heaven to earth, Al - le - lu - ia!
3. Praise the Lord, His mer - cies trace, Al - le - lu - ia!

Saints with - in His courts be - low, Al - le - lu - ia!
Tell His won - ders, sing His worth, Al - le - lu - ia!
Praise His prov - i - dence and grace, Al - le - lu - ia!

An - gels round His throne a - bove, Al - le - lu - ia!
Age to age and shore to shore, Al - le - lu - ia!
All that He for man hath done, Al - le - lu - ia!

All that see and share His love. Al - le - lu - ia!
Praise Him, praise Him ev - er - more! Al - le - lu - ia!
All He sends us through His Son. Al - le - lu - ia! A - men.

All Creatures of Our God and King   3

LASST UNS ERFREUEN 8.8.4.4.8.8. with Alleluias

St. Francis of Assisi, 1182-1226
Trans. by William H. Draper, 1855-1933

Melody from *Geistliche Kirchengesäng*, 1623

1. All crea - tures of our God and King, Lift up your voice and with us
2. Thou rush-ing wind that art so strong, Ye clouds that sail in heaven a -
3. Thou flow-ing wa - ter, pure and clear, Make mu - sic for thy Lord to
4. Dear moth-er earth, who day by day Un - fold-est bless-ings on our
5. And all ye men of ten - der heart, For - giv-ing oth - ers, take your
6. Let all things their Cre-a - tor bless, And wor-ship Him in hum-ble-

sing Al-le-lu - ia! Al-le-lu - ia! Thou burn-ing sun with
long, O praise Him! Al-le-lu - ia! Thou ris - ing morn, in
hear, Al-le-lu - ia! Al-le-lu - ia! Thou fire so mas - ter-
way, O praise Him! Al-le-lu - ia! The flowers and fruits that
part, O sing ye! Al-le-lu - ia! Ye who long pain and
ness, O praise Him! Al-le-lu - ia! Praise, praise the Fa - ther,

gold-en beam, Thou sil - ver moon with soft-er gleam! O praise Him
praise re - joice, Ye lights of eve-ning, find a voice! O praise Him
ful and bright, Thou giv-est man both warmth and light! O praise Him
in thee grow, Let them His glo-ry al - so show! O praise Him
sor - row bear, Praise God and on Him cast your care! O praise Him
praise the Son, And praise the Spir-it, Three in One! O praise Him

Al-le-lu - ia

O praise Him! Al-le-lu - ia! Al-le-lu - ia! Al-le-lu - ia! A-men.

4 Praise the Lord: Ye Heavens, Adore Him

FABEN 8.7.8.7. D.

Stanza 1 & 2 *Foundling Hospital Collection*, 1796
Stanza 3 Edward Osler, 1798-1863

John H. Willcox, 1827-1875

1. Praise the Lord, ye heavens, a-dore Him; Praise Him, an-gels, in the height;
2. Praise the Lord, for He is glo-rious; Nev-er shall His prom-ise fail:
3. Wor-ship, hon-or, glo-ry, bless-ing, Lord, we of-fer un-to Thee;

Sun and moon, re-joice be-fore Him; Praise Him, all ye stars of light.
God hath made His saints vic-to-rious; Sin and death shall not pre-vail.
Young and old, Thy praise ex-press-ing, In glad hom-age bend the knee.

Praise the Lord, for He hath spo-ken; Worlds His might-y voice o-beyed:
Praise the God of our sal-va-tion; Hosts on high, His power pro-claim;
All the saints in heaven a-dore Thee; We would bow be-fore Thy throne:

Laws which nev-er shall be bro-ken For their guid-ance He hath made.
Heaven and earth and all cre-a-tion, Laud and mag-ni-fy His Name.
As Thine an-gels serve be-fore Thee, So on earth Thy will be done. A-men.

Lord of All Being
LOUVAN 8.8.8.8.

Oliver Wendell Holmes, 1808-1894

Virgil C. Taylor, 1817-1891

1. Lord of all be-ing, throned a-far, Thy glo-ry flames from sun and star;
2. Sun of our life, Thy quick-ening ray Sheds on our path the glow of day;
3. Our mid-night is Thy smile with-drawn; Our noon-tide is Thy gra-cious dawn;
4. Grant us Thy truth to make us free, And kind-ling hearts that burn for Thee;

Cen-ter and soul of ev-ery sphere, Yet to each lov-ing heart how near!
Star of our hope, Thy soft-ened light Cheers the long watch-es of the night.
Our rain-bow arch, Thy mer-cy's sign; All, save the clouds of sin, are Thine.
Till all Thy liv-ing al-tars claim One ho-ly light, one heaven-ly flame. A-men.

Let Us with a Gladsome Mind
MONKLAND 7.7.7.7.

From Psalm 156
John Milton, 1608-1674; alt.

Moravian Melody
John B. Wilkes, 1785-1869

1. Let us, with a glad-some mind, Praise the Lord, for He is kind:
2. Let us sound His name a-broad, For of gods He is the God:
3. He, with all-com-mand-ing might, Filled the new-made world with light:
4. All things liv-ing He doth feed; His full hand sup-plies their need:
5. Let us then with glad-some mind Praise the Lord, for He is kind:

For His mer-cies shall en-dure, Ev-er faith-ful, ev-er sure. A-men.

7 I Sing the Mighty Power of God

ELLACOMBE 8.6.8.6.D.

Isaac Watts, 1674-1748
Third Stanza Alt.

Gesangbuch der Herzogl., 1784

1. I sing the might-y power of God, That made the moun-tains rise;
2. I sing the good-ness of the Lord, That filled the earth with food;
3. There's not a plant or flower be-low, But makes Thy glo-ries known;

That spread the flow-ing seas a-broad, And built the loft-y skies.
He formed the crea-tures with His word, And then pro-nounced them good.
And clouds a-rise, and tem-pests blow, By or-der from Thy throne;

I sing the wis-dom that or-dained The sun to rule the day;
Lord, how Thy won-ders are dis-played, Wher-e'er I turn my eye:
While all that bor-rows life from Thee Is ev-er in Thy care,

The moon shines full at His com-mand, And all the stars o-bey.
If I sur-vey the ground I tread, Or gaze up-on the sky!
And ev-ery-where that man can be, Thou, God, art pres-ent there. A-men.

Sing Praise to God Who Reigns Above 8

Johann J. Schütz, 1640-1690
Trans. by Frances E. Cox, 1812-1897

MIT FREUDEN ZART 8.7.8.7.8.8.7.

From the Bohemian Brethren's
Gesangbuch, 1566

In unison

1. Sing praise to God who reigns a-bove, The God of all cre - a - tion,
2. What God's al-might-y power hath made, His gra-cious mer-cy keep - eth;
3. The Lord is nev-er far a-way, But, through all grief dis - tress - ing,
4. Thus, all my toil-some way a-long, I sing a-loud Thy prais - es,

The God of power, the God of love, The God of our sal -
By morn-ing glow or eve-ning shade His watch-ful eye ne'er
An ev-er-pres-ent help and stay, Our peace, and joy, and
That men may hear the grate-ful song My voice un-wea - ried

va - tion; With heal-ing balm my soul He fills, And ev-ery faith-less
sleep - eth; With-in the king-dom of His might, Lo, all is just and
bless - ing; As with a moth-er's ten-der hand, He leads His own, His
rais - es; Be joy-ful in the Lord, my heart, Both soul and bod - y

mur-mur stills: To God all praise and glo - ry.
all is right: To God all praise and glo - ry.
cho - sen band: To God all praise and glo - ry.
bear your part: To God all praise and glo - ry. A - men.

9 Arise, and Bless the Lord

ST. THOMAS 6.6.8.6.

James Montgomery, 1771-1854
Alt: J. H. Thompson, 1858

Aaron Williams, 1731-1776

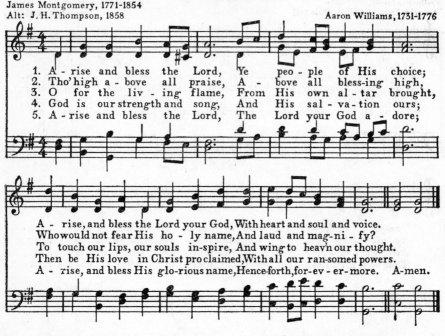

1. A - rise and bless the Lord, Ye peo - ple of His choice;
2. Tho' high a - bove all praise, A - bove all bless-ing high,
3. O for the liv - ing flame, From His own al - tar brought,
4. God is our strength and song, And His sal - va - tion ours;
5. A - rise and bless the Lord, The Lord your God a - dore;

A - rise, and bless the Lord your God, With heart and soul and voice.
Who would not fear His ho - ly name, And laud and mag-ni - fy?
To touch our lips, our souls in-spire, And wing to heav'n our thought.
Then be His love in Christ pro claimed, With all our ran-somed powers.
A - rise, and bless His glo-rious name, Hence-forth, for-ev - er-more. A-men.

10 Begin, My Tongue, Some Heavenly Theme

MANOAH 8.6.8.6.

Isaac Watts, 1674-1748

Henry W. Greatorex's "Collection," 1851

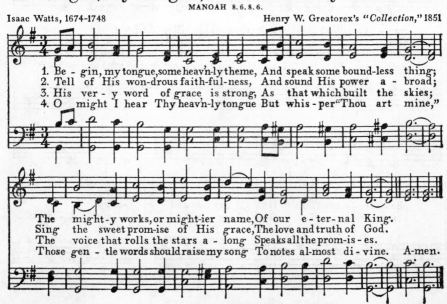

1. Be - gin, my tongue, some heav'n-ly theme, And speak some bound-less thing;
2. Tell of His won-drous faith-ful-ness, And sound His power a - broad;
3. His ver - y word of grace is strong, As that which built the skies;
4. O might I hear Thy heav'n-ly tongue But whis-per "Thou art mine,"

The might-y works, or might-ier name, Of our e - ter-nal King.
Sing the sweet prom-ise of His grace, The love and truth of God.
The voice that rolls the stars a - long Speaks all the prom-is - es.
Those gen - tle words should raise my song To notes al-most di - vine. A-men.

Praise, My Soul, the King of Heaven 11

BENEDIC ANIMA MEA 8.7. 8.7. 8.7.

From Psalm 103
Henry F. Lyte, 1793-1847

John Goss, 1800-1880

1. Praise, my soul, the King of heav - en, To His feet thy
2. Praise Him for His grace and fa - vor To our fa - thers
3. Fa - ther-like, He tends and spares us; Well our fee - ble
4. An - gels, help us to a - dore Him, Ye be - hold Him

trib - ute bring; Ran-somed, healed, re-stored, for - giv - en,
in dis - tress; Praise Him, still the same for - ev - er,
frame He knows, In His hands He gen - tly bears us,
face to face; Sun and moon, bow down be - fore Him;

Who like me, His praise should sing? Al - le - lu - ia!
Slow to chide, and swift to bless. Al - le - lu - ia!
Res - cues us from all our foes. Al - le - lu - ia!
Dwell - ers all in time and space, Al - le - lu - ia!

Al - le - lu - ia! Praise the ev - er - last - ing King!
Al - le - lu - ia! Glo - rious in His faith-ful - ness!
Al - le - lu - ia! Wide - ly as His mer - cy flows!
Al - le - lu - ia! Praise with us the God of grace! A - men.

12 Now Thank We All Our God

NUN DANKET 6. 7. 6. 7. 6. 6. 6. 6.

Martin Rinkart, 1586-1649
Trans. by Catherine Winkworth, 1829-1878

Johann Crüger, 1598-1662
Harmonized by Felix Mendelssohn, 1809-1847

1. Now thank we all our God With heart and hands and voi-ces,
2. O may this boun-teous God Through all our life be near us,
3. All praise and thanks to God The Fa-ther now be giv-en,

Who won-drous things hath done, In whom His world re- joi- ces;
With ev-er joy-ful hearts And bless-ed peace to cheer us;
The Son, and Him who reigns With Them in high-est heav- en,

Who, from our moth-ers' arms, Hath blessed us on our way
And keep us in His grace, And guide us when per- plexed,
The one e-ter-nal God, Whom earth and heaven a - dore;

With count-less gifts of love, And still is ours to - day.
And free us from all ills In this world and the next.
For thus it was, is now, And shall be ev-er-more. A-men.

A Mighty Fortress Is Our God

EIN FESTE BURG 8.7.8.7.6.6.6.6.7.

13

Martin Luther, 1483-1546
Trans. by Frederick H. Hedge, 1805-1890

Martin Luther, 1483-1546

1. A might-y for-tress is our God, A bul-wark nev-er fail - ing;
2. Did we in our own strength con-fide, Our striv-ing would be los - ing;
3. And though this world, with dev - ils filled, Should threat-en to un - do us;
4. That word a - bove all earth - ly powers, No thanks to them, a - bid - eth;

Our help-er He, a - mid the flood Of mor-tal ills pre - vail - ing:
Were not the right Man on our side, The Man of God's own choos - ing:
We will not fear, for God hath willed His truth to tri-umph through us:
The Spir-it and the gifts are ours Through Him who with us sid - eth:

For still our an - cient foe Doth seek to work us woe; His craft and power are
Dost ask who that may be? Christ Je-sus, it is He; Lord Sa - ba - oth, His
The Prince of Dark-ness grim We trem-ble not for him; His rage we can en -
Let goods and kin-dred go, This mor-tal life al - so; The bod - y they may

great, And, armed with cru - el hate, On earth is not his e - qual.
name, From age to age the same, And He must win the bat - tle.
dure, For lo! his doom is sure; One lit - tle word shall fell him.
kill: God's truth a - bid - eth still; His king-dom is for - ev - er. A-men.

14 Praise to the Lord, the Almighty

LOBE DEN HERREN 14.14.4.7.8.

Joachim Neander, 1650-1680

Trans. by Catherine Winkworth, 1829-1878

From *Praxis Pietatis Melica*, 1668

1. Praise to the Lord, the Al-might-y, the King of cre - a - tion!
2. Praise to the Lord, who o'er all things so won-drous-ly reign - eth,
3. Praise to the Lord, who doth pros-per thy work and de - fend thee;

O my soul, praise Him, for He is thy health and sal - va - tion!
Shield-eth thee un-der His wings, yea, so gen-tly sus - tain - eth.
Sure - ly His good-ness and mer-cy here dai - ly at - tend thee.

All ye who hear, Now to His tem - ple draw near;
Hast thou not seen How thy de - sires e'er have been
Pon - der a - new What the Al might-y can do,

Join me in glad ad - o - ra - tion!
Grant - ed in what He or - dain - eth?
If with His love He be - friend thee. A - men.

Bless, O My Soul, the Living God 15

ROCKINGHAM OLD 8. 8. 8. 8

Isaac Watts, 1674-1748

Edward Miller, 1731-1807

1. Bless, O my soul, the liv-ing God; Call home thy tho'ts that rove a-broad;
2. Bless, O my soul, the God of grace; His fa-vors claim thy high-est praise;
3. 'Tis He, my soul, that sent His Son To die for crimes which thou hast done;
4. Let ev-ery land His power con-fess, Let all the earth a-dore His grace;

Let all the powers with-in me join In work and wor-ship so di-vine.
Why should the won-ders He hath wrought Be lost in si-lence, and for-got?
He owns the ran-som, and for-gives The hour-ly fol-lies of our lives.
My heart and tongue with rap-ture join In work and wor-ship so di-vine. A-men

Now God Be Praised 16

GELOBT SEI GOTT 8.8.8. with Alleluias

H.W.F.-Edited by A.T.D.

Melchior Volpius 1560-1616

1. Now God be praised in heav'n a-bove, Prais-ed be He for His great love,
2. Praise Him yet more for con-qu'ring faith, Which fear-eth nei-ther pain nor death,
3. His grace de-fends us from all ill; His Christ shall be our lead-er still,

Where-in all creatures live and move, Al-le-lu-ia! ____ Al-le-lu-ia! ____ Al-le-lu-ia!
But trust-ing God, re-joic-ing saith, Al-le-lu-ia! ____ Al-le-lu-ia! ____ Al-le-lu-ia!
Till heav'n and earth shall do His will; Al-le-lu-ia! ____ Al-le-lu-ia! ____ Al-le-lu-ia!

17 Joyful, Joyful, We Adore Thee

HYMN TO JOY 8.7.8.7.D.

Henry Van Dyke, 1852-1933

Ludwig von Beethoven, 1770-1827

1. Joy - ful, joy - ful, we a - dore Thee, God of glo - ry, Lord of love;
2. All Thy works with joy sur-round Thee, Earth and heaven re-flect Thy rays,
3. Thou art giv - ing and for - giv - ing, Ev - er bless - ing, ev - er blest,
4. Mor - tals, join the hap - py cho - rus Which the morn-ing stars be-gan;

Hearts un-fold like flowers be-fore Thee, Open-ing to the sun a-bove.
Stars and an-gels sing a-round Thee, Cen - ter of un-bro-ken praise.
Well-spring of the joy of liv - ing, O - cean depth of hap - py rest!
Fa - ther love is reign-ing o'er us, Broth-er love binds man to man.

Melt the clouds of sin and sad-ness, Drive the dark of doubt a - way;
Field and for - est, vale and moun-tain, Flow-ery mead-ow, flash-ing sea,
Thou our Fa - ther, Christ our Broth-er, All who live in love are Thine;
Ev - er sing-ing, march we on-ward, Vic - tors in the midst of strife,

Giv - er of im-mor-tal glad-ness, Fill us with the light of day.
Chant-ing bird and flow-ing foun-tain, Call us to re - joice in Thee.
Teach us how to love each oth - er, Lift us to the Joy di-vine.
Joy - ful mu - sic leads us sun-ward In the tri-umph song of life. A-men.

To God Be the Glory

TO GOD BE THE GLORY 11.11.11.11. with Refrain

Fanny J. Crosby, 1820-1915

William H. Doane, 1832-1915

1. To God be the glo-ry, great things He hath done, So loved He the world that He
2. O per-fect re-demp-tion, the pur-chase of blood, To ev-ery be-liev-er the
3. Great things He hath taught us, great things He hath done, And great our re-joic-ing thro'

gave us His Son, Who yield-ed His life an a-tone-ment for sin, And o-pened the
prom-ise of God; The vil-est of-fen-der who tru-ly be-lieves, That moment from
Je-sus the Son; But pu-rer, and high-er, and great-er will be Our won-der, our

life-gate that all may go in.
Je-sus a par-don re-ceives. Praise the Lord, praise the Lord, Let the earth hear His
trans-port, when Je-sus we see.

voice! Praise the Lord, praise the Lord, Let the peo-ple re-joice! O come to the

Fa-ther thro' Je-sus the Son, And give Him the glo-ry, great things He hath done.

19 The God of Abraham Praise

LEONI (YIGDAL) 6.6.8.4.D.

Daniel Ben Judah, 14th cent.
Revised Version of the Yigdal
By Thomas Olivers, 1725-1799

Arr. from a Hebrew Melody
Meyer Leoni-1797

1. The God of Abra-ham praise, All prais-ed be His name,
2. His spir-it flow-eth free, High surg-ing where it will:
3. He hath e-ter-nal life Im-plant-ed in the soul;

Who was, and is, and is to be, And still the same!
In proph-et's word He spoke of old—He speak-eth still.
His love shall be our strength and stay, While a-ges roll.

The one e-ter-nal God, Ere aught that now ap-pears;
Es-tab-lished is His law, And change-less it shall stand,
Praise to the liv-ing God! All prais-ed be His name

The First, the Last: be-yond all thought His time-less years!
Deep writ up-on the hu-man heart, On sea, or land.
Who was, and is, and is to be, And still the same! A-men.

Thee, Holy Father, We Adore

20

LASST UNS ERFREUEN 8.8.4.4.8.8. with Alleluias

Calvin W. Laufer, 1874-1938

Geistliche Kirchengesäng, Cologne, 1623

In unison

1. Thee, ho-ly Fa-ther, we a-dore; We sing Thy prais-es o'er and o'er:
2. Thou fill-est heaven and earth and sea With sov'reign power and maj-es-ty:
3. Our souls on wings of rap-ture rise To swell the choirs of Par-a-dise:

Harmony — *Unison*

Al-le-lu-ia, Al-le-lu-ia! With ser-aph throngs join heart and voice,
Al-le-lu-ia, Al-le-lu-ia! Yet where the poor in spir-it meet,
Al-le-lu-ia, Al-le-lu-ia! Enthralled and thrilled, we Thee a-dore,

Harmony

Ac-claim Thy glo-ry, and re-joice: Al-le-lu-ia, Al-le-
There is Thy bless-ed mer-cy seat: Al-le-lu-ia, Al-le-
Who art our God for-ev-er-more. Al-le-lu-ia, Al-le-

Unison

lu-ia, Al-le-lu-ia, Al-le-lu-ia, Al-le-lu-ia!
lu-ia, Al-le-lu-ia, Al-le-lu-ia, Al-le-lu-ia!
lu-ia, Al-le-lu-ia, Al-le-lu-ia, Al-le-lu-ia! A-men.

21 From All That Dwell

DUKE STREET 8.8.8.8.

Stanzas 1,4
Isaac Watts, 1674-1748
Stanzas 2,3, Anonymous

John Hatton, d. 1793

1. From all that dwell below the skies, Let the Cre-
a - tor's praise a - rise; Let the Re - deem - er's name be.
sung, Through ev-ery land, by ev - ery tongue.

2. E - ter-nal are Thy mer - cies, Lord; E - ter-nal
truth at - tends Thy word; Thy praise shall sound from shore to
shore, Till suns shall rise and set no more.

3. Your loft-y themes, ye mor-tals, bring; In songs of
praise di - vine-ly sing; The great sal-va - tion loud pro-
claim, And shout for joy the Sav-iour's name.

4. In ev-ery land be - gin the song; To ev-ery
land the strains be-long; In cheer-ful sounds all voic-es
raise, And fill the world with loud-est praise. A - men.

22 To Thee, My Heart, Eternal King

GERMANY 8.8.8.8.

Exeter Coll.

William Gardiner's *Sacred Melodies*, 1815

1. To Thee, my heart, e - ter - nal King, Would now its thank-ful trib - ute bring;
2. All na-ture shows Thy bound-less love, In worlds be-low and worlds a-bove;
3. Here what de-light-ful truths are giv'n, Here Je-sus shows the way to heav'n;
4. For love like this, O may our song, Thro' end-less years Thy praise pro-long;

To Thee its hum-ble hom-age raise In songs of ar-dent, grate-ful praise.
But in Thy bless-ed word I trace The rich-er glo-ries of Thy grace.
His name sa - lutes my list'ning ear, Re-vives my heart, and checks my fear.
And dis-tant climes Thy name a-dore, Till time and na-ture are no more. A-men.

The Lord Is King
CREATION 8. 8. 8. 8.

Josiah Conder, 1789-1855   Arr. from F. Joseph Haydn, 1732-1809

1. The Lord is King! lift up your voice, O earth; and
2. The Lord is King! who then shall dare Re - sist His
3. The Lord is King! Child of the dust, The Judge of
4. One Lord, one em - pire, all se - cures; He reigns, and

all ye heavens re - joice: From world to world the
will, dis - trust His care, Or mur - mur at His
all the earth is just; Ho - ly and true are
life and death are yours: Through earth and heaven one

joy shall ring, "The Lord Om-nip - o-tent is King!"
wise de-crees, Or doubt His roy - al prom - is - es?
all His ways: Let ev - ery crea - ture speak His praise.
song shall ring, "The Lord Om-nip - o-tent is King!" A - men.

23

24 When All Thy Mercies, O My God

ST. PETER 8. 6. 8. 6.

Joseph Addison, 1672-1719

Alexander Reinagle, 1799-1877

1. When all Thy mer - cies, O my God, My ris - ing soul sur - veys,
2. Un - num - bered com - forts to my soul Thy ten - der care be - stowed,
3. Ten thou-sand thou-sand pre - cious gifts My dai - ly thanks em - ploy;
4. Through all e - ter - ni - ty, to Thee A joy - ful song I'll raise;

Trans - port - ed with the view, I'm lost In won-der, love, and praise.
Be - fore my in-fant heart con-ceived From whom those comforts flowed.
Nor is the least a cheer-ful heart That tastes those gifts with joy.
But O e-ter-ni-ty's too short To ut - ter all Thy praise! A-men.

25 Majestic Sweetness Sits Enthroned

ORTONVILLE 8,6,8,6.

Samuel Stennett, 1727-1795

Thomas Hastings, 1784-1872

1. Ma - jes - tic sweetness sits enthroned Up-on the Sav-iour's brow; His head with ra-diant
2. He saw me plunged in deep distress, And flew to my re - lief; For me He bore the
3. To Him I owe my life and breath, And all the joys I have; He makes me tri-umph
4. To heav'n, the place of His a-bode, He brings my weary feet, Shows me the glo-ries
5. Since from His boun-ty I re-ceive Such proofs of love di - vine, Had I a thousand

glo-ries crowned, His lips with grace o'er-flow, His lips with grace o'er-flow.
shameful cross, And carried all my grief, And car-ried all my grief.
o - ver death: He saves me from the grave, He saves me from the grave.
of my God, And makes my joys com-plete, And makes my joys com-plete.
hearts to give, Lord, they should all be Thine, Lord, they should all be Thine. A-men.

Ye Servants of God, Your Master Proclaim 26

HANOVER 10.10.11.11.

Charles Wesley, 1707-1788   William Croft, 1678-1727

1. Ye ser - vants of God, your Mas - ter pro - claim,
2. God rul - eth on high, al - might - y to save;
3. Sal - va - tion to God, who sits on the throne!
4. Then let us a - dore, and give Him His right,

And pub - lish a - broad His won - der - ful name;
And still He is nigh, His pres - ence we have;
Let all cry a - loud, and hon - or the Son;
All glo - ry and power, all wis - dom and might,

The name all vic - to - rious of Je - sus ex - tol;
The great con - gre - ga - tion His tri - umph shall sing,
The prais - es of Je - sus the an - gels pro - claim,
All hon - or and bless - ing, with an - gels a - bove,

His king - dom is glo - rious, He rules o - ver all.
As - crib - ing sal - va - tion to Je - sus our King.
Fall down on their fac - es, and wor - ship the Lamb.
And thanks nev - er ceas - ing for in - fi - nite love. A - men.

27 Crown Him with Many Crowns

DIADEMATA 6.6.8.6.D.

Matthew Bridges, 1800-1894
Godfrey Thring, 1823-1903

George J. Elvey, 1816-1893

1. Crown Him with man-y crowns, The Lamb up-on His throne;
2. Crown Him the Son of God Be-fore the worlds be-gan,
3. Crown Him the Lord of life, Who tri-umphed o'er the grave,
4. Crown Him the Lord of love; Be-hold His hands and side,

Hark! how the heaven-ly an-them drowns All mu-sic but its own!
And ye, who tread where He hath trod, Crown Him the Son of man;
And rose vic-to-rious in the strife For those He came to save;
Those wounds, yet vis-i-ble a-bove, In beau-ty glo-ri-fied:

A-wake, my soul, and sing Of Him who died for thee,
Who ev-ery grief hath known That wrings the hu-man breast,
His glo-ries now we sing Who died, and rose on high,
All hail, Re-deem-er, hail! For Thou hast died for me:

And hail Him as thy match-less King Through all e-ter-ni-ty.
And takes and bears them for His own, That all in Him may rest.
Who died, e-ter-nal life to bring, And lives that death may die.
Thy praise shall nev-er, nev-er fail Throughout e-ter-ni-ty. A-men.

Blessing and Honor and Glory and Power 28

O QUANTA QUALIA 10. 10. 10. 10.

Horatius Bonar, 1808-1889   Le Feillee's *Methode du plain-chant*, 1808

1. Bless - ing and hon - or and glo - ry and power,
2. Sound - eth the heav'n of the heav'ns with His name;
3. Ev - er as - cend - eth the song and the joy;
4. Give we the glo - ry and praise to the Lamb;

Wis - dom and rich - es and strength ev - er - more
Ring - eth the earth with His glo - ry and fame;
Ev - er de - scend - eth the love from on high;
Take we the robe and the harp and the palm;

Give ye to Him who our bat - tle hath won,
O - cean and moun - tain, stream, for - est, and flower
Bless - ing and hon - or and glo - ry and praise —
Sing we the song of the Lamb that was slain,

Whose are the King - dom, the crown, and the throne.
Ech - o His prais - es and tell of His power.
This is the theme of the hymns that we raise.
Dy - ing in weak - ness, but ris - ing to reign.

29 Jesus, My Lord, My Life, My All

ST. CHRYSOSTOM (Barnby) 8.8.8.8.8.8.

Henry Collins, 1827-1919
Stanza 1, line 1, and Refrain alt.

Joseph Barnby, 1838-1896

1. Je - sus, my Lord, my Life, my All, Hear me, blest Sav - iour,
2. Je - sus, too late I Thee have sought; How can I love Thee
3. Je - sus, what didst thou find in me, That Thou hast dealt so
4. Je - sus, of Thee shall be my song, To Thee my heart and

when I call; Hear me, and from Thy dwell - ing place
as I ought? And how ex - tol Thy match - less fame,
lov - ing - ly? How great the joy that Thou hast brought,
soul be - long; All that I have or am is Thine,

Pour down the rich - es of Thy grace. Je - sus, my Lord, I
The glo - rious beau - ty of Thy name? Je - sus, my Lord, I
So far ex - ceed - ing hope or thought. Je - sus, my Lord, I
And Thou, blest Sav - iour, Thou art mine. Je - sus, my Lord, I

Thee a - dore; O may I love Thee more and more. A - men.

Rejoice, the Lord Is King

DARWALL 6.6.6.6.8.8.

30

Charles Wesley, 1707-1788

John Darwall, 1731-1789

1. Re - joice, the Lord is King: Your Lord and King a - dore!
2. His King-dom can-not fail, He rules o'er earth and heaven;
3. He all His foes shall quell, Shall all our sins de - stroy,

Re - joice, give thanks, and sing, And tri - umph
The keys of death and hell Are to our
And ev - ery bos - om swell With pure se -

ev - er - more: Lift up your heart, lift up your voice!
Je - sus given: Lift up your heart, lift up your voice!
raph-ic joy: Lift up your heart, lift up your voice!

Re - joice, a - gain I say, re - joice!
Re - joice, a - gain I say, re - joice!
Re - joice, a - gain I say, re - joice! A - men.

31 Hark, Ten Thousand Harps and Voices

HARWELL 8.7.8.7.7.7. with Alleluias

Thomas Kelly, 1769-1854

Lowell Mason, 1792-1872

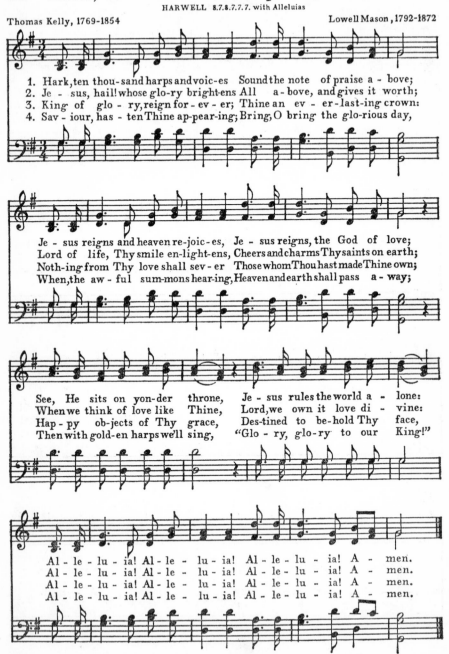

1. Hark, ten thou-sand harps and voic-es Sound the note of praise a-bove;
2. Je - sus, hail! whose glo-ry bright-ens All a-bove, and gives it worth;
3. King of glo - ry, reign for-ev - er; Thine an ev - er-last-ing crown:
4. Sav - iour, has - ten Thine ap-pear-ing; Bring, O bring the glo-rious day,

Je - sus reigns and heaven re-joic-es, Je - sus reigns, the God of love;
Lord of life, Thy smile en-light-ens, Cheers and charms Thy saints on earth;
Noth-ing from Thy love shall sev - er Those whom Thou hast made Thine own;
When, the aw - ful sum-mons hear-ing, Heaven and earth shall pass a - way;

See, He sits on yon-der throne, Je - sus rules the world a - lone:
When we think of love like Thine, Lord, we own it love di - vine:
Hap - py ob-jects of Thy grace, Des-tined to be-hold Thy face,
Then with gold-en harps we'll sing, "Glo - ry, glo-ry to our King!"

Al - le - lu - ia! Al - le - lu - ia! Al - le - lu - ia! A - men.
Al - le - lu - ia! Al - le - lu - ia! Al - le - lu - ia! A - men.
Al - le - lu - ia! Al - le - lu - ia! Al - le - lu - ia! A - men.
Al - le - lu - ia! Al - le - lu - ia! Al - le - lu - ia! A - men.

Come, Christians, Join to Sing

32

MADRID 6.6.6.6.D.

Christian H. Bateman, 1813-1889

Source Unknown

Harmonized by David Evans, 1874-1948

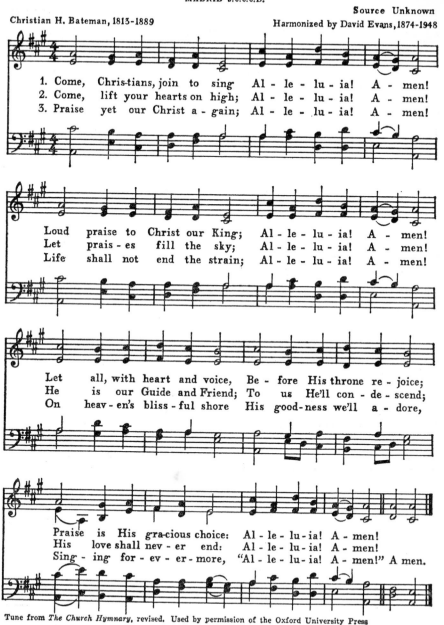

1. Come, Christians, join to sing Al - le - lu - ia! A - men!
2. Come, lift your hearts on high; Al - le - lu - ia! A - men!
3. Praise yet our Christ a - gain; Al - le - lu - ia! A - men!

Loud praise to Christ our King; Al - le - lu - ia! A - men!
Let prais - es fill the sky; Al - le - lu - ia! A - men!
Life shall not end the strain; Al - le - lu - ia! A - men!

Let all, with heart and voice, Be - fore His throne re - joice;
He is our Guide and Friend; To us He'll con - de - scend;
On heav - en's bliss - ful shore His good - ness we'll a - dore,

Praise is His gra - cious choice: Al - le - lu - ia! A - men!
His love shall nev - er end: Al - le - lu - ia! A - men!
Sing - ing for - ev - er - more, "Al - le - lu - ia! A - men!" A men.

Tune from *The Church Hymnary*, revised. Used by permission of the Oxford University Press

33 All Hail the Power of Jesus' Name

CORONATION 8.6.8.6.

Edward Perronet, 1726-1792
Alt. John Rippon, 1751-1836

Oliver Holden, 1765-1844

1. All hail the power of Je - sus' name!
2. Sin - ners, whose love can ne'er for - get
3. Let ev - ery kin - dred, ev - ery tribe,
4. O that with yon - der sa - cred throng

Let an-gels pros-trate fall; Bring forth the roy-al di-a-dem,
The worm-wood and the gall, Go, spread your tro-phies at His feet,
On this ter - res-trial ball, To Him all maj-es-ty as-cribe,
We at His feet may fall! We'll join the ev-er - last-ing song,

And crown Him Lord of all; Bring forth the roy-al di-a-dem,
And crown Him Lord of all; Go, spread your tro-phies at His feet,
And crown Him Lord of all; To Him all maj-es-ty as-cribe,
And crown Him Lord of all; We'll join the ev-er - last-ing song,

And crown Him Lord of all!
And crown Him Lord of all!
And crown Him Lord of all!
And crown Him Lord of all! A - men.

All Hail the Power of Jesus' Name   34

MILES LANE 8.6.8.6.

Edward Perronet, 1726-1792
Alt. John Rippon, 1751-1836

William Shrubsole, 1760-1806

1. All hail the power of Je - sus' name!
2. Sin - ners, whose love can ne'er for - get
3. Let ev - ery kin - dred, ev - ery tribe,
4. O that with yon - der sa - cred throng:

Let an - gels pros - trate fall; Bring forth the roy - al
The worm - wood and the gall, Go, spread your tro - phies
On this ter - res - trial ball, To Him all maj - es -
We at His feet may fall! We'll join the ev - er -

di - a - dem, And crown Him, crown Him,
at His feet, And crown Him, crown Him,
ty as - cribe, And crown Him, crown Him,
last - ing song, And crown Him, crown Him,

crown Him, crown Him Lord of all.
crown Him, crown Him Lord of all.
crown Him, crown Him Lord of all.
crown Him, crown Him Lord of all. A - men.

35 How Sweet the Name of Jesus Sounds

MANNA 8.6.8.6.

John Newton, 1725-1807

William H. Havergal, 1793-1870

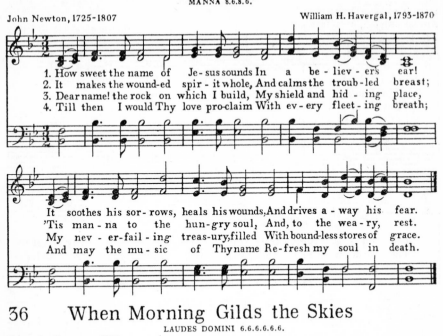

1. How sweet the name of Jesus sounds In a be-liev-ers ear!
2. It makes the wound-ed spir-it whole, And calms the troub-led breast;
3. Dear name! the rock on which I build, My shield and hid-ing place,
4. Till then I would Thy love pro-claim With ev-ery fleet-ing breath;

It soothes his sor-rows, heals his wounds, And drives a-way his fear.
'Tis man-na to the hun-gry soul, And, to the wea-ry, rest.
My nev-er-fail-ing treas-ury, filled With bound-less stores of grace.
And may the mu-sic of Thy name Re-fresh my soul in death.

36 When Morning Gilds the Skies

LAUDES DOMINI 6.6.6.6.6.6.

From the German c. 1800
Trans. by Edward Caswall, 1814-1878

Joseph Barnby, 1838-1896

1. When morn-ing gilds the skies, My heart a-wak-ing cries:
2. When sleep her balm de-nies, My si-lent spir-it sighs:
3. Does sad-ness fill my mind, A sol-ace here I find:
4. In heav'ns e-ter-nal bliss The love-liest strain is this:
5. Be this, while life is mine, My can-ti-cle di-vine,

May Je-sus Christ be praised; A-like at work and prayer
May Je-sus Christ be praised; When e-vil thoughts mo-lest,
May Je-sus Christ be praised; Or fades my earth-ly bliss,
May Je-sus Christ be praised; The powers of dark-ness fear,
May Je-sus Christ be praised; Be this th'e-ter-nal song,

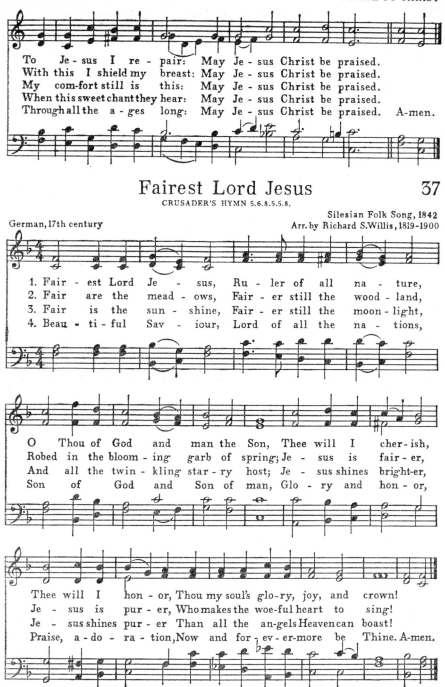

To Je - sus I re - pair: May Je - sus Christ be praised.
With this I shield my breast: May Je - sus Christ be praised.
My com-fort still is this: May Je - sus Christ be praised.
When this sweet chant they hear: May Je - sus Christ be praised.
Through all the a - ges long: May Je - sus Christ be praised. A-men.

Fairest Lord Jesus
CRUSADER'S HYMN 5.6.8.5.5.8.

37

German, 17th century

Silesian Folk Song, 1842
Arr. by Richard S. Willis, 1819-1900

1. Fair - est Lord Je - sus, Ru - ler of all na - ture,
2. Fair are the mead - ows, Fair - er still the wood - land,
3. Fair is the sun - shine, Fair - er still the moon - light,
4. Beau - ti - ful Sav - iour, Lord of all the na - tions,

O Thou of God and man the Son, Thee will I cher - ish,
Robed in the bloom - ing garb of spring; Je - sus is fair - er,
And all the twin - kling star - ry host; Je - sus shines bright - er,
Son of God and Son of man, Glo - ry and hon - or,

Thee will I hon - or, Thou my soul's glo-ry, joy, and crown!
Je - sus is pur - er, Who makes the woe-ful heart to sing!
Je - sus shines pur - er Than all the an-gels Heaven can boast!
Praise, a - do - ra - tion, Now and for - ev - er-more be Thine. A-men.

38 O Saviour, Precious Saviour

BURKE 7.6.7.6.D.

Frances R. Havergal, 1836-1879

J.H.Burke

1. O Sav - iour, pre-cious Sav - iour, Whom yet un - seen we love;
2. O bring - er of sal - va - tion, Who won-drous-ly hast wrought,
3. In Thee all ful - ness dwell-eth, All grace and power di - vine;
4. O grant the con - sum-ma - tion Of this our song a - bove,

O Name of might and fa - vor, All oth - er names a - bove!
Thy-self the rev - e - la - tion Of love be - yond our thought,
The glo - ry that ex - cel - leth, O Son of God, is Thine;
In end - less ad - o - ra - tion, And ev - er-last-ing love;

We wor - ship Thee, we bless Thee, To Thee, O Christ, we sing;
We wor - ship Thee, we bless Thee, To Thee, O Christ, we sing;
We wor - ship Thee, we bless Thee, To Thee, O Christ, we sing;
Then shall we praise and bless Thee Where per-fect prais - es ring,

We praise Thee, and con-fess Thee Our ho - ly Lord and King.
We praise Thee, and con-fess Thee Our gra-cious Lord and King.
We praise Thee, and con-fess Thee Our glo-rious Lord and King.
And ev - er-more con-fess Thee Our Sav-iour and our King. A - men.

Christ, Whose Glory Fills the Skies   39

LUX PRIMA 7.7.7.7.7.7.

Charles Wesley, 1707-1788 · Charles F. Gounod, 1818-1893

1. Christ, whose glo-ry fills the skies, Christ, the true, the
2. Dark and cheer-less is the morn Un-ac-com-pa-
3. Vis-it then this soul of mine; Pierce the gloom of

on-ly light, Sun of Right-eous-ness, a-rise,
nied by Thee; Joy-less is the day's re-turn
sin and grief; Fill me, Ra-dian-cy Di-vine;

Tri-umph o'er the shades of night; Day-spring from on
Till Thy mer-cy's beams I see; Till they in-ward
Scat-ter all my un-be-lief; More and more Thy-

high, be near; Day-star, in my heart ap-pear.
light im-part, Glad my eyes and warm my heart.
self dis-play, Shin-ing to the per-fect day. A-men.

40 Jesus Shall Reign

DUKE STREET 8.8.8.8.

Isaac Watts, 1674-1748

John Hatton, 1710-1795

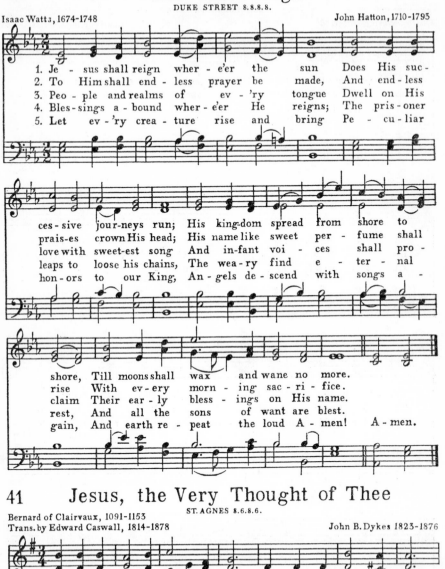

1. Je - sus shall reign wher - e'er the sun Does His suc -
2. To Him shall end - less prayer be made, And end - less
3. Peo - ple and realms of ev - 'ry tongue Dwell on His
4. Bles - sings a - bound wher - e'er He reigns; The pris - oner
5. Let ev - 'ry crea - ture rise and bring Pe - cu - liar

ces - sive jour-neys run; His king-dom spread from shore to
prais - es crown His head; His name like sweet per - fume shall
love with sweet-est song And in-fant voi - ces shall pro -
leaps to loose his chains, The wea - ry find e - ter - nal
hon - ors to our King, An - gels de - scend with songs a -

shore, Till moons shall wax and wane no more.
rise With ev - ery morn - ing sac - ri - fice.
claim Their ear - ly bless - ings on His name.
rest, And all the sons of want are blest.
gain, And earth re - peat the loud A - men! A - men.

41 Jesus, the Very Thought of Thee

ST. AGNES 8.6.8.6.

Bernard of Clairvaux, 1091-1153
Trans. by Edward Caswall, 1814-1878

John B. Dykes 1823-1876

1. Je - sus, the ver - y thought of Thee With sweet-ness fills my breast;
2. No voice can sing, no heart can frame, Nor can the mem - ory find
3. O hope of ev - ery con - trite heart, O joy of all the meek,
4. But what to those who find? ah, this No tongue or pen can show:
5. Je - sus, our on - ly joy be Thou, As Thou our prize wilt be;

But sweet-er far Thy face to see, And in Thy pres-ence rest.
A sweet-er sound than Thy blest name, O Sav-iour of man-kind!
To those who fall, how kind Thou art! How good to those who seek!
The love of Je - sus, what it is, None but His loved ones know.
Je - sus, be Thou our glo - ry now, And through e-ter - ni - ty. A - men.

Jesus, Thou Mighty Lord 42

MIGHTY LORD 6.4.6.4.D.

James Miller

William H. Doane, 1832-1915

1. Je - sus, Thou might-y Lord, Great is Thy name; Still thro' e-
2. Je - sus, Thou might-y Lord, Je - sus, our King, Praise for Thy
3. Sought by Thy mer - cy, Lord, Saved by Thy power Led by Thy

ter - nal years, Thou art the same; Change-less Thy ho - ly Word,
won-drous love Glad - ly we sing. Love in Thy di - a-dem
gra-cious hand, Kept ev-ery hour. Thine shall the hon - or be,

True ev-er-more; Thy name we glo-ri-fy, Thy name a - dore.
Shines ev-er-more; Thy name we glo-ri-fy, Thy name a - dore.
Thine ev-er-more; Thy name we glo-ri-fy, Thy name a - dore. A - men.

43 Blessed Saviour, We Adore Thee

GLORIOUS NAME 8.7.8.7. with Refrain

B.B. McKinney, 1886-1952

B.B. McKinney, 1886-1952

1. Bless-ed Sav-iour, we a-dore Thee, We Thy love and grace pro-claim;
2. Great Re-deem-er, Lord, and Mas-ter, Light of all e-ter-nal days;
3. From the throne of heav-en's glo-ry To the cross of sin and shame,
4. Come, O come, im-mor-tal Sav-iour, Come and take Thy roy-al throne;

Thou art might-y, Thou art ho-ly, Glo-rious is Thy match-less name!
Let the saints of ev-ery na-tion Sing Thy just and end-less praise!
Thou didst come to die a ran-som, Guilt-y sin-ners to re-claim!
Come, and reign, and reign for-ev-er, Be the king-dom all Thine own!

Glo ri-ous, Glo ri-ous,

Glo-rious is Thy name, O Lord! Glo-rious is Thy name, O Lord!

Glo-rious is Thy name, O Lord! Glo ri-ous,

Glo-rious is Thy name, O Lord!

rit.

Glo ri-ous, Glo-rious is Thy name, O Lord! A-men.

Glo-rious is Thy name, O Lord!

Copyright 1942, Broadman Press

Jesus What a Friend for Sinners

44

HYFRYDOL 8.7.8.7. with Refrain

J. Wilbur Chapman, 1859-1918

Rowland Hugh Prichard, 1811-1887
Arr. by Robert Harkness, 1880–

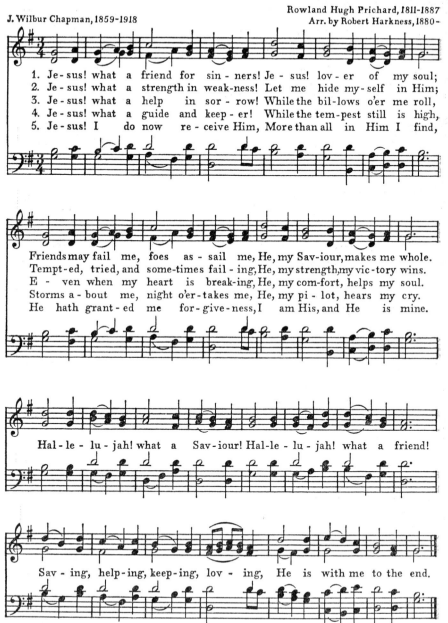

1. Je-sus! what a friend for sin-ners! Je-sus! lov-er of my soul;
2. Je-sus! what a strength in weak-ness! Let me hide my-self in Him;
3. Je-sus! what a help in sor-row! While the bil-lows o'er me roll,
4. Je-sus! what a guide and keep-er! While the tem-pest still is high,
5. Je-sus! I do now re-ceive Him, More than all in Him I find,

Friends may fail me, foes as-sail me, He, my Sav-iour, makes me whole.
Tempt-ed, tried, and some-times fail-ing, He, my strength, my vic-tory wins.
E-ven when my heart is break-ing, He, my com-fort, helps my soul.
Storms a-bout me, night o'er-takes me, He, my pi-lot, hears my cry.
He hath grant-ed me for-give-ness, I am His, and He is mine.

Hal-le-lu-jah! what a Sav-iour! Hal-le-lu-jah! what a friend!

Sav-ing, help-ing, keep-ing, lov-ing, He is with me to the end.

45 O Power of Love

ST. PETERSBURG 9.8.9.8.9.9.

Gerhard Tersteegen, 1697-1769
Trans. by H. Brueckner, 1866-1942 Alt.

Dimitri S. Bortniansky, 1752-1825

1. O power of love, all else trans-cend-ing, In Je-sus pres-ent ev-er-more, I wor-ship Thee, in hom-age bend-ing, Thy name to hon-or and a-dore: Yea, let my soul, in deep de-vo-tion, Bathe in love's might-y bound-less o-cean.

2. Thou art my rest, no earth-ly treas-ure Can sat-is-fy my yearn-ing heart, And naught can give to me the pleas-ure I find in Thee, my chos-en part, Thy love, so ten-der, so pos-sess-ing, Is joy to me, and ev-ery bless-ing.

3. To Thee my heart and life be giv-en, Thou art in truth my high-est good; For me Thy sa-cred side was riv-en, For me was shed Thy pre-cious blood. O Thou Who art the world's sal-va-tion, Be Thine my love and ad-o-ra-tion. A-men.

Shepherd of Tender Youth

KIRBY BEDON 6.6.4.6.6.6.4.

Clement of Alexandria, c.170- c.220
Trans. by Martin Dexter, 1821-1890

Edward Bunnett, 1834-1923

1. Shep - herd of ten - der youth, Guid - ing in
2. Thou art our ho - ly Lord, The all - sub -
3. Ev - er be Thou our guide, Our Shep - herd
4. So now, and till we die, Sound we Thy

love and truth, Through de - vious ways; Christ our tri -
du - ing Word, Heal - er of strife; Thou didst Thy -
and our pride, Our staff and song; Je - sus, Thou
prais - es high, And joy - ful sing; Let all the

um - phant King, We come Thy name to sing,
self a - base, That from sin's deep dis - grace
Christ of God, By Thy per - en - nial word,
ho - ly throng Who to Thy Church be - long,

Hi - ther our chil-dren bring To shout Thy praise.
Thou might-est save our race, And give us life.
Lead us where Thou hast trod, Make our faith strong.
U - nite and swell the song To Christ our King! A - men.

47 O Could I Speak the Matchless Worth

ARIEL 8.8.6.D.

Samuel Medley, 1738-1799

Wolfgang A. Mozart, 1756-1791
Arr. by Lowell Mason, 1792-1872

1. O could I speak the match-less worth, O could I sound the glo-ries forth Which in my Sav-iour shine, I'd sing His glo-rious right-eous-ness, And mag-ni-fy the won-drous grace Which made sal-va-tion mine, Which made sal-va - tion mine.

2. I'd sing the pre-cious blood He spilt, My ran-som from the dread-ful guilt Of sin, and wrath di - vine; I'd sing His glo-rious right-eous-ness, In which all-per-fect, heaven-ly dress My soul shall ev-er shine, My soul shall ev - er shine.

3. I'd sing the char-ac-ters He bears, And all the forms of love He wears, Ex - alt-ed on His throne; In loft-iest songs of sweet-est praise, I would to ev - er - last-ing days Make all His glo-ries known, Make all His glo - ries known.

4. Well, the de-light-ful day will come When my dear Lord will bring me home, And I shall see His face; Then with my Sav-iour, Broth-er, Friend, A blest e-ter-ni - ty I'll spend, Tri - umph-ant in His grace, Tri-umph-ant in His grace. A-men.

Praise Him! Praise Him!

48

JOYFUL SONG 12.10.12.10.12.10.12.10.

Fanny J. Crosby, 1820-1915

Chester G. Allen, 1838-1878

1. Praise Him! praise Him! Je-sus, our bless-ed Re-deem-er! Sing, O earth, His
2. Praise Him! praise Him! Je-sus, our bless-ed Re-deem-er! For our sins He
3. Praise Him! praise Him! Je-sus, our bless-ed Re-deem-er! Heav'n-ly por-tals

won - der-ful love pro - claim! Hail Him! hail Him! high-est arch-an-gels in glo-ry;
suf-fered and bled and died; He our rock, our hope of e - ter-nal sal-va-tion,
loud with ho-san-nas ring! Je - sus, Sav-iour, reign-eth for-ev-er and ev-er;

Strength and hon - or give to His ho - ly name! Like a shep-herd, Je-sus will
Hail Him! hail Him! Je-sus the Cru-ci - fied. Sound His prais - es! Je-sus who
Crown Him! crown Him! pro-phet, and priest, and king! Christ is com - ing! o-ver the

guard His chil-dren, In His arms He car-ries them all day long:
bore our sor-rows, Love un-bound-ed, won-der-ful, deep and strong: Praise Him! praise Him
world vic - to-rious, Power and glo - ry un - to the Lord be-long:

tell of His ex-cel-lent great-ness; Praise Him! praise Him! ev - er in joy-ful song!

49 He Hideth My Soul

KIRKPATRICK 11. 8. 11. 8. with Refrain

Fanny J. Crosby, 1820-1915   William J. Kirkpatrick, 1838-1921

1. A won-der-ful Sav-iour is Je-sus my Lord, A won-der-ful
2. A won-der-ful Sav-iour is Je-sus my Lord, He tak-eth my
3. With num-ber-less bless-ings each mo-ment He crowns, And, filled with His
4. When clothed in His bright-ness, trans-port-ed I rise To meet Him in

Sav-iour to me; He hid-eth my soul in the cleft of the rock, Where
bur-den a - way; He hold-eth me up, and I shall not be moved, He
full-ness di - vine, I sing in my rap-ture, "O, glo-ry to God, For
clouds of the sky, His per-fect sal-va-tion, His won-der-ful love, I'll

riv-ers of pleas-ure I see.
giv-eth me strength as my day. He hid-eth my soul in the cleft of the rock
such a Re-deem-er as mine!"
shout with the mil-lions on high.

That sha-dows a dry, thirst-y land; He hid-eth my life in the depths of His love,

And cov-ers me there with His hand, And cov-ers me there with His hand.

O for a Thousand Tongues 50

AZMON 8.6.8.6.

Charles Wesley, 1707-1788

Carl G. Glässer, 1784-1829
Arr. by Lowell Mason, 1792-1872

1. O   for   a thou-sand tongues to sing My great Re-deem-er's praise,
2. My   gra-cious Mas-ter and my God, As - sist me   to   pro-claim,
3. Je - sus! the name that charms our fears, That bids our sor - rows cease;
4. He   breaks the power of   can-celed sin, He sets the pris-oner free;
5. Hear Him, ye deaf; His praise, ye dumb, Your loos-ened tongues em-ploy;

The glo-ries of my God and King, The tri-umphs of His grace!
To spread through all the earth a-broad The hon-ors of Thy name.
'Tis mu-sic in the sin-ner's ears, 'Tis life and health and peace.
His blood can make the foul-est clean; His blood a-vailed for me.
Ye   blind, be-hold your Sav-iour come; And leap, ye lame, for joy.   A-men.

All People That on Earth Do Dwell 51

From Psalm 100
William Kethe, c. 1510-1594

OLD HUNDREDTH 8.8.8.8.

Louis Bourgeois, c. 1500-1561

1. All   peo-ple that on earth do dwell, Sing to the Lord with cheer-ful voice;
2. Know that the Lord is God in-deed; With-out our aid He did us make;
3. O   en-ter then His gates with praise, Ap-proach with joy His courts un - to;
4. For why? the Lord our God is good, His mer-cy is for - ev - er sure;

Him serve with fear, His praise forth tell, Come ye   be-fore Him and re - joice.
We   are His flock, He doth us feed, And for   His sheep He doth us take.
Praise, laud, and bless His name al-ways, For it   is seem-ly so to do.
His truth at all times firm-ly stood, And shall   from age to age en-dure. A-men.

52 We Gather Together

KREMSER Irregular

Anonymous
Trans. by Theodore Baker, 1851-1934

Netherlands Folk Song, 1625
Arr. by Edward Kremser, 1838-1914

1. We gath-er to-geth-er to ask the Lord's bless-ing;
2. Be-side us to guide us, our God with us join-ing,
3. We all do ex-tol Thee, Thou Lead-er tri-um-phant,

He chas-tens and has-tens His will to make known;
Or-dain-ing, main-tain-ing His king-dom di-vine;
And pray that Thou still our De-fend-er wilt be.

The wick-ed op-press-ing now cease from dis-tress-ing,
So from the be-gin-ning the fight we were win-ning:
Let Thy con-gre-ga-tion es-cape trib-u-la-tion:

Sing prais-es to His name: He for-gets not His own.
Thou, Lord, wast at our side, all glo-ry be Thine!
Thy name be ev-er praised! O Lord, make us free! A-men.

All Praise to Him Who Reigns Above 53

BLESSED NAME 8.6.8.6.

W. H. Clark, 19th century
Refrain, Ralph E. Hudson, 1843-1901

Ralph E. Hudson, 1843-1901
Arr. by William J. Kirkpatrick, 1838-1921

1. All praise to Him who reigns a-bove, In maj-es-ty su-preme,
2. His name a-bove all names shall stand, Ex-alt-ed more and more,
3. Re-deem-er, Sav-iour, Friend of man Once ru-ined by the fall,
4. His name shall be the Coun-sel-lor, The might-y Prince of Peace,

Who gave His Son for man to die, That He might man re-deem.
At God the Fa-ther's own right hand, Where an-gel hosts a-dore.
Thou hast de-vised sal-va-tion's plan, For Thou hast died for all.
Of all earth's king-doms Con-quer-or, Whose reign shall nev-er cease.

Bless-ed be the name, bless-ed be the name, Bless-ed be the name of the Lord;

Bless-ed be the name, bless-ed be the name, Bless-ed be the name of the Lord.

54 Open Now Thy Gates of Beauty
NEANDER 8. 7. 8. 7. 8. 7.

Benjamin Schmolck, 1672-1737
Trans. by Catherine Winkworth, 1829-1878

Joachim Neander, 1650-1680

1. O - pen now Thy gates of beau - ty, Zi - on, let me en - ter there,
2. Yes, my God, I come be - fore Thee, Come Thou al - so down to me;
3. Here Thy praise is glad - ly chant - ed, Here Thy seed is du - ly sown;
4. Speak, O God, and I will hear Thee, Let Thy will be done in - deed;

Where my soul in joy - ful du - ty Waits for Him who an-swers prayer:
Where we find Thee and a - dore Thee, There a heaven on earth must be.
Let my soul, where it is plant - ed, Bring forth pre-cious sheaves a - lone.
May I un - dis-turbed draw near Thee Whilst Thou dost Thy peo - ple feed.

O how bless - ed is this place, Filled with sol-ace, light, and grace.
To my heart, O en-ter Thou, Let it be Thy tem - ple now.
So that all I hear may be Fruit-ful un - to life in me.
Here of life the foun-tain flows, Here is balm for all our woes. A - men.

55 Rejoice, Ye Pure in Heart
MARION 6. 6. 8. 6. 4. 6.

Edward H. Plumptre, 1821-1891

Arthur H. Messiter, 1834-1916

1. Re - joice, ye pure in heart, Re - joice, give thanks, and sing;
2. With all the an - gel choirs, With all the saints on earth,
3. Still lift your stand - ard high, Still march in firm ar - ray;
4. Yes, on through life's long path, Still chant - ing as ye go;
5. Then on, ye pure in heart, Re - joice, give thanks, and sing;

Your fes-tal ban-ner wave on high, The cross of Christ, your King.
Pour out the strains of joy and bliss, True rap-ture, no-blest mirth!
As war-riors through the dark-ness toil Till dawns the gold-en day.
From youth to age, by night and day, In glad-ness and in woe.
Your fes-tal ban-ner wave on high, The cross of Christ, your King.

Re-joice, re-joice, Re-joice, give thanks, and sing! A-men.

Re-joice, re-joice,

Come, We That Love the Lord 56

ST. THOMAS 6.6.8.6.

Isaac Watts, 1674-1748   Aaron Williams, 1731-1776

1. Come, we that love the Lord, And let our joys be known; Join
2. Let those re-fuse to sing Who nev-er knew our God; But
3. The hill of Zi-on yields A thou-sand sa-cred sweets Be-
4. Then let our songs a-bound And ev-ery tear be dry; We're

in a song of sweet ac-cord, And thus sur-round the throne.
chil-dren of the heaven-ly King Should speak their joys a-broad.
fore we reach the heaven-ly fields, Or walk the gold-en streets.
march-ing through Em-ma-nuel's ground To fair-er worlds on high. A-men.

57 Come, Thou Almighty King

ITALIAN HYMN (Trinity) 6. 6. 4. 6. 6. 6. 4.

Anon. c. 1757

Felice de Giardini, 1716-1796

1. Come, Thou al - might - y King, Help us Thy
2. Come, Thou In - car - nate Word, Gird on Thy
3. Come, Ho - ly Com - fort - er, Thy sa - cred
4. To Thee, great One in Three, E - ter - nal

name to sing, Help us to praise!
might - y sword, Our prayer at - tend;
wit - ness bear, In this glad hour:
prais - es be, Hence, ev - er - more:

Fa - ther all glo - ri - ous, O'er all vic - to - ri - ous,
Come, and Thy peo - ple bless, And give Thy word suc - cess;
Thou who al - might - y art, Now rule in ev - ery heart,
Thy sov - 'reign maj - es - ty May we in glo - ry see,

Come, and reign o - ver us, An - cient of Days!
Spir - it of ho - li - ness, On us de - scend!
And ne'er from us de - part, Spir - it of power!
And to e - ter - ni - ty Love and a - dore! A - men.

Brethren, We Have Met to Worship 58

HOLY MANNA 8. 7. 8. 7. D.

George Atkins

William Moore

1. Breth-ren, we have met to wor - ship And a - dore the Lord our God;
2. Breth-ren, see poor sin - ners round you Slum-ber-ing on the brink of woe;
3. Sis - ters, will you join and help us? Mo - ses' sis-ter aid-ed him;
4. Let us love our God su - preme-ly, Let us love each oth-er too;

Will you pray with all your pow- er, While we try to preach the Word?
Death is com-ing, hell is mov - ing, Can you bear to let them go?
Will you help the trem-bling mour-ners Who are strug-gling hard with sin?
Let us love and pray for sin - ners, Till our God makes all things new.

All is vain un - less the Spir-it Of the Ho - ly One comes down;
See our fa - thers and our moth-ers, And our chil-dren sink-ing down;
Tell them all a - bout the Sav-iour, Tell them that He will be found;
Then He'll call us home to heav-en, At His ta-ble we'll sit down;

Breth-ren, pray, and ho - ly man-na Will be show-ered all a-round.
Breth-ren, pray, and ho - ly man-na Will be show-ered all a-round.
Sis - ters, pray, and ho - ly man-na Will be show-ered all a-round.
Christ will gird Him-self, and serve us With sweet man-na all a-round.

59 Come, Thou Fount of Every Blessing

NETTLETON 8. 7. 8. 7. D.

Robert Robinson, 1735-1790   John Wyeth, 1770-1858

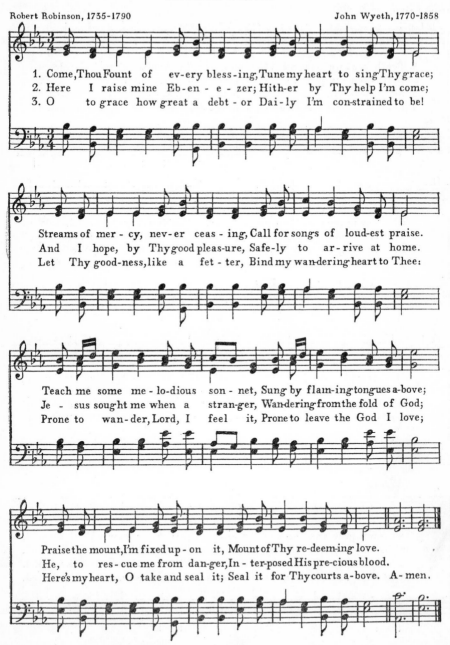

1. Come, Thou Fount of ev-ery bless-ing, Tune my heart to sing Thy grace;
2. Here I raise mine Eb-en - e - zer; Hith-er by Thy help I'm come;
3. O to grace how great a debt - or Dai-ly I'm con-strained to be!

Streams of mer - cy, nev-er ceas - ing, Call for songs of loud-est praise.
And I hope, by Thy good pleas-ure, Safe-ly to ar - rive at home.
Let Thy good-ness, like a fet - ter, Bind my wan-dering heart to Thee:

Teach me some me - lo-dious son - net, Sung by flam-ing tongues a-bove;
Je - sus sought me when a stran-ger, Wan-dering from the fold of God;
Prone to wan - der, Lord, I feel it, Prone to leave the God I love;

Praise the mount, I'm fixed up - on it, Mount of Thy re-deem-ing love.
He, to res - cue me from dan-ger, In - ter-posed His pre-cious blood.
Here's my heart, O take and seal it; Seal it for Thy courts a-bove. A-men.

Saviour, Again to Thy Dear Name 60

ELLERS 10. 10. 10. 10.

John Ellerton, 1826-1893   Edward J. Hopkins, 1818-1901

1. Sav - iour, a - gain to Thy dear name we raise
2. Grant us Thy peace up - on our home-ward way;
3. Grant us Thy peace, Lord, through the com - ing night;
4. Grant us Thy peace through-out our earth - ly life,

With one ac - cord our part - ing hymn of praise:
With Thee be - gan, with Thee shall end the day:
Turn Thou for us its dark - ness in - to light:
Our balm in sor - row, and our stay in strife:

We stand to bless Thee ere our wor - ship cease;
Guard Thou the lips from sin, the hearts from shame,
From harm and dan - ger keep Thy chil-dren free,
Then, when Thy voice shall bid our con - flict cease,

Then, still our hearts to wait Thy word of peace.
That in this house have called up - on Thy name.
For dark and light are both a - like to Thee.
Call us, O Lord, to Thine e - ter - nal peace. A - men.

61 On Our Way Rejoicing

HERMAS 6.5.6.5. D. with Refrain

Rev. John S.B. Monsell, 1811-1875
Stanza 1 alt.

Frances R. Havergal, 1836-1879

1. On our way re-joi-cing, As we home-ward move, Heark-en to our prais-es,
2. If with hon-est-heart-ed Love for God and man, Day by day Thou find us
3. On our way re-joi-cing Glad-ly let us go; Conquered hath our Lead-er,
4. Un - to God the Fa-ther Joy-ful songs we sing; Un-to God the Sav-iour

O Thou God of love! Is there grief or sad-ness? Thou our joy shalt be;
Do - ing all we can, Thou who giv'st the seed-time Wilt give large in - crease,
Van-quished is the foe; Christ with-out, our safe-ty; Christ with-in, our joy;
Thank-ful hearts we bring; Un - to God the Spir-it Bow we and a - dore;

Is our sky be-cloud-ed? There is light with Thee.
Crown the head with blessings, Fill the heart with peace. On our way re - joi - cing,
Who, if we be faith-ful, Can our hope de-stroy?
On our way re-joi-cing Now and ev - er-more.

As we home-ward move, Heark-en to our prais-es, O Thou God of love! A-men.

Once More before We Part 62

LABAN 6.6.8.6.

Joseph Hart, 1712-1768   Lowell Mason, 1792-1872

1. Once more be - fore we part, O bless the Sav - iour's name! Let
2. Lord, in Thy grace we came, That bless - ing still im - part; We
3. Still on Thy ho - ly Word Help us to feed and grow; Still
4. Now, Lord, be - fore we part, Help us to bless Thy name; Let

ev - ery tongue and ev - ery heart A - dore and praise the same.
met in Je - sus' sa - cred name, In Je - sus' name we part.
to go on to know the Lord And prac-tice what we know.
ev - ery tongue and ev - ery heart A - dore and praise the same. A - men.

Lord, Dismiss Us with Thy Blessing 63

SICILIAN MARINERS' HYMN 8.7.8.7.8.7.

John Fawcett, 1704-1817, alt.   Arr. from a Sicilian Melody

1. Lord, dis - miss us with Thy bless-ing, Fill our hearts with joy and peace;
2. Thanks we give and ad - o - ra - tion, For Thy Gos - pel's joy - ful sound;

Let us each, Thy love pos - sess-ing, Tri-umph in re - deem-ing grace;
May the fruits of Thy sal - va-tion In our hearts and lives a - bound;

O re - fresh us, O re - fresh us, Traveling through this wil-der-ness.
May Thy pres-ence, May Thy pres-ence, With us ev - er - more be found. A-men

64 Almighty God, Thy Word Is Cast

ST. FULBERT 8. 6. 8. 6.

John Cawood, 1775-1852

Henry J. Gauntlett, 1805-1876

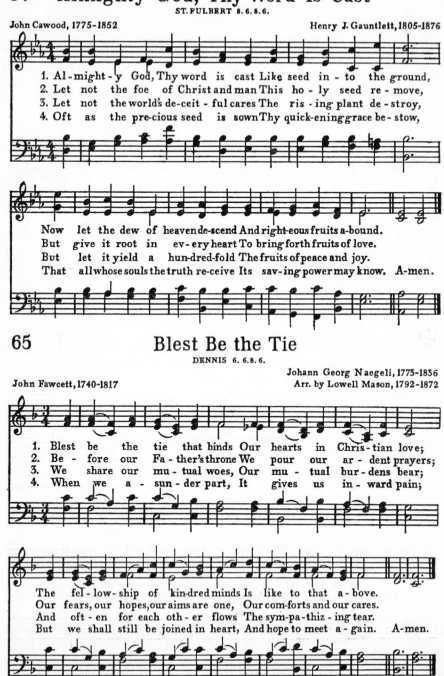

1. Al-might-y God, Thy word is cast Like seed in-to the ground,
2. Let not the foe of Christ and man This ho-ly seed re-move,
3. Let not the world's de-ceit-ful cares The ris-ing plant de-stroy,
4. Oft as the pre-cious seed is sown Thy quick-ening grace be-stow,

Now let the dew of heaven de-scend And right-eous fruits a-bound.
But give it root in ev-ery heart To bring forth fruits of love.
But let it yield a hun-dred-fold The fruits of peace and joy.
That all whose souls the truth re-ceive Its sav-ing power may know. A-men.

65 Blest Be the Tie

DENNIS 6. 6. 8. 6.

Johann Georg Naegeli, 1773-1836
Arr. by Lowell Mason, 1792-1872

John Fawcett, 1740-1817

1. Blest be the tie that binds Our hearts in Chris-tian love;
2. Be-fore our Fa-ther's throne We pour our ar-dent prayers;
3. We share our mu-tual woes, Our mu-tual bur-dens bear;
4. When we a-sun-der part, It gives us in-ward pain;

The fel-low-ship of kin-dred minds Is like to that a-bove.
Our fears, our hopes, our aims are one, Our com-forts and our cares.
And oft-en for each oth-er flows The sym-pa-thiz-ing tear.
But we shall still be joined in heart, And hope to meet a-gain. A-men.

God Be with You till We Meet   66

GOD BE WITH YOU 9.8.8.9.

Jeremiah E. Rankin, 1828-1904   William Tomer, 1832-1896

1. God be with you till we meet a-gain, By His coun-sels guide, up-hold you,
2. God be with you till we meet a-gain, 'Neath His wings se-cure-ly hide you,
3. God be with you till we meet a-gain, When life's per-ils thick con-found you,
4. God be with you till we meet a-gain, Keep love's ban-ner float-ing o'er you,

With His sheep se-cure-ly fold you: God be with you till we meet a-gain.
Dai - ly man-na still pro-vide you: God be with you till we meet a-gain.
Put His arm un-fail-ing 'round you: God be with you till we meet a-gain.
Smite death's threat'ning wave be-fore you: God be with you till we meet a-gain. A-men.

May the Mind of Christ My Saviour   67

ST. LEONARDS 8.7.8.5.

Kate B. Wilkinson, 20th century   A. Cyril Barham-Gould, 1891-1953

1. May the mind of Christ, my Sav-iour, Live in me from day to day,
2. May the Word of God dwell rich-ly In my heart from hour to hour,
3. May the peace of God, my Fa-ther, Rule my life in ev-ery-thing,
4. May the love of Je-sus fill me, As the wa-ters fill the sea;

By His love and power con-trol-ling All I do and say.
So that all may see I tri-umph On-ly through His power.
That I may be calm to com-fort Sick and sor - row-ing.
Him ex - alt-ing, self a-bas-ing, This is vic - to-ry. A-men.

Copyright, used by permission of E. W. M. Gould

68 Awake, My Soul, in Joyful Lays

LOVING KINDNESS 8.8.8.8. with Refrain

Samuel Medley, 1738-1799

Western Melody

1. A-wake, my soul, in joy-ful lays, And sing thy great Re-
2. He saw me ru-ined in the fall, Yet loved me not-with-
3. Thro' might-y hosts of cru-el foes, Where earth and hell my
4. When trou-ble like a gloom-y cloud Has gath-ered thick, and

deem-er's praise; He just-ly claims a song from me, His
stand-ing all, And saved me from my lost es-tate, His
way op-pose, He safe-ly leads my soul a-long, His
thun-dered loud, He near my soul has al-ways stood, His

lov-ing-kind-ness is so free. Lov-ing-kind-ness,
lov-ing-kind-ness is so great. Lov-ing-kind-ness,
lov-ing-kind-ness is so strong. Lov-ing-kind-ness,
lov-ing-kind-ness O, how good! Lov-ing-kind-ness,

lov-ing-kind-ness, His lov-ing-kind-ness is so free.
lov-ing-kind-ness, His lov-ing-kind-ness is so great.
lov-ing-kind-ness, His lov-ing-kind-ness is so strong.
lov-ing-kind-ness, His lov-ing-kind-ness O, how good!

Lord, in the Morning

WARWICK 8. 6. 8. 6.

69

Isaac Watts, 1674-1748

Samuel Stanley, 1767-1822

1. Lord, in the morn-ing Thou shalt hear My voice as-cend-ing high;
2. Up to the hills where Christ is gone To plead for all His saints,
3. Un-to Thy house will I re-sort To taste Thy mer-cies there;
4. O, may Thy Spir-it guide my feet In ways of right-eous-ness;

To Thee will I di-rect my prayer, To Thee lift up mine eye.
Pre-sent-ing, at His Fa-ther's throne, Our songs and our com-plaints.
I will fre-quent Thy ho-ly court, And wor-ship in Thy fear.
Make ev-ery path of du-ty straight And plain be-fore my face. A-men.

New Every Morning Is the Love

CANONBURY 8. 8. 8. 8.

70

John Keble, 1792-1866

Robert Schumann, 1810-1856

1. New ev-ery morn-ing is the love Our waken-ing and up-ris-ing prove;
2. New mer-cies, each re-turn-ing day, A-round us hov-er while we pray,
3. The triv-ial round, the com-mon task, Will fur-nish all we ought to ask:
4. On-ly, O Lord, in Thy dear love, Fit us for per-fect rest a-bove,

Thro' sleep and dark-ness safe-ly brought, Restored to life and power and thought.
New per-ils past, new sins for-given, New thoughts of God, new hopes of heaven.
Room to de-ny our-selves, a road To bring us dai-ly near-er God.
And help us, this and ev-ery day, To live more near-ly as we pray. A-men.

71 Day Is Dying in the West

CHAUTAUQUA 7.7.7.7.4. with Refrain

Mary Ann Lathbury, 1841-1913   William F. Sherwin, 1826-1888

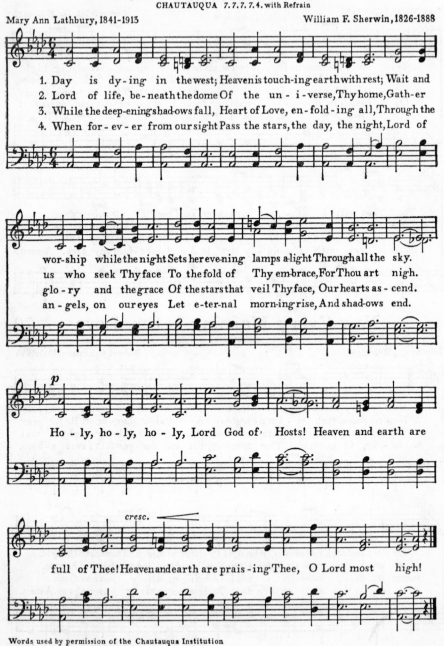

1. Day is dy-ing in the west; Heaven is touch-ing earth with rest; Wait and
2. Lord of life, be-neath the dome Of the u-ni-verse, Thy home, Gath-er
3. While the deep-en-ing shad-ows fall, Heart of Love, en-fold-ing all, Through the
4. When for-ev-er from our sight Pass the stars, the day, the night, Lord of

wor-ship while the night Sets her eve-ning lamps a-light Through all the sky.
us who seek Thy face To the fold of Thy em-brace, For Thou art nigh.
glo-ry and the grace Of the stars that veil Thy face, Our hearts as-cend.
an-gels, on our eyes Let e-ter-nal morn-ing rise, And shad-ows end.

p

Ho-ly, ho-ly, ho-ly, Lord God of Hosts! Heaven and earth are

cresc.

full of Thee! Heaven and earth are prais-ing Thee, O Lord most high!

Words used by permission of the Chautauqua Institution

Now, on Land and Sea Descending 72

VESPER HYMN 8.7.8.7.8.6.8.7.

Samuel Longfellow, 1819-1892, alt.   Dimitri S. Bortniansky, 1752-1825

1. Now, on land and sea de-scend-ing, Brings the night its peace pro-found;
2. Soon as dies the sun-set glo-ry, Stars of heaven shine out a-bove,
3. Now, our wants and bur-dens leav-ing To His care who cares for all,
4. As the dark-ness deep-ens o'er us, Lo! e-ter-nal stars a-rise;

Let our ves-per hymn be blend-ing With the ho-ly calm a-round.
Tell-ing still the an-cient sto-ry: Their Cre-a-tor's change-less love.
Cease we fear-ing, cease we griev-ing: At His touch our bur-dens fall.
Hope and faith and love rise glo-rious, Shin-ing in the spir-it's skies.

Ju-bi-la-te! Ju-bi-la-te! Ju-bi-la-te! A-men!

Let our ves-per hymn be blend-ing With the ho-ly calm a-round.
Tell-ing still the an-cient sto-ry: Their Cre-a-tor's change-less love.
Cease we fear-ing, cease we griev-ing: At His touch our bur-dens fall.
Hope and faith and love rise glo-rious, Shin-ing in the spir-it's skies. A-men.

73 Abide with Me; 'Tis Eventide

EVENTIDE 8.6.8.6.8.6. with Refrain

M. Lowrie Hofford   H. Millard

1. A-bide with me; 'tis e-ven-tide! The day is past and gone;
2. A-bide. with me; 'tis e-ven-tide! Thy walk to-day with me
3. A-bide with me; 'tis e-ven-tide! And lone will be the night,

The shad-ows of the eve-ning fall; The night is com-ing on!
Has made my heart with-in me burn, As I com-muned with Thee.
If I can-not com-mune with Thee, Nor find in Thee my light.

With-in my heart a wel-come guest, With-in my home a-bide;
Thy ear-nest words have filled my soul And kept me near Thy side;
The dark-ness of the world, I fear, Would in my home a-bide;

O Sav-iour, stay this night with me; Be-hold, 'tis e-ven-tide!

O Sav-iour, stay this night with me; Be-hold, 'tis e-ven-tide. A-men.

Softly Now the Light of Day — 74

SEYMOUR 7.7.7.7.

George W. Doane, 1799-1859   Carl M. von Weber, 1786-1826

1. Soft - ly now the light of day   Fades up - on my sight a - way;
2. Thou, whose all per - vad - ing eye   Naught es - capes, with-out, with-in,
3. Thou who, sin - less, yet hast known   All of man's in - firm - i - ty;
4. Soon for me the light of day   Shall for - ev - er pass a - way;

Free from care, from la - bor free, Lord, I would com-mune with Thee.
Par - don each in - firm - i - ty, O - pen fault, and se-cret sin.
Then, from Thine e - ter - nal throne, Je - sus, look with pity-ing eye.
Then, from sin and sor - row free, Take me, Lord, to dwell with Thee. A-men.

Now the Day Is Over — 75

MERRIAL 6.5.6.5.

Sabine Baring-Gould, 1834-1924   Joseph Barnby, 1838-1896

1. Now the day is o - ver, Night is draw - ing nigh,
2. Je - sus, give the wea - ry Calm and sweet re - pose;
3. Grant to lit - tle chil - dren Vi - sions bright of Thee;
4. Through the long night watch - es, May Thine an - gels spread
5. When the morn - ing wak - ens, Then may I a - rise

Shad - ows of the eve - ning Steal a - cross the sky.
With Thy ten - derest bless - ing May our eye - lids close.
Guard the sail - ors toss - ing On the deep, blue sea.
Their white wings a - bove me, Watch-ing round my bed.
Pure, and fresh, and sin - less In Thy ho - ly eyes. A-men.

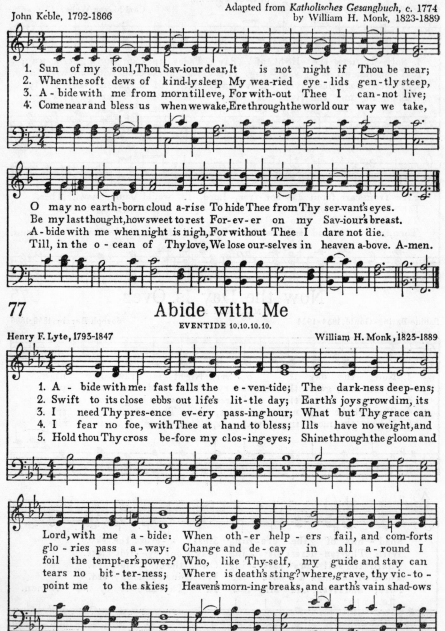

76 Sun of My Soul
HURSLEY 8.8.8.8.

John Keble, 1792-1866

Adapted from *Katholisches Gesangbuch*, c. 1774
by William H. Monk, 1823-1889

1. Sun of my soul, Thou Sav-iour dear, It is not night if Thou be near;
2. When the soft dews of kind-ly sleep My wea-ried eye - lids gen-tly steep,
3. A - bide with me from morn till eve, For with-out Thee I can-not live;
4. Come near and bless us when we wake, Ere through the world our way we take,

O may no earth-born cloud a-rise To hide Thee from Thy ser-vant's eyes.
Be my last thought, how sweet to rest For-ev-er on my Sav-iour's breast.
A-bide with me when night is nigh, For without Thee I dare not die.
Till, in the o - cean of Thy love, We lose our-selves in heaven a-bove. A-men.

77 Abide with Me
EVENTIDE 10.10.10.10.

Henry F. Lyte, 1793-1847

William H. Monk, 1823-1889

1. A - bide with me: fast falls the e - ven-tide; The dark-ness deep-ens;
2. Swift to its close ebbs out life's lit-tle day; Earth's joys grow dim, its
3. I need Thy pres-ence ev-ery pass-ing hour; What but Thy grace can
4. I fear no foe, with Thee at hand to bless; Ills have no weight, and
5. Hold thou Thy cross be-fore my clos-ing eyes; Shine through the gloom and

Lord, with me a - bide: When oth-er help - ers fail, and com-forts
glo - ries pass a - way: Change and de - cay in all a - round I
foil the tempt-er's power? Who, like Thy-self, my guide and stay can
tears no bit - ter-ness; Where is death's sting? where, grave, thy vic-to -
point me to the skies; Heaven's morn-ing breaks, and earth's vain shad-ows

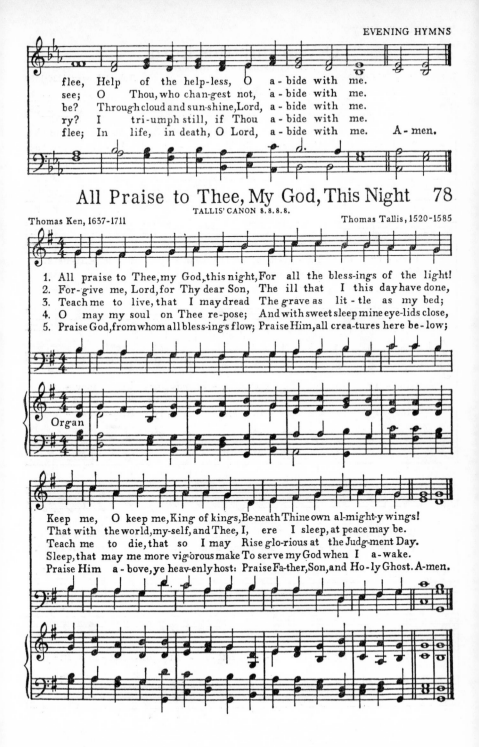

flee, Help of the help-less, O a - bide with me.
see; O Thou, who chan-gest not, a - bide with me.
be? Through cloud and sun-shine, Lord, a - bide with me.
ry? I tri-umph still, if Thou a - bide with me.
flee; In life, in death, O Lord, a - bide with me. A - men.

All Praise to Thee, My God, This Night 78
TALLIS' CANON 8.8.8.8.

Thomas Ken, 1637-1711   Thomas Tallis, 1520-1585

1. All praise to Thee, my God, this night, For all the bless-ings of the light!
2. For-give me, Lord, for Thy dear Son, The ill that I this day have done,
3. Teach me to live, that I may dread The grave as lit - tle as my bed;
4. O may my soul on Thee re-pose; And with sweet sleep mine eye-lids close,
5. Praise God, from whom all bless-ings flow; Praise Him, all crea-tures here be-low;

Organ

Keep me, O keep me, King of kings, Be-neath Thine own al-might-y wings!
That with the world, my-self, and Thee, I, ere I sleep, at peace may be.
Teach me to die, that so I may Rise glo-rious at the Judg-ment Day.
Sleep, that may me more vig-orous make To serve my God when I a-wake.
Praise Him a-bove, ye heav-enly host: Praise Fa-ther, Son, and Ho-ly Ghost. A-men.

79 O Worship the Lord

BEAUTY OF HOLINESS Irregular

Robert Lowry, 1826-1899   Robert Lowry, 1826-1899

1. O wor-ship the Lord in the beau-ty of ho-li-ness, in the
2. O wor-ship the Lord in the beau-ty of ho-li-ness, in the
3. O wor-ship the Lord in the beau-ty of ho-li-ness, in the

beau-ty of ho-li-ness, in the beau-ty of ho-li-ness.
beau-ty of ho-li-ness, in the beau-ty of ho-li-ness.
beau-ty of ho-li-ness, in the beau-ty of ho-li-ness.

Glo-ry to the Fa-ther a-bound-ing in mer-cy!
Glo-ry be to Je-sus, our gra-cious Re-deem-er!
Glo-ry to the Spir-it, the ho-ly Re-veal-er!

Be joy-ful, all ye peo-ple, and mag-ni-fy Je-ho-vah!
We praise Him, for He loved us, and brought a great sal-va-tion.
We praise Him with the Fa-ther, and with the Son our Sav-iour.

O glo-ry hal-le-lu-jah, hal-le-lu-jah, hal-le-lu-jah!

ritard

O come be-fore His pres-ence and glo-ri-fy His name.

We All Believe in One True God   80

THE APOSTLES' CREED 8.7.7.7.7.7.

Tobias Clausnitzer, 1668
Trans. by Catherine Winkworth, 1863 alt.

Kirchengesangbuch, Darmstad, 1699

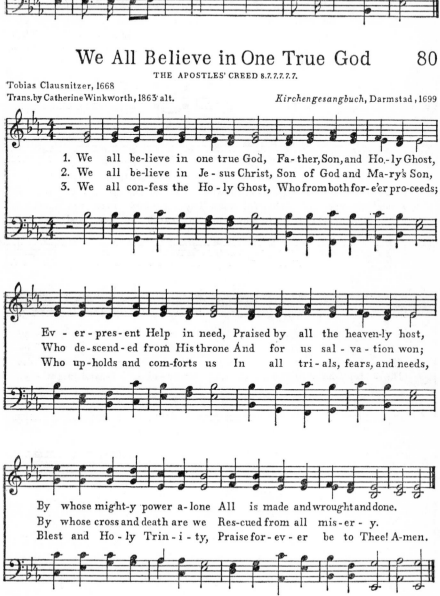

1. We all be-lieve in one true God, Fa-ther, Son, and Ho-ly Ghost,
2. We all be-lieve in Je-sus Christ, Son of God and Ma-ry's Son,
3. We all con-fess the Ho-ly Ghost, Who from both for-e'er pro-ceeds;

Ev - er-pres-ent Help in need, Praised by all the heaven-ly host,
Who de-scend-ed from His throne And for us sal-va-tion won;
Who up-holds and com-forts us In all tri-als, fears, and needs,

By whose might-y power a-lone All is made and wrought and done.
By whose cross and death are we Res-cued from all mis-er-y.
Blest and Ho-ly Trin-i-ty, Praise for-ev-er be to Thee! A-men.

81 Holy, Holy, Holy

NICAEA 11.12.12.10.

Reginald Heber, 1783-1826   John B. Dykes, 1823-1876

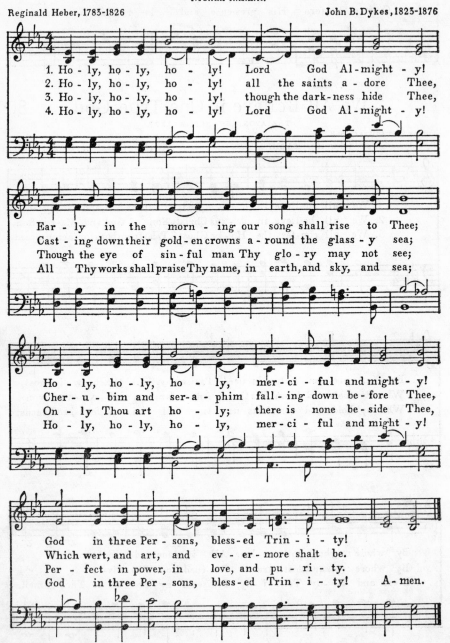

1. Ho-ly, ho-ly, ho-ly! Lord God Al-might-y!
2. Ho-ly, ho-ly, ho-ly! all the saints a-dore Thee,
3. Ho-ly, ho-ly, ho-ly! though the dark-ness hide Thee,
4. Ho-ly, ho-ly, ho-ly! Lord God Al-might-y!

Ear-ly in the morn-ing our song shall rise to Thee;
Cast-ing down their gold-en crowns a-round the glass-y sea;
Though the eye of sin-ful man Thy glo-ry may not see;
All Thy works shall praise Thy name, in earth, and sky, and sea;

Ho-ly, ho-ly, ho-ly, mer-ci-ful and might-y!
Cher-u-bim and ser-a-phim fall-ing down be-fore Thee,
On-ly Thou art ho-ly; there is none be-side Thee,
Ho-ly, ho-ly, ho-ly, mer-ci-ful and might-y!

God in three Per-sons, bless-ed Trin-i-ty!
Which wert, and art, and ev-er-more shalt be.
Per-fect in power, in love, and pu-ri-ty.
God in three Per-sons, bless-ed Trin-i-ty! A-men.

Eternal Father, When to Thee

82

WAREHAM 8.8.8.8.

Hervey G. Ganse, 1822-1891

William Knapp, 1698-1768

1. E - ter-nal Fa-ther, when to Thee, Be - yond all worlds, by faith I soar,
2. But, Sav-iour, Thou art by my side; Thy voice I hear, Thy face I see:
3. And Thou, great Spir-it, in my heart Dost make Thy tem - ple day by day;
4. Blest Trin-i - ty, in whom a-lone, All things cre - a - ted move or rest,

Be - fore Thy boundless maj-es-ty I stand in si - lence, and a - dore.
Thou art my Friend, my dai-ly Guide: God o - ver all, yet God with me.
The Ho - ly Ghost of God Thou art, Yet dwell-est in this house of clay.
High in the heav'ns Thou hast Thy throne! Thou hast Thy throne within my breast. A-men.

The King of Love My Shepherd Is

83

DOMINUS REGIT ME 8.7.8.7.

Henry W. Baker, 1821-1877

John B. Dykes, 1823-1876

1. The King of love my Shep-herd is, Whose good-ness fail - eth nev - er;
2. Where streams of liv-ing wa - ter flow My ran-somed soul He lead - eth.
3. Per-verse and fool-ish oft I strayed, But yet in love He sought me,
4. In death's dark vale I fear no ill With Thee, dear Lord, be - side me;
5. And so through all the length of days Thy good-ness fail - eth nev - er:

I noth - ing lack if I am His And He is mine for - ev - er.
And where the ver-dant pas-tures grow, With food ce - les-tial feed-eth.
And on His shoul-der gen - tly laid, And home, re-joic-ing, brought me.
Thy rod and staff my com-fort still, Thy cross be-fore to guide me.
Good Shep-herd, may I sing Thy praise With-in Thy house for - ev - er. A-men.

84 God of Our Life

SANDON 10.4.10.4.10.10.

Hugh T. Kerr, 1871-1950

Charles Henry Purday, 1799-1885

1. God of our life, through all the cir-cling years, We trust in Thee;
2. God of the past, our times are in Thy hand; With us a-bide.
3. God of the com-ing years, through paths unknown We fol-low Thee;

In all the past, through all our hopes and fears, Thy hand we see.
Lead us by faith to hope's true Prom-ised Land; Be Thou our guide.
When we are strong, Lord, leave us not a-lone; Our ref-uge be.

With each new day, when morn-ing lifts the veil,
With Thee to bless, the dark-ness shines as light,
Be Thou for us in life our Dai-ly Bread,

We own Thy mer-cies, Lord, which nev-er fail.
And faith's fair vi-sion chan-ges in-to sight.
Our heart's true Home when all our years have sped. A-men.

This Is My Father's World

TERRA BEATA 6.6.8.6.D.

Maltbie D. Babcock, 1858-1901   Franklin L. Sheppard, 1852-1930

1. This is my Fa-ther's world, And to my list-ening ears, All na-ture sings, and round me rings The mu-sic of the spheres. This is my Fa-ther's world: I rest me in the thought Of rocks and trees, of skies and seas; His hand the won-ders wrought.

2. This is my Fa-ther's world, The birds their car-ols raise, The morn-ing light, the lil-y white, De-clare their Mak-er's praise. This is my Fa-ther's world: He shines in all that's fair; In the rust-ling grass I hear Him pass, He speaks to me ev-ery-where.

3. This is my Fa-ther's world, O let me ne'er for-get That though the wrong seems oft so strong, God is the Rul-er yet. This is my Fa-ther's world: Why should my heart be sad? The Lord is King: let the heav-ens ring! God reigns: let the earth be glad. A-men.

86 Immortal, Invisible

JOANNA 11.11.11.11.

William Chalmers Smith, 1824-1908

Welsh hymn melody

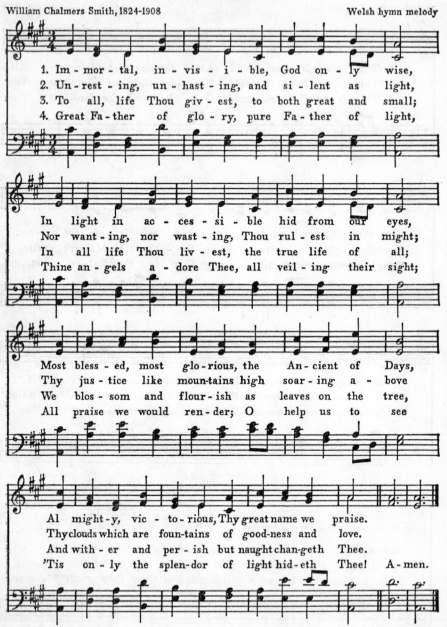

1. Im - mor - tal, in - vis - i - ble, God on - ly wise,
2. Un - rest - ing, un - hast - ing, and si - lent as light,
3. To all, life Thou giv - est, to both great and small;
4. Great Fa - ther of glo - ry, pure Fa - ther of light,

In light in ac - ces - si - ble hid from our eyes,
Nor want - ing, nor wast - ing, Thou rul - est in might;
In all life Thou liv - est, the true life of all;
Thine an - gels a - dore Thee, all veil - ing their sight;

Most bless - ed, most glo - rious, the An - cient of Days,
Thy jus - tice like moun - tains high soar - ing a - bove
We blos - som and flour - ish as leaves on the tree,
All praise we would ren - der; O help us to see

Al - might - y, vic - to - rious, Thy great name we praise.
Thy clouds which are foun - tains of good - ness and love.
And with - er and per - ish but naught chang - eth Thee.
'Tis on - ly the splen - dor of light hid - eth Thee! A - men.

God Is Love, His Mercy Brightens 87

EFFIE 8.7. 8.7.

J. Allen, 1754-1804   D. M. Click

1. God   is love; His mer-cy bright-ens   All the path in which we rove;
2. Chance and change are bus-y   ev - er; Man de - cays and a - ges move;
3. E'en the hour that dark-est seem-eth   Will His change-less good-ness prove;
4. He   with earth-ly cares en-twin-eth   Hope and com-fort from a - bove;

Bliss He wakes and woe He light-ens: God is wis-dom, God is love.
But His mer-cy wan-eth nev-er: God is wis-dom, God is love.
From the mist His brightness streameth: God is wis-dom, God is love.
Ev - ery-where His glo-ry shin-eth: God is wis-dom, God is love. A-men.

God Is the Fountain 88

6. 6. 8. 6.

Unknown   Lowell Mason, 1792-1872

1. God is the foun-tain whence Ten thou-sand bless-ings flow; To Him   my
2. The com-forts He af-fords Are nei - ther few nor small; He is   the
3. He fills my heart with joy, My lips   at - tunes for praise, And to   His

life,   my health, and friends, And ev - ery good I owe.
source of   fresh de - lights, My por-tion and my all.
glo - ry I'll   de - vote The rem-nant of my days. A-men.

89 Hallelujah, Praise Jehovah!

PRAISE JEHOVAH 8.7.8.7.D. with Refrain

Psalm XVI

Wm. J. Kirkpatrick, 1838-1921

1. Hal - le - lu - jah, praise Je - ho - vah! From the heav-ens praise His name.
2. Let them prais-es give Je - ho - vah; They were made at His com-mand.
3. All ye fruit-ful trees and ce - dars, All ye hills and moun-tains high,

Praise Je - ho - vah in the high-est; All His an-gels, praise pro-claim.
Them for - ev - er He es - tab-lished; His de-cree shall ev - er stand.
Creep-ing things and beasts and cat - tle, Birds that in the heav-ens fly;

All His hosts, to - geth - er praise Him Sun, and moon, and stars on high.
From the earth, Oh, praise Je - ho - vah, All ye floods, ye drag-ons all;
Kings of earth and all ye peo - ple, Princ-es great, earth's judg-es all;

Praise Him, O ye heaven of heav-ens, And ye floods a-bove the sky.
Fire, and hail, and snow, and va - pors, Storm-y winds that hear Him call.
Praise His name, young men and maid-ens, A - ged men, and chil-dren small.

Let them prais - es give Je - ho-vah, For His name a-lone is high,
Let them prais-es

And His glo - ry is ex-alt-ed, And His glo - ry is ex-alt-ed,
And His glo-ry   And His glo-ry

pp   *p*

And His glo - ry is ex-alt-ed Far a-bove the earth and sky.
And His glo-ry

God Moves in a Mysterious Way 90

DUNDEE 8.6.8.6.

William Cowper, 1731-1800   *Scottish Psalter*, 1615

1. God moves in a mys - te-rious way His won-ders to per- form;
2. Deep in un-fath-om - a-ble mines, Of nev - er-fail - ing skill,
3. Ye fear-ful saints, fresh cour-age take; The clouds ye so much dread
4. Blind un - be - lief is sure to err, And scan His work in vain;

He plants His foot-steps in the sea, And rides up-on the storm.
He treas-ures up His bright de-signs, And works His sov-ereign will.
Are big with mer-cy, and shall break In bless-ings on your head.
God is His own in-ter-pre-ter, And He will make it plain. A-men.

91 Come, Let Us All Unite to Sing

GOD IS LOVE Irregular with Refrain

Anonymous   Edmund S. Lorenz, 1854-1942

1. Come, let us all unite to sing, God is love; Let heaven and
2. O tell to earth's re-mot-est bound, God is love; We have in
3. How hap-py is our por-tion here, God is love; His prom-is-

earth their prais-es bring, God is love; Let ev-ery soul from
Christ re-demp-tion found, God is love; His blood has washed our
es our spir-its cheer, God is love; He is our sun and

sin a-wake; Each in his heart sweet mu-sic make, And sing with us for
sins a-way, His spir-it turned our night to day, And now we can re-
shield by day, Our help, our hope, our strength and stay; He will be with us

Je-sus' sake, For God is love.
joice to say That God is love. God is love,   God is
all the way; Our God is love.   God is love,

love.   Come, let us all u-nite to sing That God is love.
God is love.

O God, Our Help in Ages Past

ST. ANNE 8.6.8.6.

Isaac Watts, 1674-1748   **92**   William Croft, 1678-1727

1. O God, our help in a-ges past, Our hope for years to come,
2. Un-der the shad-ow of Thy throne Thy saints have dwelt se-cure;
3. Be-fore the hills in or-der stood, Or earth re-ceived her frame,
4. A thou-sand a-ges in Thy sight Are like an eve-ning gone;
5. O God, our help in a-ges past, Our hope for years to come,

Our shel-ter from the storm-y blast, And our e-ter-nal home.
Suf-fi-cient is Thine arm a-lone, And our de-fense is sure.
From ev-er-last-ing Thou art God, To end-less years the same.
Short as the watch that ends the night Be-fore the ris-ing sun.
Be Thou our guard while life shall last, And our e-ter-nal home. A-men.

My God, How Wonderful Thou Art

DUNDEE 8.6.8.6.

Frederick W. Faber, 1814-1863   **93**   *Scottish Psalter*, 1615

1. My God, how won-der-ful Thou art, Thy ma-jest-y how bright,
2. How won-der-ful, how beau-ti-ful, The sight of Thee must be,
3. Oh, how I fear Thee, liv-ing God, With deep-est, tender-est fears,
4. Yet I may love Thee, too, O Lord, Al-might-y as Thou art,

How beau-ti-ful Thy mer-cy-seat, In depths of burn-ing light!
Thine end-less wis-dom, boundless power, And aw-ful pur-i-ty.
And wor-ship Thee with trembling hope And pen-i-ten-tial tears.
For Thou hast stooped to ask of me The love of my poor heart. A-men.

94 Great Is Thy Faithfulness

FAITHFULNESS 11.10.11.10. with Refrain

Thomas O. Chisholm, 1866-   William M. Runyan, 1870-1957

1. Great is Thy faith-ful-ness, O God my Fa-ther, There is no shad-ow of
2. Sum-mer and win-ter, and spring-time and harvest, Sun, moon and stars in their
3. Par - don for sin and a peace that en - dur-eth, Thine own dear presence to

turn-ing with Thee; Thou chang-est not, Thy com-pas-sions, they fail not;
cours-es a - bove Join with all na-ture in man - i - fold wit-ness
cheer and to guide; Strength for to - day and bright hope for to - mor-row

As Thou hast been Thou for - ev- er wilt be.
To Thy great faith-ful-ness, mer-cy and love. Great is Thy faith-ful-ness!
Bless-ings all mine, with ten thou-sand be-side!

Great is Thy faith-ful-ness! Morning by morning new mercies I see; All I have

need-ed Thy hand hath pro-vid-ed; Great is Thy faith-ful-ness, Lord, un-to me!

O God of Bethel

DUNDEE 8.6.8.6.

Philip Doddridge, 1702-1751

Scottish Psalter, 1615

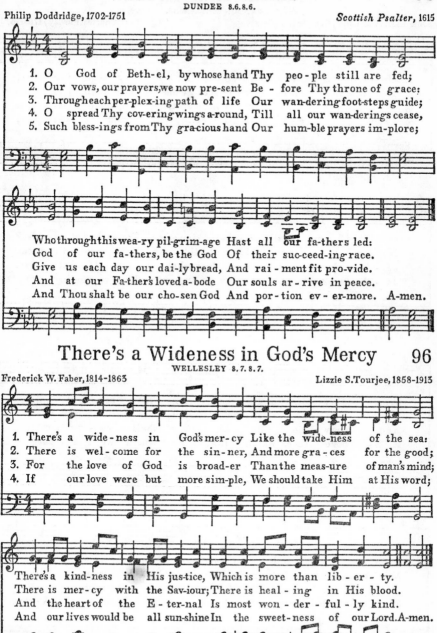

1. O God of Beth-el, by whose hand Thy peo-ple still are fed;
2. Our vows, our prayers, we now pre-sent Be - fore Thy throne of grace:
3. Through each per-plex-ing path of life Our wan-dering foot-steps guide;
4. O spread Thy cov-ering wings a-round, Till all our wan-derings cease,
5. Such bless-ings from Thy gra-cious hand Our hum-ble prayers im-plore;

Who through this wea-ry pil-grim-age Hast all our fa-thers led:
God of our fa-thers, be the God Of their suc-ceed-ing race.
Give us each day our dai-ly bread, And rai - ment fit pro-vide.
And at our Fa-ther's loved a-bode Our souls ar - rive in peace.
And Thou shalt be our cho-sen God And por - tion ev - er-more. A-men.

There's a Wideness in God's Mercy

WELLESLEY 8.7.8.7.

Frederick W. Faber, 1814-1863

Lizzie S. Tourjee, 1858-1913

95

1. There's a wide-ness in God's mer-cy Like the wide-ness of the sea:
2. There is wel-come for the sin-ner, And more gra - ces for the good;
3. For the love of God is broad-er Than the meas-ure of man's mind;
4. If our love were but more sim-ple, We should take Him at His word;

There's a kind-ness in His jus-tice, Which is more than lib - er - ty.
There is mer-cy with the Sav-iour; There is heal - ing in His blood.
And the heart of the E - ter-nal Is most won - der - ful - ly kind.
And our lives would be all sun-shine In the sweet-ness of our Lord. A-men.

97 Unto the Hills Around

SANDON 10.4.10.4.10.10.

From Psalm CXXI. John Campbell, 1845-1914   Charles Purday, 1799-1885

1. Un - to the hills a-round do I lift up My long-ing eyes;
2. He will not suf-fer that thy foot be moved: Safe shalt thou be.
3. Je - ho-vah is Him-self thy keep-er true, Thy change-less shade;
4. From ev-ery e-vil shall He keep thy soul, From ev-ery sin;

O whence for me shall my sal-va-tion come, From whence a-rise?
No care-less slum - ber shall His eye-lids close, Who keep-eth thee.
Je - ho-vah thy de-fense on thy right hand Him-self hath made.
Je - ho-vah shall pre-serve thy go-ing out, Thy com-ing in.

From God the Lord doth come my cer-tain aid,
Be - hold, He sleep-eth not, He slum-bereth ne'er,
And thee no sun by day shall ev-er smite;
A - bove thee watch-ing, He whom we a-dore

From God the Lord who heaven and earth hath made.
Who keep-eth Is - rael in His ho-ly care.
No moon shall harm thee in the si-lent night.
Shall keep thee hence-forth, yea, for-ev-er-more.   A-men.

Come, Thou Long Expected Jesus

HYFRYDOL 8.7.8.7. D.

Charles Wesley, 1707-1788

Rowland H. Pritchard, 1811-1887

1. Come, Thou long-ex-pect-ed Je-sus, Born to set Thy peo-ple free;
2. Born Thy peo-ple to de-liv-er, Born a child and yet a King,

From our fears and sins re-lease us; Let us find our rest in Thee.
Born to reign in us for-ev-er, Now Thy gra-cious king-dom bring.

Is-rael's strength and con-so-la-tion, Hope of all the earth Thou art;
By Thine own e-ter-nal Spir-it Rule in all our hearts a-lone;

Dear de-sire of ev-ery na-tion, Joy of ev-ery long-ing heart.
By Thine all - fi-cient mer-it Raise us to Thy glo-rious throne. Amen.

99 O Come, O Come, Emmanuel

VENI EMMANUEL 8.8.8.8.8.8.

Latin Hymn, 12th century
Stanza 1 tr. by John M. Neale, 1818-1866
Stanza 2,3 by Henry S. Coffin, 1877-1954

Ancient plain song, 13th century

1. O come, O come, Em - man - u - el, And ran - som cap-tive
2. O come, Thou Rod of Jes - se, free Thine own from Sa - tan's
3. O come, Thou Day-spring, come and cheer Our spir - its by Thine
4. O come, Thou Key of Da - vid, come, And o - pen wide our

Is - ra - el, That mourns in lone - ly ex - ile here
tyr - an - ny; From depths of hell Thy peo - ple save,
ad - vent here; And drive a - way the shades of night,
heaven - ly home; Make safe the way that leads on high,

Un - til the Son of God ap-pear. Re - joice! re - joice! Em-
And give them vic -tory o'er the grave. Re - joice! re - joice! Em-
And pierce the clouds and bring us light! Re - joice! re - joice! Em-
And close the path to mis - er - y. Re - joice! re - joice! Em-

man - u - el Shall come to thee, O Is - ra - el!
man - u - el Shall come to thee, O Is - ra - el!
man - u - el Shall come to thee, O Is - ra - el!
man - u - el Shall come to thee, O Is - ra - el! A - men.

O Come, All Ye Faithful

ADESTE FIDELES   Irregular

Latin 18th century
Trans. by Frederick Oakeley, 1802-1880

From John F. Wade's *Cantus Diversi*, 1751

1. O come, all ye faith - ful, Joy - ful and tri - um - phant, O
2. O sing choirs of an - gels, Sing in ex - ul - ta - tion! O
3. A - men, Lord, we greet Thee, Born this hap - py morn - ing, O

come ye, O come ye to Beth - le - hem!
sing, all ye cit - i - zens of heaven a - bove!
Je - sus, to Thee be all glo - ry given;

Come and be - hold Him, Born the King of an - gels!
Glo - ry to God, all glo - ry in the high - est!
Word of the Fa - ther, Now in flesh ap - pear - ing!

O come, let us a - dore Him, O come, let us a - dore Him,

O come, let us a - dore Him, Christ, the Lord! A - men.

Joy to the World

101

ANTIOCH 8.6.8.6.

From Psalm XCVIII
Isaac Watts, 1674-1748

Arr. from George F. Handel, 1685-1759

1. Joy to the world! the Lord is come; Let earth re-ceive her King;
2. Joy to the earth! the Sav-iour reigns; Let men their songs em-ploy;
3. No more let sins and sor-rows grow, Nor thorns in-fest the ground;
4. He rules the world with truth and grace, And makes the na-tions prove

Let ev - ery heart pre - pare Him room,
While fields and floods, rocks, hills, and plains
He comes to make His bless - ings flow
The glo - ries of His right - eous - ness,

And heaven and na - ture sing, And heaven and na - ture sing,
Re - peat the sound-ing joy, Re - peat the sound-ing joy,
Far as the curse is found, Far as the curse is found,
And won-ders of His love, And won-ders of His love

And heaven and na-ture sing,

And heaven and na-ture sing, And heaven and na-

And heaven, and heaven and na - ture sing.
Re - peat, re - peat the sound - ing joy.
Far as, far as the curse is found.
And won - ders, won - ders of His love.

ture sing,

It Came upon the Midnight Clear 102

CAROL 8.6.8.6. D

Edmund H. Sears, 1810-1876   Richard S. Willis, 1819-1900

1. It came up-on the mid-night clear, That glo-rious song of old,
2. Still thro' the clo-ven skies they come With peace-ful wings un-furled,
3. Yet with the woes of sin and strife The world hath suf-fered long;
4. For lo! the days are has-tening on By proph-et-bards fore-told,

From an-gels bend-ing near the earth To touch their harps of gold:
And still their heav'n-ly mu-sic floats O'er all the wea-ry world;
Be-neath the an-gel strain have rolled Two thou-sand years of wrong;
When with the ev-er-cir-cling years Comes round the age of gold;

"Peace on the earth, good will to men, From heav'n's all gra-cious King."
A-bove its sad and low-ly plains They bend on hover-ing wing,
And man, at war with man, hears not The words of peace they bring:
When peace shall o-ver all the earth Its an-cient splen-dors fling,

The world in sol-emn still-ness lay To hear the an-gels sing.
And ev-er o'er its Ba-bel sounds The bless-ed an-gels sing.
O hush the noise, ye men of strife, And hear the an-gels sing!
And the whole world send back the song Which now the an-gels sing. A-men.

103 Angels from the Realms of Glory

REGENT SQUARE 8.7.8.7.8.7.

James Montgomery, 1771-1854

Henry Smart, 1813-1879

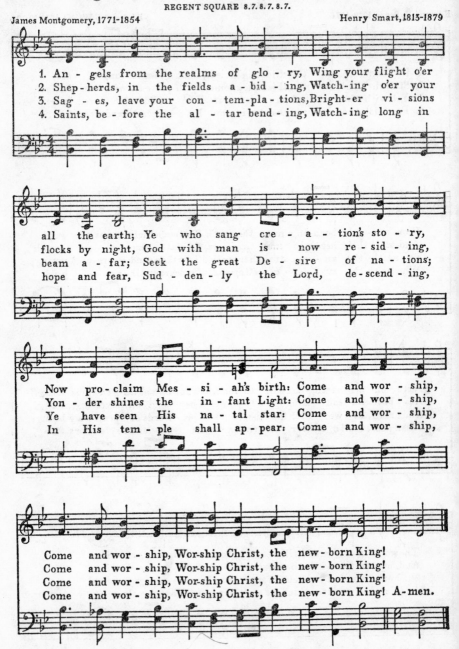

1. An - gels from the realms of glo - ry, Wing your flight o'er
2. Shep-herds, in the fields a - bid - ing, Watch-ing o'er your
3. Sag - es, leave your con - tem-pla-tions, Bright-er vi - sions
4. Saints, be - fore the al - tar bend - ing, Watch-ing long in

all the earth; Ye who sang cre - a - tion's sto - ry,
flocks by night, God with man is now re - sid - ing,
beam a - far; Seek the great De - sire of na - tions;
hope and fear, Sud - den - ly the Lord, de-scend - ing,

Now pro - claim Mes - si - ah's birth: Come and wor - ship,
Yon - der shines the in - fant Light: Come and wor - ship,
Ye have seen His na - tal star: Come and wor - ship,
In His tem - ple shall ap - pear: Come and wor - ship,

Come and wor - ship, Wor-ship Christ, the new - born King!
Come and wor - ship, Wor-ship Christ, the new - born King!
Come and wor - ship, Wor-ship Christ, the new - born King!
Come and wor - ship, Wor-ship Christ, the new - born King! A - men.

What Child Is This

GREENSLEEVES 8.7.8.7. with Refrain

William C. Dix, 1837-1898

Old English Melody

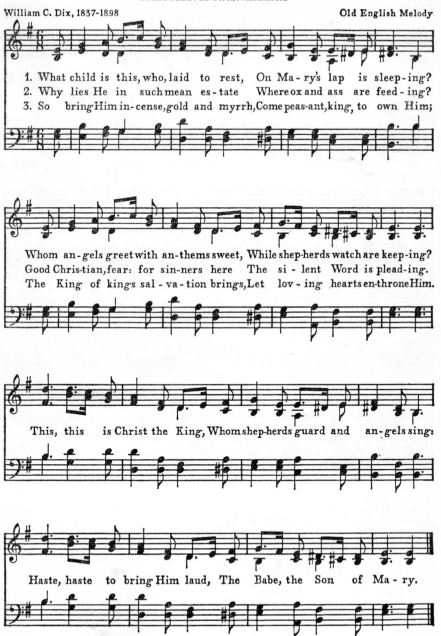

1. What child is this, who, laid to rest, On Mary's lap is sleeping?
2. Why lies He in such mean estate Where ox and ass are feeding?
3. So bring Him incense, gold and myrrh, Come peasant, king, to own Him;

Whom angels greet with anthems sweet, While shepherds watch are keeping?
Good Christian, fear: for sinners here The silent Word is pleading.
The King of kings salvation brings, Let loving hearts enthrone Him.

This, this is Christ the King, Whom shepherds guard and angels sing:

Haste, haste to bring Him laud, The Babe, the Son of Mary.

105 Good Christian Men, Rejoice

IN DULCI JUBILO 6.6.7.7.7.8.5,5.

From the Latin
Trans. by John M. Neale, 1818-1866

14th century German melody
Harmonized by Winfred Douglas, 1867-1944

1. Good Chris-tian men, re - joice, With heart and soul and voice;
2. Good Chris-tian men, re - joice, With heart and soul and voice;
3. Good Chris-tian men, re - joice, With heart and soul and voice;

Give ye heed to what we say: Je - sus Christ is born to-day;
Now ye hear of end-less bliss: Je - sus Christ was born for this!
Now ye need not fear the grave: Je - sus Christ was born to save!

Ox and ass be-fore Him bow, And He is in the man-ger now.
He hath o-pened heav-en's door, And man is bless-ed ev-er-more.
Calls you one and calls you all, To gain His ev-er-last-ing hall.

Christ is born to - day! Christ is born to - day!
Christ was born for this! Christ was born for this!
Christ was born to save! Christ was born to save!

Hark! the Herald Angels Sing 106

MENDELSSOHN 7.7.7.7.D with Refrain

Charles Wesley, 1707-1788
Alt. by George Whitefield, 1714-1770

Felix Mendelssohn, 1809-1847
William H. Cummings, 1831-1915

1. Hark! the her - ald an-gels sing, "Glo - ry to the new-born King;
2. Christ, by high - est heaven a - dored, Christ, the ev - er - last-ing Lord:
3. Hail the heav'n-born Prince of Peace! Hail the Sun of right-eous-ness!

Peace on earth, and mer-cy mild; God and sin - ners rec - on-ciled."
Long de - sired, be-hold Him come, Find-ing here His hum-ble home.
Light and life to all He brings, Risen with heal - ing in His wings.

Joy - ful, all ye na-tions rise, Join the tri-umph of the skies;
Veiled in flesh the God-head see, Hail th' In-car-nate De - i - ty!
Mild He lays His glo-ry by, Born that man no more may die,

With an - gel - ic hosts pro-claim, "Christ is born in Beth-le - hem!"
Pleased as man with men to dwell, Je - sus our Im-man-u - el.
Born to raise the sons of earth, Born to give them sec-ond birth.

Hark! the her-ald an-gels sing, "Glo - ry to the new-born King." A-men.

107 Gentle Mary Laid Her Child

TEMPUS ADEST FLORIDUM 7.6.7.6.D.

A Spring Carol c.14th century

Joseph Simpson Cook, 1859-1933

Ernest Mac Millan, 1895-

1. Gen - tle Ma - ry laid her Child Low - ly in a man - ger;
2. An - gels sang a - bout His birth; Wise men sought and found Him;
3. Gen - tle Ma - ry laid her Child Low - ly in a man - ger;

There He lay the un - de - filed, To the world a stran - ger.
Heav - en's star shone bright-ly forth Glo - ry all a - round Him.
He is still the un - de - filed, But no more a stran - ger.

Such a Babe in such a place, Can He be the Sav - iour?
Shep-herds saw the won-drous sight, Heard the an - gels sing - ing;
Son of God, of hum-ble birth, Beau - ti - ful the sto - ry;

Ask the saved of all the race Who have found His fa - vor.
All the plains were lit that night, All the hills were ring - ing.
Praise His name in all the earth, Hail the King of glo - ry!

Brightest and Best   108

Reginald Heber, 1783-1826   MORNING STAR 11. 10. 11. 10.   James P. Harding, 1861-1911

1. Bright - est and best of the sons of the morn - ing,
2. Cold on His cra - dle the dew - drops are shin - ing;
3. Shall we then yield Him, in cost - ly de - vo - tion,
4. Vain - ly we of - fer each amp - le ob - la - tion,
5. Bright - est and best of the sons of the morn - ing,

Dawn on our dark - ness, and lend us thine aid;
Low lies His head with the beasts of the stall;
O - dors of E - dom, and of - ferings di - vine,
Vain - ly with gifts would His fa - vor se - cure;
Dawn on our dark - ness, and lend us thine aid;

Star of the East, the ho - ri - zon a - dorn - ing,
An - gels a - dore Him in slum - ber re - clin - ing,
Gems of the moun - tain, and pearls of the o - cean,
Rich - er by far is the heart's a - dor - a - tion,
Star of the East, the ho - ri - zon a - dorn - ing,

Guide where our in - fant Re - deem - er is laid.
Ma - ker and Mon - arch and Sa - viour of all.
Myrrh from the for - est, and gold from the mine?
Dear - er to God are the prayers of the poor.
Guide where our in - fant Re - deem - er is laid.

109 Angels We Have Heard on High

GLORIA 7.7.7.7., with Refrain

Traditional Carol

Old French Carol

1. An - gels we have heard on high, Sweet - ly sing - ing o'er the plains,
2. Shep - herds, why this ju - bi - lee? Why your joy - ous strains pro - long?
3. Come to Beth - le - hem, and see Him whose birth the an - gels sing!
4. See with - in a man - ger laid Je - sus, Lord of heav'n and earth!

And the moun-tains in re-ply Ech - o back their joy - ous strains.
Say what may the ti - dings be Which in - spire your heav'n-ly song?
Come, a - dore on bend-ed knee Christ the Lord, the new - born King.
Ma - ry, Jo - seph, lend your aid, With us sing our Sav-iour's birth.

Glo - - - - - - - ri - a

in ex - cel - sis De - o, Glo - - - - -

- - - - ri - a in ex - cel - sis De - o.

Thou Didst Leave Thy Throne 110

MARGARET 10.8.11.8.with Refrain

Emily E.S. Elliott, 1836-1897   Timothy R.Matthews, 1826-1910

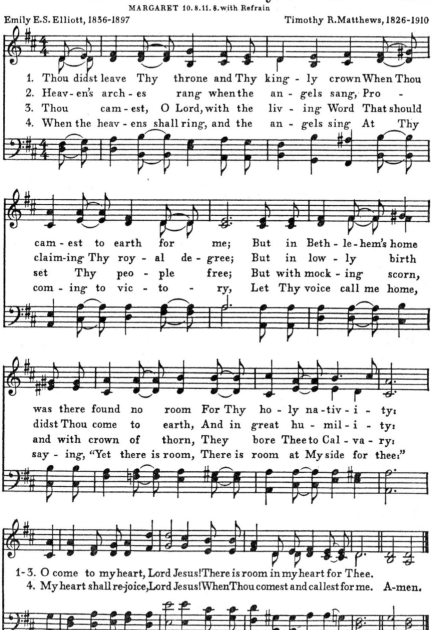

1. Thou didst leave Thy throne and Thy king - ly crown When Thou cam - est to earth for me; But in Beth - le - hem's home was there found no room For Thy ho - ly na - tiv - i - ty:
2. Heav- en's arch - es rang when the an - gels sang, Pro - claim-ing Thy roy - al de - gree; But in low - ly birth didst Thou come to earth, And in great hu - mil - i - ty:
3. Thou cam - est, O Lord, with the liv - ing Word That should set Thy peo - ple free; But with mock - ing scorn, and with crown of thorn, They bore Thee to Cal - va - ry:
4. When the heav - ens shall ring, and the an - gels sing At Thy com - ing to vic - to - ry, Let Thy voice call me home, say - ing, "Yet there is room, There is room at My side for thee:"

1-3. O come to my heart, Lord Jesus! There is room in my heart for Thee.
4. My heart shall re-joice, Lord Jesus! When Thou comest and callest for me. A-men.

The First Noel

111

THE FIRST NOEL Irregular with Refrain

Old English Carol

Traditional melody in
W. Sandys' *Christmas Carols*, 1833

1. The first No - el, the an - gel did say, Was to
2. They look - ed up and saw a star Shin - ing
3. And by the light of that same star Three
4. This star drew nigh to the north - west, O'er
5. Then en - tered in those wise men three, Full

cer-tain poor shep-herds in fields as they lay; In fields where
in the east, be - yond them far, And to the
wise - men came from coun - try far; To seek for a
Beth - le - hem it took its rest, And there it
rev - erent-ly up - on the knee, And of - fered

they lay keep - ing their sheep, On a cold win - ter's
earth it gave great light, And so it con -
king was their in - tent, And to fol - low the
did both stop and stay, Right o - ver the
there in His pres - ence, Their gold and

night that was so deep. No - el, No - el, No -
tin-ued both day and night.
star wher - ev - er it went.
place where Je - sus lay.
myrrh and frank - in - cense.

el, No - el, Born is the King of Is - ra - el.

While Shepherds Watched Their Flocks 112

CHRISTMAS 8.6.8.6.6.

Nahum Tate, 1652-1715

Arr. from George F. Handel, 1685-1759

1. While shepherds watched their flocks by night, All seat - ed on the
2. "Fear not!" said he, for might-y dread Had seized their troub - led
3. "To you, in Da - vid's town, this day Is born of Da - vid's
4. "The heav'n - ly Babe you there shall find To hu - man view dis -
5. "All glo - ry be to God on high, And to the earth be

ground, The an - gel of the Lord came down, And
mind, "Glad ti - dings of great joy I bring, To
line, The Sav - iour, who is Christ the Lord; And
played, All mean-ly wrapped in swath - ing - bands, And
peace, Good will hence-forth from heav'n to men, Be -

glo - ry shone a - round, And glo - ry shone a - round.
you and all man - kind, To you and all man - kind.
this shall be the sign, And this shall be the sign:
in a man - ger laid, And in a man - ger laid."
gin and nev - er cease! Be - gin and nev - er cease!"

113

Silent Night! Holy Night!

STILLE NACHT Irregular

Joseph Mohr, 1792-1848

Franz Grüber, 1787-1863

1. Si - lent night, ho - ly night, All is calm, all is bright
2. Si - lent night, ho - ly night, Shep - herds quake, at the sight!
3. Si - lent night, ho - ly night, Son of God, love's pure light
4. Si - lent night, ho - ly night, Won - drous star, lend Thy light,

Round yon Vir - gin Mother and Child. Ho - ly In-fant, so ten-der and mild,
Glo - ries stream from Heaven a-far, Heav'nly host sing al - le - lu - ia;
Ra - diant beams from Thy ho - ly face, With the dawn of re - deem-ing grace,
With the an - gels let us sing, Al - le - lu - ia to our King;

Sleep in heav-en-ly peace, Sleep in heav - en - ly peace.
Christ the Sav-iour is born, Christ the Sav-iour is born.
Je - sus Lord at Thy birth, Je - sus Lord at Thy birth.
Christ the Sav-iour is born, Christ the Sav-iour is born.

114

Away in a Manger

MÜELLER 11.11.11.11.

Traditional Carol

James R. Murray, 1841-1905

1. A - way in a man-ger, no crib for a bed, The lit - tle Lord
2. The cat - tle are low-ing, the Ba - by a-wakes, But lit - tle Lord
3. Be near me, Lord Je-sus, I ask Thee to stay Close by me for-

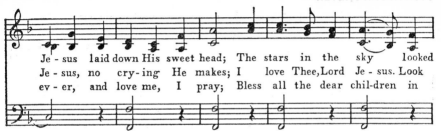

Je - sus laid down His sweet head; The stars in the sky looked
Je - sus, no cry - ing He makes; I love Thee, Lord Je - sus. Look
ev - er, and love me, I pray; Bless all the dear chil - dren in

down where He lay, The lit - tle Lord Je - sus, a - sleep on the hay.
down from the sky, And stay by my cra - dle, till morn - ing is nigh.
Thy ten - der care, Pre - pare us for heav - en, to live with Thee there.

I Heard the Bells on Christmas Day 115

CHRISTINE 8.8.8.8.

Henry W. Longfellow, 1807-1882

Melody by Franklin L. Lusk, 1929-
Harmonized by Ronald R. Sider, 1933

1. I heard the bells on Christ-mas day Their old fa - mil - iar car-ols play,
2. I thought how, as the day had come, The bel-fries of all Chris-ten-dom
3. And in de-spair I bowed my head: "There is no peace on earth," I said,
4. Then pealed the bells more loud and deep: "God is not dead, nor doth He sleep;
5. Till, ring-ing, sing-ing on its way, The world re-volved from night to day,

And wild and sweet the words re-peat Of peace on earth, good will to men.
Had rolled a - long th' unbroken song Of peace on earth, good will to men.
"For hate is strong, and mocks the song Of peace on earth, good will to men."
The wrong shall fail, the right pre-vail, With peace on earth, good will to men":
A voice, a chime, a chant sub-lime, Of peace on earth, good will to men!

116 God Rest You Merry, Gentlemen

GOD REST YOU MERRY 7.6.7.6.7.6. with Refrain

Traditional Melody
Harmonized by John Stainer, 1840-1901

English Traditional

1. God rest you mer - ry, gen - tle-men, Let noth - ing you dis - may,
2. From God our heaven-ly Fa - ther A bless - ed an - gel came;
3. "Fear not, then," said the an - gel, "Let noth - ing you af - fright,
4. Now to the Lord sing prais - es, All you with - in this place,

Re - mem - ber Christ our Sav - iour Was born on Christ-mas Day;
And un - to cer - tain shep - herds Brought ti - dings of the same;
This day is born a Sav - iour Of Vir - gin pure and bright,
And with true love and broth-er-hood Each oth - er now em - brace;

To save us all from Sa - tan's power When we were gone a - stray.
How that in Beth - le - hem was born The Son of God by name.
To free all who will trust in Him From Sa - tan's power and might."
This ho - ly tide of Christ-mas All oth - ers doth ef - face.

O ti - dings of com - fort and joy, Com-fort and joy;

O ti - dings of com - fort and joy.

Once in Royal David's City

IRBY 8.7.8.7.8.8.

Cecil F. Alexander, 1823-1895

Henry J. Gauntlett, 1805-1876

1. Once in roy-al Da-vid's cit-y Stood a low-ly cat-tle shed, Where a moth-er laid her ba-by In a man-ger for his bed: Ma-ry was that moth-er mild, Je-sus Christ, her lit-tle Child.

2. He came down to earth from heav-en, Who is God and Lord of all, And His shel-ter was a sta-ble, And His cra-dle was a stall: With the poor, and mean, and low-ly, Lived on earth our Sav-iour ho-ly.

3. Je-sus is our child-hood's pat-tern, Day by day like us He grew; He was lit-tle, weak, and help-less, Tears and smiles like us He knew; And He feel-eth for our sad-ness, And He shar-eth in our glad-ness.

4. And our eyes at last shall see Him, Thro' His own re-deem-ing love, For that Child so dear and gen-tle Is our Lord in heav'n a-bove, And He leads His chil-dren on To the place where He is gone. A-men.

118   O Little Town of Bethlehem

ST. LOUIS 8.6.8.6.7.6.8.6.

Phillips Brooks, 1835-1893   Lewis H. Redner, 1831-1908

1. O   lit - tle town of   Beth-le-hem, How still we see thee lie!
2. For Christ is born of   Ma — ry; And gath-ered all a - bove,
3. How si - lent - ly, how si - lent - ly, The won-drous gift is given!
4. O   ho - ly Child of   Beth-le-hem, De-scend on   us, we pray;

A - bove thy deep and dream-less sleep The si - lent stars go   by:
While mor-tals sleep, the an - gels keep Their watch of won-dering love.
So   God im-parts to   hu-man hearts The bless-ings of His heaven.
Cast out our sin, and en - ter in, Be born in us to - day.

Yet   in thy dark streets shin-eth The ev - er - last-ing Light; The
O   morn-ing stars, to - geth-er Pro-claim the ho - ly birth, And
No   ear may hear His com-ing, But in this world of   sin, Where
We   hear the Christ-mas an - gels The great glad ti - dings tell; O

hopes and fears of   all the years Are met in thee to - night.
prais-es sing to   God the King, And peace to men on earth.
meek souls will re - ceive Him still, The dear Christ en-ters in.
come to   us, a - bide with us, Our Lord Em-man - u - el.   A-men.

As with Gladness Men of Old 119

DIX. 7.7.7.7.7.7.

William C. Dix, 1837-1898

Abridged from a Chorale by
Conrad Kocher, 1786-1872

1. As with glad-ness men of old Did the guid-ing
2. As with joy-ous steps they sped To that low-ly
3. As they of-fered gifts most rare At that man-ger
4. Ho-ly Je-sus, ev-ery day Keep us in the

star be-hold; As with joy they hailed its light,
man-ger bed, There to bend the knee be-fore
rude and bare, So may we with ho-ly joy,
nar-row way; And, when earth-ly things are past,

Lead-ing on-ward, beam-ing bright; So, most gra-cious
Him whom heaven and earth a-dore; So may we with
Pure and free from sin's al-loy, All our cost-liest
Bring our ran-somed souls at last Where they need no

Lord, may we Ev-er-more be led to Thee.
will-ing feet Ev-er seek Thy mer-cy seat.
treas-ures bring, Christ, to Thee, our heaven-ly King.
star to guide, Where no clouds Thy glo-ry hide. A-men.

120   O Sing a Song of Bethlehem

KINGSFOLD 8.6.8.6.8.6.8.6.

Louis F. Benson, 1855-1930

English Traditional Melody
Arr. by R. Vaughn Williams, 1872-1958

1. O sing a song of Beth-le-hem, Of shep-herds watch-ing there,
2. O sing a song of Naz-a-reth, Of sun-ny days of joy,
3. O sing a song of Gal-i-lee, Of lake and woods and hill,
4. O sing a song of Cal-va-ry, Its glo-ry and dis-may;

And of the news that came to them From an-gels in the air;
O sing of fra-grant flow-ers' breath And of the sin-less Boy;
Of Him who walked up-on the sea And bade its waves be still;
Of Him who hung up-on the tree, And took our sins a-way;

The light that shone on Beth-le-hem Fills all the world to-day; Of
For now the flowers of Naz-a-reth In ev-ery heart may grow; Now
For though, like waves on Gal-i-lee, Dark seas of trou-ble roll, When
For He who died on Cal-va-ry Is ris-en from the grave, And

Je-sus' birth and peace on earth The an-gels sing al-way.
spreads the fame of His dear name On all the winds that blow.
faith has heard the Mas-ter's word, Falls peace up-on the soul.
Christ, our Lord, by heaven a-dored, Is might-y now to save. A-men.

Wonderful Birth to a Manger He Came 121

WONDERFUL 10.10.10.10.with Refrain

Alfred H. Ackley, 1887-1960   Alfred H. Ackley, 1887-1960

1. Won-der-ful birth, to a man-ger He came, Made in the like-ness of
2. Won-der-ful life, full of serv-ice so free, Friend to the poor and the
3. Won-der-ful death, for it meant not de-feat, Cal-va-ry made His great
4. Won-der-ful hope, He is com-ing a-gain, Com-ing as King o'er the

man to pro-claim God's bound-less love for a world sick with sin, Plead-ing with
need-y was He; Un-fail-ing good-ness on all He be-stowed, Un-dy-ing
mis-sion com-plete, Wrought our re-demption, and when He a-rose, Ban-ished for-
na-tions to reign; Glo-ri-ous prom-ise, His word can-not fail, His right-eous

sin-ners to let Him come in.
faith in the vil-est He showed. Won-der-ful name He bears, Won-der-ful
ev-er the last of our foes.
king-dom at last must pre-vail!

crown He wears, Won-der-ful bless-ings His tri-umphs af-ford; Won-der-ful

Cal-va-ry, Won-der-ful grace for me, Won-der-ful love of my Won-der-ful Lord!

122 Jesus, Thou Divine Companion

HYFRYDOL 8.7.8.7 D.

Henry van Dyke, 1852-1933

Rowland H. Prichard, 1811-1887

1. Je - sus, Thou di-vine com - pan-ion, By Thy low-ly hu-man birth
2. They who tread the path of la - bor Fol-low where Thy feet have trod;
3. Ev - ery task, how-ev - er sim-ple, Sets the soul that does it free;

Thou hast come to join the work-ers, Bur - den-bear-ers of the earth.
They who work with-out com-plain-ing Do the ho - ly will of God.
Ev - ery deed of love and kindness Done to man is done to Thee.

Thou, the car-pen - ter of Naz-reth, Toil-ing for Thy dai - ly food,
Thou, the peace that pass-eth knowledge, Dwell-est in the dai - ly strife;
Je - sus, Thou di-vine com-pan - ion, Help us all to work our best;

By Thy pa - tience and Thy cour - age, Thou hast taught us toil is good.
Thou, the Bread of heav'n, art bro - ken In the sa - cra-ment of life.
Bless us in our dai - ly la - bor, Lead us to our Sab-bath rest. A-men.

I Know Not How That Bethlehem's Babe 123

BOUWERIE 8.6.8.6.

Henry Webb Farrington, 1879-1930

W. A. Goldsworthy, 1941-

1. I know not how that Beth-lehem's Babe Could in the God-head be;
2. I know not how that Cal-vary's cross A world from sin could free;
3. I know not how that Jo-seph's tomb Could solve death's mys-ter-y;

I on-ly know the man-ger Child Has brought God's life to me.
I on-ly know its match-less love Has brought God's love to me.
I on-ly know a liv-ing Christ, Our im-mor-tal-i-ty. A-men.

Music Copyright 1942 by The Church Pension Fund. Words by permission of The Hymn Society.

Ride On! Ride On in Majesty 124

ST. DROSTANE 8.8.8.8.

Henry H. Milman, 1791-1868

John B. Dykes, 1823-1876

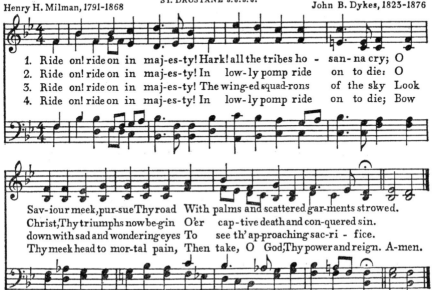

1. Ride on! ride on in maj-es-ty! Hark! all the tribes ho-san-na cry; O
2. Ride on! ride on in maj-es-ty! In low-ly pomp ride on to die: O
3. Ride on! ride on in maj-es-ty! The wing-ed squad-rons of the sky Look
4. Ride on! ride on in maj-es-ty! In low-ly pomp ride on to die; Bow

Sav-iour meek, pur-sue Thy road With palms and scattered gar-ments strowed.
Christ, Thy triumphs now be-gin O'er cap-tive death and con-quered sin.
down with sad and wondering eyes To see th' ap-proaching sac-ri-fice.
Thy meek head to mor-tal pain, Then take, O God, Thy power and reign. A-men.

125 All Glory, Laud, and Honor

ST. THEODULPH 7. 6. 7. 6. D.

Theodulph of Orleans, 760-821
Trans. by John M. Neale, 1818-1866

Melchior Teschner, 1584-1635

{All glo - ry, laud, and hon - or To Thee, Re - deem - er, King,}
{To whom the lips of chil - dren Made sweet ho - san - nas ring.}

1. Thou art the King of Is - rael, Thou, Da - vid's roy - al Son,
2. The com - pa - ny of an - gels Are prais - ing Thee on high,
3. The peo - ple of the He - brews With palms be - fore Thee went;
4. To Thee, be - fore Thy pas - sion, They sang their hymns of praise;
5. Thou didst ac - cept their prais - es, Ac - cept the prayers we bring,

Who in the Lord's name com - est, The King and Bless - ed One.
And mor - tal men, and all things Cre - at - ed, make re - ply.
Our praise and prayer and an - thems Be - fore Thee we pre - sent.
To Thee, now high ex - alt - ed, Our mel - o - dy we raise.
Who in all good de - light - est, Thou good and gra - cious King.

D. S.

{All glo - ry, laud, and hon - or To Thee, Re - deem - er, King,}
{To whom the lips of chil - dren Made sweet ho - san - nas ring.} A - men.

The ascription should be sung the first time only; the refrain should be sung after each stanza.

Hosanna, Loud Hosanna

126

ELLACOMBE 7. 6. 7. 6. D.

Jeannette Threlfall, 1821-1880

Gesangbuch der Herzogl, 1784

1. Ho - san - na, loud ho - san - na The lit - tle chil - dren sang;
2. From Ol - i - vet they fol - lowed 'Mid an ex - ult - ant crowd,
3. "Ho - san - na in the high - est!" That an - cient song we sing,

Through pil - lared court and tem - ple The love - ly an - them rang;
The vic - tor palm-branch wav - ing, And chant - ing clear and loud;
For Christ is our Re - deem - er, The Lord of heaven our King.

To Je - sus, who had blessed them Close fold - ed to His breast,
The Lord of men and an - gels Rode on in low - ly state,
O may we ev - er praise Him With heart and life and voice,

The chil - dren sang their prais - es, The sim - plest and the best.
Nor scorned that lit - tle chil - dren Should on His bid - ding wait.
And in His bliss - ful pres - ence E - ter - nal - ly re - joice! A - men.

127 When, His Salvation Bringing

TOURS 7. 6. 7. 6. D.

John King, 1789-1858　　　　　　　　　　　　　Berthold Tours, 1838-1897

1. When, His sal - va - tion bring-ing, To Zi - on Je - sus came,
2. And since the Lord re - tain - eth His love for chil - dren still,
3. For should we fail pro-claim-ing Our great Re - deem-er's praise,

The chil-dren all stood sing - ing Ho - san - nas to His name;
Though now as King He reign-eth On Zi - on's heaven-ly hill,
The stones, our si - lence sham-ing, Would their ho - san - nas raise.

Nor did their zeal of - fend Him, But, as He rode a - long,
We'll flock a - round His ban - ner, Who sits up - on His throne,
But shall we on - ly ren - der The trib - ute of our words?

He let them still at - tend Him, And smiled to hear their song.
And cry a - loud, "Ho-san-na To Da - vid's roy-al Son."
No, while our hearts are ten-der, They, too, shall be the Lord's. A-men.

O Sacred Head, Now Wounded 128

PASSION CHORALE 7.6.7.6.D.

Ascribed to Bernard of Clairvaux, 1091-1153
Trans. into German by Paul Gerhardt, 1607-1676
Trans. from German by James W. Alexander, 1804-1859

Hans Leo Hassler, 1564-1612
Har. by J.S. Bach, 1685-1750

1. O sa-cred head, now wound-ed, With grief and shame weighed down,
2. What Thou, my Lord, hast suf-fered Was all for sin-ners' gain:
3. What lan-guage shall I bor-row, To thank Thee, dear-est Friend,
4. Be near when I am dy-ing, O show Thy cross to me;

Now scorn-ful-ly sur-round-ed With thorns, Thine on-ly crown!
Mine, mine was the trans-gres-sion, But Thine the dead-ly pain.
For this Thy dy-ing sor-row, Thy pit-y with-out end?
And for my suc-cor fly-ing, Come, Lord, and set me free.

O sa-cred head, what glo-ry, What bliss, till now was Thine!
Lo, here I fall, my Sav-iour! 'Tis I de-serve Thy place;
O make me Thine for-ev-er; And should I faint-ing be,
These eyes, new faith re-ceiv-ing, From Je-sus shall not move;

Yet though de-spised and go-ry, I joy to call Thee mine.
Look on me with Thy fav-or, Vouch-safe to me Thy grace.
Lord, let me nev-er, nev-er, Out-live my love to Thee.
For he who dies be-liev-ing, Dies safe-ly through Thy love. A-men.

129 In the Cross of Christ I Glory

RATHBUN 8.7.8.7.

John Bowring, 1792-1872

Ithamar Conkey, 1815-1867

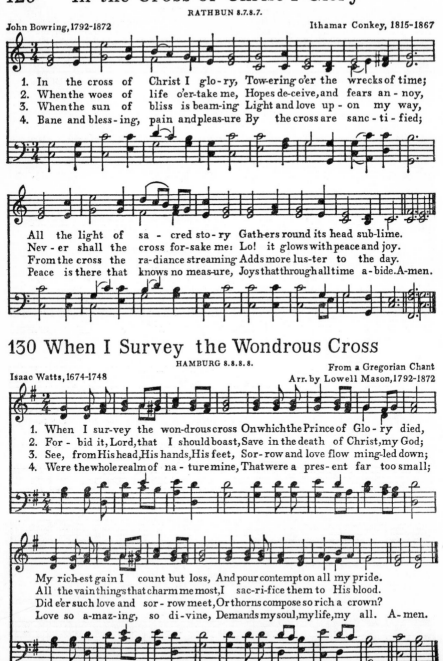

1. In   the cross of   Christ I glo-ry, Tow-ering o'er the   wrecks of time;
2. When the woes of   life o'er-take me, Hopes de-ceive, and   fears an - noy,
3. When the sun of   bliss is beam-ing Light and love up - on   my way,
4. Bane and bless-ing,   pain and pleas-ure By   the cross are   sanc - ti - fied;

All   the light of   sa - cred sto-ry Gath-ers round its head sub-lime.
Nev - er shall the   cross for-sake me: Lo! it glows with peace and joy.
From the cross the   ra-diance streaming Adds more lus-ter   to   the day.
Peace   is there that   knows no meas-ure, Joys that through all time a-bide. A-men.

130 When I Survey the Wondrous Cross

HAMBURG 8.8.8.8.

Isaac Watts, 1674-1748

From a Gregorian Chant
Arr. by Lowell Mason, 1792-1872

1. When I sur-vey the won-drous cross On which the Prince of Glo - ry died,
2. For - bid it, Lord, that I should boast, Save in the death of Christ, my God;
3. See, from His head, His hands, His feet, Sor - row and love flow ming-led down;
4. Were the whole realm of na - ture mine, That were a pres - ent far too small;

My rich-est gain I   count but loss, And pour contempt on all my pride.
All the vain things that charm me most, I   sac-ri-fice them to His blood.
Did e'er such love and sor - row meet, Or thorns compose so rich a crown?
Love so a-maz-ing, so di-vine, Demands my soul, my life, my all. A - men.

Beneath the Cross of Jesus

ST. CHRISTOPHER 7.6.8.6.8.6.8.6.

Elizabeth C. Clephane, 1830-1869

Frederick C. Maker, 1844-1927

1. Be - neath the cross of Je - sus I fain would take my stand,
2. Up - on the cross of Je - sus Mine eye at times can see
3. I take, O Cross, thy shad - ow For my a - bid - ing place;

The shad - ow of a might - y rock With - in a wea - ry land;
The ver - y dy - ing form of One Who suf-fered there for me.
I ask no oth - er sun-shine than The sun-shine of His face;

A home with-in the wil - der-ness, A rest up - on the way,
And from my smit-ten heart with tears, These won-ders I con - fess:
Con - tent to let the world go by, To know no gain nor loss,

From the burn-ing of the noon-tide heat, And the bur-den of the day.
The won-der of His glo-rious love, And my own worth-less-ness.
My sin - ful self my on - ly shame, My glo - ry all the cross.

132 Go to Dark Gethsemane

GETHSEMANE 7.7.7.7.7.7.

James Montgomery, 1771-1854   Richard Redhead, 1820-1901

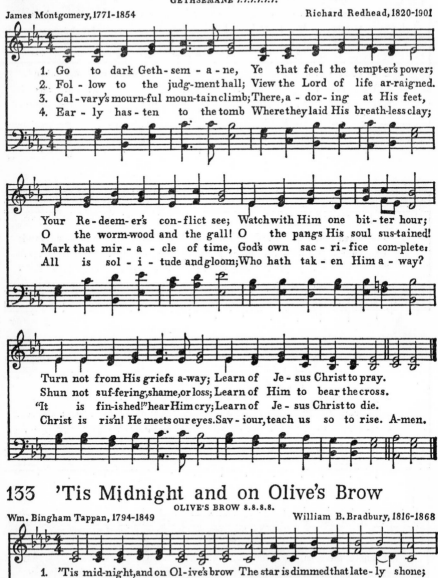

1. Go to dark Geth-sem-a-ne, Ye that feel the tempt-er's power;
2. Fol-low to the judg-ment hall; View the Lord of life ar-raigned.
3. Cal-vary's mourn-ful moun-tain climb; There, a-dor-ing at His feet,
4. Ear-ly has-ten to the tomb Where they laid His breath-less clay;

Your Re-deem-er's con-flict see; Watch with Him one bit-ter hour;
O the worm-wood and the gall! O the pangs His soul sus-tained!
Mark that mir-a-cle of time, God's own sac-ri-fice com-plete;
All is sol-i-tude and gloom; Who hath tak-en Him a-way?

Turn not from His griefs a-way; Learn of Je-sus Christ to pray.
Shun not suf-fering, shame, or loss; Learn of Him to bear the cross.
"It is fin-ished!" hear Him cry; Learn of Je-sus Christ to die.
Christ is ris'n! He meets our eyes. Sav-iour, teach us so to rise. A-men.

133 'Tis Midnight and on Olive's Brow

OLIVE'S BROW 8.8.8.8.

Wm. Bingham Tappan, 1794-1849   William B. Bradbury, 1816-1868

1. 'Tis mid-night, and on Ol-ive's brow The star is dimmed that late-ly shone;
2. 'Tis mid-night, and from all re-moved, The Sav-iour wres-tles lone with fears;
3. 'Tis mid-night, and for oth-ers' guilt The Man of Sor-rows weeps in blood;
4. 'Tis mid-night, and from heaven-ly plains Is borne the song that an-gels know;

'Tis mid-night,in the gar-den now The suf-fer-ing Sav-iour prays a-lone.
E'en that dis-ci-ple whom He loved Heeds not his Mas-ter's grief and tears.
Yet He that hath in an-guish knelt Is not for-sak-en by His God.
Un-heard by mor-tals are the strains That sweetly soothe the Sav-iour's woe. A-men.

Arise, My Soul, Arise   134

LENOX 6.6.6.6.8.8.

Charles Wesley, 1707-1788   Lewis Edson, 1748-1820

1. A - rise, my soul, a - rise, Shake off thy guilt - y fears; The bleed-ing
2. He ev - er lives a - bove, For me to in - ter-cede; His all - re -
3. Five bleeding wounds He bears, Re-ceived on Cal - va - ry; They pour ef -
4. The Fa-ther hears Him pray, His dear a - noint-ed One; He can-not
5. My God is rec - on-ciled: His pardoning voice I hear; He owns me

Sac - ri-fice In my be-half ap-pears; Be - fore the throne my Sure-ty stands,
deem-ing love, His prec-ious blood to plead; His blood a-toned for all our race,
fect-ual prayers, They strongly plead for me; "For-give Him, O for-give," they cry,
turn a - way The pres-ence of His Son: His Spir - it an-swers to the blood,
for His child: I can no long-er fear; With con-fi-dence I now draw nigh,

Be - fore the throne my Surety stands, My name is writ-ten on His hands.
His blood a-toned for all our race, And sprinkles now the throne of grace.
"For-give Him, O for-give," they cry, "Nor let that ransomed sin-ner die."
His Spir-it an-swers to the blood, And tells me I am born of God.
With con-fi-dence I now draw nigh, And, "Fa-ther, Ab-ba, Fa-ther," cry. A-men.

135 There Is a Green Hill Far Away

GREEN HILL 8.6.8.6. with Refrain

Cecil Frances Alexander, 1823-1895

George C. Stebbins, 1846-1945, alt.

1. There is a green hill far a-way, With-out a cit-y wall,
2. We may not know, we can-not tell What pains He had to bear;
3. He died that we might be for-given, He died to make us good,
4. There was no oth-er good e-nough To pay the price of sin;

Where the dear Lord was cru-ci-fied, Who died to save us all.
But we be-lieve it was for us He hung and suf-fered there.
That we might go at last to heaven, Saved by His pre-cious blood.
He on-ly could un-lock the gate Of heaven, and let us in.

O, dear-ly, dear-ly has He loved, And we must love Him, too,

And trust in His re-deem-ing blood, And try His works to do.

Down at the Cross

GLORY TO HIS NAME 9.9.9.5.with Refrain

136

Elisha A. Hoffman, 1839-1929

John H. Stockton, 1813-1877

1. Down at the cross where my Sav - iour died,
2. I am so won - drous - ly saved from sin,
3. O pre - cious foun - tain that saves from sin,
4. Come to this foun - tain, so rich and sweet;

Down where for cleans - ing from sin I cried,
Je - sus so sweet - ly a - bides with - in;
I am so glad I have en - tered in;
Cast thy poor soul at the Sav - iour's feet;

There to my heart was the blood ap - plied;
There at the cross where He took me in;
There Je - sus saves me and keeps me clean;
Plunge in to - day and be made com - plete;

Glo-ry to His name! Glo-ry to His name, Glo-ry to His name:

There to my heart was the blood ap-plied; Glo - ry to His name!

137 Blessed Redeemer

REDEEMER. 9.9.9.9. with Refrain

Avis Burgeson Christiansen, 1895- Harry Dixon Loes, 1892-

1. Up Cal-vary's moun-tain one dread-ful morn, Walked Christ my Sav-iour
2. "Fa-ther, for-give them!" thus did He pray, E'en while His life-blood
3. O how I love Him, Sav-iour and Friend, How can my prais-es

wea-ry and worn, Fac-ing for sin-ners death on the cross,
flowed fast a-way; Pray-ing for sin-ners while in such woe—
ev-er find end! Thro' years un-num-bered on heav-en's shore

That He might save them from end-less loss.
No one but Je-sus ev-er loved so. Bless-ed Re-deem-er,
My tongue shall praise Him for-ev-er-more.

pre-cious Re-deem-er! Seems now I see Him on

Cal-va-ry's tree; Wound-ed and bleed-ing, for sin-ners

plead - ing, Blind and un - heed - ing_ dy - ing for me!

How Great the Wisdom and the Love   138

Eliza R. Snow

8.6.8.6.

Thomas McIntyre

1. How great the wis - dom and the love that
2. His pre - cious blood He free - ly spilt; His
3. He marked the path and led the way, And
4. How great, how glo - rious, how com - plete Re -

filled the courts on high And sent the Sav - iour
life He free - ly gave, A sin - less sac - ri -
ev - ery point de - fines To light and life and
demp - tion's grand de - sign, Where jus - tice, love, and

from a - bove To suf - fer, bleed, and die.
fice for guilt, A dy - ing world to save.
end - less day Where God's full pres - ence shines.
mer - cy meet In har - mo - ny di - vine. A - men.

Used by permission of the Church of Jesus Christ Latter Day Saints.

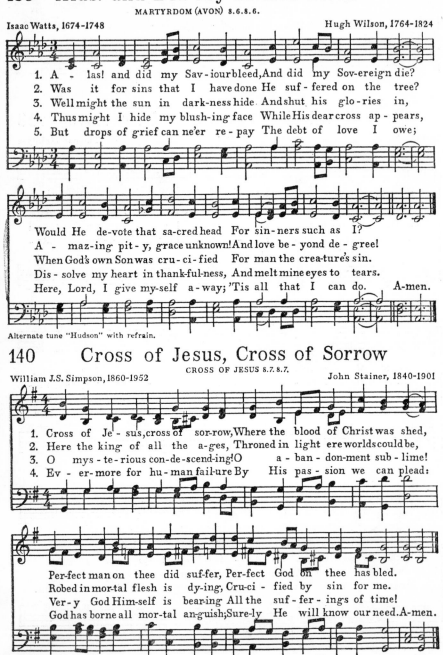

139 Alas! and Did My Saviour Bleed

MARTYRDOM (AVON) 8.6.8.6.

Isaac Watts, 1674-1748   Hugh Wilson, 1764-1824

1. A - las! and did my Sav-iour bleed, And did my Sov-ereign die?
2. Was it for sins that I have done He suf - fered on the tree?
3. Well might the sun in dark-ness hide. And shut his glo-ries in,
4. Thus might I hide my blush-ing face While His dear cross ap - pears,
5. But drops of grief can ne'er re - pay The debt of love I owe;

Would He de-vote that sa-cred head For sin-ners such as I?
A - maz-ing pit-y, grace unknown! And love be - yond de - gree!
When God's own Son was cru-ci-fied For man the crea-ture's sin.
Dis - solve my heart in thank-ful-ness, And melt mine eyes to tears.
Here, Lord, I give my-self a - way; 'Tis all that I can do. A-men.

Alternate tune "Hudson" with refrain.

140 Cross of Jesus, Cross of Sorrow

CROSS OF JESUS 8.7.8.7.

William J.S. Simpson, 1860-1952   John Stainer, 1840-1901

1. Cross of Je - sus, cross of sor-row, Where the blood of Christ was shed,
2. Here the king of all the a-ges, Throned in light ere worlds could be,
3. O mys-te-rious con-de-scend-ing! O a - ban-don-ment sub - lime!
4. Ev - er-more for hu-man fail-ure By His pas - sion we can plead:

Per-fect man on thee did suf-fer, Per-fect God on thee has bled.
Robed in mor-tal flesh is dy-ing, Cru-ci - fied by sin for me.
Ver-y God Him-self is bear-ing All the suf - fer - ings of time!
God has borne all mor-tal an-guish; Sure-ly He will know our need. A-men.

When I See the Blood

141

REDEEMER 9.9.10.9.with Refrain

Unknown

J. G. Foote.

1. Christ our Re-deem - er died on the cross, Died for the sin - ner,
2. Chief - est of sin - ners, Je - sus will save; All He has prom-ised,
3. Judg-ment is com - ing, all will be there, Each one re-ceiv - ing
4. O great com-pas - sion! O bound-less love! O lov - ing-kind-ness,

paid all his due: Sprin - kle your soul with the blood of the Lamb,
that will He do; Wash in the foun - tain o - pened for sin,
just - ly his due; Hide in the sav - ing, sin-cleans-ing blood,
faith - ful and true! Find peace and shel - ter un - der the blood,

And I will pass, will pass o - ver you. When I see the
When I

blood, When I see the blood, When I see the
see the blood, When I see the blood, When I

blood I will pass, I will pass, o - ver you.
see the blood o - ver you.

142 "Man of Sorrows," What a Name

MAN OF SORROWS 7.7.7.8.

Philip P. Bliss, 1838-1876   Philip P. Bliss, 1838-1876

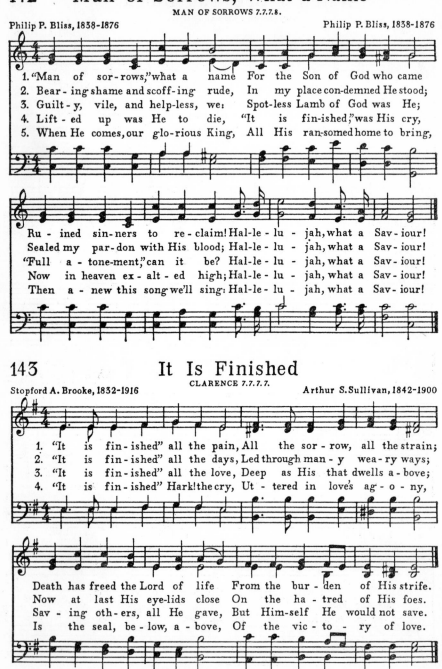

1. "Man of sor-rows," what a name For the Son of God who came
2. Bear-ing shame and scoff-ing rude, In my place con-demned He stood;
3. Guilt-y, vile, and help-less, we: Spot-less Lamb of God was He;
4. Lift-ed up was He to die, "It is fin-ished," was His cry,
5. When He comes, our glo-rious King, All His ran-somed home to bring,

Ru-ined sin-ners to re-claim! Hal-le-lu-jah, what a Sav-iour!
Sealed my par-don with His blood; Hal-le-lu-jah, what a Sav-iour!
"Full a-tone-ment," can it be? Hal-le-lu-jah, what a Sav-iour!
Now in heaven ex-alt-ed high; Hal-le-lu-jah, what a Sav-iour!
Then a-new this song we'll sing: Hal-le-lu-jah, what a Sav-iour!

143 It Is Finished

CLARENCE 7.7.7.7.

Stopford A. Brooke, 1832-1916   Arthur S. Sullivan, 1842-1900

1. "It is fin-ished" all the pain, All the sor-row, all the strain;
2. "It is fin-ished" all the days, Led through man-y wea-ry ways;
3. "It is fin-ished" all the love, Deep as His that dwells a-bove;
4. "It is fin-ished" Hark! the cry, Ut-tered in love's ag-o-ny,

Death has freed the Lord of life From the bur-den of His strife.
Now at last His eye-lids close On the ha-tred of His foes.
Sav-ing oth-ers, all He gave, But Him-self He would not save.
Is the seal, be-low, a-bove, Of the vic-to-ry of love.

Jesus Christ Is Risen Today   144

LLANFAIR 7.7.7.7.with Alleluias

Latin Hymn, 14th century
Stanza Three, Charles Wesley, 1707-1788

Robert Williams, 1781-1821

1. Je - sus Christ is risen to day, Al - le - lu - ia!
2. Hymns of praise then let us sing, Al - le - lu - ia!
3. Sing we to our God a bove, Al - le - lu - ia!

Our tri - um-phant ho - ly day, Al - le - lu - ia!
Un - to Christ, our heaven-ly King, Al - le - lu - ia!
Praise e - ter - nal as His love; Al - le - lu - ia!

Who did once, up - on the cross, Al - le - lu - ia!
Who en - dured the cross and grave, Al - le - lu - ia!
Praise Him, all ye heaven-ly host, Al - le - lu - ia!

Suf - fer to re - deem our loss. Al - le - lu - ia!
Sin - ners to re - deem and save. Al - le - lu - ia!
Fa - ther, Son, and Ho - ly Ghost. Al - le - lu - ia! A - men.

145 Welcome, Happy Morning

HERMAS 6.5.6.5.D. with Refrain

Venantius Fortunatus, c. 530-609
John Ellerton, 1826-1893

Frances R. Havergal, 1836-1879

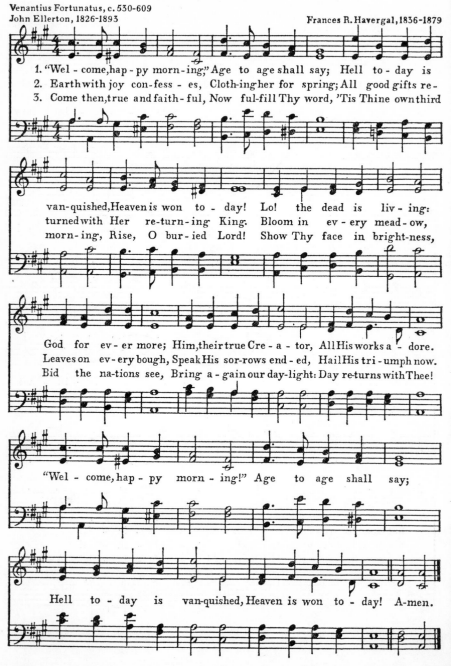

1. "Wel - come, hap - py morn - ing," Age to age shall say; Hell to - day is
2. Earth with joy con - fess - es, Cloth - ing her for spring; All good gifts re -
3. Come then, true and faith - ful, Now ful - fill Thy word, 'Tis Thine own third

van - quished, Heaven is won to - day! Lo! the dead is liv - ing:
turned with Her re - tur - ning King. Bloom in ev - ery mead - ow,
morn - ing, Rise, O bur - ied Lord! Show Thy face in bright - ness,

God for ev - er more; Him, their true Cre - a - tor, All His works a - dore.
Leaves on ev - ery bough, Speak His sor - rows end - ed, Hail His tri - umph now.
Bid the na - tions see, Bring a - gain our day - light: Day re - turns with Thee!

"Wel - come, hap - py morn - ing!" Age to age shall say;

Hell to - day is van - quished, Heaven is won to - day! A - men.

Low in the Grave He Lay

146

CHRIST AROSE 6.5.6.4. with Refrain

Robert Lowry, 1826-1899   Robert Lowry, 1826-1899

1. Low   in the grave He lay, Je-sus, my Sav-iour! Wait-ing the com-ing day,
2. Vain - ly they watch His bed, Je-sus, my Sav-iour! Vain - ly they seal the dead,
3. Death can-not keep His prey, Je-sus, my Sav-iour! He   tore the bars a - way,

Je - sus, my Lord! Up from the grave He a - rose,   With a
                                                  He a - rose,

might - y tri - umph o'er His foes;   He   a -
                                   He   a - rose;

rose a vic - tor from the dark do - main, And He

lives for - ev - er with His saints to reign: He a -

rose!   He a - rose!   Hal - le - lu - jah! Christ a - rose!
He a-rose!   He a-rose!

147 Alleluia! Alleluia!

HYFRYDOL 8.7.8.7.D.

Christopher Wordsworth, 1807-1885   Rowland H. Prichard, 1811-1887

1. Al - le - lu - ia! Al - le - lu - ia! Hearts to heaven and voic-es raise;
2. Now the i - ron bars are bro-ken, Christ from death to life is born,
3. Al - le - lu - ia! Al - le - lu - ia! Glo - ry be to God on high;

Sing to God a hymn of glad-ness, Sing to God a hymn of praise:
Glo - rious life, and life im - mor-tal, On this ho - ly Eas-ter morn:
Al - le - lu - ia to the Sav-iour Who has won the vic - to - ry;

He who on the cross as Sav-iour For the world's sal - va - tion bled,
Christ has tri-umphed, and we con-quer By His might - y en - ter - prise;
Al - le - lu - ia to the Spir-it, Fount of love and sanc - ti - ty;

Je - sus Christ, the King of Glo - ry Now is ris-en from the dead.
We with Him to life e - ter - nal By His res-ur-rec-tion rise.
Al - le - lu - ia! Al - le - lu - ia! To the Tri-une Maj-es-ty. A - men.

Christ, the Lord, Is Risen Today 148

EASTER HYMN 7.7.7.7. with Alleluias

Charles Wesley, 1707-1788   *Lyra Davidica*, 1708

1. Christ the Lord is risen to - day, Al - le - lu - ia!
2. Lives a - gain our glo - rious King: Al - le - lu - ia!
3. Love's re - deem - ing work is done, Al - le - lu - ia!
4. Soar we now where Christ has led, Al - le - lu - ia!

Sons of men and an - gels say: Al - le - lu - ia!
Where, O death, is now thy sting? Al - le - lu - ia!
Fought the fight, the bat - tle won; Al - le - lu - ia!
Fol - lowing our ex - alt - ed Head; Al - le - lu - ia!

Raise your joys and tri - umphs high, Al - le - lu - ia!
Dy - ing once, He all doth save: Al - le - lu - ia!
Death in vain for - bids Him rise; Al - le - lu - ia!
Made like Him, like Him we rise; Al - le - lu - ia!

Sing ye heav'ns, and earth re - ply, Al - le - lu - ia!
Where thy vic - to - ry, O grave? Al - le - lu - ia!
Christ has o - pened Par - a - dise. Al - le - lu - ia!
Ours the cross, the grave, the skies. Al - le - lu - ia! A - men.

149 The Day of Resurrection

GREENLAND 7.6.7.6.D.

John of Damascus, 8th century
John Mason Neale, 1818-1866

Arr. from J. Michael Haydn, 1737-1806

1. The day of res-ur-rec-tion, Earth, tell it out a-broad,
2. Our hearts be pure from e-vil, That we may see a-right
3. Now let the heavens be joy-ful, Let earth her song be-gin,

The Pass-o-ver of glad-ness, The Pass-o-ver of God.
The Lord in rays e-ter-nal Of res-ur-rec-tion light;
Let the round world keep tri-umph And all that is there-in;

From death to life e-ter-nal, From earth un-to the sky,
And, lis-tening to His ac-cents, May hear, so calm and plain,
Let all things seen and un-seen Their notes in glad-ness blend;

Our Christ hath brought us o-ver With hymns of vic-to-ry.
His own "All hail!" and, hear-ing, May raise the vic-tor-strain.
For Christ the Lord hath ris-en, Our joy that hath no end. A-men.

Come, Ye Faithful, Raise the Strain   150

ST. KEVIN 7.6.7.6.D.

John of Damascus, 8th century
John Mason Neale, 1818-1866

Arthur S. Sullivan, 1842-1900

1. Come, ye faith-ful, raise the strain Of tri - um-phant glad - ness:
2. 'Tis the spring of souls to - day: Christ hath burst His pris - on,
3. "Al - le - lu - ia!" now we cry To our King Im-mor - tal,

God hath brought His peo - ple forth In - to joy from sad - ness.
And from three days' sleep in death As a sun hath ris - en;
Who, tri - um - phant, burst the bars Of the tomb's dark por - tal;

Now re - joice, Je - ru - sa - lem, And with true af - fec - tion
All the win - ter of our sins, Long and dark, is fly - ing
"Al - le - lu - ia!" with the Son, God the Fa - ther prais-ing;

Wel - come in un-wea-ried strains Je - sus' res - ur - rec-tion.
From His light, to whom we give Laud and praise un - dy - ing.
"Al - le - lu - ia!" yet a-gain To the Spir - it rais-ing. A-men.

151 The Strife Is O'er

VICTORY 8.8.8.4. with Alleluias

Author Unknown
Trans. by Francis Pott, 1832-1909

Giovanni P. da Palestrina, 1525-1594
Adapted by William H. Monk, 1823-1889

Alleluia! Alleluia! Alleluia!

1. The strife is o'er, the battle done;
2. The powers of death have done their worst,
3. The three sad days have quickly sped;
4. He closed the yawning gates of hell;
5. Lord, by the stripes which wounded Thee,

The victory of life is won; The song of
But Christ their legions hath dispersed: Let shouts of
He rises glorious from the dead: All glory
The bars from heaven's high portals fell: Let hymns of
From death's dread sting Thy servants free, That we may

triumph has begun. Alleluia!
holy joy outburst. Alleluia!
to our risen Head! Alleluia!
praise His triumphs tell. Alleluia!
live and sing to Thee. Alleluia! Amen.

Look, Ye Saints! the Sight Is Glorious 152

CORONAE 8.7.8.7.4.7.

Thomas Kelly, 1769-1854

William H. Monk, 1823-1889

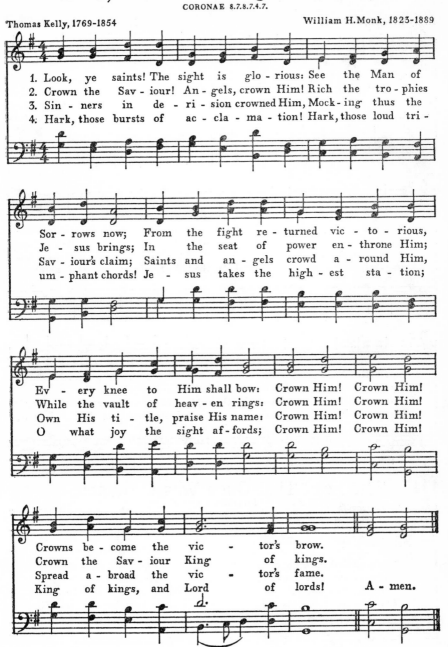

1. Look, ye saints! The sight is glo - rious: See the Man of
2. Crown the Sav - iour! An - gels, crown Him! Rich the tro - phies
3. Sin - ners in de - ri - sion crowned Him, Mock - ing thus the
4. Hark, those bursts of ac - cla - ma - tion! Hark, those loud tri -

Sor - rows now; From the fight re - turned vic - to - rious,
Je - sus brings; In the seat of power en - throne Him;
Sav - iour's claim; Saints and an - gels crowd a - round Him,
um - phant chords! Je - sus takes the high - est sta - tion;

Ev - ery knee to Him shall bow: Crown Him! Crown Him!
While the vault of heav - en rings: Crown Him! Crown Him!
Own His ti - tle, praise His name: Crown Him! Crown Him!
O what joy the sight af - fords; Crown Him! Crown Him!

Crowns be - come the vic - tor's brow.
Crown the Sav - iour King of kings.
Spread a - broad the vic - tor's fame.
King of kings, and Lord of lords! A - men.

153 Lift Up Your Glad Voices

Irregular

Henry Ware, Jr., 1794-1843   John Edgar Gould, 1822-1875

1. Lift up your glad voic - es in tri-umph on high, For Je - sus hath
2. He burst from the fet - ters of dark-ness that bound Him, Re-splen-dent in
3. All glo - ry to God, in full an-thems of joy, The be - ing He
4. But Je - sus hath cheered the dark val - ley of sor - row, And bade us, im-

ris - en and man shall not die; Vain were the ter-rors that gath-ered a -
glo - ry, to live and to save; Loud was the cho-rus of an - gels on
gave us death can-not de-stroy; Sad were the life we may part with to -
mor-tal, to heav-en as-cend; Lift then your voi-ces in tri-umph on

round Him, And short the do - min - ion of death and the grave.
high, The Sav-iour hath ris - en and man shall not die.
mor - row, If tears were our birth-right, and death were our end.
high, For Je - sus hath ris - en, and man shall not die. A-men.

154 The Head That Once Was Crowned

ST. MAGNUS 8.6.8.6.

Thomas Kelly, 1769-1854   Jeremiah Clark, 1670-1707

1. The head that once was crowned with thorns Is crowned with glo - ry now;
2. The high-est place that heaven af-fords Is His, is His by right,
3. The joy of all who dwell a - bove; The joy of all be - low,
4. The cross He bore is life and health, Though shame and death to Him:

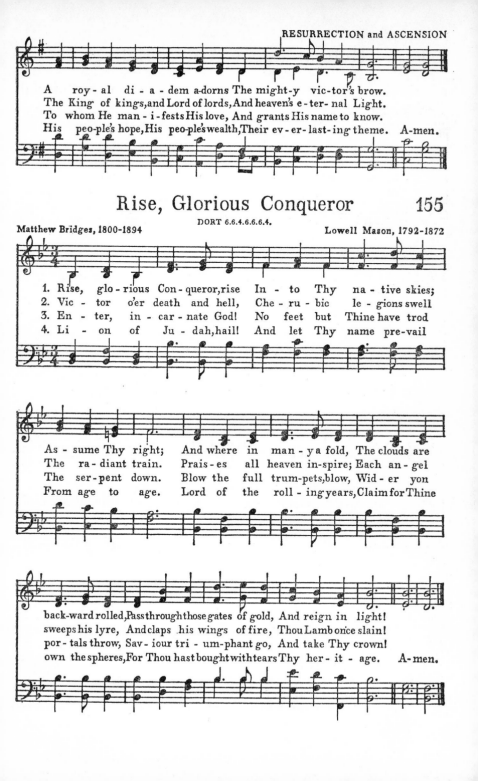

A roy-al di-a-dem a-dorns The might-y vic-tor's brow.
The King of kings, and Lord of lords, And heaven's e-ter-nal Light.
To whom He man-i-fests His love, And grants His name to know.
His peo-ple's hope, His peo-ple's wealth, Their ev-er-last-ing theme. A-men.

Rise, Glorious Conqueror 155

DORT 6.6.4.6.6.6.4.

Matthew Bridges, 1800-1894

Lowell Mason, 1792-1872

1. Rise, glo-rious Con-queror, rise In-to Thy na-tive skies;
2. Vic-tor o'er death and hell, Che-ru-bic le-gions swell
3. En-ter, in-car-nate God! No feet but Thine have trod
4. Li-on of Ju-dah, hail! And let Thy name pre-vail

As-sume Thy right; And where in man-y a fold, The clouds are
The ra-diant train. Prais-es all heaven in-spire; Each an-gel
The ser-pent down. Blow the full trum-pets, blow, Wid-er yon
From age to age. Lord of the roll-ing years, Claim for Thine

back-ward rolled, Pass through those gates of gold, And reign in light!
sweeps his lyre, And claps his wings of fire, Thou Lamb once slain!
por-tals throw, Sav-iour tri-um-phant go, And take Thy crown!
own the spheres, For Thou hast bought with tears Thy her-it-age. A-men.

156 Golden Harps Are Sounding

HERMAS 6.5.6.5.D. with Refrain

Frances R. Havergal, 1836-1879   Frances R. Havergal, 1836-1879

1. Gold-en harps are sounding, An-gel voic-es ring, Pearl-y gates are o-pened
2. He who came to save us, He who bled and died, Now is crowned with glo-ry
3. Pray-ing for His chil-dren In that bless-ed place, Call-ing them to glo-ry,

O-pened for the King: Christ the King of glo-ry, Je-sus, King of love,
At His Fa-ther's side; Nev-er-more to suf-fer, Nev-er-more to die,
Send-ing them His grace; His bright home pre-par-ing, Faith-ful ones, for you;

Is gone up in tri-umph To His throne a-bove.
Je-sus, King of glo-ry, Is gone up on high. All His work is end-ed,
Je-sus ev-er liv-eth, Ev-er lov-eth too.

Joy-ful-ly we sing; Je-sus hath as-cend-ed: Glo-ry to our King!

Rejoice, Rejoice, Believers

GREENLAND 7.6.7.6.D.

Laurentius Laurenti, 1660-1722
Sarah B. Findlater, 1823-1907

Johann Michael Haydn, 1737-1806

1. Re - joice, re - joice, be - liev - ers, And let your lights ap - pear;
2. See that your lamps are burn - ing; Re - plen - ish them with oil;
3. Our hope and ex - pec - ta - tion, O Je - sus, now ap - pear!

The eve-ning is ad - van - cing, And dark - er night is near:
And wait for your sal - va - tion, The end of earth-ly toil.
A - rise, Thou sun so longed for, O'er this be - night-ed sphere!

The Bride-groom is a - ris - ing, And soon He draw-eth nigh;
The watch - ers on the moun-tain Pro-claim the Bride-groom near,
With hearts and hands up - lift - ed, We plead, O Lord, to see

Up, pray, and watch, and wres - tle: At mid-night comes the cry.
Go meet Him as He com - eth, With al - le - lu - ias clear.
The day of earth's re-demp-tion That brings us un - to Thee. A-men.

158 Lo! He Comes with Clouds Descending

HOLYWOOD 8.7.8.7.8.7.

John Cennick, 1718-1755
Alt. by Charles Wesley, 1707-1788

J.F. Wade's *Cantus Diversi*, 1751

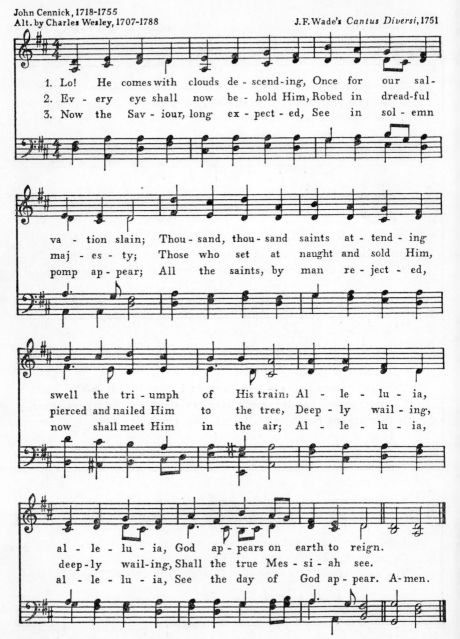

1. Lo! He comes with clouds de-scend-ing, Once for our sal-va-tion slain; Thou-sand, thou-sand saints at-tend-ing swell the tri-umph of His train: Al-le-lu-ia, al-le-lu-ia, God ap-pears on earth to reign.

2. Ev-ery eye shall now be-hold Him, Robed in dread-ful maj-es-ty; Those who set at naught and sold Him, pierced and nailed Him to the tree, Deep-ly wail-ing, deep-ly wail-ing, Shall the true Mes-si-ah see.

3. Now the Sav-iour, long ex-pect-ed, See in sol-emn pomp ap-pear; All the saints, by man re-ject-ed, now shall meet Him in the air; Al-le-lu-ia, al-le-lu-ia, See the day of God ap-pear. A-men.

Is It the Crowning Day?

GLAD DAY Irregular, with Refrain

159

Henry Ostrom, 19th century

Charles H. Marsh, 1886-1956

1. Je - sus may come to - day, Glad day, glad day! And I would see my Friend; Dan-gers and troub-les would end If Je-sus should come to - day.
2. I may go home to - day, Glad day, glad day! Seem-eth I hear their song; Hail to the ra - di - ant throng! If I should go home to - day.
3. Why should I anx - ious be? Glad day, glad day! Lights ap-pear on the shore, Storms will af-fright nev-er - more, For He is at hand to - day.
4. Faith-ful I'll be to - day, Glad day, glad day! And I will free-ly tell Why I should love Him so well, For He is my all to - day.

Glad day, glad day! Is it the crown-ing day? I'll live for to - day, nor anx-ious be, Je - sus, my Lord, I soon shall see; Glad day, glad day! Is it the crown - ing day?

rit.

160 It May Be at Morn

CHRIST RETURNETH 12.12.12.8.with Refrain

H.L.Turner, 19th century   James McGranahan, 1840-1907

1. It may be at morn, when the day is a wak-ing, When sun-light through dark-ness and shad-ow is break-ing, That Je-sus will come in the full-ness of glo-ry, To re-ceive from the world His own.

2. It may be at mid-day, it may be at twi-light, It may be, per-chance, that the black-ness of mid-night Will burst in-to light in the blaze of His glo-ry, When Je-sus re-ceives His own.

3. While hosts cry Ho-san-na from heav-en de-scend-ing, With glo-ri-fied saints and the an-gels at-tend-ing, With grace on His brow, like a ha-lo of glo-ry, Will Je-sus re-ceive His own.

4. O joy! O de-light! should we go with-out dy-ing, No sick-ness, no sad-ness, no dread and no cry-ing, Caught up thro' the clouds with our Lord in-to glo-ry, When Je-sus re-ceives His own.

O Lord Je-sus, how long, how long Ere we shout the glad song, Christ re-turn-eth! Hal-le-lu-jah! hal-le-lu-jah! A-men, Hal-le-lu-jah! A-men.

He Is Coming

NEWCASTLE 9.6.9.6.with Refrain

Fanny J. Crosby, 1820-1915

Ira D. Sankey, 1840-1908

1. He is com - ing, the Man of Sor-rows, Now ex - alt - ed on high;
2. He is com - ing, our lov-ing Sav-iour, Bless-ed Lamb that was slain;
3. He is com - ing, our Lord and Mas-ter, Our Re-deem-er and King;
4. He shall gath - er His cho-sen peo-ple, Who are called by His name;

He is com - ing with loud ho - san-nas, In the clouds of the sky.
In the glo - ry of God the Fa-ther, On the earth He shall reign.
We shall see Him in all His beau-ty, And His praise we shall sing.
And the ran-somed of ev-ery na-tion For His own He shall claim.

Hal-le - lu - jah! hal-le - lu - jah! He is com-ing a - gain;

And with joy we shall gath-er round Him, At His com-ing to reign.

162 Lift Up Your Heads, Pilgrims Aweary

HE IS COMING AGAIN 4.5.4.5.4.5.6.5.with Refrain

Mabel Johnston Camp, 1871-1937   Mabel Johnston Camp, 1871-1937

1. Lift up your heads, pil-grims a-wea-ry, See day's ap-proach,now
2. Dark was the night, sin warred a-gainst us; Heav-y the load of
3. O bless-ed hope! O bliss-ful prom-ise! Fill-ing our hearts with
4. E-ven so come, pre-cious Lord Je-sus; Cre-a-tion waits re-

crim-son the sky; Night sha-dows flee, and your Be-lov-ed,
sor-row we bore; But now we see signs of His com-ing;
rap-ture di-vine; O day of days! hail Thy ap-pear-ing!
demp-tion to see; Caught up in clouds, soon we shall meet Thee;

A-wait-ed with long-ing, at last draw-eth nigh.
Our hearts glow with-in us, joy's cup run-neth o'er!
Thy tran-scen-dent glo-ry for-ev-er shall shine!
O bless-ed as-sur-ance, for-ev-er with Thee!

He is com-ing a-gain, He is com-ing a-gain, The ver-y same

Je-sus, re-ject-ed of men; He is com-ing a-gain, He is com-ing a-gain!

With power and great glo - ry, He is com-ing a - gain!
is com-ing a - gain!

Christ Is Coming! Let Creation   163

CWM RHONDDA 8.7.8.7.8.7.7.

John R. MacDuff, 1818-1895

Welsh Hymn melody
John Hughes, 1873-1932

1. Christ is com - ing! let cre - a - tion From her groans and
2. Earth can now but tell the sto - ry Of Thy bit - ter
3. Long Thine ex - iles have been pin - ing, Far from rest, and
4. With that bless - ed hope be - fore us, Let no harp re -

tra - vail cease; Let the glo - rious proc - la - ma - tion
cross and pain; She shall yet be - hold Thy glo - ry
home, and Thee: But, in heaven - ly ves - tures shin - ing,
main un - strung; Let the might - y ad - vent cho - rus

Hope re-store and faith in-crease: Christ is com-ing! Christ is com-ing!
When Thou com-est back to reign: Christ is com-ing! Christ is com-ing!
They their lov - ing Lord shall see: Christ is com-ing! Christ is com-ing!
On-ward roll from tongue to tongue: Christ is com-ing! Christ is com-ing!

Come, Thou bless-ed Prince of Peace! Come, Thou bless - ed Prince of Peace.
Let each heart re-peat the strain. Let each heart re - peat the strain.
Haste the joy-ous ju - bi - lee. Haste the joy - ous ju - bi - lee.
Come, Lord Je-sus, quick-ly come! Come, Lord Je - sus, quick-ly come.

Music used by permission of G.D. Hughes and Dilys S. Webb

164 One Day

CHAPMAN 11.10.11.10. with Refrain

J. Wilbur Chapman, 1859-1918

Charles H. Marsh, 1886-1956

1. One day when heav - en was filled with His prais-es, One day when
2. One day they led Him up Cal - va-ry's moun-tain, One day they
3. One day they left Him a - lone in the gar - den, One day He
4. One day the grave could con-ceal Him no long - er, One day the
5. One day the trum - pet will sound for His com - ing, One day the

sin was as black as could be, Je - sus came forth to be
nailed Him to die on the tree; Suf-fer-ing an-guish, de -
rest - ed, from suf-fer-ing free; An - gels came down o'er His
stone rolled a - way from the door; Then He a - rose, o - ver
skies with His glo - ry will shine; Won-der-ful day, my be-

born of a vir - gin, Dwelt a-mong men, my ex-am-ple is He!
spised and re - ject - ed, Bear-ing our sins, my Re-deem-er is He!
tomb to keep vig - il; Hope of the hope-less, my Sav-iour is He!
death He has con-quered; Now is as-cend-ed, my Lord ev-er-more!
lov - ed ones bring-ing; Glo - ri - ous Sav-iour, this Je-sus is mine!

Liv-ing, He loved me; dy - ing, He saved me; Bur - ied, He

car - ried my sins far a - way; Ris - ing, He jus - ti - fied

free - ly for - ev - er: One day He's com - ing O, glo - ri - ous day!

The King Shall Come 165
ST. STEPHEN 8.6.8.6.

Greek Hymn
Trans. by John Brownlie, 1859-1925

William Jones, 1726-1800

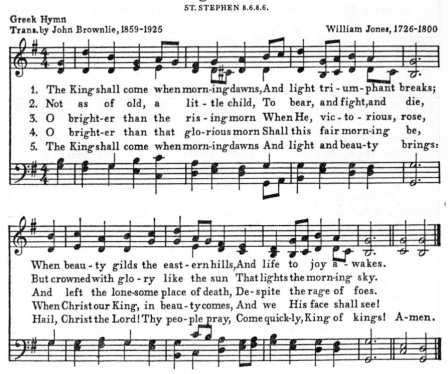

1. The King shall come when morn-ing dawns, And light tri - um - phant breaks;
2. Not as of old, a lit - tle child, To bear, and fight, and die,
3. O bright-er than the ris - ing morn When He, vic - to - rious, rose,
4. O bright-er than that glo-rious morn Shall this fair morn-ing be,
5. The King shall come when morn-ing dawns And light and beau - ty brings:

When beau - ty gilds the east - ern hills, And life to joy a - wakes.
But crowned with glo - ry like the sun That lights the morn-ing sky.
And left the lone-some place of death, De - spite the rage of foes.
When Christ our King, in beau-ty comes, And we His face shall see!
Hail, Christ the Lord! Thy peo-ple pray, Come quick-ly, King of kings! A-men.

166 Holy Spirit, Faithful Guide

FAITHFUL GUIDE 7.7.7.7.D.

Marcus M. Wells, 1815-1895   Marcus M. Wells, 1815-1895

1. Ho - ly Spir - it, faith-ful Guide, Ev - er near the Christian's side,
2. Ev - er-pres-ent, tru - est Friend, Ev - er near Thine aid to lend,
3. When our days of toil shall cease, Wait-ing still for sweet re - lease,

Gen - tly lead us by Thy hand, Pil - grims in a des - ert land;
Leave us not to doubt and fear, Grop-ing on in dark-ness drear;
Noth-ing left but heaven and prayer, Trust-ing that our names are there;

Wea - ry souls for - e'er re - joice, While they hear that sweet-est voice
When the storms are rag-ing sore, Hearts grow faint, and hopes give o'er,
Fear - ing not the dis - mal flood, Plead - ing naught but Je - sus' blood,

Whis-pering soft-ly, "Wan-derer, come! Fol-low me, I'll guide thee home."
Whis-per soft - ly, "Wan-derer, come! Fol-low me, I'll guide thee home."
Whis-per soft - ly, "Wan-derer, come! Fol-low me, I'll guide thee home." A-men.

Our Blest Redeemer, Ere He Breathed 167

ST. CUTHBERT 8.6.8.4.

Harriet Auber, 1773-1862　　　　　　　　　John Bacchus Dykes, 1823-1876

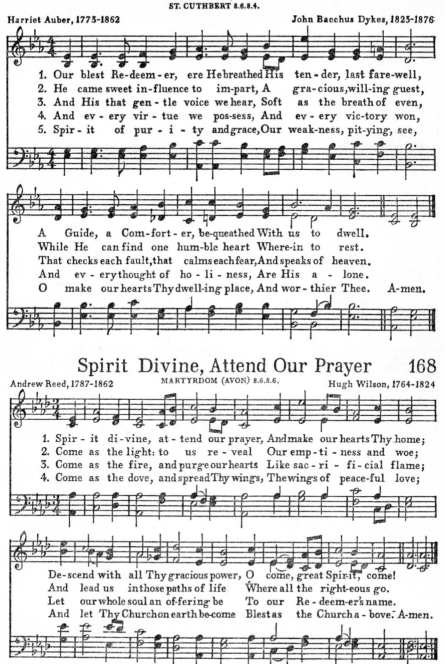

1. Our blest Re-deem-er, ere He breathed His ten-der, last fare-well,
2. He came sweet in-fluence to im-part, A gra-cious, will-ing guest,
3. And His that gen-tle voice we hear, Soft as the breath of even,
4. And ev-ery vir-tue we pos-sess, And ev-ery vic-tory won,
5. Spir-it of pur-i-ty and grace, Our weak-ness, pit-ying, see,

A Guide, a Com-fort-er, be-queathed With us to dwell.
While He can find one hum-ble heart Where-in to rest.
That checks each fault, that calms each fear, And speaks of heaven.
And ev-ery thought of ho-li-ness, Are His a-lone.
O make our hearts Thy dwell-ing place, And wor-thier Thee. A-men.

Spirit Divine, Attend Our Prayer 168

Andrew Reed, 1787-1862　　　MARTYRDOM (AVON) 8.6.8.6.　　Hugh Wilson, 1764-1824

1. Spir-it di-vine, at-tend our prayer, And make our hearts Thy home;
2. Come as the light: to us re-veal Our emp-ti-ness and woe;
3. Come as the fire, and purge our hearts Like sac-ri-fi-cial flame;
4. Come as the dove, and spread Thy wings, The wings of peace-ful love;

De-scend with all Thy gracious power, O come, great Spir-it, come!
And lead us in those paths of life Where all the right-eous go.
Let our whole soul an of-fering be To our Re-deem-er's name.
And let Thy Church on earth be-come Blest as the Church a-bove. A-men.

169 Spirit of God, Descend

MORECAMBE 10.10.10.10.

George Croly, 1780-1860   Frederick C. Atkinson, 1841-1897

1. Spir - it of God, de - scend up - on my heart;
2. I ask no dream, no proph - et ec - sta - sies,
3. Hast Thou not bid us love Thee, God and King?
4. Teach me to feel that Thou art al - ways nigh;
5. Teach me to love Thee as Thine an - gels love,

Wean it from earth, through all its puls - es move;
No sud - den rend - ing of the veil of clay,
All, all Thine own: soul, heart, and strength, and mind.
Teach me the strug - gles of the soul to bear,
One ho - ly pas - sion fill - ing all my frame;

Stoop to my weak - ness, might - y as Thou art,
No an - gel vis - it - ant, no o - pening skies;
I see Thy cross, there teach my heart to cling;
To check the ris - ing doubt, the reb - el sigh;
The bap - tism of the heaven - de - scend - ed Dove,

And help me love Thee as I ought to love.
But take the dim - ness of my soul a - way.
O let me seek Thee, and O let me find.
Teach me the pa - tience of un - an - swered prayer.
My heart an al - tar, and Thy love the flame. A - men.

Thy Holy Spirit, Lord, Alone   170
HOLY SPIRIT 8.6.8.6.

Henrietta E. Blair, 19th century

Wm. J. Kirkpatrick, 1838-1921

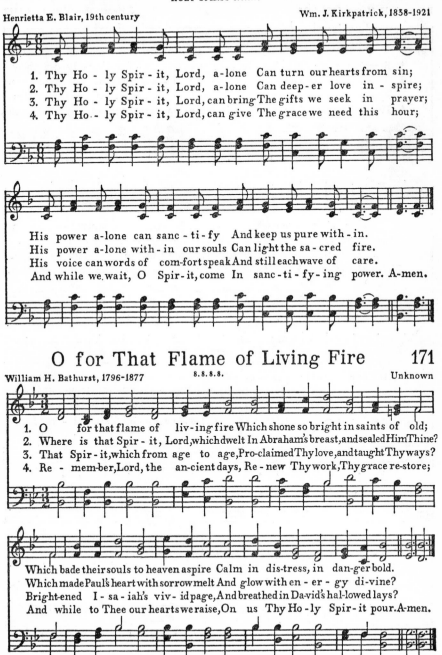

1. Thy Ho - ly Spir - it, Lord, a - lone Can turn our hearts from sin;
2. Thy Ho - ly Spir - it, Lord, a - lone Can deep - er love in - spire;
3. Thy Ho - ly Spir - it, Lord, can bring The gifts we seek in prayer;
4. Thy Ho - ly Spir - it, Lord, can give The grace we need this hour;

His power a-lone can sanc - ti - fy And keep us pure with - in.
His power a-lone with - in our souls Can light the sa - cred fire.
His voice can words of com-fort speak And still each wave of care.
And while we wait, O Spir-it, come In sanc-ti-fy-ing power. A-men.

O for That Flame of Living Fire   171
8.8.8.8.

William H. Bathurst, 1796-1877

Unknown

1. O for that flame of liv-ing fire Which shone so bright in saints of old;
2. Where is that Spir - it, Lord, which dwelt In Abraham's breast, and sealed Him Thine?
3. That Spir - it, which from age to age, Pro-claimed Thy love, and taught Thy ways?
4. Re - mem-ber, Lord, the an-cient days, Re - new Thy work, Thy grace re-store;

Which bade their souls to heaven aspire Calm in dis-tress, in dan-ger bold.
Which made Paul's heart with sorrow melt And glow with en - er - gy di-vine?
Bright-ened I - sa - iah's viv - id page, And breathed in Da-vid's hal-lowed lays?
And while to Thee our hearts we raise, On us Thy Ho - ly Spir - it pour. A-men.

172 Breathe upon Us, Holy Spirit

SHOWALTER 8.7.8.7. D.

Elisha A. Hoffman, 1839-1929 J. Henry Showalter, 1864-1947

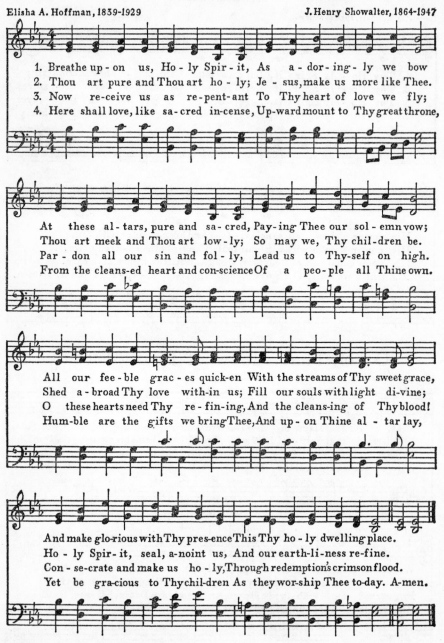

1. Breathe up-on us, Ho-ly Spir-it, As a-dor-ing-ly we bow
2. Thou art pure and Thou art ho-ly; Je-sus, make us more like Thee.
3. Now re-ceive us as re-pent-ant To Thy heart of love we fly;
4. Here shall love, like sa-cred in-cense, Up-ward mount to Thy great throne,

At these al-tars, pure and sa-cred, Pay-ing Thee our sol-emn vow;
Thou art meek and Thou art low-ly; So may we, Thy chil-dren be.
Par-don all our sin and fol-ly, Lead us to Thy-self on high.
From the cleans-ed heart and con-science Of a peo-ple all Thine own.

All our fee-ble grac-es quick-en With the streams of Thy sweet grace,
Shed a-broad Thy love with-in us; Fill our souls with light di-vine;
O these hearts need Thy re-fin-ing, And the cleans-ing of Thy blood!
Hum-ble are the gifts we bring Thee, And up-on Thine al-tar lay,

And make glo-rious with Thy pres-ence This Thy ho-ly dwelling place.
Ho-ly Spir-it, seal, a-noint us, And our earth-li-ness re-fine.
Con-se-crate and make us ho-ly, Through redemption's crimson flood.
Yet be gra-cious to Thy chil-dren As they wor-ship Thee to-day. A-men.

Holy Ghost, with Light Divine

173

MERCY 7.7.7.7.

Andrew Reed, 1787-1862

Louis M. Gottschalk, 1829-1869

1. Ho - ly Ghost, with light di-vine, Shine up - on this heart of mine;
2. Ho - ly Ghost, with power di-vine, Cleanse this guilt - y heart of mine;
3. Ho - ly Ghost, with joy di-vine, Cheer this sad-dened heart of mine;
4. Ho - ly Spir - it, all di-vine, Dwell with-in this heart of mine;

Chase the shades of night a - way; Turn my dark-ness in-to day.
Long has sin, with-out con-trol, Held do - min-ion o'er my soul.
Bid my man - y woes de-part, Heal my wound-ed, bleeding heart.
Cast down ev - ery i - dol throne; Reign su-preme, and reign a-lone. A-men.

Holy Spirit, Hear Us

174

ERNSTEIN 6.5.6.5.

William H. Parker, 1845-1929

James F. Swift, 1847-1931

1. Ho - ly Spir - it, hear us; Help us while we sing;
2. Ho - ly Spir - it, prompt us When we kneel to pray;
3. Ho - ly Spir - it, shine Thou On the Book we read;
4. Ho - ly Spir - it, give us Each a low-ly mind;

Breathe in - to the mu - sic Of the praise we bring.
Near - er come and teach us What we ought to say.
Gild its ho - ly pa - ges With the light we need.
Make us more like Je - sus, Gen - tle, pure, and kind. A-men.

175 O Spread the Tidings 'Round

Frank Bottome, 1823-1894   COMFORTER 12.12.12.6.with Refrain   William J. Kirkpatrick, 1838-1921

1. O spread the ti-dings 'round, wher-ev-er man is found, Wher-ev-er hu-man
2. O bound-less love di-vine! how shall this tongue of mine To wondering mortals
3. Sing, till the ech-oes fly a-bove the vault-ed sky, And all the saints a-

hearts and hu-man woes a-bound; Let ev-ery Christian tongue proclaim the joy-ful
tell the matchless grace di-vine That I, a child of hell, should in His im-age
bove to all be-low re-ply, In strains of end-less love, the song that ne'er will

sound: The Com-fort-er has come!
shine! The Com-fort-er has come! The Com-fort-er has come, the Com-fort-er has
die: The Com-fort-er has come!

come! The Ho-ly Ghost from Heaven, the Fa-ther's prom-ise given; O spread the

ti-dings 'round, wher-ev-er man is found: The Com-fort-er has come!

Come, Holy Ghost, Our Hearts Inspire   176
WINCHESTER OLD 8.6.8.6.

Charles Wesley, 1707-1788   *Este's Psalter,* 1592

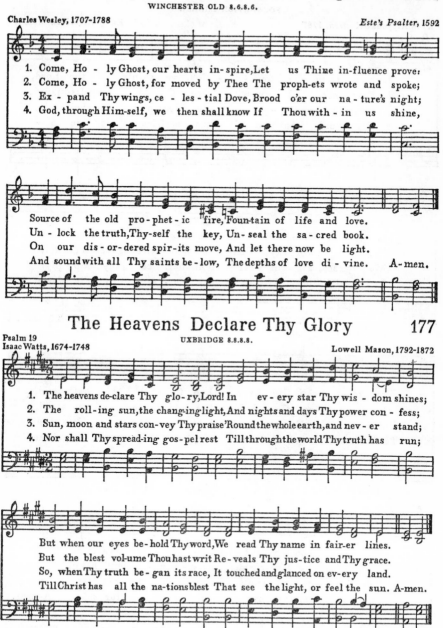

1. Come, Ho - ly Ghost, our hearts in - spire, Let   us Thine in - fluence prove:
2. Come, Ho - ly Ghost, for moved by Thee The   proph - ets wrote and   spoke;
3. Ex - pand Thy wings, ce - les - tial Dove, Brood   o'er our   na - ture's night;
4. God, through Him - self, we   then shall know If   Thou with - in   us   shine,

Source of   the old pro - phet - ic   fire, Foun-tain of   life and   love.
Un - lock   the truth, Thy - self   the   key, Un - seal   the   sa - cred book.
On   our   dis - or - dered spir - its move, And let there now be   light.
And sound with all Thy saints be - low, The depths of   love di - vine.   A - men.

The Heavens Declare Thy Glory   177
UXBRIDGE 8.8.8.8.

Psalm 19
Isaac Watts, 1674-1748   Lowell Mason, 1792-1872

1. The heavens de - clare Thy   glo - ry, Lord! In   ev - ery star Thy wis - dom shines;
2. The   roll - ing sun, the chang - ing light, And nights and days Thy power con - fess;
3. Sun, moon and stars con - vey Thy praise 'Round the whole earth, and nev - er   stand;
4. Nor shall Thy spread - ing gos - pel rest Till through the world Thy truth has   run;

But when our eyes be - hold Thy word, We read Thy name in fair - er   lines.
But   the blest vol - ume Thou hast writ Re - veals Thy jus - tice and Thy grace.
So, when Thy truth be - gan its race, It touched and glanced on ev - ery land.
Till Christ has   all the na - tions blest That see   the light, or feel the sun. A - men.

178 How Firm a Foundation

FOUNDATION 11.11.11.11.

"K" in Rippon's *Selection*, 1787

Early American Melody

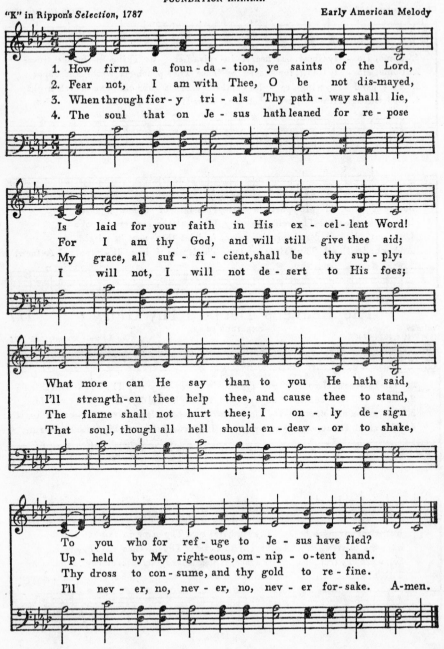

1. How firm a foun-da-tion, ye saints of the Lord,
2. Fear not, I am with Thee, O be not dis-mayed,
3. When through fier-y tri-als Thy path-way shall lie,
4. The soul that on Je-sus hath leaned for re-pose

Is laid for your faith in His ex-cel-lent Word!
For I am thy God, and will still give thee aid;
My grace, all suf-fi-cient, shall be thy sup-ply:
I will not, I will not de-sert to His foes;

What more can He say than to you He hath said,
I'll strength-en thee help thee, and cause thee to stand,
The flame shall not hurt thee; I on-ly de-sign
That soul, though all hell should en-deav-or to shake,

To you who for ref-uge to Je-sus have fled?
Up-held by My right-eous, om-nip-o-tent hand.
Thy dross to con-sume, and thy gold to re-fine.
I'll nev-er, no, nev-er, no, nev-er for-sake. A-men.

O Word of God Incarnate

MUNICH (MEININGEN) 7.6.7.6.D.

William Walsham How, 1823-1897

*Neuvermehrtes Meiningisches Gesangbuch,*1693
Arr. by Felix Mendelssohn-Bartholdy, 1809-1847

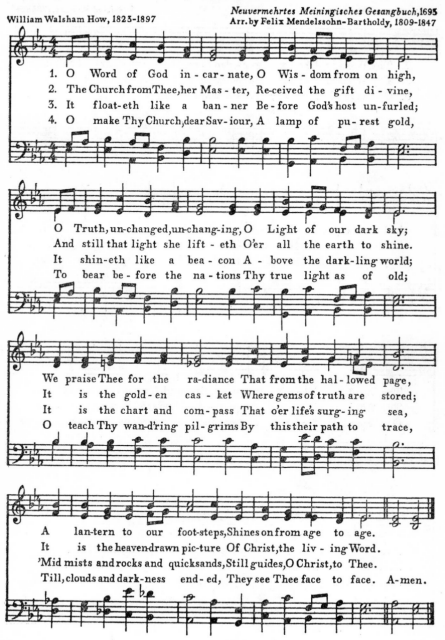

1. O Word of God in - car - nate, O Wis - dom from on high,
2. The Church from Thee, her Mas - ter, Re-ceived the gift di - vine,
3. It float-eth like a ban - ner Be - fore God's host un-furled;
4. O make Thy Church, dear Sav-iour, A lamp of pu - rest gold,

O Truth, un-changed, un-chang-ing, O Light of our dark sky;
And still that light she lift - eth O'er all the earth to shine.
It shin-eth like a bea - con A - bove the dark-ling world;
To bear be - fore the na - tions Thy true light as of old;

We praise Thee for the ra-diance That from the hal - lowed page,
It is the gold - en cas - ket Where gems of truth are stored;
It is the chart and com - pass That o'er life's surg-ing sea,
O teach Thy wan-d'ring pil - grims By this their path to trace,

A lan-tern to our foot-steps, Shines on from age to age.
It is the heaven-drawn pic-ture Of Christ, the liv - ing Word.
'Mid mists and rocks and quicksands, Still guides, O Christ, to Thee.
Till, clouds and dark-ness end - ed, They see Thee face to face. A-men.

180 Thy Word Is Like a Garden, Lord

BETHLEHEM (SERAPH) 8.6.8.6.D.

Edwin Hodder, 1837-1904

Gottfried W. Fink, 1783-1846

1. Thy Word is like a gar-den, Lord, With flow-ers bright and fair;
2. Thy Word is like a star-ry host: A thou-sand rays of light
3. O may I love Thy pre-cious Word, May I ex-plore the mine,

And ev-ery-one who seeks may pluck A love-ly clus-ter there.
Are seen to guide the trav-el-er, And make his path-way bright.
May I its fra-grant flow-ers glean, May light up-on me shine.

Thy Word is like a deep, deep mine; And jew-els rich and rare
Thy Word is like an ar-mor-y, Where sol-diers may re-pair,
O may I find my ar-mor there, Thy word my trust-y sword;

Are hid-den in its might-y depths For ev-ery search-er there.
And find, for life's long bat-tle day, All need-ful weap-ons there.
I'll learn to fight with ev-ery foe The bat-tle of the Lord. A-men.

Thy Word Is a Lamp to My Feet   181

SELLERS 8.7.8.7. with Refrain

Psalm 119
Adapted by Ernest O. Sellers, 1869-1952

Ernest O. Sellers, 1869-1952

1. Thy Word is a lamp to my feet, A light to my path al-
2. For - ev - er, O Lord, is Thy Word Es - tab-lished and fixed on
3. At morn-ing, at noon, and at night, I ev - er will give Thee

way, To guide and to save me from sin, And show me the
high; Thy faith-ful-ness un - to all men A - bid-eth for-
praise; For Thou art my por-tion, O Lord, And shalt be through

heaven-ly way.
ev - er nigh. Thy Word have I hid in my heart,
all my days. in my heart,

That I might not sin a-gainst Thee, That I might not sin,
a-gainst Thee,

That I might not sin, Thy Word have I hid in my heart.

182 O God of Light

ANCIENT OF DAYS 11.10.11.10.

Sarah E. Taylor, 1883-1954

J. Albert Jeffery, 1855-1929

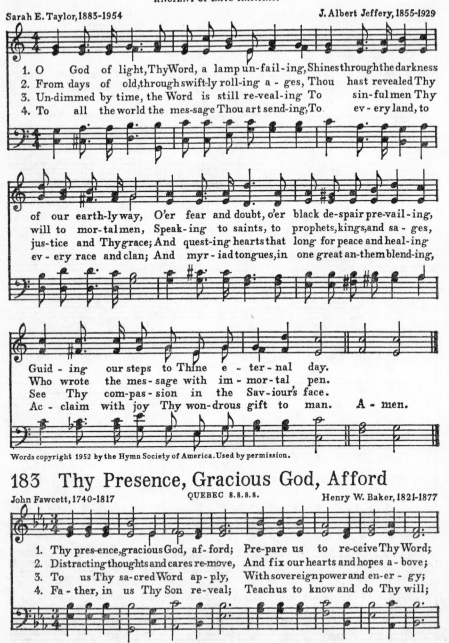

1. O God of light, Thy Word, a lamp un-fail-ing, Shines through the darkness
2. From days of old, through swift-ly roll-ing a-ges, Thou hast revealed Thy
3. Un-dimmed by time, the Word is still re-veal-ing To sin-ful men Thy
4. To all the world the mes-sage Thou art send-ing, To ev-er y land, to

of our earth-ly way, O'er fear and doubt, o'er black de-spair pre-vail-ing,
will to mor-tal men, Speak-ing to saints, to prophets, kings, and sa-ges,
jus-tice and Thy grace; And quest-ing hearts that long for peace and heal-ing
ev-er y race and clan; And myr-iad tongues, in one great an-them blend-ing,

Guid-ing our steps to Thine e-ter-nal day.
Who wrote the mes-sage with im-mor-tal pen.
See Thy com-pas-sion in the Sav-iour's face.
Ac-claim with joy Thy won-drous gift to man. A-men.

Words copyright 1952 by the Hymn Society of America. Used by permission.

183 Thy Presence, Gracious God, Afford

John Fawcett, 1740-1817

QUEBEC 8.8.8.8.

Henry W. Baker, 1821-1877

1. Thy pres-ence, gracious God, af-ford; Pre-pare us to re-ceive Thy Word;
2. Distracting thoughts and cares re-move, And fix our hearts and hopes a-bove;
3. To us Thy sa-cred Word ap-ply, With sovereign power and en-er-gy;
4. Fa-ther, in us Thy Son re-veal; Teach us to know and do Thy will;

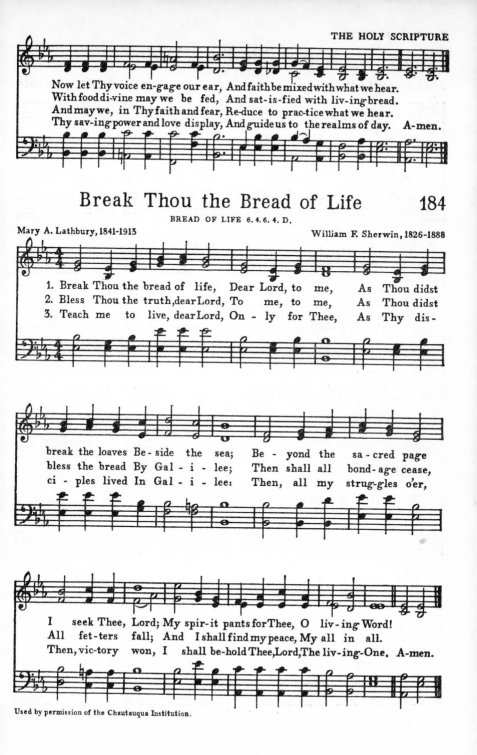

Now let Thy voice en-gage our ear, And faith be mixed with what we hear.
With food di-vine may we be fed, And sat-is-fied with liv-ing bread.
And may we, in Thy faith and fear, Re-duce to prac-tice what we hear.
Thy sav-ing power and love dis play, And guide us to the realms of day. A-men.

Break Thou the Bread of Life 184

BREAD OF LIFE 6. 4. 6. 4. D.

Mary A. Lathbury, 1841-1913

William F. Sherwin, 1826-1888

1. Break Thou the bread of life, Dear Lord, to me, As Thou didst
2. Bless Thou the truth, dear Lord, To me, to me, As Thou didst
3. Teach me to live, dear Lord, On - ly for Thee, As Thy dis-

break the loaves Be - side the sea; Be - yond the sa - cred page
bless the bread By Gal - i - lee; Then shall all bond-age cease,
ci - ples lived In Gal - i - lee: Then, all my strug-gles o'er,

I seek Thee, Lord; My spir-it pants for Thee, O liv-ing Word!
All fet-ters fall; And I shall find my peace, My all in all.
Then, vic-tory won, I shall be-hold Thee, Lord, The liv-ing-One. A-men.

Used by permission of the Chautauqua Institution.

185 Holy Bible, Book Divine

ALETTA 7. 7. 7. 7.

John Burton, 1773-1822

William B. Bradbury, 1816-1868

1. Ho - ly Bi - ble, book di - vine, Pre - cious treas-ure, thou art mine:
2. Mine to chide me when I rove; Mine to show a Sav-iour's love;
3. Mine to com-fort in dis-tress, Suf-fering in this wil - der-ness;
4. Mine to tell of joys to come, And the reb - el sin-ner's doom:

Mine to tell me whence I came; Mine to teach me what I am;
Mine thou art to guide and guard; Mine to pun-ish or re-ward;
Mine to show by liv - ing faith, Man can tri-umph o - ver death;
O thou ho - ly book di - vine, Pre-cious treas-ure, thou art mine. A-men.

186 Lamp of Our Feet, Whereby We Trace

LAMBETH 8. 6. 8. 6.

Bernard Barton, 1784-1849

Wilhelm A. F. Schulthes, 1816-1879

1. Lamp of our feet, where-by we trace Our path when wont to stray;
2. Bread of our souls, where-on we feed, True man-na from on high;
3. Pil - lar of fire, through watches dark, Or ra-diant cloud by day;
4. Word of the ev - er - liv - ing God, Will of His glo-rious Son;

Stream from the fount of heaven-ly grace, Brook by the trav-eler's way;
Our guide and chart where-in we read Of realms be-yond the sky;
When waves would whelm our toss-ing bark, Our an-chor and our stay;
With - out Thee how could earth be trod, Or heaven it-self be won? A-men.

Revealing Word, Thy Light Portrays 187

ST. PETERSBURG 8.8.8.8.8.8.

M. Elmore Turner, 1906–

Dimitri Bortniansky, 1752-1825

1. Re - veal - ing Word, thy light por - trays The work of
2. In - spir - ing Word, thy truth im - parts Tri - um - phant
3. En - dur - ing Word, thy strength a - bides Like moun-tains

God through end-less days; We view His wis - dom, power, and love,
hope to hu - man hearts; Through thee, en-slaved men find re - lease,
firm, and o - cean tides; Man's fee - ble works grow old with time,

That show the form of things a - bove: How splen - did are the
Earth's bur - dened ones find wel - come peace: What deeps the sons of
But thou art age - less and sub - lime: What last - ing splen - dor

plans di - vine Which through thy sa - cred pag - es shine!
God dis - cern When from thy sa - cred page they learn!
crowns the page Where-in God writes our her - it - age! A - men.

188 How I Love Thy Law, O Lord!

SPANISH HYMN 7. 7. 7. 7. with Refrain   Unknown

Psalm 119   Arr. by Benjamin Carr, 1769-1831

1. How I love Thy law, O Lord! Dai - ly joy its truths af-ford;
2. Thy com-mand-ments in my heart Tru - est wis - dom can im-part;
3. While my heart Thy word o-beys, I am kept from e - vil ways;

In its con-stant light I go, Wise to con-quer ev - ery foe.
To mine eyes Thy pre-cepts show Wis - dom more than sa - ges know.
From Thy law, with Thee to guide, I shall nev - er turn a - side.

Sweet - er are Thy words to me Than all oth - er good can be;

Safe I walk, Thy truth my light, Hat-ing false-hood, lov-ing right.

189 Jesus, Thy Blood and Righteousness

GERMANY 8. 8. 8. 8.

Nicolaus L. Zinzendorf, 1700-1760
Trans. by John Wesley, 1703-1791

William Gardiner, *Sacred Melodies*, 1815

1. Je-sus, Thy blood and right-eous-ness My beau-ty are, my glo-rious dress;
2. Bold shall I stand in Thy great day, For who aught to my charge shall lay?
3. Lord, I be-lieve Thy pre-cious blood, Which, at the mer-cy seat of God,
4. Lord, I be-lieve were sin - ners more Than sands up-on the o - cean shore,

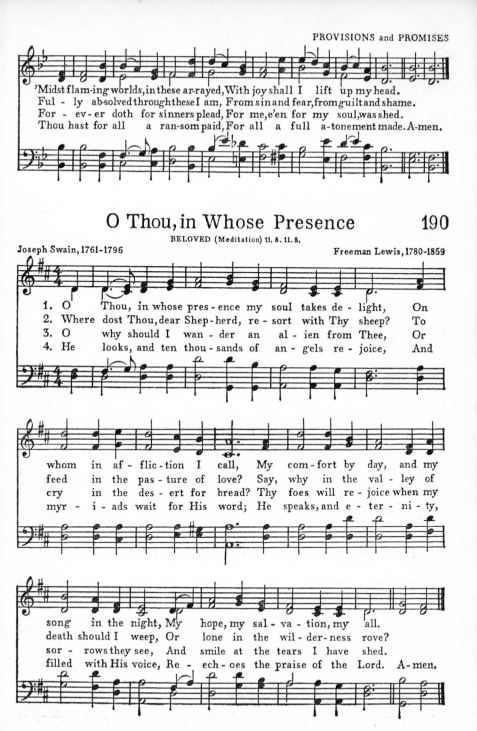

'Midst flam-ing worlds, in these ar-rayed, With joy shall I lift up my head.
Ful - ly ab-solved through these I am, From sin and fear, from guilt and shame.
For - ev - er doth for sinners plead, For me, e'en for my soul, was shed.
Thou hast for all a ran-som paid, For all a full a-tonement made. A-men.

O Thou, in Whose Presence   190

BELOVED (Meditation) 11. 8. 11. 8.

Joseph Swain, 1761-1796   Freeman Lewis, 1780-1859

1. O   Thou, in whose pres-ence my soul takes de - light,   On
2. Where dost Thou, dear Shep-herd, re - sort with Thy sheep?   To
3. O   why should I wan - der an   al - ien from Thee,   Or
4. He   looks, and ten thou-sands of an - gels re - joice,   And

whom   in af - flic - tion I call,   My com - fort by day, and my
feed   in the pas - ture of love?   Say, why in the val - ley of
cry   in the des - ert for bread? Thy foes will re - joice when my
myr - i - ads wait for His word;   He speaks, and e - ter - ni - ty,

song   in the night, My hope, my sal - va - tion, my all.
death should I weep, Or lone in the wil - der - ness rove?
sor - rows they see, And smile at the tears I have shed.
filled with His voice, Re - ech - oes the praise of the Lord. A - men.

191 Would You Live for Jesus?

NUSBAUM Irregular with Refrain

Cyrus S. Nusbaum, 1861-1937   Cyrus S. Nusbaum, 1861-1937

1. Would you live for Je - sus and be al-ways pure and good?
2. Would you have Him make you free, and fol - low at His call?
3. Would you in His king-dom find a place of con-stant rest?

Would you walk with Him with-in the nar-row road? Would you have Him
Would you know the peace that comes by giv-ing all? Would you have Him
Would you prove Him true each prov-i - den-tial test? Would you in His

bear your bur-den, car-ry all your load? Let Him have His way with thee.
save you, so that you need nev-er fall? Let Him have His way with thee.
serv - ice la - bor al-ways at your best? Let Him have His way with thee.

His power can make you what you ought to be; His

blood can cleanse your heart and make you free; His love can fill your soul, and

you will see 'Twas best for Him to have His way with thee.

Jesus Paid It All 192

ALL TO CHRIST 6.6.7.7. with Refrain

Elvina M. Hall, 1820–1889

John T. Grape, 1835–1915

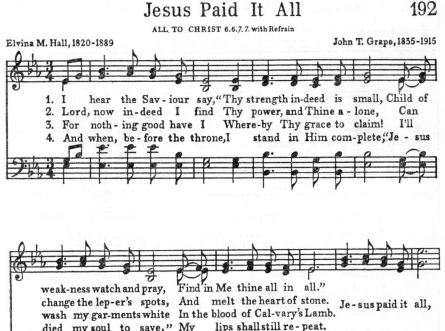

1. I hear the Sav-iour say,"Thy strength in-deed is small, Child of
2. Lord, now in-deed I find Thy power, and Thine a - lone, Can
3. For noth - ing good have I Where-by Thy grace to claim! I'll
4. And when, be - fore the throne, I stand in Him com-plete;"Je - sus

weak-ness watch and pray, Find in Me thine all in all."
change the lep-er's spots, And melt the heart of stone. Je-sus paid it all,
wash my gar-ments white In the blood of Cal-vary's Lamb.
died my soul to save," My lips shall still re-peat.

All to Him I owe; Sin had left a crim-son stain, He washed it white as snow.

193 Not All the Blood of Beasts

BOYLSTON 6.6.8.6.

Isaac Watts, 1674-1748

Lowell Mason, 1792-1872
Arr. *Wes. H. Bk.*, 1875

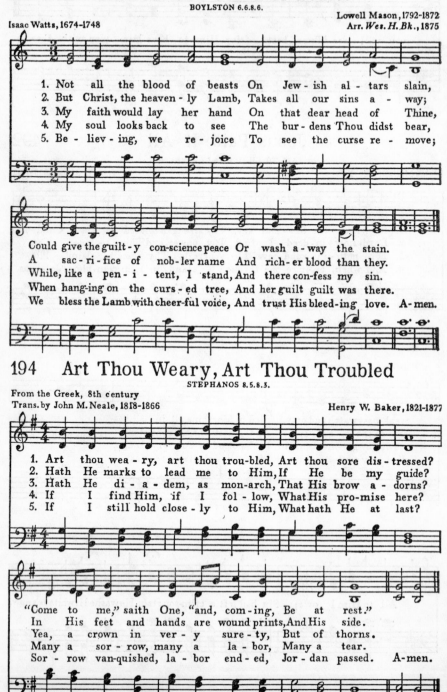

1. Not all the blood of beasts On Jew-ish al-tars slain,
2. But Christ, the heaven-ly Lamb, Takes all our sins a - way;
3. My faith would lay her hand On that dear head of Thine,
4. My soul looks back to see The bur-dens Thou didst bear,
5. Be - liev-ing, we re - joice To see the curse re - move;

Could give the guilt-y con-science peace Or wash a-way the stain.
A sac-ri-fice of nob-ler name And rich-er blood than they.
While, like a pen-i - tent, I stand, And there con-fess my sin.
When hang-ing on the curs-ed tree, And her guilt guilt was there.
We bless the Lamb with cheer-ful voice, And trust His bleed-ing love. A-men.

194 Art Thou Weary, Art Thou Troubled

STEPHANOS 8.5.8.3.

From the Greek, 8th century
Trans. by John M. Neale, 1818-1866

Henry W. Baker, 1821-1877

1. Art thou wea - ry, art thou trou-bled, Art thou sore dis-tressed?
2. Hath He marks to lead me to Him, If He be my guide?
3. Hath He di - a - dem, as mon-arch, That His brow a - dorns?
4. If I find Him, if I fol - low, What His pro-mise here?
5. If I still hold close-ly to Him, What hath He at last?

"Come to me," saith One, "and, com-ing, Be at rest."
In His feet and hands are wound prints, And His side.
Yea, a crown in ver - y sure-ty, But of thorns.
Many a sor - row, many a la - bor, Many a tear.
Sor - row van-quished, la - bor end - ed, Jor - dan passed. A-men.

Years I Spent in Vanity and Pride 195

CALVARY 9. 9. 9. 4. with Refrain

William R. Newell, 1868-1956

Daniel B. Towner, 1850-1919

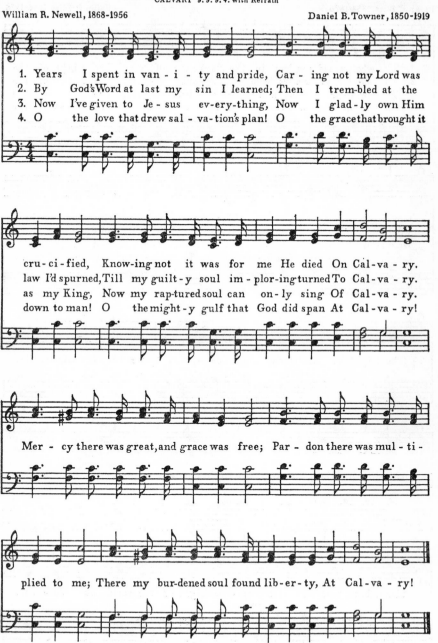

1. Years   I spent in van - i - ty and pride, Car - ing not my Lord was
2. By   God's Word at last my   sin I learned; Then I trem-bled at the
3. Now   I've given to Je - sus   ev-ery-thing, Now   I glad-ly own Him
4. O   the love that drew sal - va-tion's plan! O   the grace that brought it

cru - ci - fied, Know-ing not it was for me He died On Cal-va - ry.
law I'd spurned, Till my guilt-y soul im - plor-ing turned To Cal-va - ry.
as my King, Now my rap-tured soul can   on - ly sing Of Cal-va - ry.
down to man! O   the might-y gulf that God did span At Cal-va - ry!

Mer - cy there was great, and grace was free; Par - don there was mul - ti -

plied to me; There my bur-dened soul found lib-er-ty, At Cal-va - ry!

196 The Light of the World Is Jesus

LIGHT OF THE WORLD .11.8.11.8. with Refrain

Philip P. Bliss, 1838-1876   Philip P. Bliss, 1838-1876

1. The whole world was lost in the dark-ness of sin, The Light of the
2. No dark-ness have we who in Je-sus a-bide, The Light of the
3. Ye dwell-ers in dark-ness with sin-blind-ed eyes, The Light of the
4. No need of the sun-light in heav-en, we're told, The Light of the

world is Je-sus; Like sun-shine at noon-day His glo-ry shone in,
world is Je-sus; We walk in the light when we fol-low our guide,
world is Je-sus; Go, wash, at His bid-ding, and light will a-rise,
world is Je-sus; The Lamb is the Light in the Cit-y of Gold,

The Light of the world is Je-sus. Come to the Light, 'tis

shin-ing for thee; Sweet-ly the Light has dawned up-on me; Once I was

blind, but now I can see; The Light of the world is Je-sus.

Standing on the Promises

PROMISES 11.11.11.9. with Refrain

R. Kelso Carter, 1849-1928   R. Kelso Carter, 1849-1928

1. Stand-ing on the prom-is-es of Christ my King, Through e-ter-nal a-ges let His
2. Stand-ing on the prom-is-es that can-not fail, When the howling storms of doubt and
3. Stand-ing on the prom-is-es of Christ the Lord, Bound to Him e-ter-nal-ly by
4. Stand-ing on the prom-is-es I can-not fall, Listening every moment to the

prais-es ring; Glo-ry in the high-est, I will shout and sing, Stand-ing on the
fear as-sail, By the liv-ing word of God I shall pre-vail, Stand-ing on the
love's strong cord, O-ver-com-ing dai-ly with the Spir-it's sword, Stand-ing on the
Spir-it's call, Rest-ing in my Sav-iour, as my all in all, Stand-ing on the

prom-is-es of God. Stand - ing, stand - ing,
Stand-ing on the prom-is-es, stand-ing on the prom-is-es,

Stand-ing on the prom-is-es of God my Sav-iour, Stand - ing,
Stand-ing on the prom-is-es,

stand - ing, I'm stand-ing on the prom-is-es of God.
stand-ing on the prom-is-es,

198   In Tenderness He Sought Me

GORDON   7. 6. 7. 6. 8. 8. with Refrain

W. Spencer Walton, 19th century, Alt.   A. J. Gordon, 1836–1895

1. In ten-der-ness He sought me, For-get-ful of His pain,
2. He washed the bleed-ing sin-wounds, And poured in oil and wine;
3. He point-ed to the nail-prints; For me His blood was shed;
4. I'm sit-ting in His pres-ence, The sun-shine of His face,
5. So while the hours are pass-ing, All now is per-fect rest;

And on His shoul-ders brought me Back to His fold a-gain. While
He whis-pered to as-sure me, "I've found thee, thou art Mine;" I
A mock-ing crown so thorn-y Was placed up-on His head: I
While with a-dor-ing won-der His bless-ings I re-trace. I
I'm wait-ing for the morn-ing, The bright-est and the best, When

an-gels in His pres-ence sang Un-til the courts of heav-en rang.
nev-er heard a sweet-er voice; It made my ach-ing heart re-joice.
won-dered what He saw in me To suf-fer such deep ag-o-ny.
know I'll find e-ter-nal days Are far too short to sound His praise.
He will call us to His side To be with Him, His spot-less bride.

O, the love that sought me! O, the blood that bought me! O, the grace that

brought me to the fold, Won-drous grace that brought me to the fold!

There Is Power in the Blood
199

POWER IN THE BLOOD 10. 9. 10. 8. with Refrain

Lewis E. Jones, 1865-1936   Lewis E. Jones, 1865-1936

1. Would you be free from the bur-den of sin? There's power in the blood,
2. Would you be free from your pas-sion and pride? There's power in the blood,
3. Would you be whit-er, much whit-er than snow? There's power in the blood,
4. Would you do serv-ice for Je-sus, your King? There's power in the blood,

power in the blood; Would you o'er e-vil a vic-to-ry win? There's
power in the blood; Come for a cleans-ing to Cal-va-ry's tide; There's
power in the blood; Sin-stains are lost in its life-giv-ing flow; There's
power in the blood; Would you live dai-ly His prais-es to sing? There's

won-der-ful power in the blood. There is power, power,
there is

Won-der-work-ing power In the blood of the Lamb; There is
In the blood of the Lamb;

power, power, Won-der-work-ing power In the pre-cious blood of the Lamb.
there is

200 Grace Greater Than Our Sin

MOODY 9. 9. 9. 9. with Refrain

Julia H. Johnston, 1849-1919   Daniel B. Towner, 1850-1919

1. Mar-vel-ous grace of our lov-ing Lord, Grace that ex-ceeds our
2. Sin and de-spair, like the sea waves cold, Threat-en the soul with
3. Dark is the stain that we can-not hide, What can a-vail to
4. Mar-vel-ous, in-fi-nite, match-less grace, Free-ly be-stowed on

sin and our guilt, Yon-der on Cal-va-ry's mount out-poured,
in-fi-nite loss; Grace that is great-er, yes, grace un-told,
wash it a-way? Look! there is flow-ing a crim-son tide;
all who be-lieve; You that are long-ing to see His face,

There where the blood of the Lamb was spilt. Grace, grace,
Points to the ref-uge, the might-y Cross.
Whit-er than snow you may be to-day.
Will you this mo-ment His grace re-ceive? Mar-vel-ous grace,

God's grace, Grace that will par-don and cleanse with-in; Grace,
in-fi-nite grace,   Mar-vel-ous

grace, God's grace, Grace that is great-er than all our sin.
grace, in-fi-nite grace,

Whosoever Heareth

WHOSOEVER Irregular, with Refrain·

Philip P. Bliss, 1838-1876   Philip P. Bliss, 1838-1876

1. "Who - so - ev - er hear - eth," shout, shout the sound! Spread the bless-ed ti-dings
2. Who - so - ev - er com - eth need not de - lay, Now the door is o - pen,
3. "Who - so - ev - er will," the promise is se - cure! "Who - so - ev - er will," for-

all the world a - round; Tell the joy-ful news wher - ev - er man is found,
en - ter while you may; Je - sus is the true, the on - ly liv - ing Way;
ev - er must en-dure; "Who-so-ev-er will!" 'tis life for - ev - er-more;

"Who-so-ev-er will may come." "Who-so-ev-er will, who - so - ev - er will!"

Send the proc - la - ma - tion o - ver vale and hill; 'Tis a lov-ing

Fa-ther calls the wan-derer home: "Who - so - ev - er will may come."

202 Full Salvation

CWM RHONDDA 8.7.8.7.8.7.7.

Francis Bottome, 1823-1894

John Hughes, 1873-1932

1. Full sal - va - tion! Full sal - va - tion! Lo, the foun - tain
2. Love's re - sist - less cur - rent sweep-ing All the re - gions
3. Life im - mor - tal, hea - ven de-scending, Lo! my heart the

o-pened wide, Streams through ev - ery land and na - tion From the Sav - iour's
deep with-in; Thought, and wish, and sens - es keep-ing Now and ev - ery
Spir-it's shrine: God and man in one - ness blend-ing, O what fel - low -

wound - ed side. Full sal - va - tion! Full sal - va - tion!
in - stant, clean: Full sal - va - tion! Full sal - va - tion!
ship is mine! Full sal - va - tion! Full sal - va - tion!

Streams an end-less crim-son tide. Streams an end - less crim-son tide.
From the guilt and power of sin. From the guilt and power of sin.
Raised in Christ to life di - vine! Raised in Christ to life di - vine! A-men.

Music used by permission of G.D. Hughes and Dilys S. Webb.

Grace, Enough for Me

FATHOMLESS GRACE 8. 6. 8. 6. with Refrain

Edwin O. Excell, 1851-1921

Edwin O. Excell, 1851-1921

1. In look-ing through my tears one day, I saw Mount Cal-va-ry;
2. When I be-held my ev-ery sin Nailed to the cru-el tree,
3. When I am safe with-in the veil, My por-tion there will be

Be-neath the cross there flowed a stream Of grace, e-nough for me.
I felt a flood go through my soul Of grace, e-nough for me.
To sing through all the years to come Of grace, e-nough for me.

Grace is flow-ing from Cal-va-ry, Grace as fath-om-less as the sea,

Grace for time and e-ter-ni-ty, Grace, e-nough for me.

204   He Is Able to Deliver Thee

DELIVERANCE 10.10.10.10. with Refrain

William A. Ogden, 1841-1897   William A. Ogden, 1841-1897

1. 'Tis the grand-est theme through the a-ges rung, 'Tis the grandest theme for a
2. 'Tis the grand-est theme in the earth or main, 'Tis the grandest theme for a
3. 'Tis the grand-est theme, let the ti-dings roll, To the guilt-y heart, to the

mor-tal tongue; 'Tis the grand-est theme that the world e'er sung, Our God is
mor-tal strain; 'Tis the grand-est theme, tell the world a-gain, Our God is
sin-ful soul; Look to God in faith, He will make thee whole, Our God is

a-ble to de-liv-er thee. He is a - ble to de-liv-er thee,
a-ble, He is a-ble

He is a - ble to de-liv-er thee; Though by sin op-prest,
a-ble, He is a-ble

Go to Him for rest; Our God is a-ble to de-liv-er thee.

Under the Atoning Blood

9.9.9.7. with Refrain

Haldor Lillenas, 1885-1959

Haldor Lillenas, 1885-1959

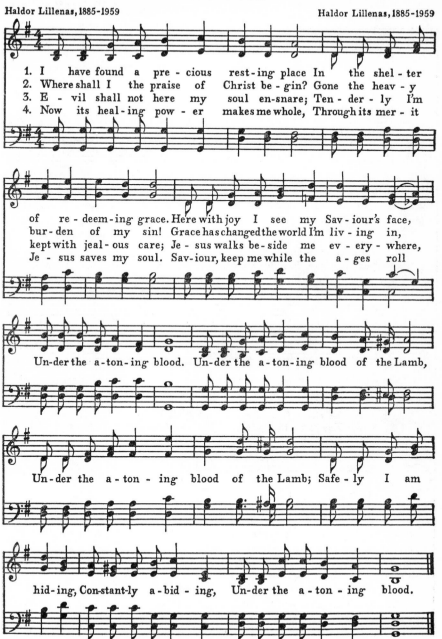

1. I have found a pre - cious rest-ing place In the shel - ter
2. Where shall I the praise of Christ be - gin? Gone the heav - y
3. E - vil shall not here my soul en-snare; Ten - der - ly I'm
4. Now its heal - ing pow - er makes me whole, Through its mer - it

of re - deem-ing grace. Here with joy I see my Sav - iour's face,
bur - den of my sin! Grace has changed the world I'm liv - ing in,
kept with jeal - ous care; Je - sus walks be - side me ev - ery - where,
Je - sus saves my soul. Sav-iour, keep me while the a - ges roll

Un-der the a-ton-ing blood. Un-der the a-ton-ing blood of the Lamb,

Un - der the a - ton - ing blood of the Lamb; Safe - ly I am

hid-ing, Con-stant-ly a-bid-ing, Un-der the a - ton - ing blood.

Copyright 1918. Renewal 1946 by Nazarene Publishing House.

206 There Is a Fountain

CLEANSING FOUNTAIN 8.6.8.6.6.6.8.6.

William Cowper, 1731-1800

Early American Melody
Arr. by Lowell Mason, 1792-1872

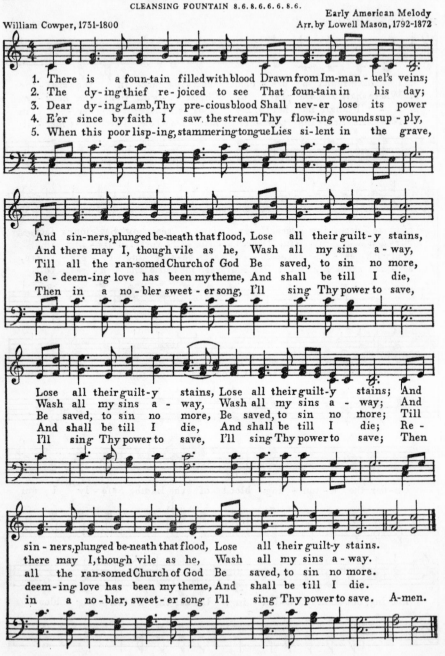

1. There is a foun-tain filled with blood Drawn from Im-man-uel's veins;
2. The dy-ing thief re-joiced to see That foun-tain in his day;
3. Dear dy-ing Lamb, Thy pre-cious blood Shall nev-er lose its power
4. E'er since by faith I saw the stream Thy flow-ing wounds sup-ply,
5. When this poor lisp-ing, stammering tongue Lies si-lent in the grave,

And sin-ners, plunged be-neath that flood, Lose all their guilt-y stains,
And there may I, though vile as he, Wash all my sins a-way,
Till all the ran-somed Church of God Be saved, to sin no more,
Re-deem-ing love has been my theme, And shall be till I die,
Then in a no-bler sweet-er song, I'll sing Thy power to save,

Lose all their guilt-y stains, Lose all their guilt-y stains; And
Wash all my sins a-way, Wash all my sins a-way; And
Be saved, to sin no more, Be saved, to sin no more; Till
And shall be till I die, And shall be till I die; Re-
I'll sing Thy power to save, I'll sing Thy power to save; Then

sin-ners, plunged be-neath that flood, Lose all their guilt-y stains.
there may I, though vile as he, Wash all my sins a-way.
all the ran-somed Church of God Be saved, to sin no more.
deem-ing love has been my theme, And shall be till I die.
in a no-bler, sweet-er song I'll sing Thy power to save. A-men.

Wonderful Words of Life

WORDS OF LIFE 8.6.8.6.6.6. with Refrain

207

Philip P. Bliss, 1838-1876

Philip P. Bliss, 1838-1876

1. Sing them o - ver a - gain to me, Won-der - ful words of life;
2. Christ, the bless - ed One, gives to all Won-der - ful words of life;
3. Sweet - ly ech - o the gos-pel call, Won-der - ful words of life;

Let me more of their beau - ty see, Won-der - ful words of life.
Sin - ner, list to the lov - ing call, Won-der - ful words of life.
Of - fer par - don and peace to all, Won-der - ful words of life.

Words of life and beau - ty, Teach me faith and du - ty:
All so free - ly giv - en, Woo - ing us to heav - en:
Je - sus, on - ly Sav - iour, Sanc - ti - fy for - ev - er:

Beau - ti - ful words, won-der-ful words, Won-der-ful words of life;

Beau - ti - ful words, won-der-ful words, Won-der - ful words of life.

208 Wonderful Story of Love

WONDERFUL STORY 7.6.7.6.8.8.8.7. with Refrain

J.M. Driver
J.M. Driver

1. Won-der-ful sto-ry of love; Tell it to me a - gain; Won-der-ful
2. Won-der-ful sto-ry of love; Though you are far a - way; Won-der-ful
3. Won-der-ful sto-ry of love; Je - sus pro-vides a rest; Won-der-ful

sto-ry of love; Wake the immor-tal strain! An-gels with rapture announce it,
sto-ry of love; Still He doth call to - day; Call-ing from Cal-va-ry's moun-tain,
sto-ry of love; For all the pure and blest, Rest in those mansions a-bove us,

Shepherds with wonder re - ceive it; Sin - ner, O won't you be - lieve it?
Down from the crys-tal bright foun-tain, E'en from the dawn of cre - a - tion,
With those who've gone on be - fore us, Sing-ing the rap-tur-ous cho - rus,

Won-der-ful sto-ry of love. Won - der - ful! Won - der -
Won-der-ful sto-ry of love; Wonder-ful sto-ry of

ful! Won - der - ful! Won-der-ful sto-ry of love!
love; Won-der-ful sto-ry of love;

And Can It Be That I Should Gain? 209

SAGINA 8.8.8.8.D.

Charles Wesley, 1707-1788

Thomas Campbell, 1777-1844

1. And can it be that I should gain An in-terest in the
2. He left His Fa-ther's throne a-bove, So free, so in-fi-
3. No con-dem-na-tion now I dread, I am my Lord's and

Sav-iour's blood? Died He for me who caused His pain? For me, who
nite His grace! Emp-tied Him-self of all but love, And bled for
He is mine; A-live in Him, my liv-ing Head, And clothed in

Him to death pur-sued?
A-dam's help-less race? A-maz-ing love! How can it be
right-eous-ness di-vine.

That Thou, my God, shouldst die for me? A-maz-ing love! How
A-maz-ing love!

rit.

can it be That Thou, my God, shouldst die for me?
How can it be That Thou, my God,

210 The Way of the Cross Leads Home

WAY OF THE CROSS 11.7.10.8. with Refrain

Jessie Brown Pounds, 1861-1921   Charles H. Gabriel, 1856-1932

1. I must needs go home by the way of the cross, There's no oth-er
2. I must needs go on in the blood-sprin-kled way, The path that the
3. Then I bid fare-well to the way of the world, To walk in it

way but this; I shall ne'er get sight of the gates of light,
Sav-iour trod, If I ev-er climb to the heights sub-lime,
nev-er-more, For my Lord says "Come," and I seek my home,

If the way of the cross I miss.
Where the soul is at home with God. The way of the cross leads
Where He waits at the o-pen door.

home, The way of the cross leads home; It is
leads home, leads home;

sweet to know as I on-ward go, The way of the cross leads home.

Come to the Saviour Now

211

INVITATION 6.6.6.6.D.

John M. Wigner, 1844-1911

Frederick C. Maker, 1844-1927

1. Come to the Sav-iour now, He gent-ly call-eth thee;
2. Come to the Sav-iour now, Ye who have wan-dered far;
3. Come to the Sav-iour, all, What-e'er your bur-dens be;

In true re-pent-ance bow, Be-fore Him bend the knee;
Re-new your sol-emn vow, For His by right you are;
Hear now His lov-ing call, "Cast all your care on Me."

He wait-eth to be-stow Sal-va-tion, peace, and love,
Come, like poor wan-dering sheep Re-turn-ing to His fold;
Come, and for ev-ery grief In Je-sus you will find

True joy on earth be-low, A home in heaven a-bove.
His arm will safe-ly keep, His love will ne'er grow cold.
A sure and safe re-lief, A lov-ing friend and kind. A-men.

212   I Lay My Sins on Jesus

ST. HILDA 7. 6. 7. 6. D.

Justin H. Knecht, 1752-1817

Edward Husband, 1843-1908

Horatius Bonar, 1808-1889

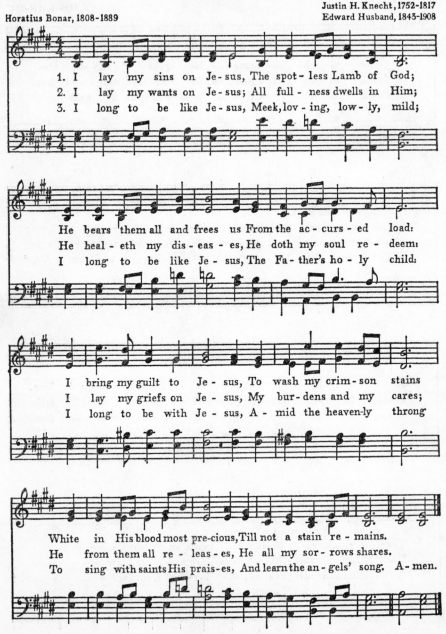

1. I lay my sins on Je-sus, The spot-less Lamb of God;
2. I lay my wants on Je-sus; All full-ness dwells in Him;
3. I long to be like Je-sus, Meek, lov-ing, low-ly, mild;

He bears them all and frees us From the ac-curs-ed load:
He heal-eth my dis-eas-es, He doth my soul re-deem:
I long to be like Je-sus, The Fa-ther's ho-ly child:

I bring my guilt to Je-sus, To wash my crim-son stains
I lay my griefs on Je-sus, My bur-dens and my cares;
I long to be with Je-sus, A-mid the heaven-ly throng

White in His blood most pre-cious, Till not a stain re-mains.
He from them all re-leas-es, He all my sor-rows shares.
To sing with saints His prais-es, And learn the an-gels' song. A-men.

Lord Jesus, I Long to Be Perfectly Whole 213

FISCHER 11.11.11.11. with Refrain

James Nicholson, c. 1828-1896   William G. Fischer, 1835-1912

1. Lord Je - sus, I long to be per - fect - ly whole, I
2. Lord Je - sus, for this I most hum - bly en - treat; I
3. Lord Je - sus, Thou se - est I pa - tient - ly wait; Come

want Thee for - ev - er to live in my soul. Break down ev - ery
wait, bless - ed Lord, at Thy cru - ci - fied feet. By faith, for my
now, and with - in me a new heart cre - ate. To those who have

i - dol, cast out ev - ery foe; Now wash me, and I shall be
cleans-ing I see Thy blood flow; Now wash me, and I shall be
sought Thee, Thou nev - er saidst "No" Now wash me, and I shall be

whit - er than snow.
whit - er than snow. Whit - er than snow, yes, whit - er than snow;
whit - er than snow.

Now wash me, and I shall be whit - er than snow.

214 I Will Arise and Go to Jesus

ARISE 8.7.8.7.

Joseph Hart, 1712-1768

Early American Tune

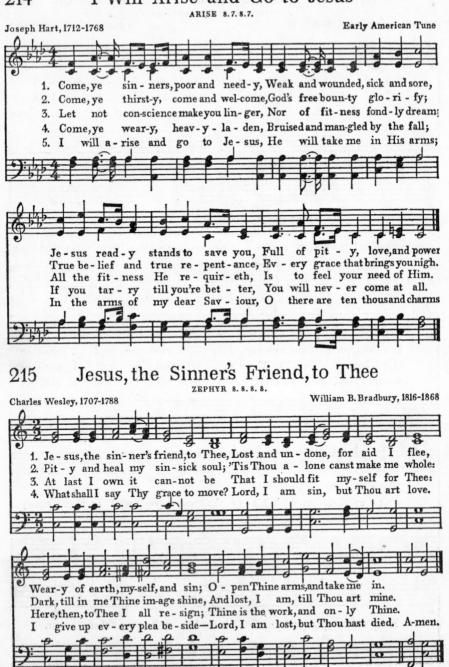

1. Come, ye sin-ners, poor and need-y, Weak and wounded, sick and sore,
2. Come, ye thirst-y, come and wel-come, God's free boun-ty glo-ri-fy;
3. Let not con-science make you lin-ger, Nor of fit-ness fond-ly dream;
4. Come, ye wear-y, heav-y-la-den, Bruised and man-gled by the fall;
5. I will a-rise and go to Je-sus, He will take me in His arms;

Je-sus read-y stands to save you, Full of pit-y, love, and power
True be-lief and true re-pent-ance, Ev-ery grace that brings you nigh.
All the fit-ness He re-quir-eth, Is to feel your need of Him.
If you tar-ry till you're bet-ter, You will nev-er come at all.
In the arms of my dear Sav-iour, O there are ten thousand charms

215 Jesus, the Sinner's Friend, to Thee

ZEPHYR 8.8.8.8.

Charles Wesley, 1707-1788

William B. Bradbury, 1816-1868

1. Je-sus, the sin-ner's friend, to Thee, Lost and un-done, for aid I flee,
2. Pit-y and heal my sin-sick soul; 'Tis Thou a-lone canst make me whole:
3. At last I own it can-not be That I should fit my-self for Thee:
4. What shall I say Thy grace to move? Lord, I am sin, but Thou art love.

Wear-y of earth, my-self, and sin; O-pen Thine arms, and take me in.
Dark, till in me Thine im-age shine, And lost, I am, till Thou art mine.
Here, then, to Thee I all re-sign; Thine is the work, and on-ly Thine.
I give up ev-ery plea be-side—Lord, I am lost, but Thou hast died. A-men.

O Jesus, Thou Art Standing

ST. HILDA 7.6.7.6.D.

William W. How, 1823-1897

Justin H. Kr...
Edward Hus...

1. O Je-sus, Thou art stand-ing Out-side the fast-closed door,
2. O Je-sus, Thou art knock-ing; And lo! Thy hand is scarred,
3. O Je-sus, Thou art plead-ing In ac-cents meek and low,

In low-ly pa-tience wait-ing To pass the thresh-old o'er.
And thorns Thy brow en-cir-cle, And tears Thy face have marred.
"I died for you, My chil-dren, And will ye treat Me so?"

We bear the name of Chris-tian, His name and sign we bear;
O love that pass-eth knowl-edge, So pa-tient-ly to wait!
O Lord, with shame and sor-row We o-pen now the door;

O shame, thrice shame up-on us, To keep Him stand-ing there!
O sin that hath no e-qual, So fast to bar the gate!
Dear Say-iour, en-ter, en-ter, And leave us nev-er-more! A-men.

7

Speak to My Heart

HOLCOMB 7. 6. 7. 6. with Refrain

B. B. McKinney, 1886-1952   B. B. McKinney, 1886-1952

1. Speak to my heart, Lord Je-sus, Speak that my soul may hear;
2. Speak to my heart, Lord Je-sus, Purge me from ev-ery sin;
3. Speak to my heart, Lord Je-sus, It is no long-er mine:

Speak to my heart, Lord Je-sus, Calm ev-ery doubt and fear.
Speak to my heart, Lord Je-sus, Help me the lost to win.
Speak to my heart, Lord Je-sus, I would be whol-ly Thine.

Speak to my heart, O speak to my heart, Speak to my heart, I pray;

Yield-ed and still, seek-ing Thy will, O speak to my heart to-day.

Jesus Is Standing in Pilate's Hall 218

PILATE Irregular

Unknown

M. L. Stocks

1. Je-sus is stand-ing in Pi - late's hall—Friendless, for-sak-en, be-trayed by all:
2. Je-sus is stand-ing on tri - al still, You can be false to Him if you will,
3. Will you e - vade Him as Pi - late tried? Or will you choose Him, what-e'er be-tide?
4. Will you, like Pe-ter, your Lord de - ny? Or will you scorn from His foes to fly,
5. "Je-sus, I give Thee my heart to-day! Je-sus, I'll fol-low Thee all the way,

Heark-en! what mean-eth the sud - den call! What will you do with Je - sus?
You can be faith-ful through good or ill: What will you do with Je - sus?
Vain-ly you strug-gle from Him to hide: What will you do with Je - sus?
Dar - ing for Je - sus to live or die? What will you do with Je - sus?
Glad - ly o - bey-ing Thee!" will you say: "This will I do with Je - sus!"

What will you do with Je - sus? Neu-tral you can - not be;

Some-day your heart will be ask - ing, "What will He do with me?"

219 Out of My Bondage, Sorrow, and Night

JESUS, I COME Irregular

William T. Sleeper, 1819-1904

George C. Stebbins, 1846-1945

1. Out of my bond-age, sor-row, and night, Je-sus, I come, Je-sus, I come;
2. Out of my shame-ful fail-ure and loss, Je-sus, I come, Je-sus, I come;
3. Out of un-rest and ar-ro-gant pride, Je-sus, I come, Je-sus, I come;
4. Out of the fear and dread of the tomb, Je-sus, I come, Je-sus, I come;

In - to Thy free-dom, glad-ness, and light, Je-sus, I come to Thee; Out of my
In - to the glo-rious gain of Thy cross, Je-sus, I come to Thee; Out of earth's
In - to Thy bless-ed will to a-bide, Je-sus, I come to Thee; Out of my
In - to the joy and light of Thy home, Je-sus, I come to Thee; Out of the

sick-ness in - to Thy health, Out of my want and in-to Thy wealth,
sor - rows in - to Thy balm, Out of life's storms and in-to Thy calm,
self to dwell in Thy love, Out of de-spair in-to rap-tures a-bove,
depths of ru-in un-told, In-to the peace of Thy shel-ter-ing fold,

Out of my sin and in-to Thy-self, Je-sus, I come to Thee.
Out of dis-tress to ju-bi-lant psalm, Je-sus, I come to Thee.
Up-ward to soar on wings like a dove, Je-sus, I come to Thee.
Ev - er Thy glo-rious face to be-hold, Je-sus, I come to Thee.

Come Every Soul by Sin Oppressed   220

STOCKTON 8.6.8.6. with Refrain

John H. Stockton, 1813-1877   John H. Stockton, 1813-1877

1. Come, ev - ery soul by sin oppressed, There's mer-cy with the Lord,
2. For Je - sus shed His pre-cious blood Rich bless-ings to be - stow;
3. Yes, Je - sus is the Truth, the Way, That leads you in - to rest;
4. Come then, and join this ho - ly band And on to glo - ry go,

And He will sure - ly give you rest, By trust-ing in His word.
Plunge now in - to the crim-son flood That wash-es white as snow.
Be - lieve in Him with-out de-lay, And you are ful - ly blest.
To dwell in that ce - les-tial land, Where joys im-mor-tal flow.

On - ly trust Him, on - ly trust Him, On - ly trust Him now;

He will save you, He will save you, He will save you now.

221 If You Are Tired of the Load of Your Sin

McCONNELSVILLE 10.8.10.8. with Refrain

Mrs. C. H. Morris, 1862-1929   Mrs. C. H. Morris, 1862-1929

1. If you are tired of the load of your sin, Let Je-sus come in-to your heart; If you de-sire a new life to be-gin,
2. If 'tis for pu-ri-ty now that you sigh, Let Je-sus come in-to your heart; Foun-tains for cleans-ing are flow-ing near by,
3. If there's a tem-pest your voice can-not still, Let Je-sus come in-to your heart; If there's a void this world nev-er can fill,
4. If you would join the glad songs of the blest, Let Je-sus come in-to your heart; If you would en-ter the man-sions of rest,

Let Je-sus come in-to your heart. Just now, your doubt-ings give o'er; Just now, re-ject Him no more; Just now, throw o-pen the door; Let Je-sus come in-to your heart.

Have You Been to Jesus

WASHED IN THE BLOOD 11. 9. 11. 9. with Refrain

Elisha A. Hoffman, 1859-1929

Elisha A. Hoffman, 1859-1929

1. Have you been to Je-sus for the cleansing power? Are you washed in the
2. Are you walk-ing dai-ly by the Sav-iour's side? Are you washed in the
3. When the bridegroom cometh will your robes be white, Pure and white in the
4. Lay a-side the garments that are stained with sin, And be washed in the

blood of the Lamb? Are you ful-ly trust-ing in His grace this hour? Are you
blood of the Lamb? Do you rest each mo-ment in the Cru-ci-fied? Are you
blood of the Lamb? Will your soul be read-y for the man-sions bright, And be
blood of the Lamb; There's a foun-tain flowing for the soul un-clean, O be

washed in the blood of the Lamb? Are you washed in the
Are you washed

blood, In the soul-cleans-ing blood of the Lamb?
in the blood, of the Lamb?

Are your garments spotless? Are they white as snow? Are you washed in the blood of the Lamb?

223 Almost Persuaded Now to Believe

ALMOST PERSUADED Irregular

Philip P. Bliss, 1838-1876   Philip P. Bliss, 1838-1876

1. Al-most per-suad-ed now to be-lieve; Al-most per-suad-ed,
2. Al-most per-suad-ed, come, come to-day; Al-most per-suad-ed,
3. Al-most per-suad-ed; har-vest is past! Al-most per-suad-ed;

Christ to re-ceive; Seems now some soul to say, "Go Spir-it,
turn not a-way; Je-sus in-vites you here, An-gels are
doom comes at last! "Al-most" can-not a-vail; "Al-most" is

go Thy way, Some more con-ven-ient day On Thee I'll call."
lin-gering near, Prayers rise from hearts so dear; O wan-derer, come!
but to fail! Sad, sad that bit-ter wail— "Al-most," but lost!

224 Just As I Am

WOODWORTH 8. 8. 8. 8.

Charlotte Elliot, 1789-1871   William B. Bradbury, 1816-1868

1. Just as I am, with-out one plea, But that Thy blood was shed for me,
2. Just as I am, and wait-ing not To rid my soul of one dark blot,
3. Just as I am, though tossed a-bout With ma-ny a con-flict, many a doubt,
4. Just as I am, poor, wretched, blind. Sight, rich-es, heal-ing of the mind,
5. Just as I am, Thou wilt receive, Wilt wel-come, par-don, cleanse, relieve;
6. Just as I am, Thy love unknown Hath bro-ken ev-ery bar-rier down;

And that Thou bidd'st me come to Thee, O Lamb of God, I come, I come!
To Thee whose blood can cleanse each spot, O Lamb of God, I come, I come!
Fighting with-in, and fears with-out, O Lamb of God, I come, I come!
Yea, all I need in Thee to find, O Lamb of God, I come, I come!
Be-cause Thy prom-ise I be-lieve, O Lamb of God, I come, I come!
Now to be Thine, yea, Thine a-lone, O Lamb of God, I come, I come!

While Jesus Whispers to You 225

COME, SINNER, COME 7. 4. 7. 4. D.

William E. Witter, b. 1854

Horatio R. Palmer, 1834-1907

1. While Je - sus whis-pers to you, Come, sin-ner, come! While we are
2. Are you too heav-y-la-den? Come, sin-ner, come! Je - sus will
3. O, hear His ten-der pleading, Come, sin-ner, come! Come and re-

pray-ing for you, Come, sin-ner, come! Now is the time to own Him,
bear your bur-den, Come, sin-ner, come! Je - sus will not de-ceive you,
ceive the bless-ing, Come, sin-ner, come! While Je-sus whis-pers to you,

Come, sin-ner, come! Now is the time to know Him, Come, sin-ner, come!
Come, sin-ner, come! Je - sus can now re-lieve you, Come, sin-ner, come!
Come, sin-ner, come! While we are pray-ing for you, Come, sin-ner, come!

226 Lord, I'm Coming Home

COMING HOME 8.5.8.5. with Refrain

William J. Kirkpatrick, 1838-1921   William J. Kirkpatrick, 1838-1921

1. I've wan-dered far a - way from God, Now I'm com-ing home;
2. I've wast - ed man - y pre - cious years, Now I'm com-ing home;
3. I'm tired of sin and stray - ing, Lord, Now I'm com-ing home;
4. My soul is sick, my heart is sore, Now I'm com-ing home;
5. My on - ly hope, my on - ly plea, Now I'm com-ing home;

The paths of sin too long I've trod, Lord, I'm com-ing home.
I now re-pent with bit - ter tears, Lord, I'm com-ing home.
I'll trust Thy love, be - lieve Thy Word, Lord, I'm com-ing home.
My strength re-new, my hope re-store, Lord, I'm com-ing home.
That Je - sus died, and died for me, Lord, I'm com-ing home.

Com-ing home, com-ing home, Nev - er-more to roam;

O - pen wide Thine arms of love, Lord, I'm com-ing home.

Softly and Tenderly

THOMPSON 11.7.11.7.with Refrain

Will L. Thompson, 1847-1909   Will L. Thompson, 1847-1909

1. Soft-ly and ten-der-ly Je-sus is call-ing, Call-ing for you and for me;
2. Why should we tarry when Je-sus is plead-ing, Pleading for you and for me?
3. Time is now fleeting, the moments are passing, Pass-ing from you and from me;
4. O, for the won-der-ful love He has prom-ised, Promised for you and for me;

See, on the por-tals He's waiting and watching, Watching for you and for me.
Why should we linger and heed not His mer-cies, Mer-cies for you and for me?
Shadows are gather-ing, death-beds are com-ing, Com-ing for you and for me.
Though we have sinned, He has mercy and par-don, Par-don for you and for me.

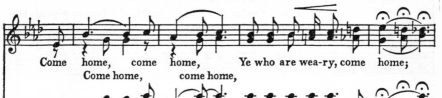

Come home,   come home,   Ye who are wea-ry, come home;
Come home,   come home,

Ear-nest-ly, ten-der-ly, Je-sus is call-ing, Call-ing, O sin-ner, come home!

228 Give Me Thy Heart

BOURNE 10.10.10.10. with Refrain

Eliza E. Hewitt, 1851-1920

William J. Kirkpatrick, 1838-1921

1. "Give Me thy heart," says the Fa-ther a-bove, No gift so pre-cious to
2. "Give Me thy heart," says the Sav-iour of men, Call-ing in mer-cy a-
3. "Give Me thy heart," says the Spir-it di-vine, "All that thou hast to My

Him as our love; Soft-ly He whis-pers wher-ev-er thou art,
gain and a-gain; "Turn now from sin, and from e-vil de-part,
keep-ing re-sign; Grace more a-bound-ing is Mine to im-part,

"Grate-ful-ly trust Me and give Me thy heart.
Have I not died for thee? give Me thy heart. Give Me thy heart, give Me thy
Make full sur-ren-der and give Me thy heart.

heart," Hear the soft whisper, wher-ev-er thou art; From this dark world He would

draw thee a-part; Speak-ing so ten-der-ly, "Give Me thy heart."

Jesus Is Calling

229

CALLING TODAY 10.8.10.7.with Refrain

Fanny J. Crosby, 1820-1915

George C. Stebbins, 1846-1945

1. Je-sus is ten-der-ly call-ing thee home, Call-ing to-day, call-ing to-day;
2. Je-sus is call-ing the wea-ry to rest, Call-ing to-day, call-ing to-day;
3. Je-sus is wait-ing, O come to Him now, Wait-ing to-day, wait-ing to-day;
4. Je-sus is plead-ing, O list to His voice, Hear Him to-day, hear Him to-day;

Why from the sun-shine of love wilt thou roam Far-ther and far-ther a - way?
Bring Him thy bur-den and thou shalt be blest; He will not turn thee a - way.
Come with thy sins, at His feet low-ly bow; Come, and no long-er de - lay.
They who be-lieve on His name shall re-joice; Quick-ly a-rise and a - way.

Call - ing to - day! Call - ing to - day!
Call-ing, call-ing to - day, to-day! Call-ing, call-ing to - day, to-day!

Je - sus is call - ing, Is ten-der-ly call-ing to - day.
Je-sus is ten-der-ly call-ing to-day,

230   I Am Coming to the Cross

TRUSTING 7.7.7.7. with Refrain

William McDonald, 1820-1901   William G. Fischer, 1835-1912

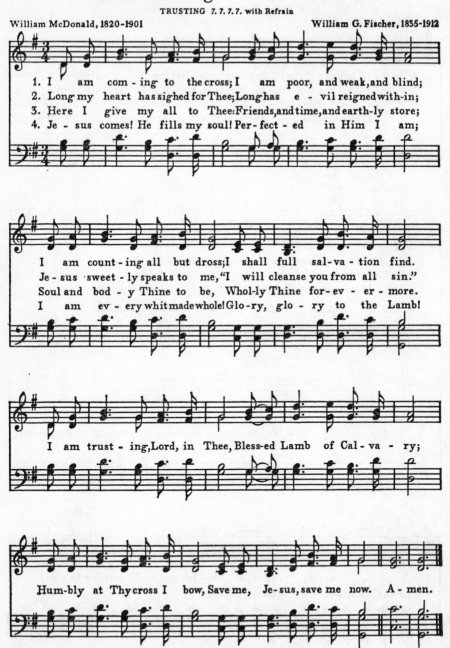

1. I am com-ing to the cross; I am poor, and weak, and blind;
2. Long my heart has sighed for Thee; Long has e - vil reigned with-in;
3. Here I give my all to Thee: Friends, and time, and earth-ly store;
4. Je - sus comes! He fills my soul! Per-fect-ed in Him I am;

I am count-ing all but dross; I shall full sal-va-tion find.
Je - sus sweet-ly speaks to me, "I will cleanse you from all sin."
Soul and bod-y Thine to be, Whol-ly Thine for-ev-er-more.
I am ev - ery whit made whole! Glo-ry, glo-ry to the Lamb!

I am trust-ing, Lord, in Thee, Bless-ed Lamb of Cal-va-ry;

Hum-bly at Thy cross I bow, Save me, Je-sus, save me now. A-men.

Have You Any Room for Jesus 231

ROOM FOR JESUS 8.7.8.7. with Refrain

Scource Unknown
Alt. by Daniel W. Whittle, 1840-1901

C. C. Williams, 19th century

1. Have you an-y room for Je-sus, He who bore your load of sin?
2. Room for pleas-ure, room for busi-ness, But for Christ the Cru-ci-fied,
3. Have you an-y room for Je-sus, As in grace He calls a-gain?
4. Room and time now give to Je-sus, Soon will pass God's day of grace;

As He knocks and asks ad-mis-sion, Sin-ner, will you let Him in?
Not a place that He can en-ter, In the heart for which He died?
O to-day is time ac-cept-ed, La-ter you may call in vain.
Soon thy heart left cold and si-lent, And thy Sav-iour's plead-ing cease.

Room for Je-sus, King of glo-ry! Has-ten now, His word o-bey;

Swing your heart's door wide-ly o-pen, Bid Him en-ter while you may.

232 Father, I Stretch My Hands to Thee

CAMP MEETING 8.6.8.6.C.

Charles Wesley, 1707-1788

Early American Melody

1. Fa - ther, I stretch my hands to Thee; No oth-er help I know;
2. What did Thine on - ly Son en-dure Be - fore I drew my breath!
3. Au - thor of faith, to Thee I lift My wea - ry, long-ing eyes;
4. Sure - ly Thou canst not let me die; O speak, and I shall live;
5. How would my faint-ing soul re-joice Could I but see Thy face!
6. I do be - lieve, I now be-lieve That Je - sus died for me;

If Thou with-draw Thy-self from me, Ah, whith-er shall I go?
What pain, what la - bor, to se-cure My soul from end-less death!
O let me now re - ceive that gift; My soul with-out it dies.
And here I will un - wea-ried lie, Till Thou Thy Spir-it give.
Now let me hear Thy quickening voice; And taste Thy par-doning grace.
And through His blood, His pre-cious blood, I shall from sin be free.

233 Lord of Mercy, God of Might

SEYMOUR 7.7.7.7.

Wilson T. Hogue, 1852-1920

Carl M. von Weber, 1786-1826

1. Lord of mer - cy, God of might, Dwell-ing in ef - ful-gence bright,
2. Lord of grace and truth and love, Fit me here for worlds a - bove,
3. Lord of earth and heav'n a - bove, Fill me now with per-fect love;
4. Lord of an - gels and of men, Com-ing soon to earth a - gain,

Shed Thy gra-cious beams on me, In Thy free - dom make me free.
Let me lose my will in thine, In Thine im - age let me shine.
Sanc - ti - fy by power di - vine, And from dross my heart re - fine.
For that day my soul pre - pare, In that glo - ry let me share.

All to Jesus I Surrender

234

SURRENDER 8.7.8.7. with Refrain

Judson W. Van DeVenter, 1855-1939

Winfield S. Weeden, 1847-1908

1. All to Je-sus I sur-ren-der, All to Him I free-ly give;
2. All to Je-sus I sur-ren-der, Hum-bly at His feet I bow,
3. All to Je-sus I sur-ren-der, Make me, Sav-iour, whol-ly Thine;
4. All to Je-sus I sur-ren-der, Lord, I give my-self to Thee;

I will ev-er love and trust Him, In His pres-ence dai-ly live.
World-ly pleas-ures all for-sak-en, Take me, Je-sus, take me now.
Let me feel the Ho-ly Spir-it, Tru-ly know that Thou art mine.
Fill me with Thy love and pow-er, Let Thy bless-ing fall on me.

I sur-ren-der all. I sur-ren-der all,

All to Thee, my bless-ed Sav-iour, I sur-ren-der all.

235 Help Me to Be Holy

TOWNER 6.5.6.5.D.

Adoniram J. Gordon, 1836-1895

Daniel B. Towner, 1850-1919

1. Help me to be ho-ly, O Fa-ther of Light;
2. Help me to be ho-ly, O Sav-iour di-vine;
3. Help me to be ho-ly, O Spir-it di-vine;

Guilt!—bur-dened and low-ly, I bow in Thy sight;
Why con-quer so slow-ly This na-ture of mine?
Come, sanc-ti-fy whol-ly This tem-ple of Thine;

How shall a stained con-science Dare gaze on Thy face,
Stamp deep-ly Thy like-ness Where Sa-tan's hath been;
Now cast out each i-dol, Here set up Thy throne,

E'en though in Thy pres-ence Thou grant me a place?
Ex - pel with Thy bright-ness My dark-ness and sin!
Reign, reign with-out ri-val, Su-preme and a-lone! A-men.

Hover O'er Me, Holy Spirit

236

FILL ME NOW 8.7.8.7. with Refrain

Elwood H. Stokes, 1815-1895

John R. Sweeney, 1837-1899

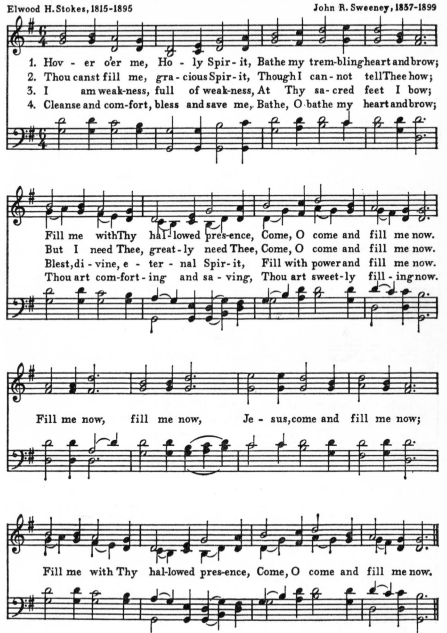

1. Hov - er o'er me, Ho - ly Spir - it, Bathe my trem-bling heart and brow;
2. Thou canst fill me, gra - cious Spir - it, Though I can - not tell Thee how;
3. I am weak-ness, full of weak-ness, At Thy sa - cred feet I bow;
4. Cleanse and com-fort, bless and save me, Bathe, O bathe my heart and brow;

Fill me with Thy hal-lowed pres-ence, Come, O come and fill me now.
But I need Thee, great-ly need Thee, Come, O come and fill me now.
Blest, di - vine, e - ter - nal Spir-it, Fill with power and fill me now.
Thou art com-fort-ing and sa - ving, Thou art sweet-ly fill - ing now.

Fill me now, fill me now, Je - sus, come and fill me now;

Fill me with Thy hal-lowed pres-ence, Come, O come and fill me now.

237 I Gave My Life for Thee

KENOSIS 6.6.6.6.8.6. with Repeat

Frances R. Havergal, 1836-1879

Philip P. Bliss, 1838-1876

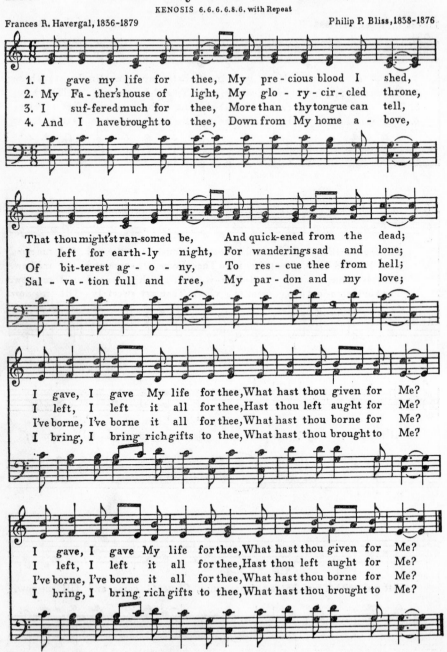

1. I gave my life for thee, My pre-cious blood I shed,
2. My Fa-ther's house of light, My glo-ry-cir-cled throne,
3. I suf-fered much for thee, More than thy tongue can tell,
4. And I have brought to thee, Down from My home a-bove,

That thou might'st ran-somed be, And quick-ened from the dead;
I left for earth-ly night, For wanderings sad and lone;
Of bit-terest ag-o-ny, To res-cue thee from hell;
Sal-va-tion full and free, My par-don and my love;

I gave, I gave My life for thee, What hast thou given for Me?
I left, I left it all for thee, Hast thou left aught for Me?
I've borne, I've borne it all for thee, What hast thou borne for Me?
I bring, I bring rich gifts to thee, What hast thou brought to Me?

I gave, I gave My life for thee, What hast thou given for Me?
I left, I left it all for thee, Hast thou left aught for Me?
I've borne, I've borne it all for thee, What hast thou borne for Me?
I bring, I bring rich gifts to thee, What hast thou brought to Me?

Where He Leads I'll Follow 238

6.4.12.6.4.12. with Refrain

William A. Ogden, 1841-1897

William A. Ogden, 1841-1897

1. Sweet are the prom-is-es, Kind is the word, Dear-er far than
2. Sweet is the ten-der love Je-sus hath shown, Sweet-er far than
3. List to His lov-ing words, "Come un-to Me!" Wea-ry, heav-y-

an-y mes-sage man ev-er heard; Pure was the mind of Christ,
an-y love that mor-tals have known; Kind to the err-ing one,
la-den, there is sweet rest for thee; Trust in His prom-is-es,

Sin-less was He; He the great ex-am-ple is, and pat-tern for me.
Faith-ful is He; He the great ex-am-ple is, and pat-tern for me.
Faith-ful and sure; Lean up-on the Sav-iour, and thy soul is se-cure.

Where He leads I'll fol-low, Fol-low all the way;

Where He leads I'll fol-low, Fol-low Je-sus ev-ery day.

239 All for Jesus

WYCLIFF 8.7.8.7.

Mary D. James, 19th century

John Stainer, 1840-1901

1. All for Je - sus! All for Je - sus! All my be - ing's
2. Let my hands per - form His bid - ding, Let my feet run
3. World-lings prize their gems of beau - ty, Cling to gild - ed
4. Since mine eyes were fixed on Je - sus, I've lost sight of
5. O what won - der! how a - maz - ing! Je - sus, glo - rious

ran - somed powers; All my thoughts and words and do - ings,
in His ways; Let mine eyes see Je - sus on - ly;
toys of dust; Boast of wealth, and fame, and pleas - ure;
all be - side, So en - chained my spir - it's vi - sion,
King of kings, Deigns to call me His be - lov - ed,

All my days and all my hours.
Let my lips speak forth His praise.
On - ly Je - sus will I trust.
Look - ing at the Cru - ci - fied.
Lets me rest be - neath His wings. A - men.

240 Have Thine Own Way, Lord

POLLARD 5.4.5.4.D.

Adelaide A. Pollard, 1862-1934

George C. Stebbins, 1846-1945

1. Have Thine own way, Lord, Have Thine own way!
2. Have Thine own way, Lord, Have Thine own way!
3. Have Thine own way, Lord, Have Thine own way!
4. Have Thine own way, Lord, Have Thine own way!

Thou art the pot-ter; I am the clay. Mould me and make me
Search me and try me, Mas-ter, to-day. Whit-er than snow, Lord,
Wound-ed and wear-y, Help me, I pray. Pow-er, all pow-er
Hold o'er my be-ing Ab-so-lute sway. Fill with Thy Spir-it

Aft-er Thy will, While I am wait-ing, Yield-ed and still.
Wash me just now, As in Thy pres-ence Hum-bly I bow.
Sure-ly is Thine! Touch me and heal me, Sav-iour di-vine!
Till all shall see Christ on-ly, al-ways, Liv-ing in me!

Search Me, O Lord 241

ELLERS 10.10.10.10.

Fanny Jane Crosby, 1820-1915   Edward J. Hopkins, 1818-1901

1. Search me, O Lord, and try this heart of mine, Search me, and prove if
2. Search me, O Lord, sub-due each vain de-sire, And in my soul a
3. Search me, O Lord, and from the dross of sin, Re-fine as gold, and
4. Search me, O Lord, let faith, through grace divine, Thy-self re-flect in

I in-deed am Thine. Test by Thy Word, that nev-er changed can be,
deep-er love in-spire. Hide Thou my life, that I, su-preme-ly blest,
keep me pure with-in. Search Thou my thoughts whose springs Thine eyes can see
ev-ery act of mine, Till at Thy call my wait-ing soul shall rise,

My strength of hope and liv-ing faith in Thee.
Be-neath Thy wings in per-fect peace may rest.
From se-cret faults, O Sav-iour, cleanse Thou me.
Caught up with joy, to meet Thee whom I prize. A-men.

242 Open the Wells of Salvation

10.9.10.9.D.

E. A. Hoffman, 1839-1929

Chas. Edw. Pollock

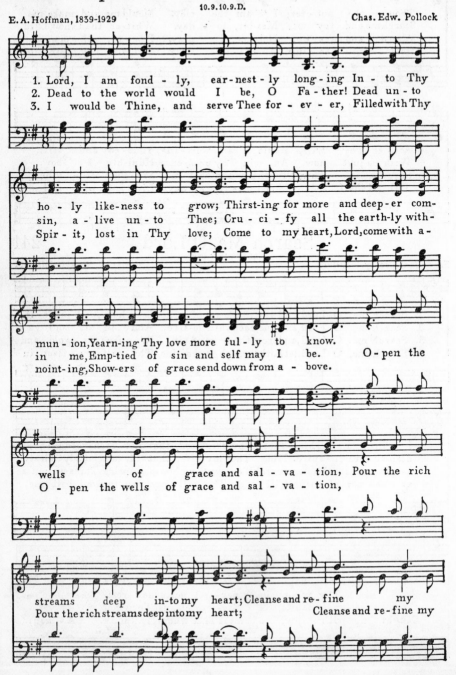

1. Lord, I am fond-ly, ear-nest-ly long-ing In-to Thy ho-ly like-ness to grow; Thirst-ing for more and deep-er com-mun-ion, Yearn-ing Thy love more ful-ly to know. O-pen the wells of grace and sal-va-tion, Pour the rich streams deep in-to my heart; Cleanse and re-fine my

2. Dead to the world would I be, O Fa-ther! Dead un-to sin, a-live un-to Thee; Cru-ci-fy all the earth-ly with-in me, Emp-tied of sin and self may I be. O-pen the wells of grace and sal-va-tion, Pour the rich streams deep into my heart;

3. I would be Thine, and serve Thee for-ev-er, Filled with Thy Spir-it, lost in Thy love; Come to my heart, Lord, come with a-noint-ing, Show-ers of grace send down from a-bove.

Cleanse and re-fine my

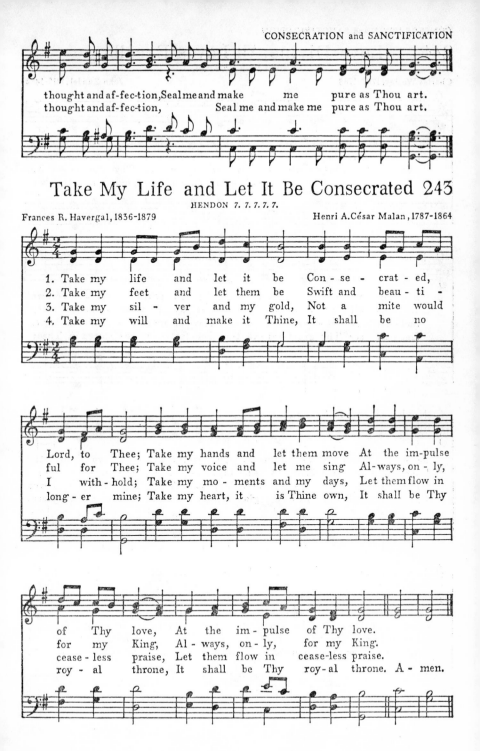

thought and af-fec-tion, Seal me and make me pure as Thou art.
thought and af-fec-tion, Seal me and make me pure as Thou art.

Take My Life and Let It Be Consecrated 243

HENDON 7. 7. 7. 7. 7.

Frances R. Havergal, 1836-1879   Henri A. César Malan, 1787-1864

1. Take my life and let it be Con - se - crat - ed,
2. Take my feet and let them be Swift and beau - ti -
3. Take my sil - ver and my gold, Not a mite would
4. Take my will and make it Thine, It shall be no

Lord, to Thee; Take my hands and let them move At the im-pulse
ful for Thee; Take my voice and let me sing Al-ways, on - ly,
I with - hold; Take my mo - ments and my days, Let them flow in
long - er mine; Take my heart, it is Thine own, It shall be Thy

of Thy love, At the im - pulse of Thy love.
for my King, Al - ways, on - ly, for my King.
cease - less praise, Let them flow in cease-less praise.
roy - al throne, It shall be Thy roy-al throne. A - men.

244 Love Divine, All Loves Excelling

BEECHER 8.7.8.7.D.

Charles Wesley, 1707-1788

John Zundel, 1815-1882

1. Love di - vine, all loves ex - cel - ling, Joy of heaven, to earth come down,
2. Breathe, O breathe Thy lov - ing Spir - it In - to ev - ery trou - bled breast!
3. Come, Al - might - y to de - liv - er, Let us all Thy life re - ceive;
4. Fin - ish, then, Thy new cre - a - tion; Pure and spot - less let us be;

Fix in us Thy hum - ble dwell - ing, All Thy faith - ful mer - cies crown!
Let us all in Thee in - her - it, Let us find the prom - ised rest;
Sud - den - ly re - turn, and nev - er, Nev - er more Thy tem - ples leave.
Let us see Thy great sal - va - tion Per - fect - ly re - stored in Thee;

Je - sus, Thou art all com - pas - sion, Pure, un - bound - ed love Thou art;
Take a - way our bent to sin - ing; Al - pha and O - me - ga be;
Thee we would be al - ways bless - ing, Serve Thee as Thy hosts a - bove;
Changed from glo - ry in - to glo - ry, Till in heaven we take our place,

Vis - it us with Thy sal - va - tion, En - ter ev - ery trem - bling heart.
End of faith, as its be - gin - ning, Set our hearts at lib - er - ty.
Pray, and praise Thee with - out ceas - ing, Glo - ry in Thy per - fect love.
Till we cast our crowns be - fore Thee, Lost in won - der, love, and praise. A - men.

Make Me a Captive, Lord

LEOMINSTER 6.6.8.6.D.

George Matheson, 1842-1906

George William Martin, 1828-1881
Arr. by Arthur S. Sullivan, 1842-1900

245

1. Make me a cap-tive, Lord, And then I shall be free;
2. My heart is weak and poor Till it a mas-ter find;
3. My power is faint and low Till I have learned to serve;
4. My will is not my own Till Thou hast made it Thine;

Force me to ren-der up my sword, And I shall con-queror be.
It has no spring of ac-tion sure—It va-ries with the wind.
It wants the need-ed fire to glow, It wants the breeze to nerve;
If it would reach a mon-arch's throne It must its crown re-sign;

I sink in life's a-larms When by my-self I stand;
It can-not free-ly move Till Thou hast wrought its chain;
It can-not drive the world Un-til it-self be driven;
It on-ly stands un-bent A-mid the clash-ing strife,

Im-pris-on me with-in Thine arms, And strong shall be my hand.
En-slave it with Thy match-less love, And death-less it shall reign.
Its flag can on-ly be un-furled When Thou shalt breathe from heaven.
When on Thy bos-om it has leant, And found in Thee its life. A-men.

246 Take Thou Our Minds

HALL 10.10.10.10.

William H. Foulkes, b. 1877

Calvin W. Laufer, 1874-1958

1. Take Thou our minds, dear Lord, we hum-bly pray;
2. Take Thou our hearts, O Christ, they are Thine own;
3. Take Thou our wills, Most High! Hold Thou full sway;
4. Take Thou our-selves, O Lord— heart, mind, and will;

Give us the mind of Christ each pass-ing day;
Come Thou with-in our souls and claim Thy throne;
Have in our in-most souls Thy per-fect way;
Through our sur-ren-dered souls Thy plans ful-fill.

Teach us to know the truth that sets us free;
Help us to shed a-broad Thy death-less love;
Guard Thou each sa-cred hour from self-ish ease;
We yield our-selves to Thee— time, tal-ents, all;

Grant us in all our thoughts to hon-or Thee.
Use us to make the earth like heaven a-bove.
Guide Thou our or-dered lives as Thou dost please.
We hear, and hence-forth heed, Thy sov-ereign call. A-men.

Fill Me with Thy Spirit, Lord

247

7. 7. 7. 7. with Refrain

Daniel S. Warner

Andrew L. Byers

1. Fill me with Thy Spir-it, Lord, Sanc-ti-fy my long-ing soul;
2. Fill me with Thy ho-ly light, I would have a sin-gle eye;
3. Fill me with Thy per-fect love, Naught of self would I re-tain;
4. Fill me with Thy might-y power, Fa-ther, Son and Spir-it, come;
5. Fill me with Thy pres-ence now, Lord, Thy-self in me re-veal;

Through the pre-cious cleans-ing blood Pu-ri-fy and make me whole.
Make me per-fect in Thy sight, 'Tis Thy will to sanc-ti-fy.
Los-ing all, Thy love to prove, Lord, I count a hap-py gain.
In my soul the unc-tion pour, Make me ev-er all Thine own.
At Thy feet I hum-bly bow To re-ceive the ho-ly seal.

Come, O Spir-it, seal me Thine, Come, Thy full-ness now be-stow;

Let Thy glo-ry in me shine, Make me whit-er than the snow.

248 Lead Me to Calvary

LEST I FORGET 8.6.8.6. with Refrain

Jennie Evelyn Hussey, 1874–   William J. Kirkpatrick, 1838–1921

1. King of my life I crown Thee now, Thine shall the glo - ry be;
2. Show me the tomb where Thou wast laid, Ten - der - ly mourned and wept;
3. Let me like Ma - ry, through the gloom, Come with a gift to Thee;
4. May I be will - ing, Lord, to bear Dai - ly my cross for Thee;

Lest I for - get Thy thorn-crowned brow, Lead me to Cal - va - ry.
An - gels in robes of light ar - rayed Guard-ed Thee while Thou slept.
Show to me now the emp - ty tomb, Lead me to Cal - va - ry.
E - ven Thy cup of grief to share: Thou hast borne all for me.

Lest I for - get Geth - sem - a - ne, Lest I for - get Thine ag - o - ny,

Lest I for - get Thy love for me, Lead me to Cal - va - ry.

O Now I See the Crimson Wave   249

KNAPP 8.6.8.6. with Refrain

Mrs. Phoebe Palmer, 1807-1874   Mrs. Joseph Knapp, 1839-1908

1. O now I see the crim-son wave, The foun-tain deep and wide;
2. I see the new cre - a - tion rise, I hear the speak-ing blood;
3. I rise to walk in hea-ven's light, A - bove the world and sin;
4. A - maz-ing grace! 'tis heaven be-low To feel the blood ap - plied;

Je - sus, my Lord, might - y to save, Points to His wound-ed side.
It speaks! pol-lut - ed na-ture dies, Sinks 'neath the crim-son flood.
With heart made pure and gar-ments white, And Christ en-throned with - in.
And Je - sus - on - ly Je - sus know, My Je - sus, cru - ci - fied.

The cleans-ing stream I see, I see! I plunge, and O, it cleans-eth me;

O praise the Lord, it cleans-eth me, It cleans-eth me, yes, cleans-eth me.

250 Lord, Possess Me Now, I Pray

WITH THY SPIRIT FILL ME 7. 7. 7. 6. with Refrain

Oswald J. Smith, 1890-   Bentley D. Ackley, 1872-1958

1. Lord, pos-sess me now, I pray, Make me whol-ly Thine to-day;
2. Lord, I yield my-self to Thee, All I am or hope to be
3. Lord, com-mis-sion me, I pray, Souls are dy-ing ev-ery day;

Glad-ly do I own Thy sway, With Thy Spir-it fill me.
Now and through e-ter-ni-ty, With Thy Spir-it fill me.
Help me lead them in Thy way, With Thy Spir-it fill me.

With Thy Spir-it fill me, With Thy Spir-it fill me;

Make me whol-ly Thine, I pray, With Thy Spir-it fill me.

I Will Be True to Thee

251

8. 6. 8. 6. with Refrain

Mrs. C. H. Morris, 1862-1929   Mrs. C. H. Morris, 1862-1929

1. Ful - ly sur - ren - dered, Lord di - vine, I will be true to Thee;
2. Tho' it may cost me friends and home, I will be true to Thee;
3. Now to the world I bid fare-well, I will be true to Thee;
4. I will go with Thee all the way, I will be true to Thee;

All that I am or have is Thine, I will be true to Thee.
Cause me in lands a - far to roam, I will be true to Thee.
Bro-ken for - ev - er its deep spell, I will be true to Thee.
All of Thy bid - ding will o - bey, I will be true to Thee.

I will be true to Thee, Lord, I will be true to Thee;

Where Thou lead-est me, I will fol-low Thee, I will be true to Thee.

252 Seal Us, O Holy Spirit

CARSON 7.7.8.7. with Refrain

Isaac H. Meredith, 1872-

Isaac H. Meredith, 1872-

1. Seal us, O Ho - ly Spir - it, Grant us Thine im-press, we pray;
2. Seal us, O Ho - ly Spir - it, Help us Thy like-ness to show;
3. Seal us, O Ho - ly Spir - it, Make us Thine own from this hour;

We would be more like the Sav - iour, Stamped with His im-age to - day.
Then from our life un - to oth - ers Streams of rich bless-ings shall flow.
Let us be use - ful, dear Mas - ter, Seal us with wit-ness-ing power.

Seal us, seal us, Seal us just now, we pray;

Seal us, O Ho - ly Spir - it, Seal us for ser - vice to - day.

I Saw the Cross of Jesus

WHITFIELD 7. 6. 7. 6. D.

Frederick Whitfield, 1829-1904

Unknown

1. I saw the cross of Je-sus, When bur-dened with my sin;
2. I love the cross of Je-sus, It tells me what I am—
3. I trust the cross of Je-sus, In ev-ery try-ing hour,
4. Safe in the cross of Je-sus! There let my wea-ry heart

I sought the cross of Je-sus, To give me peace with-in;
A vile and guilt-y crea-ture, Saved on-ly through the Lamb;
My sure and cer-tain ref-uge, My nev-er-fail-ing tower;
Still rest in peace un-shak-en, Till with Him, ne'er to part;

I brought my soul to Je-sus, He cleansed it in His blood;
No right-eous-ness nor mer-it, No beau-ty can I plead;
In ev-ery fear and con-flict, I more than con-queror am;
And then in strains of glo-ry I'll sing His won-drous power,

And in the cross of Je-sus I found my peace with God.
Yet in the cross I glo-ry, My ti-tle there I read.
Liv-ing, I'm safe, or dy-ing, Through Christ, the ris-en Lamb.
Where sin can nev-er en-ter, And death is known no more.

254 Complete in Thee

IN CHRIST 8.8.8.8. with Refrain

Aaron R. Wolfe, 1821-1902
Refrain, James M. Gray, 1851-1935

T.J. Bittikofer, b.1892-

1. Com-plete in Thee! no work of mine May take, dear Lord, the place of Thine;
2. Com-plete in Thee! no more shall sin, Thy grace hath con-quered, reign with-in;
3. Com-plete in Thee—each want sup-plied, And no good thing to me de - nied;
4. Dear Sav-iour! when be-fore Thy bar All tribes and tongues as-sem-bled are,

Thy blood hath par-don bought for me, And I am now com-plete in Thee.
Thy voice shall bid the tempt-er flee, And I shall stand com-plete in Thee.
Since Thou my por-tion, Lord, wilt be, I ask no more, com-plete in Thee.
A-mong Thy cho-sen will I be, At Thy right hand, com-plete in Thee.

Yea, jus-ti-fied! O bless-ed thought! And sanc-ti-fied! Sal-va-tion wrought!

Thy blood hath par-don bought for me, And glo-ri-fied, I too shall be!

I Love to Tell the Story

HANKEY 7.6.7.6.D. with Refrain

Katherine Hankey, 1834-1911

William G. Fischer, 1835-1912

1. I love to tell the sto-ry Of unseen things a-bove, Of Je-sus and His
2. I love to tell the sto-ry; More won-der-ful it seems Than all the gold-en
3. I love to tell the sto-ry; 'Tis pleas-ant to re-peat What seems, each time I
4. I love to tell the sto-ry; For those who know it best Seem hung-er-ing and

glo - ry, Of Je-sus and His love: I love to tell the sto-ry Be-
fan-cies Of all our gold-en dreams: I love to tell the sto-ry, It
tell it, More won-der-ful-ly sweet: I love to tell the sto-ry, For
thirst-ing To hear it, like the rest: And when, in scenes of glo-ry, I

cause I know 'tis true; It sat-is-fies my longings As noth-ing else can do.
did so much for me; And that is just the rea-son I tell it now to thee.
some have nev-er heard The message of sal - va-tion From God's own Holy Word.
sing the new, new song, 'Twill be the old, old sto-ry That I have loved so long.

I love to tell the sto-ry, 'Twill be my theme in glo - ry

To tell the old, old sto - ry Of Je - sus and His love.

256

He Included Me

SEWELL 9.9.9.7. with Refrain

Johnson Oatman, Jr., 1856-1922

Hampton H. Sewell, 1874-1937

1. I am so hap-py in Christ to-day That I go sing-ing a-long my way;
2. Glad-ly I read, Who-so-ev-er may Come to the foun-tain of life to-day;
3. Ev-er God's Spir-it is say-ing, "Come!" Hear the Bride saying, "No long-er roam";
4. "Free-ly come drink," words the soul to thrill! O with what joy they my heart do fill!

Yes I'm so hap-py to know and say, Je-sus in-clud-ed me too.
But when I read it I al-ways say, Je-sus in-clud-ed me too.
But I am sure while they're call-ing home Je-sus in-clud-ed me too.
For when He said, "Who-so-ev-er will," Je-sus in-clud-ed me too.

Je-sus in-clud-ed me, Yes, He in-clud-ed me, When the Lord said,

"Who-so-ev-er," He in-clud-ed me; Je-sus in-clud-ed me, Yes, He in-

clud-ed me, When the Lord said, "Who-so-ev-er," He in-clud-ed me.

I Am a Stranger Here

CASSEL 12.12.12.8.with Refrain

E. Taylor Cassel, 1849-1930

Flora H. Cassel, 1852-1911

1. I am a strang-er here, with-in a for-eign land, My home is far a-way up-on a gold-en strand; Am-bas-sa-dor to be of realms be-yond the sea, I'm here on business for my King.

2. This is the King's command, that all men ev-ery-where, Re-pent and turn a-way from sin's se-duc-tive snare; That all who will o-bey, with Him shall reign for aye, And that's my business for my King.

3. My home is bright-er far than Sharon's ros-y plain, E-ter-nal life and joy throughout its vast do-main; My Sovereign bids me tell how mor-tals there may dwell, And that's my business for my King.

This is the mes-sage that I bring, A message an-gels fain would sing: "O be ye re-conciled," Thus saith my Lord and King, "O be ye re-conciled to God."

258 There Is Never a Day so Dreary

NEW ORLEANS Irregular with Refrain

Anna B. Russell, 1862-1954

Ernest O. Sellers, 1869-1952

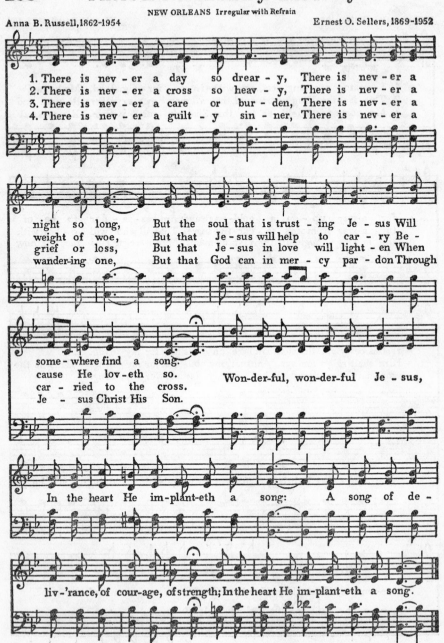

1. There is nev-er a day so drear-y, There is nev-er a
2. There is nev-er a cross so heav-y, There is nev-er a
3. There is nev-er a care or bur-den, There is nev-er a
4. There is nev-er a guilt-y sin-ner, There is nev-er a

night so long, But the soul that is trust-ing Je-sus Will
weight of woe, But that Je-sus will help to car-ry Be-
grief or loss, But that Je-sus in love will light-en When
wander-ing one, But that God can in mer-cy par-don Through

some-where find a song.
cause He lov-eth so.   Won-der-ful, won-der-ful Je-sus,
car-ried to the cross.
Je-sus Christ His Son.

In the heart He im-plant-eth a song: A song of de-

liv-'rance, of cour-age, of strength; In the heart He im-plant-eth a song.

Jesus Is All the World to Me

Will L. Thompson, 1847-1909   Will L. Thompson, 1847-1909

1. Je-sus is all the world to me, My life, my joy, my all;
2. Je-sus is all the world to me, My friend in tri-als sore;
3. Je-sus is all the world to me, I want no bet-ter friend;

He is my strength from day to day, With-out Him I would fall.
I go to Him for bless-ings, and He gives them o'er and o'er.
I trust Him now, I'll trust Him when Life's fleet-ing days shall end.

When I am sad to Him I go, No oth-er one can cheer me so;
He sends the sun-shine and the rain, He sends the har-vest's gold-en grain;
Beau-ti-ful life with such a friend; Beau-ti-ful life that has no end;

When I am sad He makes me glad, He's my friend.
Sun-shine and rain, har-vest of grain, He's my friend.
E-ter-nal life, e-ter-nal joy, He's my friend.

260 There's Within My Heart a Melody

SWEETEST NAME 9.7.9.7. with Refrain

Luther B. Bridgers, 1884-1948   Luther B. Bridgers, 1884-1948

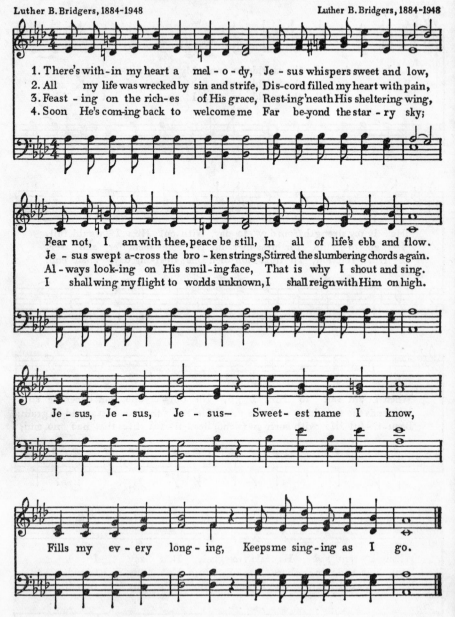

1. There's with-in my heart a mel - o - dy, Je - sus whispers sweet and low,
2. All my life was wrecked by sin and strife, Dis-cord filled my heart with pain,
3. Feast - ing on the rich - es of His grace, Rest-ing 'neath His sheltering wing,
4. Soon He's com-ing back to welcome me Far be-yond the star - ry sky;

Fear not, I am with thee, peace be still, In all of life's ebb and flow.
Je - sus swept a-cross the bro - ken strings, Stirred the slumbering chords a-gain.
Al - ways look-ing on His smil-ing face, That is why I shout and sing.
I shall wing my flight to worlds unknown, I shall reign with Him on high.

Je - sus, Je - sus, Je - sus— Sweet-est name I know,

Fills my ev - ery long - ing, Keeps me sing-ing as I go.

What Can Wash Away My Sin?

PLAINFIELD 7. 8. 7. 8. with Refrain

Robert Lowry, 1826-1899

Robert Lowry, 1826-1899

1. What can wash a - way my sin? Noth-ing but the blood of Je-sus;
2. For my par-don this I see— Noth-ing but the blood of Je-sus;
3. Noth - ing can for sin a - tone, Noth-ing but the blood of Je-sus;
4. This is all my hope and peace, Noth-ing but the blood of Je-sus;

What can make me whole a - gain? Noth-ing but the blood of Je-sus.
For my cleans-ing, this my plea— Noth-ing but the blood of Je-sus.
Naught of good that I have done, Noth-ing but the blood of Je-sus.
This is all my right-eous-ness, Noth-ing but the blood of Je-sus.

O, pre-cious is the flow That makes me white as snow;

No oth - er fount I know, Noth-ing but the blood of Je - sus.

262   I Have a Song I Love to Sing

OTHELLO 8.6.8.6. with Refrain

Edwin O. Excell, 1851-1921   Edwin O. Excell, 1851-1921

1. I have a song I love to sing, Since I have been re-deemed,
2. I have a Christ that sat-is-fies, Since I have been re-deemed,
3. I have a wit-ness bright and clear, Since I have been re-deemed,
4. I have a home pre-pared for me, Since I have been re-deemed,

Of my Re-deem-er, Sav-iour, King, Since I have been re-deemed.
To do His will my high-est prize, Since I have been re-deemed.
Dis-pell-ing ev-e-ry doubt and fear, Since I have been re-deemed.
Where I shall dwell e-ter-nal-ly, Since I have been re-deemed.

Since I have been re-deemed, Since I have been re-deemed, I will

glo-ry in His name; Since I have been re-deemed, I will glo-ry in my Saviour's name.

I Know God's Promise Is True

263

PROMISE 8.6.8.6. with Refrain

Mrs. C. H. Morris, 1862-1929

Mrs. C. H. Morris, 1862-1929

1. For God so loved this sin - ful world, His Son He free - ly gave,
2. I was a way-ward, wandering child, A slave to sin and fear,
3. The "who - so - ev - er" of the Lord, I trust - ed was for me;
4. E - ter - nal life, be-gun be - low, Now fills my heart and soul;

That who - so - ev - er would be-lieve, E - ter - nal life should have.
Un - til this bless - ed prom-ise fell Like mu - sic on my ear.
I took Him at His gra-cious word, From sin He set me free.
I'll sing His praise for - ev - er more, Who has re-deemed my soul.

'Tis true, O yes, 'tis true, God's won-der-ful prom-ise is true;

For I've trust-ed, and test-ed, and tried it, And I know God's promise is true.

264 Saved by the Blood

SAVED 10.11.11.10.with Refrain

S.J.Henderson, 19th century

Daniel B.Towner, 1850-1919

1. Saved by the blood of the Cru-ci-fied One! Now ran-somed from sin and a new work be-gun; Sing praise to the Fa-ther and praise to the Son, Saved by the blood of the Cru-ci-fied One!

2. Saved by the blood of the Cru-ci-fied One! The an-gels re-joic-ing be-cause it is done; A child of the Fa-ther, joint-heir with the Son, Saved by the blood of the Cru-ci-fied One!

3. Saved by the blood of the Cru-ci-fied One! The Fa-ther has spok-en; His will has been done; Great price of my par-don His own pre-cious Son; Saved by the blood of the Cru-ci-fied One!

4. Saved by the blood of the Cru-ci-fied One! All hail to the Fa-ther, all hail to the Son, All hail to the Spir-it, the great Three in One! Saved by the blood of the Cru-ci-fied One!

Saved! saved! My sins are all pardoned, my guilt is all gone!
Glo-ry, I'm saved! glo-ry, I'm saved!

Saved! saved! I am saved by the blood of the Cru-ci-fied One!
Glo-ry, I'm saved! glo-ry, I'm saved!

In the Service of the King

11.8.11.7. with Refrain

A.H.Ackley, 1887-1960

Bentley D. Ackley, 1872-1958

1. I am hap-py in the serv-ice of the King, I am
2. I am hap-py in the serv-ice of the King, I am
3. I am hap-py in the serv-ice of the King, I am
4. I am hap-py in the serv-ice of the King, I am

hap-py, O so hap-py; I have peace and joy that
hap-py, O so hap-py; Through the sun-shine and the
hap-py, O so hap-py; To His guid-ing hand for-
hap-py, O so hap-py; All that I pos-sess to

noth-ing else can bring, In the serv-ice of the King.
shad-ow I can sing, In the serv-ice of the King.
ev-er I will cling, In the serv-ice of the King.
Him I glad-ly bring, In the serv-ice of the King.

In the serv-ice of the King, Ev-ery tal-ent I will bring;

I have peace and joy and bless-ing In the serv-ice of the King.

266　Wonderful Love That Rescued Me

12.12.12.12. with Refrain

Avis B. Christiansen, 1895-

Harry Dixon Loes, 1892-

1. Won-der-ful love that res-cued me, Sunk deep in sin, Guilt-y and
2. Love brought my Saviour here to die On Cal-va-ry, For such a
3. Love o-pened wide the gates of light To heaven's do-main, Where in e-

vile as I could be— No hope within; When ev-ery ray of light had fled,
sin-ful wretch as I, How can it be? Love bridged the gulf 'twixt me and heaven,
ter-nal power and might Je-sus shall reign; Love lift-ed me from depths of woe

O glo-rious day! Rais-ing my soul from out the dead, Love found a way.
Taught me to pray; I am redeemed, set free, forgiven, Love found a way.
To end-less day, There was no help in earth be-low, Love found a way.

Love found a way to re-deem my soul, Love found a
a way, to re-deem my soul,

way that could make me whole; Love sent my Lord to the
a way could make me whole; my Lord

cross of shame; Love found a way, O praise His ho-ly name!
to the cross of shame,

Come Let Us Sing of a Wonderful Love 267

WONDERFUL LOVE 10.8.10.7.8.10.

Robert Walmsley, 1831-1905

Adam Watson

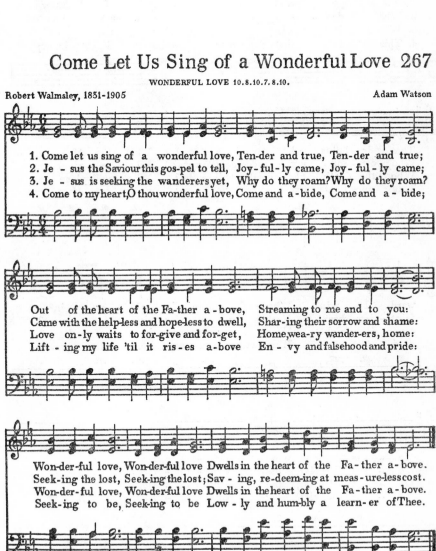

1. Come let us sing of a wonderful love, Ten-der and true, Ten-der and true;
2. Je - sus the Saviour this gos-pel to tell, Joy-ful-ly came, Joy-ful-ly came;
3. Je - sus is seeking the wanderers yet, Why do they roam? Why do they roam?
4. Come to my heart, O thou wonderful love, Come and a-bide, Come and a-bide;

Out of the heart of the Fa-ther a-bove, Streaming to me and to you:
Came with the help-less and hope-less to dwell, Shar-ing their sorrow and shame:
Love on-ly waits to for-give and for-get, Home, wea-ry wander-ers, home:
Lift-ing my life 'til it ris-es a-bove En-vy and falsehood and pride:

Won-der-ful love, Won-der-ful love Dwells in the heart of the Fa-ther a-bove.
Seek-ing the lost, Seek-ing the lost; Sav-ing, re-deem-ing at meas-ure-less cost.
Won-der-ful love, Won-der-ful love Dwells in the heart of the Fa-ther a-bove.
Seek-ing to be, Seek-ing to be Low-ly and hum-bly a learn-er of Thee.

268 Ask Ye What Great Thing

HENDON 7.7.7.7.7.

Johann C. Schwedler, 1672-1730
Trans. by Benjamin H. Kennedy, 1804-1889

H.A. César Malan, 1787-1864

1. Ask ye what great thing I know
2. Who de-feats my fier-cest foes?
3. Who is life in life to me?
4. This is that great thing I know;

That de-lights and stirs me so? What the high re-
Who con-soles my sad-dest woes? Who re-vives my
Who the death of death will be? Who will place me
This de-lights and stirs me so: Faith in Him who

ward I win? Whose the name I glo-ry in?
faint-ing heart, Heal-ing all its hid-den smart?
on His right, With the count-less hosts of light?
died to save, Him who tri-umphed o'er the grave,

Je-sus Christ, the Cru-ci-fied.
Je-sus Christ, the Cru-ci-fied.
Je-sus Christ, the Cru-ci-fied.
Je-sus Christ, the Cru-ci-fied. A-men.

O Happy Day That Fixed My Choice 269

HAPPY DAY 8.8.8.8. with Refrain

Philip Doddridge, 1702-1751   Edward F. Rimbault, 1816-1876

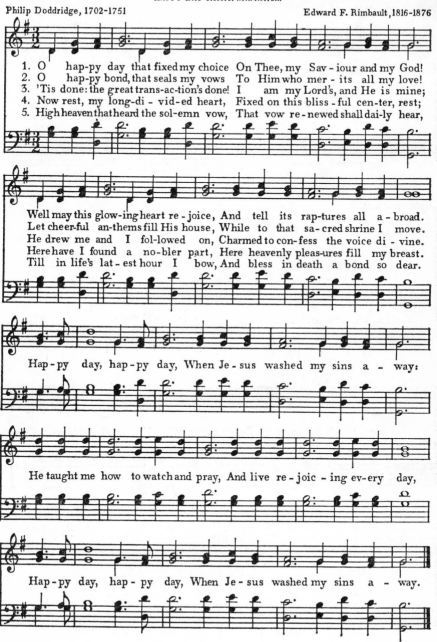

1. O hap-py day that fixed my choice On Thee, my Sav-iour and my God!
2. O hap-py bond, that seals my vows To Him who mer-its all my love!
3. 'Tis done: the great trans-ac-tion's done! I am my Lord's, and He is mine;
4. Now rest, my long-di-vid-ed heart, Fixed on this bliss-ful cen-ter, rest;
5. High heaven that heard the sol-emn vow, That vow re-newed shall dai-ly hear,

Well may this glow-ing heart re-joice, And tell its rap-tures all a-broad.
Let cheer-ful an-thems fill His house, While to that sa-cred shrine I move.
He drew me and I fol-lowed on, Charmed to con-fess the voice di-vine.
Here have I found a no-bler part, Here heavenly pleas-ures fill my breast.
Till in life's lat-est hour I bow, And bless in death a bond so dear.

Hap-py day, hap-py day, When Je-sus washed my sins a-way:

He taught me how to watch and pray, And live re-joic-ing ev-ery day,

Hap-py day, hap-py day, When Je-sus washed my sins a-way.

270 I Will Sing of My Redeemer

MY REDEEMER 8.7.8.7. with Refrain

Philip P. Bliss, 1838-1876

James McGranahan, 1840-1907

1. I will sing of my Re-deem-er And His won-drous love to me;
2. I will tell the won-drous sto-ry, How my lost es-tate to save,
3. I will praise my dear Re-deem-er, His tri-um-phant power I'll tell,
4. I will sing of my Re-deem-er, And His heaven-ly love to me;

On the cru-el cross He suf-fered, From the curse to set me free.
In His boundless love and mer-cy, He the ran-som free-ly gave.
How the vic-to-ry He giv-eth O-ver sin, and death, and hell.
He from death to life hath brought me, Son of God with Him to be.

Sing, O sing of my Re-deem-er, With His blood He pur-chased

me; On the cross He sealed my par-don, Paid the debt and made me free.

Jesus Has Lifted Me

LIFTED 10.10.10.7. with Refrain

Avis B. Christiansen, 1895–

Haldor Lillenas, 1885-1959

1. Out of the depths to the glo - ry a - bove, I have been
2. Out of the world in - to heav - en - ly rest, In - to the
3. Out of my - self in - to Him I a - dore, There to a -

lift - ed in won - der - ful love; From ev - ery fet - ter my
land of the ran-somed and blest; There in the glo - ry with
bide in His love ev - er -more; Through end-less a - ges His

spir - it is free For Je - sus has lift - ed me!
Him I shall be For Je - sus has lift - ed me!
glo - ry to see My Je - sus has lift - ed me!
lift - ed me!

Je - sus has lift - ed me! Je - sus has lift - ed me!
lift- ed me! lift - ed me!

Out of the night in - to glo - ri - ous light, Yes, Je-sus has lift- ed me!
lift-ed me!

272 What a Wonderful Change

McDANIEL 12.8.12.8. with Refrain

Rufus H. McDaniel, 1850-1940

Charles H. Gabriel, 1856-1932

1. What a won-der-ful change in my life has been wrought Since Je-sus came
2. I have ceased from my wandering and go-ing a-stray Since Je-sus came
3. There's a light in the val-ley of death now for me Since Je-sus came
4. I shall go there to dwell in that cit-y, I know, Since Je-sus came

in-to my heart! I have light in my soul for which long I had sought,
in-to my heart! And my sins, which were man-y, are all washed a-way,
in-to my heart! And the gates of the ci-ty be-yond I can see,
in-to my heart! And I'm hap-py, so hap-py, as on-ward I go,

Since Je-sus came in-to my heart! Since Je-sus came in-to my
Since Je-sus came in, came

heart, Since Je-sus came in-to my heart, Floods of joy o'er my
in-to my heart Since Je-sus came in, came in-to my heart,

soul like the sea bil-lows roll, Since Je-sus came in-to my heart.

In Loving Kindness Jesus Came

HE LIFTED ME 8.8.8.6. with Refrain

Charles H. Gabriel, 1856-1932   Charles H. Gabriel, 1856-1932

1. In lov-ing kind-ness Je-sus came My soul in mer-cy to re-claim,
2. He called me long be-fore I heard, Be-fore my sin-ful heart was stirred,
3. His brow was pierced with many a thorn, His hands by cru-el nails were torn,
4. Now on a high-er plane I dwell, And with my soul I know 'tis well;

And from the depths of sin and shame Through grace He lift-ed me.
But when I took Him at His word, For-given, He lift ed me
When from my guilt and grief, for-lorn, In love He lift-ed me.
Yet how or why I can-not tell He should have lift-ed me.

He lift-ed me.

From sink-ing sand He lift-ed me, With ten-der hand He lift-ed me,

From shades of night to plains of light, O praise His name, He lift-ed me!

274 Naught Have I Gotten

GRACE 10.10.9.9. with Refrain

James M. Gray, 1851-1935

Daniel B. Towner, 1850-1919

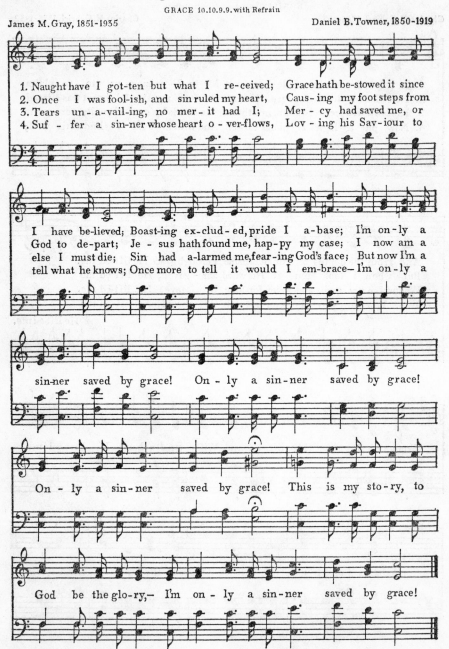

1. Naught have I got-ten but what I re-ceived; Grace hath be-stowed it since I have be-lieved; Boast-ing ex-clud-ed, pride I a-base; I'm on-ly a

2. Once I was fool-ish, and sin ruled my heart, Caus-ing my foot steps from God to de-part; Je-sus hath found me, hap-py my case; I now am a

3. Tears un-a-vail-ing, no mer-it had I; Mer-cy had saved me, or else I must die; Sin had a-larmed me, fear-ing God's face; But now I'm a

4. Suf-fer a sin-ner whose heart o-ver-flows, Lov-ing his Sav-iour to tell what he knows; Once more to tell it would I em-brace—I'm on-ly a

sin-ner saved by grace! On-ly a sin-ner saved by grace!

On-ly a sin-ner saved by grace! This is my sto-ry, to

God be the glo-ry,— I'm on-ly a sin-ner saved by grace!

Glorious Freedom

JUDSON 10.9.10.9.with Refrain

275

Haldor Lillenas, 1885-1959

Alfred Judson

1. Once I was bound by sin's gall-ing fet-ters; Chained like a slave, I
2. Free-dom from all the car-nal af - fec-tions; Free-dom from en - vy,
3. Free-dom from pride and all sin-ful fol-lies; Free-dom from love and
4. Free-dom from fear with all of its torments; Free-dom from care with

strug-gled in vain, But I re-ceived a glo-ri-ous free-dom
ha - tred, and strife; Free-dom from vain and world-ly am - bi - tions;
glit-ter of gold; Free-dom from e - vil tem-per and an-ger—
all of its pain; Free-dom in Christ, my bless-ed Re - deem-er,

When Je-sus broke my fet-ters in twain.
Free-dom from all that saddened my life.
Glo - ri-ous free-dom rap-ture un-told!
He who has rent my fet-ters in twain.

Glo - ri - ous free-dom!

Won-der-ful free-dom! No more in chains of sin I re-pine! Je-sus, the

glo-rious E-man-ci - pa-tor! Now and for-ev - er He shall be mine.

276   There Is a Name I Love to Hear

O, HOW I LOVE JESUS 8.6.8.6.with Refrain

Frederick Whitfield, 1829-1904   Traditional Melody

1. There is a name I love to hear, I love to sing its worth;
2. It tells me of a Sav-iour's love, Who died to set me free;
3. It tells me what my Fa-ther hath In store for ev - 'ry day,
4. It tells of One whose lov-ing heart Can feel my deep-est woe,

It sounds like mu-sic in mine ear, The sweet-est name on earth.
It tells me of His pre-cious blood, The sin-ner's per-fect plea.
And though I tread a darksome path, Yields sun-shine all the way.
Who in each sor-row bears a part, That none can bear be - low.

O how I love Je - sus, O how I love Je - sus,

O how I love Je - sus, Be-cause He first loved me.

Saved to the Uttermost

UTTERMOST 10.10.10.10.with Refrain

William J. Kirkpatrick, 1838-1921   William J. Kirkpatrick, 1838-1921

1. Saved to the ut - ter-most; I am the Lord's; Je - sus my
2. Saved to the ut - ter-most; Je - sus is near; Keep - ing me
3. Saved to the ut - ter-most; this I can say, Once all was
4. Saved to the ut - ter-most; cheer - ful - ly sing Loud hal - le -

Sav - iour sal - va - tion af-fords; Gives me His Spir - it, a
safe - ly, He cast - eth out fear; Trust-ing His prom - is - es,
dark-ness, but now it is day; Beau - ti - ful vi - sions of
lu - jahs to Je - sus my King; Ran - somed and par-doned, re -

wit - ness with - in, Whis-pering of par - don, and sav-ing from sin.
now I am blest; Lean - ing up - on Him, how sweet is my rest.
glo - ry I see, Je - sus in bright-ness re - vealed un - to me,
deemed by His blood, Cleansed from un-right-eous-ness; glo - ry to God!

Saved, saved, saved to the ut-ter-most; Saved, saved by pow-er di - vine;

Saved, saved, saved to the ut-ter-most; Je-sus, the Sav-iour, is mine!

278   I Heard the Voice of Jesus Say

GERALD 8.6.8.6.D

Horatius Bonar, 1808-1889   Louis Spohr, 1784-1859

1. I heard the voice of Je-sus say, "Come un-to Me and rest;
2. I heard the voice of Je-sus say, "Be-hold, I free-ly give
3. I heard the voice of Je-sus say, "I am this dark world's light:

Lay down, thou wear-y one, lay down Thy head up-on My breast." I
The liv-ing wa-ter; thirst-y one, Stoop down, and drink, and live." I
Look un-to Me; thy morn shall rise, And all thy day be bright." I

came to Je-sus as I was, Wear-y, and worn, and sad; I
came to Je-sus and I drank Of that life-giv-ing stream: My
looked to Je-sus and I found In Him my star, my sun; And

found in Him a rest-ing place, And He has made me glad.
thirst was quenched, my soul revived, And now I live in Him.
in that light of life I'll walk Till trav-el-ing days are done. A-men.

Amazing Grace 279

AMAZING GRACE 8. 6. 8. 6.

John Newton, 1725-1807

Early American Melody
Arr. Edwin O. Excell, 1851-1921

1. A - maz - ing grace! how sweet the sound, That saved a wretch like me!
2. 'Twas grace that taught my heart to fear, And grace my fears re-lieved;
3. Through man-y dan-gers, toils and snares, I have al - read-y come;
4. The Lord has prom-ised good to me, His word my hope se-cures;
5. When we've been there ten thou-sand years, Bright shin-ing as the sun,

I once was lost, but now am found, Was blind, but now I see.
How pre - cious did that grace ap - pear The hour I first be-lieved.
'Tis grace hath brought me safe thus far, And grace will lead me home.
He will my shield and por-tion be As long as life en-dures.
We've no less days to sing God's praise Than when we'd first be-gun. A-men.

Peace, Perfect Peace 280

PAX TECUM 10. 10.

Edward H. Bickersteth, 1825-1906

George T. Caldbeck, 1852-c.1912
Arr. by Charles J. Vincent, 1852-1934

1. Peace, per - fect peace, in this dark world of sin?
2. Peace, per - fect peace, by throng-ing du - ties pressed?
3. Peace, per - fect peace, with sor - rows surg - ing round?
4. Peace, per - fect peace, our fu - ture all un - known?
5. Peace, per - fect peace, death shad - 'wing us and ours?

The blood of Je-sus whis-pers peace with - in.
To do the will of Je-sus— this is rest.
On Je-sus' bos - om naught but calm is found.
Je - sus we know, and He is on the throne.
Je - sus has van-quished death and all its powers. A-men.

Tune copyright by The Proprietors of the *Church Hymnal for the Christian Year.*

281 We Have an Anchor

ANCHOR 10.9.10.9. with Refrain

Priscilla J. Owens, 1829-1907

William J. Kirkpatrick, 1838-1921

1. Will your an-chor hold in the storms of life, When the clouds un-fold
2. It is safe-ly moored, 'twill the storm withstand, For 'tis well se-cured
3. It will firm-ly hold in the straits of fear, When the breakers have told
4. When our eyes be-hold, through the gathering night, The cit-y of gold,

their wings of strife? When the strong tides lift, and the ca-bles strain,
by the Sav-iour's hand; And the ca-bles passed from His heart to mine
the reef is near; Though the tem-pest rave and the wild winds blow,
our har-bor bright; We shall an-chor fast by the heaven-ly shore,

Will your an-chor drift, or firm re-main?
Can de-fy that blast through strength di-vine.
Not an an-gry wave shall our bark o'er-flow. We have an an-chor that
With the storms all past for - ev-er-more.

keeps the soul Stead-fast and sure while the bil-lows roll, Fas-tened to the

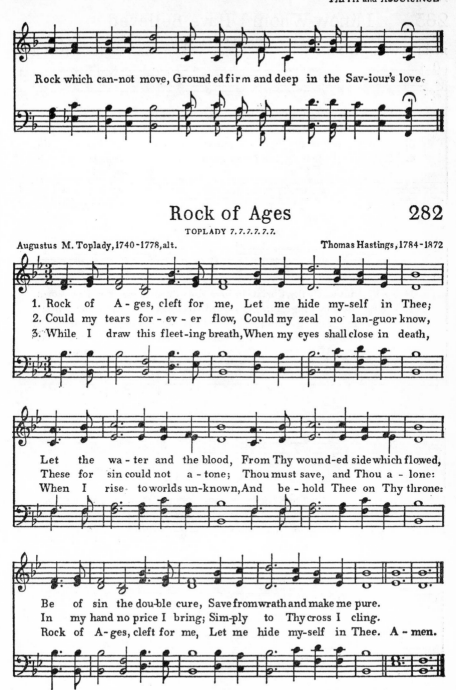

Rock which can-not move, Ground ed firm and deep in the Sav-iour's love.

Rock of Ages 282

TOPLADY 7.7.7.7.7.7.

Augustus M. Toplady, 1740-1778, alt.   Thomas Hastings, 1784-1872

1. Rock of A - ges, cleft for me, Let me hide my-self in Thee;
2. Could my tears for - ev - er flow, Could my zeal no lan-guor know,
3. While I draw this fleet-ing breath, When my eyes shall close in death,

Let the wa - ter and the blood, From Thy wound-ed side which flowed,
These for sin could not a - tone; Thou must save, and Thou a - lone:
When I rise to worlds un-known, And be - hold Thee on Thy throne:

Be of sin the dou-ble cure, Save from wrath and make me pure.
In my hand no price I bring; Sim-ply to Thy cross I cling.
Rock of A-ges, cleft for me, Let me hide my-self in Thee. A - men.

283 I Know Whom I Have Believed

EL NATHAN 8.6.8.6. with Refrain

Daniel W. Whittle, 1840-1901

James McGranahan, 1840-1907

1. I know not why God's won-drous grace To me He hath made known,
2. I know not how this sav - ing faith To me He did im - part,
3. I know not how the Spir - it moves, Con - vinc - ing men of sin,
4. I know not when my Lord may come, At night or noon-day fair,

Nor why, un-wor - thy, Christ in love Re - deemed me for His own.
Nor how be - liev - ing in His Word Wrought peace within my heart.
Re - veal - ing Je - sus through the Word, Cre - at - ing faith in Him.
Nor if I'll walk the vale with Him, Or meet Him in the air.

But "I know whom I have be - liev - ed, and am per - suad - ed that He is

a-ble To keep that which I've com-mit-ted Un-to Him a-gainst that day."

My Hope Is Built

SOLID ROCK 8.8.8.8. with Refrain

Edward Mote, 1797-1874   William B. Bradbury, 1816-1868

1. My hope is built on noth-ing less Than Je-sus' blood and righteousness;
2. When dark-ness seems to hide His face, I rest on His unchanging grace;
3. His oath, His cov - e - nant, His blood Sup-port me in the whelming flood;
4. When He shall come with trumpet sound, O may I then in Him be found,

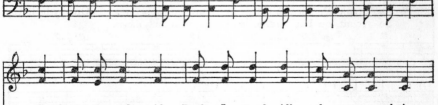

I dare not trust the sweet-est frame, But whol-ly lean on Je-sus' name.
In ev-ery high and storm-y gale, My an-chor holds with-in the veil.
When all a-round my soul gives way, He then is all my hope and stay.
Dressed in His righteous-ness a-lone, Fault-less to stand be-fore the throne.

On Christ, the sol-id Rock, I stand; All oth-er ground is

sink-ing sand, All oth-er ground is sink-ing sand.

285 Fear Not, Little Flock

LITTLE FLOCK 11.10.10.11. with Refrain

Paul Rader, 1879-1938   Paul Rader, 1879-1938

1. Fear not, lit-tle flock, from the cross to the throne, From death in-to
2. Fear not, lit-tle flock, He go-eth a-head, Your shep-herd se-
3. Fear not, lit-tle flock, what-ev-er your lot, He en-ters all

life He went for His own; All pow-er in earth, all pow-er a-bove,
lect-eth the path you must tread; The wa-ters of Ma-rah He'll sweeten for thee,
rooms, "the doors be-ing shut," He nev-er forsakes; He nev-er is gone,

Is giv-en to Him for the flock of His love.
He drank all the bit-ter in Geth-sem-a-ne.   On-ly be-lieve,
So count on His pres-ence in dark-ness and dawn.

on-ly be-lieve; All things are pos-si-ble, on-ly be-lieve:

On-ly be-lieve, on-ly be-lieve; All things are pos-si-ble, on-ly be-lieve.

Blessed Assurance, Jesus Is Mine

ASSURANCE 9.10.9.9.with Refrain

Fanny J. Crosby, 1820-1915

Phoebe P. Knapp, 1839-1908

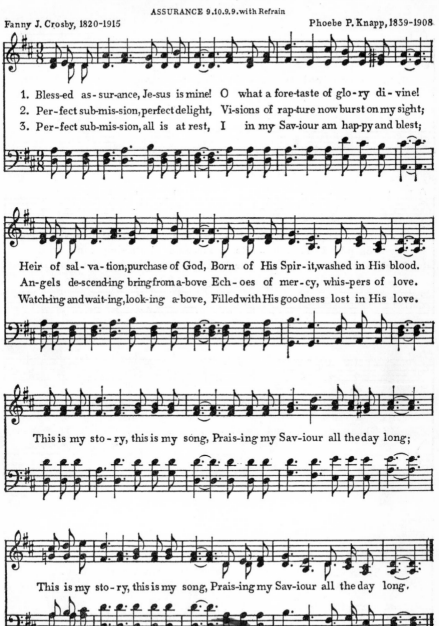

1. Bless-ed as-sur-ance, Je-sus is mine! O what a fore-taste of glo-ry di-vine!
2. Per-fect sub-mis-sion, perfect delight, Vi-sions of rap-ture now burst on my sight;
3. Per-fect sub-mis-sion, all is at rest, I in my Sav-iour am hap-py and blest;

Heir of sal-va-tion, purchase of God, Born of His Spir-it, washed in His blood.
An-gels de-scend-ing bring from a-bove Ech-oes of mer-cy, whis-pers of love.
Watch-ing and wait-ing, look-ing a-bove, Filled with His goodness lost in His love.

This is my sto-ry, this is my song, Prais-ing my Sav-iour all the day long;

This is my sto-ry, this is my song, Prais-ing my Sav-iour all the day long.

287 In Heavenly Love Abiding

SEASONS 7.6.7.6.D.

Anna L. Waring, 1820-1910   Felix Mendelssohn, 1809-1847

1. In heaven-ly love a-bid-ing, No change my heart shall fear;
2. Where-ev-er He may guide me, No want shall turn me back;
3. Green pas-tures are be-fore me, Which yet I have not seen;

And safe is such con-fid-ing, For noth-ing chang-es here.
My Shep-herd is be-side me, And noth-ing can I lack.
Bright skies will soon be o'er me, Where the dark clouds have been.

The storm may roar with-out me, My heart may low be laid,
His wis-dom ev-er wak-eth, His sight is nev-er dim;
My hope I can-not meas-ure, My path to life is free;

But God is round a-bout me, And can I be dis-mayed?
He knows the way He tak-eth, And I will walk with Him.
My Sav-iour has my treas-ure, And He will walk with me. A-men.

Let My Faith Take Hold on Thee 288

8.7.8.7. with Refrain

Fanny J. Crosby, 1820-1915

Bentley D. Ackley, 1872-1958

1. Thou who know-est all my weak-ness, Thou whose eye my heart can see,
2. Faith that smiles when skies are frown-ing, Faith that moun-tains can re - move,
3. While I feel Thy pres-ence with me, While I feel Thy gra-cious hand,
4. Till the storms of life are o - ver, This my dai - ly prayer shall be:

In my hour of deep-est tri - al, Let my faith take hold on Thee.
Faith that pur - i - fies by suf-fering, Calm-ly, sweet - ly works by love.
Glad-ly will I do Thy bid-ding, On - ly wait - ing Thy com-mand.
Lord, up - hold me with Thy Spir - it, Let my faith a - bide in Thee.

Firm and fear-less may I ev - er Tread the path de-signed for me;

And though thorns may sometimes pierce me, Let my faith take hold on Thee.

289 Jesus Is Always There

NEVER A BURDEN 10.9.10.6. with Refrain

Bertha Mae Lillenas

Bertha Mae Lillenas

1. Some-times our skies are cloud-y and drear-y, Some-times our hearts are
2. When in the midst of life with its prob-lems, Bent with our toil and
3. "Lo, I am with you al-way," is writ-ten, God will not fail to

bur-dened with care; But we may know, what-e'er may be-fall us,
bur-dens we bear, Won-der-ful thought and deep con-so-la-tion:
an-swer our prayer; Trust-ing His word we rest in His prom-ise—

Je-sus is al-ways there. Nev-er a bur-den that

He doth not car-ry, Nev-er a sor-row that He doth not share;

Wheth-er the days may be sun-ny or drear-y, Je-sus is al-ways there.

The Haven of Rest

HAVEN OF REST Irregular.

Henry L. Gilmour, 1837-1920

George D. Moore

1. My soul in sad ex-ile was out on life's sea, So bur-dened with
2. I yield-ed my-self to His ten-der em-brace, And, faith tak-ing
3. The song of my soul, since the Lord made me whole, Has been the old
4. O come to the Sav-iour, He pa-tient-ly waits To save by His

sin and dis-trest, Till I heard a sweet voice say-ing, "Make me your choice."
hold of the Word, My fet-ters fell off, and I an-chored my soul;
sto-ry so blest, Of Je-sus, who'll save who-so - ev - er will have
pow-er di-vine; Come, an-chor your soul in the hav-en of rest,

And I en-tered the hav - en of rest.
The hav - en of rest is my Lord.
A home in the hav - en of rest.
And say, "My Be-lov - ed is mine."

I've an-chored my soul

in the hav - en of rest, I'll sail the wide seas no more;

The temp-est may sweep o'er the wild storm-y deep, In Je-sus I'm safe ev-er-more.

291 If Thou but Suffer God to Guide Thee

NEUMARK 9.8.9.8.8.8.

Georg Neumark, 1621-1681
Catherine Winkworth, 1829-1878

Georg Neumark, 1621-1681

1. If thou but suf - fer God to guide thee And hope in Him through all thy ways, He'll give thee strength, what-e'er be - tide thee, And bear thee through the e - vil days; Who trusts in God's un - chang-ing love Builds on the rock that naught can move.

2. On - ly be still and wait His lei - sure In cheer-ful hope, with heart con - tent To take what-e'er thy Fa-ther's pleas-ure And all dis-cern - ing love hath sent; Nor doubt our in-most wants are known To Him who chose us for His own.

3. Sing, pray, and swerve not from His ways, But do thine own part faith-ful - ly; Trust His rich prom - is - es of grace, So shall they be ful - filled in thee; God nev - er yet for-sook at need The soul that trust - ed Him in - deed. A - men.

Lead, Kindly Light

292

LUX BENIGNA 10.4.10.4.10.10.

John H. Newman, 1801-1890

John B. Dykes, 1823-1876

1. Lead, kind - ly Light, a - mid th'en - cir - cling gloom,
2. I was not ev - er thus, nor prayed that Thou
3. So long Thy power hath blessed me, sure it still

Lead Thou me on! The night is dark and I am far from home,
Shouldst lead me on; I loved to choose and see my path, but now
Will lead me on O'er moor and fen, o'er crag and tor-rent, till

Lead Thou me on! Keep Thou my feet; I do not ask to see
Lead Thou me on! I loved the gar - ish day, and, spite of fears,
The night is gone; And with the morn those an-gel fac - es smile

The dis - tant scene— one step e - nough for me.
Pride ruled my will; Re-mem-ber not past years!
Which I have loved long since, and lost a - while. A - men.

293 Children of the Heavenly Father

Lina Sandell, b.1856
Ernst W. Olson, h.1870

8.8.8.8.

Swedish Folk Tune

1. Chil - dren of the heaven-ly Fa-ther Safe-ly in His bos - om gath-er;
2. God His own doth tend and nour-ish, In His ho - ly courts they flour-ish;
3. Neith - er life nor death shall ev - er From the Lord His chil-dren sev - er;
4. Lo, their ver - y hairs He num-bers, And no dai - ly care en-cum-bers
5. Praise the Lord in joy-ful num-bers: Your Pro-tect - or nev-er slum-bers;
6. Though He giv - eth or He tak-eth, God His chil-dren ne'er for - sak-eth,

Nest-ling bird nor star in heav-en Such a ref-uge e'er was giv-en.
From all e - vil things He spares them, In His might-y arms He bears them.
Un - to them His grace He showeth, And their sor-rows all He know-eth.
Them that share His ev-ery bless-ing, And His help in woes dis - tress-ing.
At the will of your De - fend-er Ev-ery foe-man must sur - ren-der.
His the lov-ing pur-pose sole-ly To pre-serve them pure and ho - ly.

294 The Lord's My Shepherd

CRIMOND 8.6.8.6.

Psalm 23, "Scottish Psalter." 1650

Jessie Seymour Irvine, 1836-1887

1. The Lord's my Shep - herd, I'll not want; He makes me down to lie
2. My soul He doth re - store a - gain, And me to walk doth make
3. Yea, though I walk in death's dark vale, Yet will I fear no ill;
4. My ta - ble Thou hast fur - nish-ed In pres-ence of my foes;
5. Good-ness and mer - cy all my life Shall sure-ly fol - low me;

In pas-tures green, He lead-eth me The qui - et wa-ters by.
With - in the paths of right-eous-ness, E'en for His own name's sake.
For Thou art with me, and Thy rod And staff me com-fort still.
My head Thou dost with oil a-noint, And my cup o - ver-flows.
And in God's house for - ev - er-more My dwell-ing place shall be. A - men.

Guide Me, O Thou Great Jehovah 295

CWM RHONDDA 8.7.8.7.8.7.7.

William Williams, 1717-1791
Stanza 1 trans. Peter Williams, 1722-1796
Stanza 2,3, trans, William Williams

Welsh Hymn Melody
John Hughes, 1873-1932

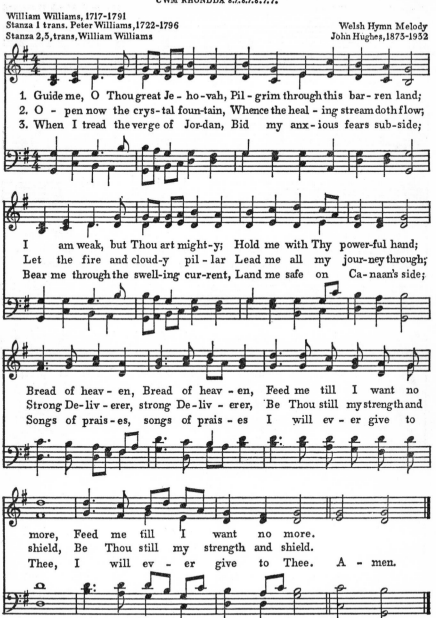

1. Guide me, O Thou great Je - ho - vah, Pil - grim through this bar - ren land;
2. O - pen now the crys - tal foun - tain, Whence the heal - ing stream doth flow;
3. When I tread the verge of Jor - dan, Bid my anx - ious fears sub - side;

I am weak, but Thou art might - y; Hold me with Thy power-ful hand;
Let the fire and cloud-y pil - lar Lead me all my jour-ney through;
Bear me through the swell-ing cur-rent, Land me safe on Ca - naan's side;

Bread of heav - en, Bread of heav - en, Feed me till I want no
Strong De - liv - er - er, strong De - liv - er - er, Be Thou still my strength and
Songs of prais - es, songs of prais - es I will ev - er give to

more, Feed me till I want no more.
shield, Be Thou still my strength and shield.
Thee, I will ev - er give to Thee. A - men.

296 Jesus, Lover of My Soul

MARTYN 7.7.7.7.D.

Charles Wesley, 1707-1788

Simeon B. Marsh, 1798-1875

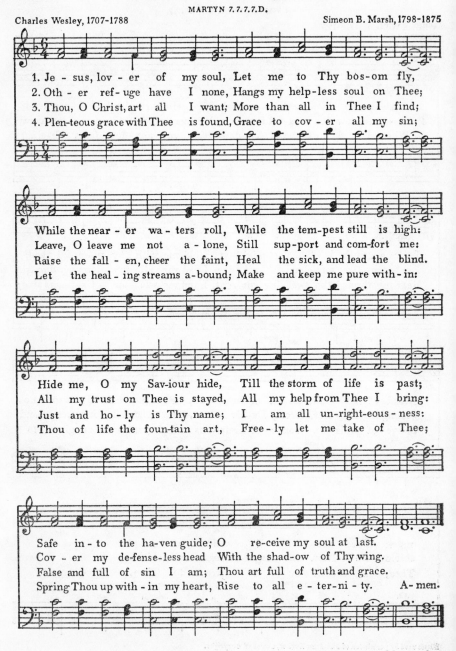

1. Je - sus, lov - er of my soul, Let me to Thy bos-om fly,
2. Oth - er ref - uge have I none, Hangs my help-less soul on Thee;
3. Thou, O Christ, art all I want; More than all in Thee I find;
4. Plen-teous grace with Thee is found, Grace to cov - er all my sin;

While the near - er wa - ters roll, While the tem-pest still is high;
Leave, O leave me not a - lone, Still sup-port and com-fort me:
Raise the fall - en, cheer the faint, Heal the sick, and lead the blind.
Let the heal - ing streams a-bound; Make and keep me pure with-in:

Hide me, O my Sav-iour hide, Till the storm of life is past;
All my trust on Thee is stayed, All my help from Thee I bring:
Just and ho - ly is Thy name; I am all un-right-eous - ness:
Thou of life the foun-tain art, Free - ly let me take of Thee;

Safe in - to the ha-ven guide; O re-ceive my soul at last.
Cov - er my de-fense-less head With the shad-ow of Thy wing.
False and full of sin I am; Thou art full of truth and grace.
Spring Thou up with-in my heart, Rise to all e - ter-ni - ty. A - men.

Jesus, Lover of My Soul 297

ABERYSTWYTH 7.7.7.7.D.

Charles Wesley, 1707-1788   Joseph Parry, 1841-1903

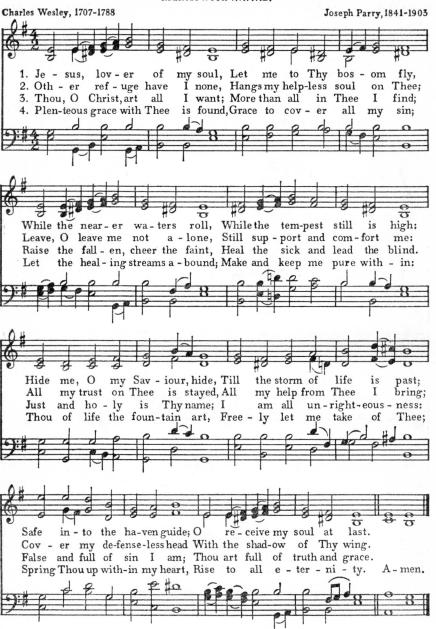

1. Je - sus, lov - er of my soul, Let me to Thy bos - om fly,
2. Oth - er ref - uge have I none, Hangs my help-less soul on Thee;
3. Thou, O Christ, art all I want; More than all in Thee I find;
4. Plen-teous grace with Thee is found, Grace to cov - er all my sin;

While the near - er wa - ters roll, While the tem-pest still is high;
Leave, O leave me not a - lone, Still sup - port and com - fort me:
Raise the fall - en, cheer the faint, Heal the sick and lead the blind.
Let the heal - ing streams a - bound; Make and keep me pure with - in:

Hide me, O my Sav - iour, hide, Till the storm of life is past;
All my trust on Thee is stayed, All my help from Thee I bring;
Just and ho - ly is Thy name; I am all un - right-eous - ness:
Thou of life the foun-tain art, Free - ly let me take of Thee;

Safe in - to the ha-ven guide; O re - ceive my soul at last.
Cov - er my de-fense-less head With the shad-ow of Thy wing.
False and full of sin I am; Thou art full of truth and grace.
Spring Thou up with-in my heart, Rise to all e - ter - ni - ty. A - men.

298 He Leadeth Me

HE LEADETH ME 8.8.8.8. with Refrain

Joseph H. Gilmore, 1834-1918   William B. Bradbury, 1816-1868

1. He lead-eth me! O bless-ed thought! O words with heav'n-ly com-fort fraught!
2. Sometimes 'mid scenes of deep-est gloom, Sometimes where Eden's bow-ers bloom,
3. Lord, I would clasp Thy hand in mine, Nor ev-er mur-mur nor re-pine,
4. And when my task on earth is done, When, by Thy grace, the vic-t'ry's won,

What-e'er I do, wher-e'er I be, Still 'tis God's hand that lead-eth me.
By wa-ters still, o'er troubled sea, Still 'tis His hand that lead-eth me.
Con-tent, what-ev-er lot I see, Since 'tis Thy hand that lead-eth me.
E'en death's cold wave I will not flee, Since God through Jor-dan lead-eth me.

He lead-eth me, He lead-eth me, By His own hand He lead-eth me!

His faith-ful fol-l'wer I would be, For by His hand He lead-eth me.

Saviour, Like a Shepherd

BRADBURY 8.7.8.7.D.

From *Hymns for the Young* 1836
Ascribed to Dorothy A. Thrupp, 1779-1847

William B. Bradbury, 1816-1868

1. Sav-iour, like a shep-herd lead us, Much we need Thy ten-der care;
2. We are Thine, do Thou be-friend us, Be the guard-ian of our way;
3. Thou hast prom-ised to re-ceive us, Poor and sin-ful though we be;
4. Ear-ly let us seek Thy fa-vor, Ear-ly let us do Thy will;

In Thy pleas-ant pas-tures feed us, For our use Thy folds pre-pare:
Keep Thy flock from sin, de-fend us, Seek us when we go a-stray:
Thou hast mer-cy to re-lieve us, Grace to cleanse, and power to free:
Bless-ed Lord and on-ly Sav-iour, With Thy love our bos-oms fill:

Bless-ed Je-sus, bless-ed Je-sus, Thou hast bought us, Thine we are;
Bless-ed Je-sus, bless-ed Je-sus, Hear, O hear us when we pray;
Bless-ed Je-sus, bless-ed Je-sus, Ear-ly let us turn to Thee;
Bless-ed Je-sus, bless-ed Je-sus, Thou hast loved us, love us still;

Bless-ed Je-sus, bless-ed Je-sus, Thou hast bought us, Thine we are.
Bless-ed Je-sus, bless-ed Je-sus, Hear, O hear us when we pray.
Bless-ed Je-sus, bless-ed Je-sus, Ear-ly let us turn to Thee.
Bless-ed Je-sus, bless-ed Je-sus, Thou hast loved us, love us still. A-men.

300   All the Way My Saviour Leads Me

ALL THE WAY 8.7.8.7.D.

Fanny J. Crosby, 1820-1915   Robert Lowry, 1826-1899

1. All the way my Sav-iour leads me; What have I to ask be-side?
2. All the way my Sav-iour leads me, Cheers each wind-ing path I tread,
3. All the way my Sav-iour leads me; O the full-ness of His love!

Can I doubt His ten-der mer-cy, Who through life has been my guide?
Gives me grace for ev-ery tri-al, Feeds me with the liv-ing bread.
Per-fect rest to me is prom-ised In my Fa-ther's house a-bove.

Heaven-ly peace, di-vin-est com-fort, Here by faith in Him to dwell!
Though my wea-ry steps may fal-ter, And my soul a-thirst may be,
When my spir-it, clothed im-mor-tal, Wings its flight to realms of day,

For I know, what-e'er be-fall me, Je-sus do-eth all things well.
Gush-ing from the Rock be-fore me, Lo! a spring of joy I see.
This my song through end-less a-ges: Je-sus led me all the way. A-men.

Under His Wings

301

UNDER HIS WINGS 11.10.11.10. with Refrain

William O. Cushing, 1823-1902

Ira D. Sankey, 1840-1908

1. Un-der His wings I am safe-ly a-bid-ing; Though the night deep-ens and tem-pests are wild, Still I can trust Him; I know He will keep me; He has re-deemed me, and I am His child.

2. Un-der His wings, what a ref-uge in sor-row! How the heart yearn-ing-ly turns to its rest! Oft-en, when earth has no balm for my heal-ing, There I find com-fort, and there I am blest.

3. Un-der His wings, O what pre-cious en-joy-ment! There will I hide till life's tri-als are o'er; Shel-tered, pro-tect-ed, no e-vil can harm me; Rest-ing in Je-sus I'm safe ev-er-more.

Un-der His wings, un-der His wings, Who from His love can sev-er! Un-der His wings my soul shall a-bide, Safe-ly a-bide for-ev-er.

302 Precious Promise God Hath Given

I WILL GUIDE THEE 8.7.8.7. with Refrain

Nathaniel Niles, b.1835-

Philip P. Bliss, 1838-1876

1. Pre - cious prom-ise God hath giv - en To the wea-ry pass - er -by,
2. When temp-ta-tions al-most win thee, And thy trust-ed watch-ers fly,
3. When thy se-cret hopes have per-ished In the grave of years gone by,
4. When the shades of life are fall-ing, And the hour has come to die,

On the way from earth to heav-en, "I will guide thee with Mine eye."
Let this prom-ise ring with-in thee, "I will guide thee with Mine eye."
Let this prom-ise still be cher-ished, "I will guide thee with Mine eye."
Hear the trust-y Pi - lot call-ing, "I will guide thee with Mine eye."

I will guide thee, I will guide thee, I will guide thee with Mine eye;

On the way from earth to heav-en, I will guide thee with Mine eye.

Saviour, Lead Me, Lest I Stray 303

LEAD ME 7. 7. 7. 7. with Refrain

Frank M. Davis, 1839-1896

Frank M. Davis, 1839-1896
Arr. by Perry L. Huffaker, 1902-

1. Sav-iour, lead me, lest I stray, (lest I stray,) Gen - tly lead me all the
2. Thou the ref-uge of my soul, (of my soul,) When life's storm-y bil-lows
3. Sav-iour, lead me then at last, (then at last,) When the storm of life is

way; I am safe when by Thy side, (by Thy side,) I would in Thy love a -
roll, I am safe when Thou art nigh, (Thou art nigh,) All my hopes on Thee re -
past, To the land of end-less day, (end-less day,) Where all tears are wiped a -

(would
(my
(all

bide. Lead me, lead me, Sav-iour, lead me, lest I stray;
ly.
in Thy love a-bide.)
hopes on Thee re-ly.)
tears are wiped a-way.)

Gen - tly down the stream of time, Lead me, Sav-iour, all the way.

Musical arrangement copyright 1950 by the Brethren Press.

304 Hiding in Thee

HIDING 12.11.12.11. with Refrain

William O. Cushing, 1823-1902

Ira D. Sankey, 1840-1908

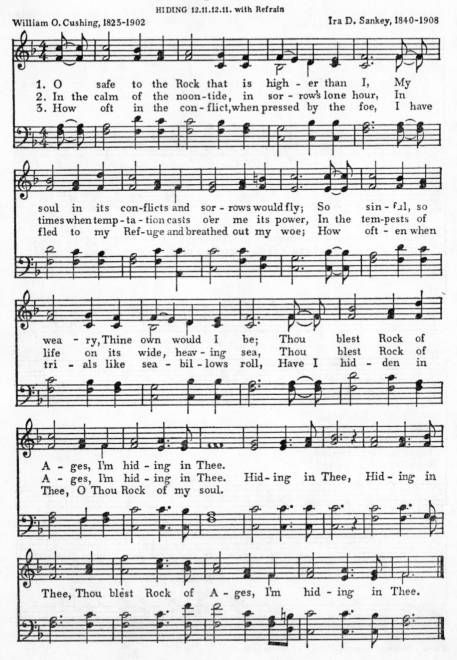

1. O safe to the Rock that is high-er than I, My
soul in its con-flicts and sor-rows would fly; So
wea-ry, Thine own would I be; Thou blest Rock of
A-ges, I'm hid-ing in Thee.

2. In the calm of the noon-tide, in sor-row's lone hour, In
times when temp-ta-tion casts o'er me its power, In the
life on its wide, heav-ing sea, Thou blest Rock of
A-ges, I'm hid-ing in Thee.

3. How oft in the con-flict, when pressed by the foe, I have
fled to my Ref-uge and breathed out my woe; How
tri-als like sea-bil-lows roll, Have I hid-den in
Thee, O Thou Rock of my soul.

Hid-ing in Thee, Hid-ing in Thee, Thou blest Rock of A-ges, I'm hid-ing in Thee.

Just When I Need Him

305

GABRIEL 9.9.9.6. with Refrain

William C. Poole, 1875-1949

Charles H. Gabriel, 1856-1932

1. Just when I need Him, Je-sus is near, Just when I fal-ter, just when I fear; Read-y to help me, read-y to cheer, Just when I need Him most.

2. Just when I need Him, Je-sus is true, Nev-er for-sak-ing all the way through; Giv-ing for bur-dens pleas-ures a-new, Just when I need Him most,

3. Just when I need Him, Je-sus is strong, Bear-ing my bur-dens all the day long; For all my sor-row giv-ing a song,

4. Just when I need Him, He is my all, An-swer-ing when up-on Him I call; Ten-der-ly watch-ing lest I should fall,

Just when I need Him most, Je-sus is near to com-fort and cheer: Just when I need Him most.

306 A Shelter in the Time of Storm

8.8.8.8. with Refrain

Vernon J. Charlesworth, b.1839
Alt. by Ira D. Sankey, 1840-1908

Ira D. Sankey, 1840-1908

1. The Lord's our Rock, in Him we hide, A shel-ter in the time of storm;
2. A shade by day, de-fense by night, A shel-ter in the time of storm;
3. The rag-ing storms may round us beat, A shel-ter in the time of storm;
4. O Rock di-vine, O Ref-uge dear, A shel-ter in the time of storm;

Se-cure what-ev-er ill be-tide, A shel-ter in the time of storm.
No fears a-larm, no foes af-fright, A shel-ter in the time of storm.
We'll nev-er leave our safe re-treat, A shel-ter in the time of storm.
Be Thou our help-er ev-er near, A shel-ter in the time of storm.

O Je-sus is a Rock in a wea-ry land, A wea-ry land, A wea-ry land;

O Je-sus is a Rock in a wea-ry land, A shel-ter in the time of storm.

The Nail-Scarred Hand

LUBBOCK 11.8.11.8. with Refrain

B. B. McKinney, 1886-1952

B. B. McKinney, 1886-1952

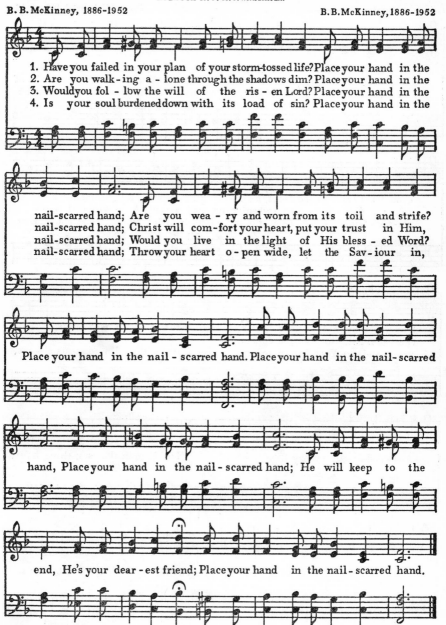

1. Have you failed in your plan of your storm-tossed life? Place your hand in the
2. Are you walk-ing a-lone through the shadows dim? Place your hand in the
3. Would you fol-low the will of the ris-en Lord? Place your hand in the
4. Is your soul burdened down with its load of sin? Place your hand in the

nail-scarred hand; Are you wea-ry and worn from its toil and strife?
nail-scarred hand; Christ will com-fort your heart, put your trust in Him,
nail-scarred hand; Would you live in the light of His bless-ed Word?
nail-scarred hand; Throw your heart o-pen wide, let the Sav-iour in,

Place your hand in the nail-scarred hand. Place your hand in the nail-scarred

hand, Place your hand in the nail-scarred hand; He will keep to the

end, He's your dear-est friend; Place your hand in the nail-scarred hand.

308

I Need Jesus

Irregular

George O. Webster, 1866-1942

Charles H. Gabriel, 1856-1932

1. I need Jesus, my need I now con-fess; No friend like Him in times of
deep dis-tress; I need Je-sus, the need I glad-ly own, Though some may bear their
load a-lone, Yet, I need Je-sus. I need Je-sus, I need Je-sus,

2. I need Jesus, I need a friend like Him, A friend to guide when paths of
life are dim; I need Jesus, when foes my soul as-sail; A-lone I know I
can but fail, So I need Je-sus.

3. I need Jesus, I need Him to the end; No one like Him, He is the
sin-ner's friend; I need Je-sus no oth-er friend will do; So con-stant, kind, so
strong and true, Yes, I need Je-sus. I need Je-sus with me, I need Je-sus al-ways,

I need Je-sus ev-ery day; ev-ery day; Need Him in the sun-shine hour,

Need Him when the storm-clouds lower; Every day a-long my way, Yes, I need Je-sus.

Be Not Dismayed Whate'er Betide

GOD CARES 8.6.8.6. with Refrain

Civilla D. Martin, 1869-1948   W. Stillman Martin, 1862-1935

1. Be not dis-mayed what-e'er be-tide, God will take care of you;
2. Through days of toil when heart doth fail, God will take care of you;
3. All you may need He will pro-vide, God will take care of you;
4. No mat-ter what may be the test, God will take care of you;

Be-neath His wings of love a-bide, God will take care of you.
When dan-gers fierce your path as-sail, God will take care of you.
Noth-ing you ask will be de-nied, God will take care of you.
Lean, wea-ry one, up-on His breast, God will take care of you.

God will take care of you, Through ev-ery day, o'er all the way;

He will take care of you, God will take care of you.

310 Jesus, Saviour, Pilot Me

PILOT 7.7.7.7.7.7.

Edward Hopper, 1818-1888

John E. Gould, 1822-1875

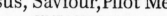

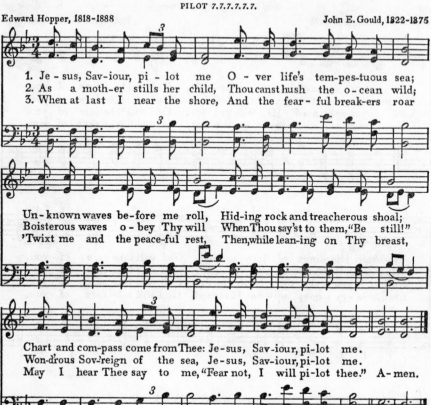

1. Je - sus, Sav-iour, pi - lot me O - ver life's tem-pes-tuous sea;
2. As a moth-er stills her child, Thou canst hush the o - cean wild;
3. When at last I near the shore, And the fear - ful break-ers roar

Un - known waves be-fore me roll, Hid-ing rock and treacherous shoal;
Boisterous waves o - bey Thy will When Thou say'st to them, "Be still!"
'Twixt me and the peace-ful rest, Then, while lean-ing on Thy breast,

Chart and com-pass come from Thee: Je-sus, Sav-iour, pi - lot me.
Won-d'rous Sov-'reign of the sea, Je-sus, Sav-iour, pi-lot me.
May I hear Thee say to me, "Fear not, I will pi-lot thee." A-men.

311 Children of the Heavenly King

PLEYEL'S HYMN 7.7.7.7.

John Cennick, 1718-1755

Ignace J. Pleyel, 1757-1831

Chil-dren of the heaven-ly King, As ye jour-ney, sweet-ly sing;
We are trav-'ling home to God, In the way the fa-thers trod;
Fear not, breth-ren, joy - ful stand On the bor - ders of your land;
Lord, o - be-dient - ly we go, Glad - ly leav - ing all be-low;

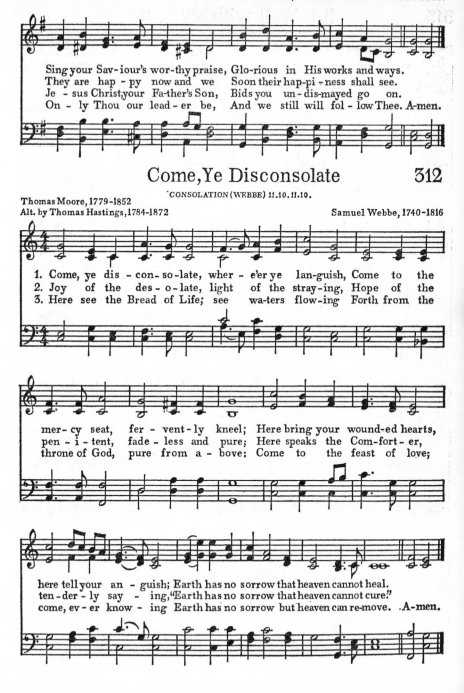

Sing your Sav-iour's wor-thy praise, Glo-rious in His works and ways.
They are hap - py now and we   Soon their hap-pi - ness shall see.
Je - sus Christ, your Fa-ther's Son, Bids you un - dis-mayed go   on.
On - ly Thou our lead - er be,   And we still will fol - low Thee. A-men.

Come, Ye Disconsolate   312

CONSOLATION (WEBBE) 11.10.11.10.

Thomas Moore, 1779-1852
Alt. by Thomas Hastings, 1784-1872

Samuel Webbe, 1740-1816

1. Come, ye dis - con - so-late, wher - e'er ye lan-guish, Come to the
2. Joy of the des - o-late, light of the stray-ing, Hope of the
3. Here see the Bread of Life; see wa-ters flow-ing Forth from the

mer-cy seat, fer - vent-ly kneel; Here bring your wound-ed hearts,
pen - i - tent, fade - less and pure; Here speaks the Com-fort-er,
throne of God, pure from a - bove: Come to the feast of love;

here tell your an - guish; Earth has no sorrow that heaven cannot heal.
ten-der - ly say - ing, "Earth has no sorrow that heaven cannot cure."
come, ev - er know - ing Earth has no sorrow but heaven can re-move. A-men.

313

It Is Well with My Soul

VILLE DE HAVRE 11.8.11.9. with Refrain

Horatio G. Spafford, 1828-1888   Philip P. Bliss, 1838-1876

1. When peace, like a riv-er, at-tend-eth my way, When
2. Though Sa-tan should buf-fet, though tri-als should come, Let
3. My sin— O the bliss of this glo-ri-ous thought— My
4. And, Lord, haste the day when the faith shall be sight, The

sor-rows like sea-bil-lows roll; What-ev-er my lot, Thou hast
this blest as-sur-ance con-trol, That Christ hath re-gard-ed my
sin, not in part but the whole, Is nailed to His cross and I
clouds be rolled back as a scroll, The trump shall re-sound and the

taught me to say, It is well, it is well with my soul.
help-less es-tate, And hath shed His own blood for my soul.
bear it no more, Praise the Lord, praise the Lord, O my soul!
Lord shall de-scend, "E-ven so"— it is well with my soul.

It is well   with my soul,   It is well, it is well with my soul.
It is well,   with my soul,

Wonderful Peace

Irregular

Haldor Lillenas, 1885-1959

Haldor Lillenas, 1885-1959

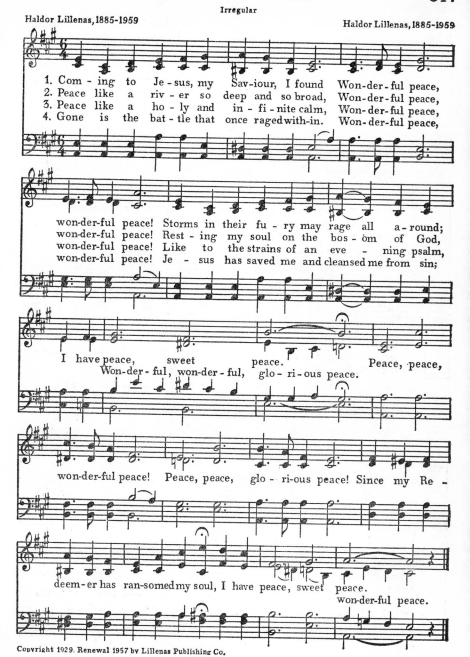

1. Com - ing to Je - sus, my Sav-iour, I found Won-der-ful peace,
2. Peace like a riv - er so deep and so broad, Won-der-ful peace,
3. Peace like a ho - ly and in - fi - nite calm, Won-der-ful peace,
4. Gone is the bat - tle that once raged with-in. Won-der-ful peace,

won-der-ful peace! Storms in their fu - ry may rage all a - round;
won-der-ful peace! Rest - ing my soul on the bos - om of God,
won-der-ful peace! Like to the strains of an eve - ning psalm,
won-der-ful peace! Je - sus has saved me and cleansed me from sin;

I have peace, sweet peace. Peace, peace,
Won-der - ful, won-der - ful, glo - ri-ous peace.

won-der-ful peace! Peace, peace, glo - ri-ous peace! Since my Re -

deem-er has ran-somed my soul, I have peace, sweet peace.
won-der-ful peace.

Heavenly Sunlight

COOK 10.9.10.9.with Refrain

H. J. Zelley

G. H. Cook

1. Walk-ing in sun-light, all of my jour-ney, O - ver the moun-tains, through the deep vale; Je - sus has said, "I'll nev-er for-sake thee," Prom-ise di - vine that nev-er shall fail.

2. Shad-ows a - round me, shad-ows a - bove me, Nev - er con-ceal my Sav - iour and Guide; He is the light, in Him is no dark-ness, Ev - er I'm walk-ing close to His side.

3. In the bright sun-light ev - er re - joic - ing, Press-ing my way to man-sions a - bove; Sing-ing His prais-es, glad-ly I'm walk-ing, Walk-ing in sun-light, sun-light of love.

Heav-en-ly sun-light, heav-en-ly sun-light, Flood-ing my soul with glo-ry di - vine; Hal - le - lu-jah! I am re-joic-ing, Sing-ing His prais-es, Je-sus is mine.

There Comes to My Heart One Sweet Strain 316

SWEET PEACE 8.8.8.7. with Refrain

Peter Philip Bilhorn, 1861-1936   Peter Philip Bilhorn, 1861-1936

1. There comes to my heart one sweet strain, A
2. Through Christ on the cross peace was made, My
3. When Jesus as Lord I had crowned, My
4. In Jesus for peace I abide, And

glad and a joy-ous re-frain; I sing it a-
debt by His death was all paid; No oth-er foun-
heart with this peace did a-bound; In Him the rich
as I keep close to His side, There's noth-ing but

gain and a-gain: Sweet peace, the gift of God's love.
da-tion is laid For peace, the gift of God's love.
bless-ing I found, Sweet peace, the gift of God's love.
peace doth be-tide, Sweet peace, the gift of God's love.

Peace, peace, sweet peace! Won-der-ful gift from a-bove! O

won-der-ful, won-der-ful peace! Sweet peace, the gift of God's love!

317 How Tedious and Tasteless the Hours

CONTRAST 8.8.8.8.D.

John Newton, 1725-1807

Early American Melody

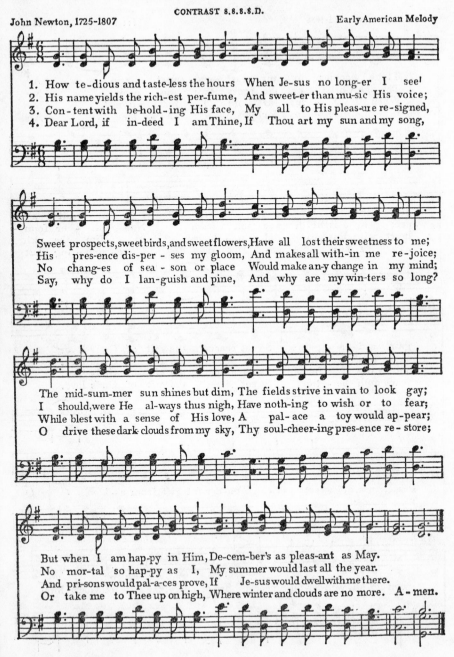

1. How te-dious and taste-less the hours When Je-sus no long-er I see!
2. His name yields the rich-est per-fume, And sweet-er than mu-sic His voice;
3. Con-tent with be-hold-ing His face, My all to His pleas-ure re-signed,
4. Dear Lord, if in-deed I am Thine, If Thou art my sun and my song,

Sweet prospects, sweet birds, and sweet flowers, Have all lost their sweetness to me;
His pres-ence dis-per - ses my gloom, And makes all with-in me re-joice;
No chang-es of sea - son or place Would make an-y change in my mind;
Say, why do I lan-guish and pine, And why are my win-ters so long?

The mid-sum-mer sun shines but dim, The fields strive in vain to look gay;
I should, were He al-ways thus nigh, Have noth-ing to wish or to fear;
While blest with a sense of His love, A pal-ace a toy would ap-pear;
O drive these dark clouds from my sky, Thy soul-cheer-ing pres-ence re - store;

But when I am hap-py in Him, De-cem-ber's as pleas-ant as May.
No mor-tal so hap-py as I, My summer would last all the year.
And pri-sons would pal-a-ces prove, If Je-sus would dwell with me there.
Or take me to Thee up on high, Where winter and clouds are no more. A - men.

The Trusting Heart to Jesus Clings 318

Eliza Edmunds Hewitt, 1851-1920   William J. Kirkpatrick, 1838-1921

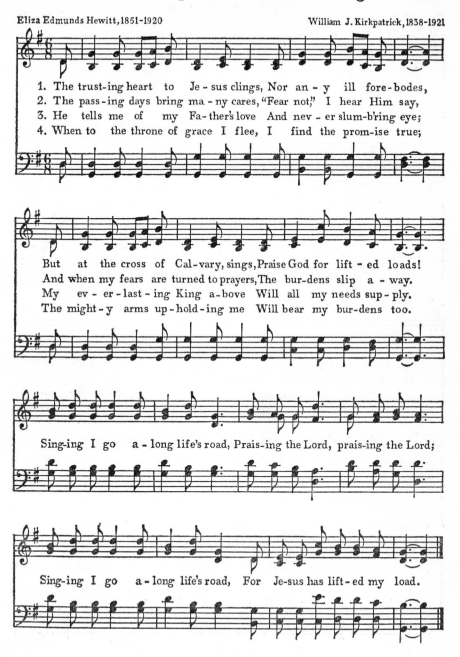

1. The trust-ing heart to Je-sus clings, Nor an-y ill fore-bodes,
2. The pass-ing days bring ma-ny cares, "Fear not," I hear Him say,
3. He tells me of my Fa-ther's love And nev-er slum-b'ring eye;
4. When to the throne of grace I flee, I find the prom-ise true;

But at the cross of Cal-vary, sings, Praise God for lift-ed loads!
And when my fears are turned to prayers, The bur-dens slip a-way.
My ev-er-last-ing King a-bove Will all my needs sup-ply.
The might-y arms up-hold-ing me Will bear my bur-dens too.

Sing-ing I go a-long life's road, Prais-ing the Lord, prais-ing the Lord;

Sing-ing I go a-long life's road, For Je-sus has lift-ed my load.

319 Living for Jesus

LIVING FOR JESUS 8.8.8.8. with Refrain

C. F. Weigle

C. F. Weigle

1. Liv-ing for Je-sus, O what peace, Riv-ers of pleas-ure
2. Liv-ing for Je-sus, O what rest, Pleas-ing my Sa-viour
3. Liv-ing for Je-sus ev-ery-where, All of my bur-dens
4. Liv-ing for Je-sus till at last In-to His glo-ry

nev-er cease; Tri-als may come, yet I'll not fear,
I am blest; On-ly to live for Him a-lone,
He doth bear; Friends may for-sake me, He'll be true,
I have passed, There to be-hold Him on His throne,

Liv-ing for Je-sus, He is near.
Do-ing His will till life is done. Help me to serve Thee
Trust-ing in Him, He'll guide me through.
Hear from His lips, "My child, well done."

more and more, Help me to praise Thee o'er and o'er, Live in Thy

pres-ence day by day, Nev-er to turn from Thee a-way.

Far Away in the Depths of My Spirit   320

COOPER 12.9.12.9.with Refrain

W.D.Cornell, 19th century, alt.

W.G.Cooper, 19th century

1. Far a - way in the depths of my spir - it to-night Rolls a
2. What a treas - ure I have in this won-der - ful peace, Bur - ied
3. I am rest - ing to-night in this won-der - ful peace, Rest - ing
4. And me-thinks when I rise to that Cit - y of peace, Where the
5. Ah! soul are you here with-out com-fort or rest, March-ing

mel - o - dy sweet-er than psalm; In ce - les - tial-like strains it un-
deep in the heart of my soul, So se - cure that no pow-er can
sweet-ly in Je - sus con - trol, For I'm kept from all dan-ger by
Au - thor of peace I shall see, That one strain of the song which the
down the rough path-way of time? Make Je - sus your friend ere the

ceas - ing - ly falls O'er my soul like an in - fi - nite calm.
mine it a - way, While the years of e - ter - ni - ty roll.
night and by day, And His glo - ry is flood-ing my soul.
ran - somed will sing In that heav - en - ly king-dom shall be:
shad - ows grow dark; O ac - cept this sweet peace so sub - lime.

Peace! peace! won-der-ful peace, Com-ing down from the Fa-ther a-bove; Sweep

o - ver my spir-it for - ev - er, I pray, In fath-om-less bil-lows of love.

321 Like a River Glorious

WYE VALLEY 6.5.6.5.D. with Refrain

Frances R. Havergal, 1836-1879   James Mountain, 1844-1933

1. Like a riv-er glo-rious Is God's per-fect peace, O - ver all vic - to-rious
2. Hid-den in the hol - low Of His bless-ed hand, Nev - er foe can fol-low,
3. Ev-ery joy or tri - al Fall-eth from a - bove, Traced up-on our di - al

In its bright in-crease; Per-fect, yet it flow-eth Full-er ev-ery day;
Nev-er trai - tor stand; Not a surge of wor - ry, Not a shade of care,
By the Sun of love. We may trust Him ful - ly All for us to do;

Per-fect, yet it grow-eth Deep - er all the way.
Not a blast of hur - ry Touch the spir - it there. Stayed up-on Je - ho - vah,
They who trust Him whol-ly Find Him whol-ly true.

Hearts are ful - ly blest, Find-ing, as He prom-ised, Per-fect peace and rest.

Hidden Peace

8.6.8.6.D.

322

John S. Brown

L. O. Brown

1. I can-not tell thee whence it came, This peace with-in my breast;
2. Be-neath the toil and care of life, This hid-den stream flows on;
3. I can-not tell the half of love, Un-feigned, su-preme, di-vine,
4. I can-not tell thee why He chose To suf-fer and to die,

But this I know, there fills my soul A strange and tran-quil rest.
My wea-ry soul no long-er thirsts, Nor am I sad and lone.
That caused my dark-est, in-most self With beams of hope to shine.
But if I suf-fer here with Him I'll reign with Him on high.

There's a deep, set-tled peace in my soul, (in my soul,) There's a

deep, set-tled peace in my soul; (in my soul;) Though the

bil-lows of sin near me roll, He a-bides, Christ a-bides.

323 In My Heart There Rings a Melody

MELODY 9.7.9.7. with Refrain

Elton M. Roth, 1891-1951   Elton M. Roth, 1891-1951

1. I have a song that Je-sus gave me, It was sent from
2. I love the Christ who died on Cal-vary, For He washed my
3. 'Twill be my end-less theme in glo-ry; With the an-gels

heaven a-bove; There nev-er was a sweet-er mel-o-dy, 'Tis a
sins a-way; He put with-in my heart a mel-o-dy, And I
I will sing; 'Twill be a song with glo-rious har-mo-ny, When the

mel-o-dy of love.
know it's there to stay. In my heart there rings a mel-o-dy, There
courts of heav-en ring.

rings a mel-o-dy with heav-en's har-mo-ny; In my heart there

rings a mel-o-dy; There rings a mel-o-dy of love.

"Whosoever" Meaneth Me

McCONNELL 11.7.10.6. with Refrain

J. Edwin McConnell, 1892-1954

J. Edwin McConnell, 1892-1954

1. I am hap-py to-day and the sun shines bright, The clouds have been
2. All my hopes have been raised, O His name be praised, His glo-ry has
3. O what won-der-ful love, O what grace di-vine, That Je-sus should

rolled a-way; For the Sav-ior said, Who-so-ev-er will, May
filled my soul; I've been lift-ed up and from sin set free, His
die for me; I was lost in sin, for the world I pined, But

come with Him (to stay to stay.)
blood hath made (me whole me whole.) "Who-so-ev-er" sure-ly mean-eth me,
now I am (set free set free.)

Sure-ly mean-eth me, O sure-ly mean-eth me; "Who-so-ev-er"

sure-ly mean-eth me, "Who-so-ev-er" mean-eth me.
mean-eth me.

325

He Lives

ACKLEY Irregular with Refrain

Alfred H. Ackley, 1887-1960   Alfred H. Ackley, 1887-1960

1. I serve a ris-en Sav-iour, He's in the world to-day; I know that He is
2. In all the world a-round me I see His lov-ing care, And tho' my heart grows
3. Re-joice, re-joice, O Christian, lift up your voice and sing E-ter-nal hal-le-

liv-ing, what-ev-er men may say; I see His hand of mer-cy, I
wea-ry, I nev-er will de-spair; I know that He is lead-ing through
lu-jahs to Je-sus Christ the King! The hope of all who seek Him, the

hear His voice of cheer, And just the time I need Him He's al-ways near.
all the storm-y blast, The day of His ap-pear-ing will come at last.
help of all who find, None oth-er is so lov-ing, so good and kind.

He lives, He lives, Christ Je-sus lives to-day! He walks with me and
He lives, He lives,

talks with me a-long life's nar-row way. He lives, He lives, sal-
He lives, He lives,

va-tion to im-part! You ask me how I know He lives: He lives within my heart.

Fade, Fade, Each Earthly Joy   326

LUNDIE 11.12.12.12.

Jane C. Bonar, 1821-1884   Theodore E. Perkins, b. 1831

1. Fade, fade, each earth-ly joy; Je-sus is mine. Break ev-ery
2. Tempt not my soul a-way; Je-sus is mine. Here would I
3. Fare-well, ye dreams of night; Je-sus is mine. Lost in this
4. Fare-well, mor-tal-i-ty; Je-sus is mine. Wel-come, e-

ten-der tie; Je-sus is mine. Dark is the wil-der-ness,
ev-er stay; Je-sus is mine. Per-ish-ing things of clay,
dawn-ing bright, Je-sus is mine. All that my soul has tried
ter-ni-ty; Je-sus is mine. Wel-come, O loved and blest,

Earth has no rest-ing place, Je-sus a-lone can bless; Je-sus is mine.
Born but for one brief day, Pass from my heart a-way; Je-sus is mine.
Left but a dis-mal void; Je-sus has sat-is-fied; Je-sus is mine.
Wel-come, sweet scenes of rest, Welcome, my Sav-iour's breast; Je-sus is mine.

327 I Need Thee Every Hour

NEED 6.4. 6.4. with Refrain

Annie S. Hawks, 1835-1918

Robert Lowry, 1826-1899

1. I need Thee ev-ery hour, Most gra - cious Lord;
2. I need Thee ev-ery hour, Stay Thou near by;
3. I need Thee ev-ery hour, In joy or pain;
4. I need Thee ev-ery hour, Teach me Thy will;
5. I need Thee ev-ery hour, Most ho - ly One;

No ten - der voice like Thine Can peace af - ford.
Temp - ta - tions lose their power When Thou art nigh.
Come quick - ly and a - bide, Or life is vain.
And Thy rich prom-is - es In me ful - fil.
O make me Thine in-deed, Thou bless - ed Son.

I need Thee, O I need Thee, Ev - ery hour I need Thee;

O bless me now, my Sav - iour, I come to Thee. A - men.

From Every Stormy Wind That Blows 328

RETREAT 8. 8. 8. 8.

Hugh Stowell, 1799-1865

Thomas Hastings, 1784-1872

1. From ev-ery storm-y wind that blows, From ev-ery swell-ing tide of woes,
2. There is a place where Je-sus sheds The oil of glad-ness on our heads,
3. There is a scene where spirits blend, Where friend holds fel-low-ship with friend;
4. Ah! whith-er could we flee for aid, When tempt-ed, des - o-late, dis-mayed,
5. Ah! there on ea - gle wings we soar, And sin and sense mo-lest no more,

There is a calm, a sure re-treat: 'Tis found be-neath the mer-cy seat.
A place than all be-sides more sweet: It is the blood-bought mer-cy seat.
Though sundered far, by faith they meet A - round one com-mon mer-cy seat.
Or how the hosts of hell de-feat, Had suf-fer-ing saints no mer-cy seat?
And heaven comes down our souls to greet, While glo-ry crowns the mer-cy seat. A-men.

Breathe on Me, Breath of God 329

TRENTHAM 6. 6. 8. 7.

Edwin Hatch, 1835-1889

Robert Jackson, 1842-1914

1. Breathe on me, Breath of God, Fill me with life a - new,
2. Breathe on me, Breath of God, Un - til my heart is pure,
3. Breathe on me, Breath of God, Till I am whol - ly Thine,
4. Breathe on me, Breath of God, So shall I nev - er die,

That I may love what Thou dost love, And do what Thou wouldst do.
Un - til with Thee I will one will, To do and to en - dure.
Un - til this earth-ly part of me Glows with Thy fire di - vine.
But live with Thee the per-fect life Of Thine e - ter - ni - ty. A-men.

Music used by permission of Mrs. Ethel Taylor

330 Be Thou My Vision

SLANE 10. 10. 9. 10.

Ancient Irish
Trans. by Mary Byrne, 1880-1931
Versified by Eleanor Hull, 1860-1935

Ancient Irish Traditional Melody
Harmonized by David Evans, 1874-1948

1. Be Thou my vi - sion, O Lord of my heart;
2. Be Thou my wis - dom, and Thou my true word;
3. Rich - es I heed not, nor man's emp - ty praise,
4. High King of heav - en, my vic - to - ry won,

Naught be all else to me, save that Thou art:
I ev - er with Thee and Thou with me, Lord;
Thou mine in - her - it - ance, now and al - ways:
May I reach heav - en's joys, O bright heaven's Sun!

Thou my best thought, by day or by night,
Thou my great Fa - ther, I Thy true son,
Thou and Thou on - ly, first in my heart,
Heart of my own heart, what - ev - er be - fall,

Wak - ing or sleep - ing, Thy pres - ence my light.
Thou in me dwell - ing, and I with Thee one.
High King of heav - en, my treas - ure Thou art.
Still be my vi - sion, O Rul - er of all. A - men.

Breathe on Me

TRUETT 7. 6. 8. 6. with Refrain

Edwin Hatch, 1835-1889
Alt. by B. B. McKinney, 1886-1952

B. B. McKinney, 1886-1952

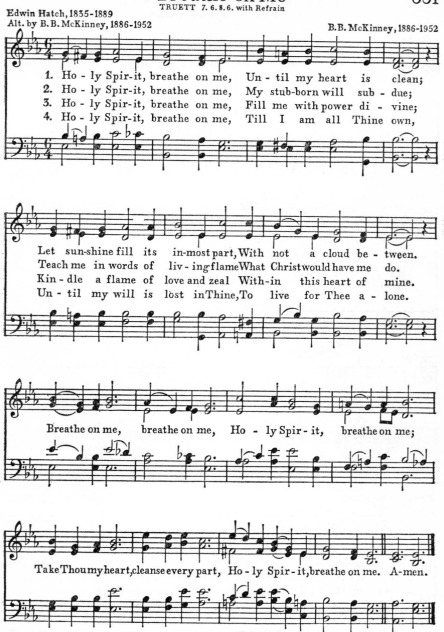

1. Ho - ly Spir-it, breathe on me, Un - til my heart is clean;
2. Ho - ly Spir-it, breathe on me, My stub-born will sub - due;
3. Ho - ly Spir-it, breathe on me, Fill me with power di - vine;
4. Ho - ly Spir-it, breathe on me, Till I am all Thine own,

Let sun-shine fill its in-most part, With not a cloud be - tween.
Teach me in words of liv-ing flame What Christ would have me do.
Kin - dle a flame of love and zeal With-in this heart of mine.
Un - til my will is lost in Thine, To live for Thee a - lone.

Breathe on me, breathe on me, Ho - ly Spir-it, breathe on me;

Take Thou my heart, cleanse every part, Ho - ly Spir-it, breathe on me. A-men.

332 More Love to Thee, O Christ

MORE LOVE TO THEE 6. 4. 6. 4. 6. 4. 4.

Elizabeth Prentiss, 1818-1878

William H. Doane, 1832-1915

1. More love to Thee, O Christ, More love to Thee! Hear Thou the
2. Once earth-ly joy I craved, Sought peace and rest; Now Thee a-
3. Let sor-row do its work, Send grief and pain; Sweet are Thy
4. Then shall my lat-est breath Whis-per Thy praise; This be the

prayer I make On bend-ed knee; This is my ear-nest plea:
lone I seek, Give what is best; This all my prayer shall be:
mes-sen-gers, Sweet their re-frain, When they can sing with me:
part-ing cry My heart shall raise; This still its prayer shall be:

More love, O Christ, to Thee, More love to Thee, More love to Thee! A-men.

333 They Who Seek the Throne of Grace

SEYMOUR 7. 7. 7. 7.

Oliver Holden, 1765-1844

Carl M. von Weber, 1786-1826

1. They who seek the throne of grace Find that throne in ev-ery place;
2. In our sick-ness and our health, In our want or in our wealth,
3. When our earth-ly com-forts fail, When the woes of life pre-vail,
4. Then, my soul, in ev-ery strait, To thy Fa-ther come, and wait;

If we live a life of prayer, God is pres-ent ev-ery-where.
If we look to God in prayer, God is pres-ent ev-ery-where.
'Tis the time for ear-nest prayer; God is pres-ent ev-ery-where.
He will an-swer ev-ery prayer; God is pres-ent ev-ery-where. A-men.

Take Time to Be Holy 334

HOLINESS 6.5.6.5.D.

William D. Longstaff, 1822-1894

George C. Stebbins, 1846-1945

1. Take time to be ho-ly, Speak oft with thy Lord; A-bide in Him
2. Take time to be ho-ly, The world rush-es on; Spend much time in
3. Take time to be ho-ly, Let Him be thy guide, And run not be-
4. Take time to be ho-ly, Be calm in thy soul; Each thought and each

al-ways, And feed on His Word: Make friends of God's chil-dren,
se-cret With Je-sus a-lone: By look-ing to Je-sus,
fore Him What-ev-er be-tide; In joy or in sor-row
mo-tive Be-neath His con-trol; Thus led by His Spir-it

Help those who are weak; For-get-ting in noth-ing His bless-ing to seek.
Like Him thou shalt be; Thy friends in thy con-duct His like-ness shall see.
Still fol-low thy Lord, And, look-ing to Je-sus, Still trust in His Word.
To foun-tains of love, Thou soon shalt be fit-ted For serv-ice a-bove.

335 Nearer, Still Nearer

MORRIS 9.10.9.10.10.

Lelia N. Morris, 1862-1929   Lelia N. Morris, 1862-1929

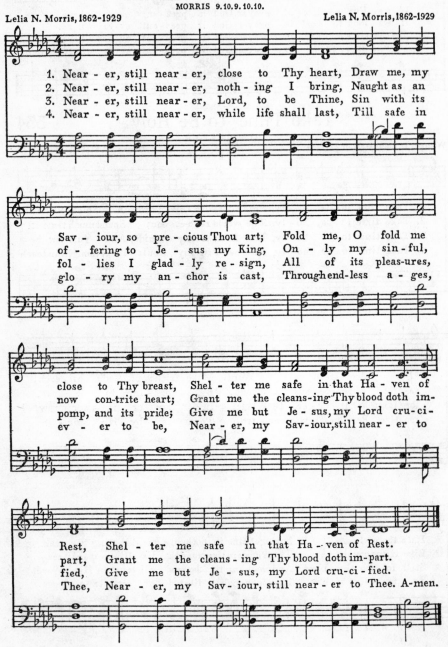

1. Near - er, still near - er, close to Thy heart, Draw me, my
2. Near - er, still near - er, noth - ing I bring, Naught as an
3. Near - er, still near - er, Lord, to be Thine, Sin with its
4. Near - er, still near - er, while life shall last, Till safe in

Sav - iour, so pre - cious Thou art; Fold me, O fold me
of - fering to Je - sus my King, On - ly my sin - ful,
fol - lies I glad - ly re - sign, All of its pleas-ures,
glo - ry my an - chor is cast, Through end-less a - ges,

close to Thy breast, Shel - ter me safe in that Ha - ven of
now con-trite heart; Grant me the cleans-ing Thy blood doth im-
pomp, and its pride; Give me but Je - sus, my Lord cru-ci-
ev - er to be, Near - er, my Sav-iour, still near - er to

Rest, Shel - ter me safe in that Ha - ven of Rest.
part, Grant me the cleans - ing Thy blood doth im-part.
fied, Give me but Je - sus, my Lord cru-ci-fied.
Thee, Near - er, my Sav - iour, still near - er to Thee. A-men.

My Faith Has Found a Resting Place 336

8.6.8.6. with Refrain

Lidie H. Edmunds, 19th century

Norse Air
Arr. by W. J. Kirkpatrick, 1838-1921

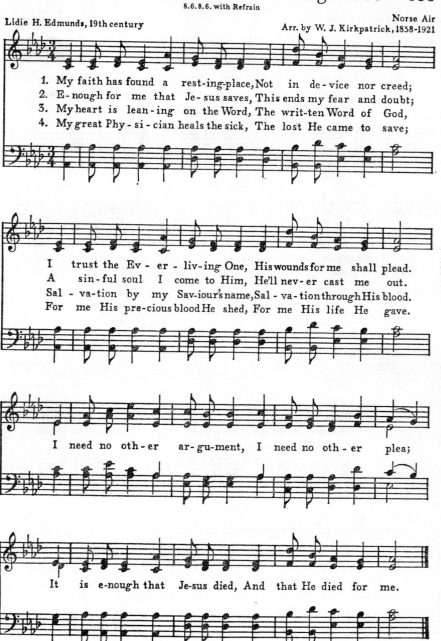

1. My faith has found a rest-ing-place, Not in de-vice nor creed;
2. E-nough for me that Je-sus saves, This ends my fear and doubt;
3. My heart is lean-ing on the Word, The writ-ten Word of God,
4. My great Phy-si-cian heals the sick, The lost He came to save;

I trust the Ev-er-liv-ing One, His wounds for me shall plead.
A sin-ful soul I come to Him, He'll nev-er cast me out.
Sal-va-tion by my Sav-iour's name, Sal-va-tion through His blood.
For me His pre-cious blood He shed, For me His life He gave.

I need no oth-er ar-gu-ment, I need no oth-er plea;

It is e-nough that Je-sus died, And that He died for me.

337 What a Friend We Have in Jesus

CONVERSE 8. 7. 8. 7. D.

Joseph Scriven, 1820-1886   Charles C. Converse, 1832-1918

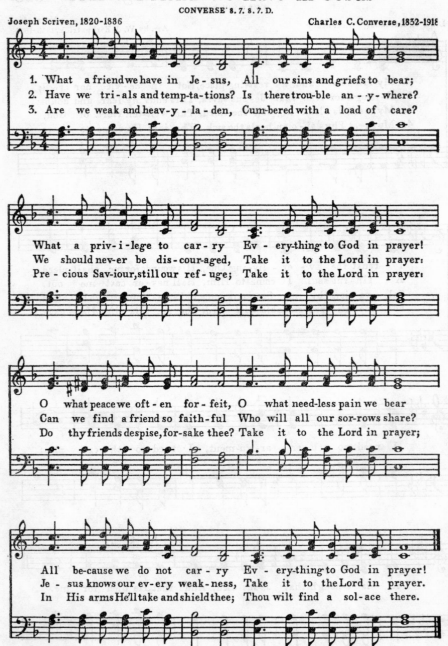

1. What a friend we have in Je-sus, All our sins and griefs to bear;
2. Have we tri-als and temp-ta-tions? Is there trou-ble an-y-where?
3. Are we weak and heav-y-la-den, Cum-bered with a load of care?

What a priv-i-lege to car-ry Ev-ery-thing to God in prayer!
We should nev-er be dis-cour-aged, Take it to the Lord in prayer:
Pre-cious Sav-iour, still our ref-uge; Take it to the Lord in prayer:

O what peace we oft-en for-feit, O what need-less pain we bear
Can we find a friend so faith-ful Who will all our sor-rows share?
Do thy friends despise, for-sake thee? Take it to the Lord in prayer;

All be-cause we do not car-ry Ev-ery-thing to God in prayer!
Je-sus knows our ev-ery weak-ness, Take it to the Lord in prayer.
In His arms He'll take and shield thee; Thou wilt find a sol-ace there.

'Tis the Blessed Hour of Prayer

BLESSED HOUR Irregular with Refrain

Fanny J. Crosby, 1820-1915

William H. Doane, 1852-1915

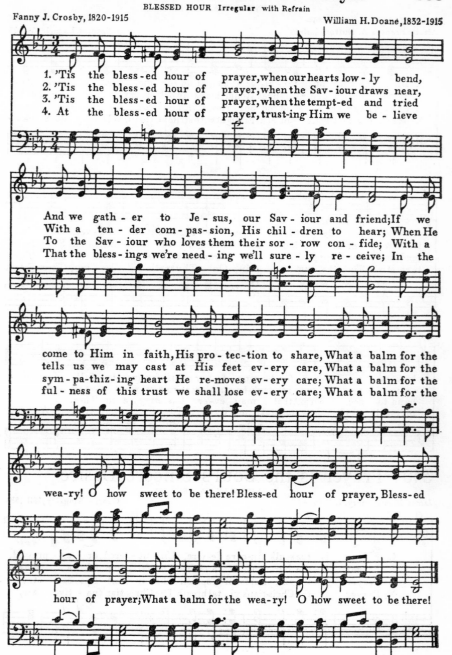

1. 'Tis the bless-ed hour of prayer, when our hearts low-ly bend,
2. 'Tis the bless-ed hour of prayer, when the Sav-iour draws near,
3. 'Tis the bless-ed hour of prayer, when the tempt-ed and tried
4. At the bless-ed hour of prayer, trust-ing Him we be-lieve

And we gath-er to Je-sus, our Sav-iour and friend; If we
With a ten-der com-pas-sion, His chil-dren to hear; When He
To the Sav-iour who loves them their sor-row con-fide; With a
That the bless-ings we're need-ing we'll sure-ly re-ceive; In the

come to Him in faith, His pro-tec-tion to share, What a balm for the
tells us we may cast at His feet ev-ery care, What a balm for the
sym-pa-thiz-ing heart He re-moves ev-ery care; What a balm for the
ful-ness of this trust we shall lose ev-ery care; What a balm for the

wea-ry! O how sweet to be there! Bless-ed hour of prayer, Bless-ed

hour of prayer; What a balm for the wea-ry! O how sweet to be there!

339 In the Hour of Trial

PENITENCE 6.5.6.5.D.

James Montgomery, 1771-1854
Alt. by Frances A. Hutton, 1811-1877

Spencer Lane, 1843-1903

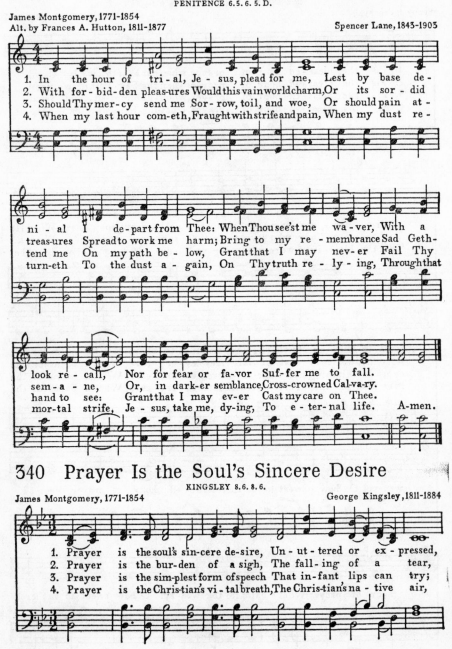

1. In the hour of tri-al, Je-sus, plead for me, Lest by base de-
2. With for-bid-den pleas-ures Would this vain world charm, Or its sor-did
3. Should Thy mer-cy send me Sor-row, toil, and woe, Or should pain at-
4. When my last hour com-eth, Fraught with strife and pain, When my dust re-

ni-al I de-part from Thee: When Thou see'st me wa-ver, With a
treas-ures Spread to work me harm; Bring to my re-membrance Sad Geth-
tend me On my path be-low, Grant that I may nev-er Fail Thy
turn-eth To the dust a-gain, On Thy truth re-ly-ing, Through that

look re-call, Nor for fear or fa-vor Suf-fer me to fall.
sem-a-ne, Or, in dark-er semblance, Cross-crowned Cal-va-ry.
hand to see: Grant that I may ev-er Cast my care on Thee.
mor-tal strife, Je-sus, take me, dy-ing, To e-ter-nal life. A-men.

340 Prayer Is the Soul's Sincere Desire

KINGSLEY 8.6.8.6.

James Montgomery, 1771-1854

George Kingsley, 1811-1884

1. Prayer is the soul's sin-cere de-sire, Un-ut-tered or ex-pressed,
2. Prayer is the bur-den of a sigh, The fall-ing of a tear,
3. Prayer is the sim-plest form of speech That in-fant lips can try;
4. Prayer is the Chris-tian's vi-tal breath, The Chris-tian's na-tive air,

The mo - tion of a hid-den fire, That trembles in the breast.
The up - ward glanc-ing of an eye, When none but God is near.
Prayer, the sub-lim est strains that reach The Maj-es - ty on high.
His watch-word at the gates of death; He en-ters heaven with prayer. A-men.

We Praise Thee, O God   341

REVIVE US AGAIN 11.11. with Refrain

William P. Mackay, 1839-1885   John J. Husband, 1760-1825

1. We praise Thee, O God! for the Son of Thy love, For   Je - sus who
2.. We praise Thee, O God! for Thy Spir-it of light, Who has shown us our
3. All glo - ry and praise to the Lamb that was slain, Who has borne all our
4. Re - vive us a - gain; fill each heart with Thy love; May each soul be re-

died, and is now gone a - bove.
Sav-iour, and scat-tered our night. Hal-le - lu - jah! Thine the glo - ry, Hal-le-
sins, and has cleansed ev-ery stain.
kin-dled with fire from a - bove.

lu - jah! A-men; Hal-le - lu - jah! Thine the glo - ry, Re-vive us a - gain.

342
Prayer Is the Key
THE GOLDEN KEY 5.5.7.5.5.7.

Unknown

John R. Sweney, 1837-1899

1. Prayer is the key For the bend-ing knee To op-en the morn's first hours;
2. Not a soul so sad, Nor a heart so glad, When com-eth the shades of night,
3. Take the gold-en key In your hand and see, As the night-tide drifts a - way,
4. When the shad-ows fall, And the ves-per call Is sob-bing its low re - frain,
5. Soon our toils will cease, And will come re-lease; Life's tears shall be wiped a - way,

See the in-cense rise To the star-ry skies, Like per-fume from the flowers.
But the day-break song Will the joy prolong, And some darkness turn to light.
How its bless-ed hold Is a crown of gold, Thro' the wear-y hours of day.
'Tis a gar-land sweet To the toil-dent feet, And an an-ti-dote for pain.
As the pearl gates swing; And the gold harps ring; And we en-ter e-ter-nal day. A-men.

343
O Lord, Help Me to Live
CROWN OF LIFE 6. 6. 8. 6.

Anna Zeigler Hess, 1834-1867

Harry D. Rotz, 1878-1946

1. O Lord, help me to live, while here on earth I stay,
2. Help me to win the prize That Christ has set be - fore,
3. Temp-ta-tions oft a-rise, Here in this wil-der-ness,
4. I put my trust while here, My faith, my all in Thee,
5. Sus-tain my hope and faith To walk with Thee in love;

That I the crown of life re-ceive, When done with life's dark day.
And be with Him in par-a-dise, When time shall be no more.
And Sa-tan by his craft oft tries To rob our haven of bliss.
For Thou hast made a way for all, Hast made a way for me.
Pre-pare my soul in time of grace, To dwell with Thee a-bove. A-men.

Lord, What a Change Within Us 344

MORECAMBE 10. 10. 10. 10.

Richard C. Trench, 1807-1886
Arr. by William P. Merrill, 1867-1954

Frederick C. Atkinson, 1841-1897

1. Lord, what a change with - in us one short hour
2. We kneel, and all a - round us seems to lower;
3. Why should we ev - er weak or heart-less be,

Spent in Thy pres - ence will pre - vail to make,
We rise, and all, the dis - tant and the near,
Why are we ev - er o - ver-borne with care,

What heav - y bur - dens from our bos - oms take,
Stands forth in sun - ny out - line, brave and clear;
Anx - ious or trou - bled, when with us is prayer,

What parch-ed fields re - fresh as with a shower.
We kneel how weak; we rise how full of power.
And joy, and strength, and cour - age are with Thee? A - men.

345 Jesus, Thy Boundless Love to Me

STELLA 8. 8. 8. 8. 8. 8.

Paul Gerhardt, 1607-1676
Trans. by John Wesley, 1703-1791
Altered and revised 1931

Old English Melody

1. Je - sus, Thy bound-less love to me No thought can
2. O grant that noth - ing in my soul May dwell, but
3. O Love, how gra - cious is Thy way! All fear be -

reach, no tongue de-clare; U - nite my thank-ful heart to Thee,
Thy pure love a - lone; O may Thy love pos - sess me whole,
fore Thy pres - ence flies; Care, an - guish, sor - row, melt a - way,

And reign with - out a ri - val there! Thine whol - ly,
My joy, my treas - ure, and my crown! All cold - ness
Wher-e'er Thy heal - ing beams a - rise. O Je - sus,

Thine a - lone, I'd live, My-self to Thee en - tire - ly give.
from my heart re-move; May ev - ery act, word, thought, be love.
noth - ing may I see, Noth-ing de - sire, or seek, but Thee. A - men.

Jesus, Keep Me Near the Cross 346

NEAR THE CROSS. 7. 6. 7. 6. with Refrain

Fanny J. Crosby, 1820-1915

William H. Doane, 1832-1915

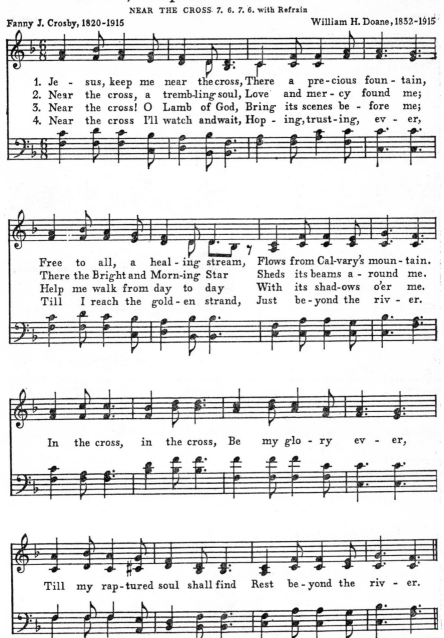

1. Je - sus, keep me near the cross, There a pre-cious foun - tain,
2. Near the cross, a trem-bling soul, Love and mer - cy found me;
3. Near the cross! O Lamb of God, Bring its scenes be - fore me;
4. Near the cross I'll watch and wait, Hop - ing, trust-ing, ev - er,

Free to all, a heal - ing stream, Flows from Cal-vary's moun - tain.
There the Bright and Morn-ing Star Sheds its beams a - round me.
Help me walk from day to day With its shad-ows o'er me.
Till I reach the gold - en strand, Just be - yond the riv - er.

In the cross, in the cross, Be my glo - ry ev - er,

Till my rap-tured soul shall find Rest be - yond the riv - er.

347 Teach Me Yet More of Thy Blest Ways

MARTYRDOM 8. 6. 8. 6.

Unknown

Hugh Wilson, 1764-1824

1. Teach me yet more of Thy blest ways, Thou ho-ly Lamb of God,
2. O tell me of-ten of each wound, Of ev-ery grief and pain,
3. For this, O may I free-ly count What-e'er I have but loss,
4. En-grave this deep-ly on my heart With an e-ter-nal pen,

And fix and root me in the grace So dear-ly bought with blood.
And let my heart with joy con-fess, From hence comes all my gain.
And ev-ery name and ev-erything, Com-pared with Thee but dross.
That I may, in some small de-gree, Re-turn Thy love a-gain. A-men.

348 Prince of Peace, Control My Will

ALETTA 7. 7. 7. 7.

Mary A. S. Barber, 1801-1864

William B. Bradbury, 1816-1868

1. Prince of Peace, con-trol my will; Bid this strug-gling heart be still:
2. Thou hast bought me with Thy blood, O-pened wide the gate to God:
3. May Thy will, not mine, be done; May Thy will and mine be one:
4. Sav-iour, at Thy feet I fall, Thou my life, my God, my all!

Bid my fears and doubt-ings cease, Hush my spir-it in-to peace.
Peace I ask, but peace must be, Lord, in be-ing one with Thee.
Chase these doubt-ings from my heart, Now Thy per-fect peace im-part.
Let Thy hap-py ser-vant be One for-ev-er-more with Thee! A-men.

O Master, Let Me Walk with Thee 349

MARYTON 8. 8. 8. 8.

Washington Gladden, 1836-1918

H. Percy Smith, 1825-1898

1. O Mas-ter, let me walk with Thee In low-ly paths of serv-ice free;
2. Help me the slow of heart to move By some clear, win-ning word of love;
3. Teach me Thy pa-tience; still with Thee In clo-ser, dear-er com-pa-ny,
4. In hope that sends a shin-ing ray Far down the fu-ture's broad 'ning way,

Tell me Thy se-cret, help me bear The strain of toil, the fret of care.
Teach me the way-ward feet to stay, And guide them in the homeward way.
In work that keeps faith sweet and strong, In trust that triumphs o - ver wrong.
In peace that on-ly Thou canst give, With Thee, O Mas-ter, let me live. A-men.

O for a Heart to Praise My God 350

MARTYRDOM 8. 6. 8. 6.

Charles Wesley, 1707-1788

Hugh Wilson, 1764-1824

1. O for a heart to praise my God, A heart from sin set free,
2. A heart re-signed, sub - mis - sive, meek, My great Re - deem - er's throne,
3. A hum-ble, low - ly, con-trite heart, Be - liev - ing, true, and clean,
4. A heart in ev - ery thought renewed, And full of love di - vine,
5. Thy na - ture, gra - cious Lord, im-part; Come quick-ly from a - bove;

A heart that al-ways feels Thy blood, So free - ly shed for me!
Where on - ly Christ is heard to speak, Where Je - sus reigns a-lone;
Which neith-er life nor death can part From Him that dwells with-in;
Per - fect and right and pure and good, A cop - y, Lord, of Thine!
Write Thy new name up - on my heart, Thy new, best name of Love. A-men.

351 I'm Pressing On the Upward Way

HIGHER GROUND 8. 8. 8. 8. with Refrain

Johnson Oatman, Jr., 1856-1922   Charles H. Gabriel, 1856-1932

1. I'm press-ing on the up-ward way, New heights I'm gain-ing ev-ery day;
2. My heart has no de-sire to stay Where doubts a-rise and fears dis-may;
3. I want to live a-bove the world, Though Sa-tan's darts at me are hurled;
4. I want to scale the ut-most height And catch a gleam of glo-ry bright;

Still pray-ing as I on-ward bound, "Lord, plant my feet on high-er ground."
Though some may dwell where these a-bound, My prayer, my aim, is high-er ground.
For faith has caught the joy-ful sound, The song of saints on high-er ground.
But still I'll pray till heaven I've found, "Lord, lead me on to high-er ground."

Lord, lift me up and let me stand, By faith, on heav-en's ta-ble-land,

A high-er plane than I have found; Lord, plant my feet on high-er ground.

I Am Thine, O Lord

I AM THINE 10.7.10.7. with Refrain

Fanny J. Crosby, 1820-1915

William H. Doane, 1832-1915

1. I am Thine, O Lord, I have heard Thy voice, And it
2. Con - se - crate me now to Thy serv - ice, Lord, By the
3. O, the pure de - light of a sin - gle hour That be -
4. There are depths of love that I can - not know Till I

told Thy love to me; But I long to rise in the
power of grace di - vine; Let my soul look up with a
fore Thy throne I spend, When I kneel in prayer, and with
cross the nar - row sea; There are heights of joy that I

arms of faith, And be clos - er drawn to Thee.
stead - fast hope, And my will be lost in Thine. Draw me near - er,
Thee, my God, I com-mune as friend with friend. near-er, near-er,
may not reach Till I rest in peace with Thee.

near - er, bless-ed Lord, To the cross where Thou hast died;. Draw me

near - er, near - er, near- er, bless-ed Lord, To Thy pre-cious, bleed-ing side.

353   I Would Be True

PEEK 11. 10. 11. 10. 10.

Howard Arnold Walter, 1883-1918
(Author of third stanza unknown)

Joseph Yates Peek, 1843-1911

1. I would be true, for there are those who trust me; I would be pure, for there are those who care; I would be strong, for there is much to suf-fer; I would be brave, for there is much to dare, I would be brave, for there is much to dare.

2. I would be friend of all—the foe, the friend-less; I would be giv - ing, and for-get the gift; I would be hum - ble, for I know my weak-ness; I would look up, and laugh, and love, and lift, I would look up, and laugh, and love, and lift.

3. I would be prayer-ful through each bus-y mo-ment; I would be con - stant-ly in touch with God; I would be tuned to hear His slight-est whis-per; I would have faith to keep the path Christ trod, I would have faith to keep the path Christ trod.

Open My Eyes, That I May See

35⁴

SCOTT Irregular

Clara H. Scott, 1841-1897

Clara H. Scott, 1841-1897

1. O-pen my eyes, that I may see Glimps-es of truth Thou hast for me;
2. O-pen my ears, that I may hear Voic - es of truth Thou send-est clear;
3. O-pen my mouth, and let me bear Glad - ly the warm truth ev-ery-where;
4. O-pen my mind, that I may read More of Thy love in word and deed;

Place in my hands the won-der-ful key That shall un-clasp, and
And while the wave-notes fall on my ear Ev - ery-thing false will
O - pen my heart, and let me pre-pare Love with Thy chil - dren
What shall I fear while yet Thou dost lead? On - ly for light from

set me free. Si-lent-ly now I wait for Thee, Read-y, my God, Thy
dis - ap-pear. Si-lent-ly now I wait for Thee, Read-y, my God, Thy
thus to share. Si-lent-ly now I wait for Thee, Read-y, my God, Thy
Thee I plead. Si-lent-ly now I wait for Thee, Read-y, my God, Thy

will to see; O-pen my eyes, il - lu-mine me, Spir - it di - vine!
will to see; O-pen my ears, il - lu-mine me, Spir - it di - vine!
will to see; O-pen my heart, il - lu-mine me, Spir - it di - vine!
will to see; O-pen my mind, il - lu-mine me, Spir - it di - vine!

Go Carry Thy Burden to Jesus

STEAL AWAY 9..8.9.8. with Refrain

Eliza Edmunds Hewitt, 1851-1920   William J. Kirkpatrick, 1838-1921

1. Go car-ry Thy bur-den to Je-sus, And lay down thy load at His feet;
2. Re-joice in His won-der-ful mer-cy, Thy soul from its sor-row re-lieved;
3. Let Christ be thy gracious com-pan-ion, Keep close to His side day by day;
4. O fel-low-ship precious and ho-ly, His life, o-ver-flow-ing in love,

Where Cal-va-ry's cross is up-lift-ed, Find par-don and com-fort-ing sweet.
Then turn-ing in love to thy neigh-bor, Give free-ly as thou hast re-ceived.
The Foun-tain, un-seen, of the bless-ings That brighten and glad-den the way.
Shall bring to the need-y a-round thee Fair sunbeams and bloom from a-bove.

O steal a-way soft-ly to Je-sus, To Him let thy heart be out-poured;

Thy Fa-ther, who se-eth in se-cret, Shall give thee a gra-cious re-ward.

Fill All My Vision

9. 9. 9. 10. with Refrain

356

Avis B. Christiansen, 1895 –

Homer Hammontree, 1884 –

1. Fill all my vi - sion, Sav-iour, I pray, Let me see on - ly
2. Fill all my vi - sion: ev - ery de - sire Keep for Thy glo - ry;
3. Fill all my vi - sion: let naught of sin Shad-ow the bright-ness

Je - sus to - day; When through the val - ley Thou lead-est me,
my soul in - spire With Thy per - fec - tion, Thy ho - ly love,
shin-ing with - in; Let me see on - ly Thy bless-ed face,

Give me Thy glo - ry and beau-ty to see. Fill all my vi - sion,
Flood-ing my path-way with light from a - bove.
Feast-ing my soul on Thy in - fi - nite grace.

Sav-iour di - vine, Till with Thy glo - ry my spir-it shall shine: Fill all my

vi - sion, that all may see Thy ho - ly im-age re-flect-ed in me.

357 Thou, My Everlasting Portion

CLOSE TO THEE 8.7.8.7. with Refrain

Fanny J. Crosby, 1820-1915

Silas J. Vail, 1818-1884

1. Thou, my ev - er - last-ing por - tion, More than friend or life to me;
2. Not for ease or world-ly pleas-ure, Nor for fame my prayer shall be;
3. Lead me through the vale of shad-ows, Bear me o'er life's fit - ful sea;

All a - long my pil-grim jour-ney, Sav-iour, let me walk with Thee.
Glad-ly will I toil and suf-fer, On - ly let me walk with Thee.
Then the gate of life e - ter-nal May I en - ter, Lord, with Thee.

Close to Thee, close to Thee, Close to Thee, close to Thee; All a -
Close to Thee, close to Thee, Close to Thee, close to Thee; Glad - ly
Close to Thee, close to Thee, Close to Thee, close to Thee; Then the

long my pil-grim jour-ney, Sav-iour, let me walk with Thee.
will I toil and suf-fer, On - ly let me walk with Thee.
gate of life e - ter-nal May I en - ter, Lord, with Thee. A - men.

O for a Faith That Will Not Shrink 358

ARLINGTON 8. 6. 8. 6.

William H. Bathurst, 1796-1877

Thomas A. Arne, 1710-1778

1. O   for a faith that will not shrink, Though pressed by ev - ery   foe,
2. That will not mur-mur nor com-plain Be - neath the chas-ten-ing rod,
3. A   faith that shines more bright and clear When tem-pests rage with - out;
4. Lord, give me such a faith as this; And then, what-e'er may   come,

That will not trem-ble on the brink Of an - y earth - ly woe!
But, in the hour of grief or pain, Will lean up-on its God.
That when in dan - ger knows no fear, In dark-ness feels no doubt.
I'll   taste, e'en now, the hal-lowed bliss Of an' e - ter - nal home. A - men.

Lord Jesus, Think on Me 359

SOUTHWELL 6. 6. 8. 6.

Synesius of Cyrene c. 375-430
Trans. by Allen W. Chatfield, 1808-1896

Damon's Psalms, 1579

1. Lord Je - sus, think on me, And purge a - way my sin;
2. Lord Je - sus, think on me, A - mid the bat - tle's strife;
3. Lord Je - sus, think on me, Nor let me go a - stray;
4. Lord Je - sus, think on me, That, when this life is past,

From earth-born pas-sions set me free, And make me pure with - in.
In   all my pain and mis-er - y Be Thou my health and life.
Through dark-ness and per - plex - i - ty Point Thou the heaven-ly way.
I   may e - ter - nal bright-ness see, And share Thy joy at last. A - men.

360 More About Jesus

SWENEY 8. 8. 8. 8. with Refrain

Eliza E. Hewitt, 1851-1920   John R. Sweney, 1837-1899

1. More a-bout Je - sus   I would know, More of His grace to oth-ers show,
2. More a-bout Je - sus   let me learn, More of His ho - ly will dis-cern;
3. More a-bout Je - sus   in His Word, Hold-ing com-mun-ion with my Lord,
4. More a-bout Je - sus   on His throne, Rich-es in glo - ry all His own;

More of His sav - ing full-ness see, More of His love who died for me.
Spir - it of God, my teach-er be, Show-ing the things of Christ to me.
Hear-ing His voice in ev - ery line, Mak-ing each faith-ful say - ing mine.
More of His king-dom's sure in-crease, More of His com - ing, Prince of Peace.

More, more a-bout Je - sus, More, more a-bout Je - sus;

More of His sav - ing full - ness see, More of His love who died for me.

Sweet Hour of Prayer   361

SWEET HOUR 8.8.8.8.D.

William W. Walford, 1772-1850

William B. Bradbury, 1816-1868

1. Sweet hour of prayer, sweet hour of prayer, That calls me from a world of care,
2. Sweet hour of prayer, sweet hour of prayer, The joys I feel, the bliss I share
3. Sweet hour of prayer, sweet hour of prayer, Thy wings shall my pe - ti - tion bear

And bids me at my Fa-ther's throne, Make all my wants and wish-es known;
Of those whose anx-ious spir-its burn With strong de-sires for thy re-turn;
To Him, whose truth and faith-ful-ness En-gage the wait-ing soul to bless;

In sea-sons of dis-tress and grief, My soul has of-ten found re-lief,
With such I has-ten to the place Where God my Sav-iour shows His face,
And since He bids me seek His face, Be-lieve His word, and trust His grace,

And oft es-caped the temp-ter's snare By thy re-turn, sweet hour of prayer.
And glad-ly take my sta-tion there, And wait for thee, sweet hour of prayer.
I'll cast on Him my ev-ery care, And wait for thee, sweet hour of prayer.

362 Nearer, My God, to Thee
BETHANY 6.4.6.4.6.6.6.4.

Sara Flower Adams, 1805-1848   Lowell Mason, 1792-1872

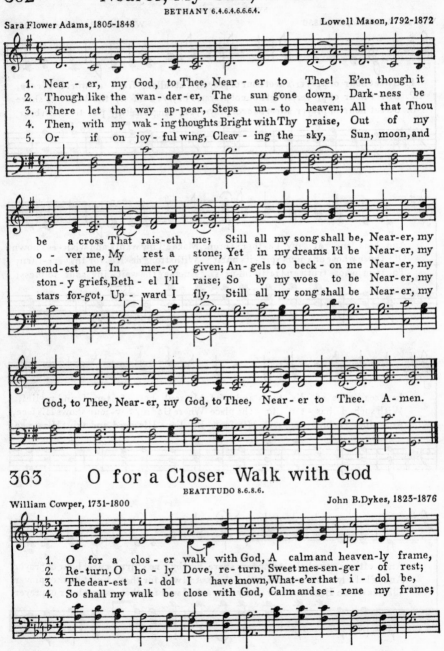

1. Near - er, my God, to Thee, Near - er to Thee! E'en though it
2. Though like the wan - der - er, The sun gone down, Dark - ness be
3. There let the way ap - pear, Steps un - to heaven; All that Thou
4. Then, with my wak - ing thoughts Bright with Thy praise, Out of my
5. Or if on joy - ful wing, Cleav - ing the sky, Sun, moon, and

be a cross That rais - eth me; Still all my song shall be, Near - er, my
o - ver me, My rest a stone; Yet in my dreams I'd be Near - er, my
send - est me In mer - cy given; An - gels to beck - on me Near - er, my
ston - y griefs, Beth - el I'll raise; So by my woes to be Near - er, my
stars for - got, Up - ward I fly, Still all my song shall be Near - er, my

God, to Thee, Near - er, my God, to Thee, Near - er to Thee. A - men.

363 O for a Closer Walk with God
BEATITUDO 8.6.8.6.

William Cowper, 1731-1800   John B. Dykes, 1823-1876

1. O for a clos - er walk with God, A calm and heaven-ly frame,
2. Re - turn, O ho - ly Dove, re - turn, Sweet mes - sen - ger of rest;
3. The dear - est i - dol I have known, What - e'er that i - dol be,
4. So shall my walk be close with God, Calm and se - rene my frame;

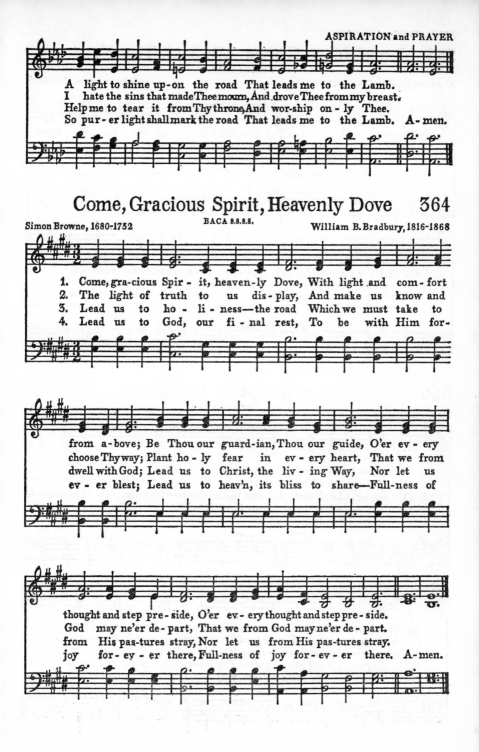

365 Lord Jesus Christ, We Seek Thy Face

HOLLEY 8.8.8.8.

Alexander Stewart, 1843-1923

George Hews, 1806-1873

1. Lord Jesus Christ, we seek Thy face, With-in the veil we bow the knee;
2. We thank Thee for the pre-cious blood That purged our sins and brought us nigh,
3. Shut in with Thee, far, far a - bove The rest-less world that wars be - low;
4. The brow that once with thorns was bound, Thy hands, Thy side, we fain would see;

O, let Thy glo-ry fill the place, And bless us while we wait on Thee.
All cleansed and sanc-ti-fied to God, Thy ho-ly name to mag-ni - fy.
We seek to learn and prove Thy love, Thy wis-dom and Thy grace to know.
Draw near, Lord Je-sus, glo-ry-crowned, And bless us while we wait on Thee. A-men.

366 Lord, Speak to Me

CANONBURY 8.8.8.8.

Frances R. Havergal, 1836-1879

Robert Schumann, 1810-1856

1. Lord, speak to me, that I may speak In liv-ing ech-oes of Thy tone;
2. O lead me, Lord, that I may lead The wan-dering and the wav-ering feet;
3. O teach me, Lord, that I may teach The pre-cious things Thou dost im-part;
4. O fill me with Thy full-ness, Lord, Un-til my ver - y heart o'er-flow
5. O use me, Lord, use e - ven me, Just as Thou wilt, and when, and where;

As Thou hast sought, so let me seek Thy err-ing chil-dren lost and lone.
O feed me, Lord, that I may feed Thy hun-gering ones with man-na sweet.
And wing my words, that they may reach The hid-den depths of many a heart.
In kin-dling thought and glow-ing word, Thy love to tell, Thy praise to show.
Un - til Thy bless-ed face I see, Thy rest, Thy joy, Thy glo-ry share. A-men.

Send a Revival

367

MATTHEWS 9.9.9.7. with Refrain

B.B. McKinney, 1886-1952

B.B. McKinney, 1886-1952

1. Send a re-viv-al, O Christ, my Lord, Let it go o-ver the land and sea;
2. Send a re-viv-al a-mong Thine own, Help us to turn from our sins a-way;
3. Send a re-viv-al to those in sin, Help them, O Je-sus, to turn to Thee;
4. Send a re-viv-al in ev-ery heart, Draw the world near-er, O Lord, to Thee;

Send it ac-cord-ing to Thy dear Word, And let it be-gin in me.
Let us get near-er the Fa-ther's throne, Re-vive us a-gain, we pray.
Let them the new life in Thee be-gin, Oh, give them the vic-to - ry.
Let Thy sal-va-tion true joy im-part, And let it be-gin in me.

Lord, send a re - viv - al, Lord, send a re - viv - al,

Lord, send a re - viv - al, And let it be-gin in me.

368 Our Father in Heaven

ST. MICHEL'S 11.11.11.11.

Sarah J. Hale, 1795-1879   William Gawler's *Hymns and Psalms,* 1789

1. Our Father in heaven we hallow Thy name;
2. Forgive our transgressions, and teach us to know

May Thy kingdom holy on earth be the same:
That humble compassion which pardons each foe;

O give to us daily our portion of bread;
Keep us from temptation, from evil and sin,

It is from Thy bounty that all must be fed.
And Thine be the glory, forever! Amen! Amen.

The Hem of His Garment

10.6.10.6.with Refrain

George F. Root, 1820-1895

George F. Root, 1820-1895

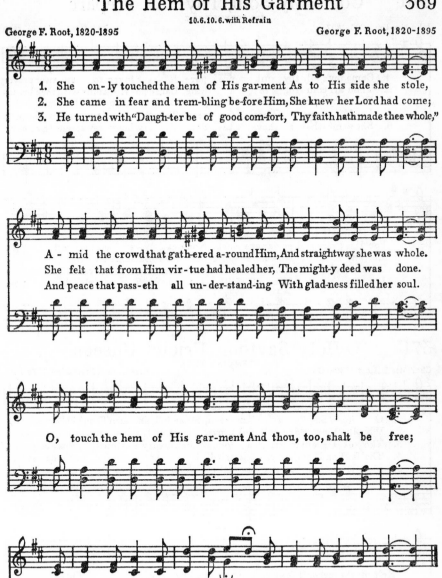

1. She on-ly touched the hem of His gar-ment As to His side she stole,
2. She came in fear and trem-bling be-fore Him, She knew her Lord had come;
3. He turned with "Daugh-ter be of good com-fort, Thy faith hath made thee whole,"

A - mid the crowd that gath-ered a-round Him, And straightway she was whole.
She felt that from Him vir-tue had healed her, The might-y deed was done.
And peace that pass-eth all un-der-stand-ing With glad-ness filled her soul.

O, touch the hem of His gar-ment And thou, too, shalt be free;

His sav-ing power this ve-ry hour Shall give new life to thee.

370   Come, My Soul, Thy Suit Prepare
INNOCENTS 7.7.7.7.

John Newton, 725-1807   *The Parish Choir, 1850*

1. Come, my soul, thy suit pre - pare, Je - sus loves to an - swer prayer;
2. Thou art com - ing to a King, Large pe - ti - tions with thee bring;
3. With my bur - den I be - gin: Lord, re - move this load of sin!
4. Lord, I come to Thee for rest; Take pos - ses - sion of my breast;
5. Show me what I have to do; Ev - ery hour my strength re - new;

He Him - self has bid thee pray, There - fore will not say thee nay.
For His grace and power are such, None can ev - er ask too much.
Let Thy blood, for sin - ners spilt, Set my con - science free from guilt.
There, Thy blood-bought right maintain, And with - out a ri - val reign.
Let me live a life of faith, Let me die Thy peo - ple's death. A - men.

371   O Holy Saviour, Friend Unseen
FLEMMING 8.8.8.6.

Charlotte Elliott, 1789-1871   Friedrich F. Flemming, 1778-1813

1. O ho - ly Sav - iour, friend un - seen, Since on Thine arm Thou bidd'st me lean,
2. What tho' the world de - ceit - ful prove, And earth - ly friends and hopes re - move;
3. Tho' oft I seem to tread a - lone Life's dreary waste with thorns o'er-grown,
4. Tho' faith and hope are of - ten tried, I ask not, need not, aught be - side;
5. Blest is my lot, what - e'er be - fall; What can dis - turb me, who ap - pall,

Help me throughout life's chang - ing scene, By faith to cling to Thee.
With pa - tient, un - com - plain - ing love, Still would I cling to Thee.
Thy voice of love in gen - tlest tone, Still whispers, "Cling to Me!"
So safe, so calm, so sat - is - fied, The soul that clings to Thee.
While as my strength, my rock, my all, Sav - iour, I cling to Thee? A - men.

I Stand Amazed in the Presence   372

MY SAVIOUR'S LOVE 8.7.8.7. with Refrain

Charles H. Gabriel, 1856-1932   Charles H. Gabriel, 1856-1932

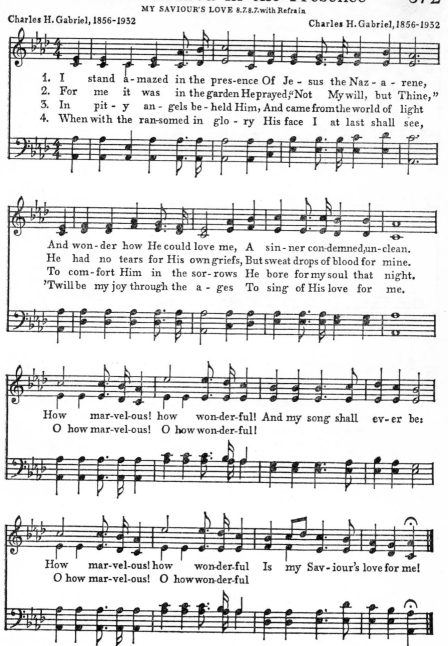

1. I stand a-mazed in the pres-ence Of Je - sus the Naz - a - rene,
2. For me it was in the garden He prayed, "Not My will, but Thine,"
3. In pit - y an - gels be - held Him, And came from the world of light
4. When with the ran-somed in glo - ry His face I at last shall see,

And won-der how He could love me, A sin - ner con-demned, un-clean.
He had no tears for His own griefs, But sweat drops of blood for mine.
To com-fort Him in the sor-rows He bore for my soul that night.
'Twill be my joy through the a - ges To sing of His love for me.

How mar-vel-ous! how won-der-ful! And my song shall ev-er be:
O how mar-vel-ous! O how won-der-ful!

How mar-vel-ous! how won-der-ful Is my Sav-iour's love for me!
O how mar-vel-ous! O how won-der-ful

373 I've Found a Friend

FRIEND 8.7.8.7. D.

James G. Small, 1817-1888

George C. Stebbins, 1846-1945

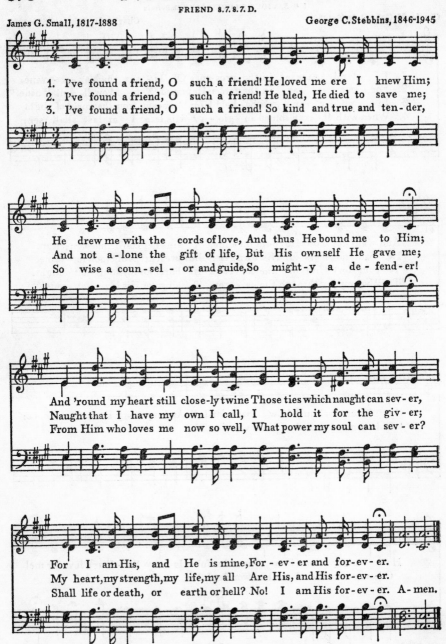

1. I've found a friend, O such a friend! He loved me ere I knew Him;
He drew me with the cords of love, And thus He bound me to Him;
And 'round my heart still close-ly twine Those ties which naught can sev-er,
For I am His, and He is mine, For-ev-er and for-ev-er.

2. I've found a friend, O such a friend! He bled, He died to save me;
And not a-lone the gift of life, But His own self He gave me;
Naught that I have my own I call, I hold it for the giv-er;
My heart, my strength, my life, my all Are His, and His for-ev-er.

3. I've found a friend, O such a friend! So kind and true and ten-der,
So wise a coun-sel-or and guide, So might-y a de-fend-er!
From Him who loves me now so well, What power my soul can sev-er?
Shall life or death, or earth or hell? No! I am His for-ev-er. A-men.

Christ Has for Sin Atonement Made 374

BENTON HARBOR 8.7.8.7. with Refrain

Elisha A. Hoffman, 1859-1929

Elisha A. Hoffman, 1859-1929

1. Christ has for sin a-tone-ment made, What a won-der-ful Sav-iour!
2. I praise Him for the cleans-ing blood, What a won-der-ful Sav-iour!
3. He cleansed my heart from all its sin, What a won-der-ful Sav-iour!
4. He gives me o-ver-com-ing power, What a won-der-ful Sav-iour!

We are re-deemed! the price is paid; What a won-der-ful Sav-iour!
That rec-on-ciled my soul to God; What a won-der-ful Sav-iour!
And now He reigns and rules there-in; What a won-der-ful Sav-iour!
And tri-umph in each try-ing hour; What a won-der-ful Sav-iour!

What a won-der-ful Sav-iour Is Je-sus, my Je-sus!

What a won-der-ful Sav-iour Is Je-sus, my Lord!

375 O Love That Wilt Not Let Me Go

ST. MARGARET 8.8.8.8.6.

George Matheson, 1842-1906

Albert L. Peace, 1844-1912

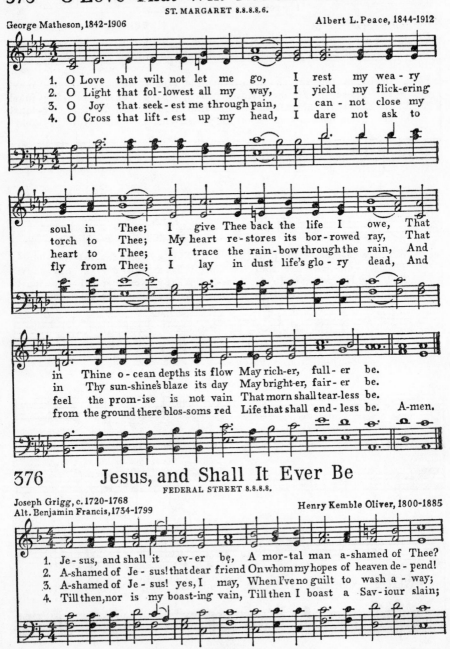

1. O Love that wilt not let me go, I rest my wea-ry
2. O Light that fol-lowest all my way, I yield my flick-ering
3. O Joy that seek-est me through pain, I can-not close my
4. O Cross that lift-est up my head, I dare not ask to

soul in Thee; I give Thee back the life I owe, That
torch to Thee; My heart re-stores its bor-rowed ray, That
heart to Thee; I trace the rain-bow through the rain, And
fly from Thee; I lay in dust life's glo-ry dead, And

in Thine o-cean depths its flow May rich-er, full-er be.
in Thy sun-shine's blaze its day May bright-er, fair-er be.
feel the prom-ise is not vain That morn shall tear-less be.
from the ground there blos-soms red Life that shall end-less be. A-men.

376 Jesus, and Shall It Ever Be

FEDERAL STREET 8.8.8.8.

Joseph Grigg, c. 1720-1768
Alt. Benjamin Francis, 1734-1799

Henry Kemble Oliver, 1800-1885

1. Je-sus, and shall it ev-er be, A mor-tal man a-shamed of Thee?
2. A-shamed of Je-sus! that dear friend On whom my hopes of heaven de-pend!
3. A-shamed of Je-sus! yes, I may, When I've no guilt to wash a-way;
4. Till then, nor is my boast-ing vain, Till then I boast a Sav-iour slain;

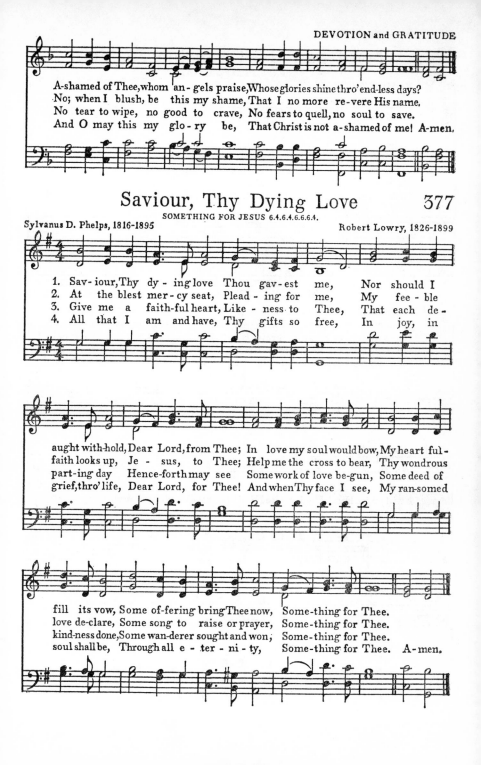

A-shamed of Thee, whom an-gels praise, Whose glories shine thro' end-less days?
No; when I blush, be this my shame, That I no more re-vere His name.
No tear to wipe, no good to crave, No fears to quell, no soul to save.
And O may this my glo-ry be, That Christ is not a-shamed of me! A-men.

Saviour, Thy Dying Love 377

SOMETHING FOR JESUS 6.4.6.4.6.6.6.4.

Sylvanus D. Phelps, 1816-1895

Robert Lowry, 1826-1899

1. Sav-iour, Thy dy-ing love Thou gav-est me, Nor should I
2. At the blest mer-cy seat, Plead-ing for me, My fee-ble
3. Give me a faith-ful heart, Like-ness to Thee, That each de-
4. All that I am and have, Thy gifts so free, In joy, in

aught with-hold, Dear Lord, from Thee; In love my soul would bow, My heart ful-
faith looks up, Je-sus, to Thee; Help me the cross to bear, Thy wondrous
part-ing day Hence-forth may see Some work of love be-gun, Some deed of
grief, thro' life, Dear Lord, for Thee! And when Thy face I see, My ran-somed

fill its vow, Some of-fering bring Thee now, Some-thing for Thee.
love de-clare, Some song to raise or prayer, Some-thing for Thee.
kind-ness done, Some wan-derer sought and won; Some-thing for Thee.
soul shall be, Through all e-ter-ni-ty, Some-thing for Thee. A-men.

378 When I Saw the Cleansing Fountain

HARRIS 8.7.8.7. with Refrain

Mrs. M. J. Harris   Mrs. M. J. Harris

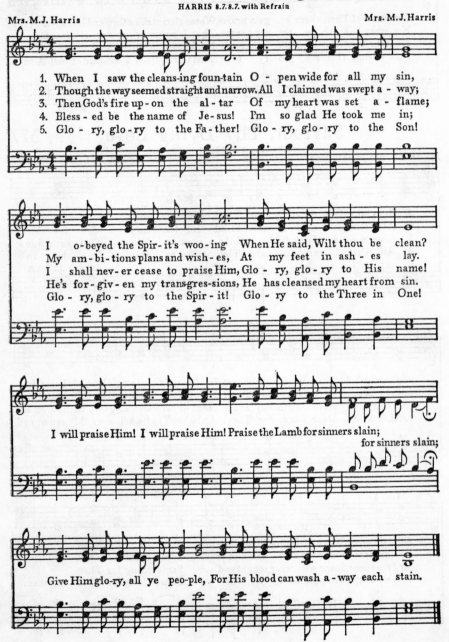

1. When I saw the cleans-ing foun-tain O - pen wide for all my sin,
2. Though the way seemed straight and narrow, All I claimed was swept a - way;
3. Then God's fire up-on the al - tar Of my heart was set a - flame;
4. Bless - ed be the name of Je - sus! I'm so glad He took me in;
5. Glo - ry, glo - ry to the Fa - ther! Glo - ry, glo - ry to the Son!

I o-beyed the Spir-it's woo-ing When He said, Wilt thou be clean?
My am - bi - tions plans and wish - es, At my feet in ash - es lay.
I shall nev - er cease to praise Him, Glo - ry, glo - ry to His name!
He's for - giv - en my trans-gres-sions, He has cleansed my heart from sin.
Glo - ry, glo - ry to the Spir - it! Glo - ry to the Three in One!

I will praise Him! I will praise Him! Praise the Lamb for sinners slain;

for sinners slain;

Give Him glo-ry, all ye peo-ple, For His blood can wash a - way each stain.

There Is a Place of Quiet Rest

McAFEE 8.6.8.6. with Refrain

Cleland B. McAfee, 1866-1944

Cleland B. McAfee, 1866-1944

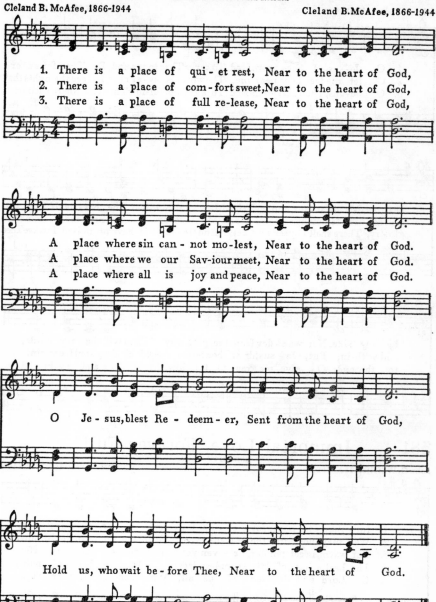

1. There is a place of qui-et rest, Near to the heart of God,
2. There is a place of com-fort sweet, Near to the heart of God,
3. There is a place of full re-lease, Near to the heart of God,

A place where sin can-not mo-lest, Near to the heart of God.
A place where we our Sav-iour meet, Near to the heart of God.
A place where all is joy and peace, Near to the heart of God.

O Je-sus, blest Re-deem-er, Sent from the heart of God,

Hold us, who wait be-fore Thee, Near to the heart of God.

380   O Jesus, I Have Promised

ANGEL'S STORY 7.6.7.6.D.

John E. Bode, 1816-1874   Arthur H. Mann, 1850-1929

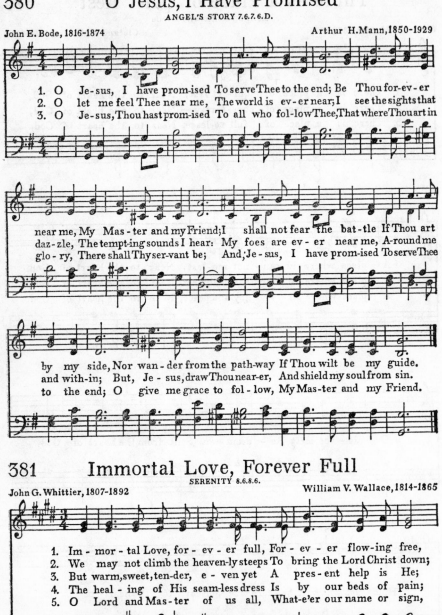

1. O Je-sus, I have prom-ised To serve Thee to the end; Be Thou for-ev-er
2. O let me feel Thee near me, The world is ev-er near; I see the sights that
3. O Je-sus, Thou hast prom-ised To all who fol-low Thee, That where Thou art in

near me, My Mas-ter and my Friend; I shall not fear the bat-tle If Thou art
daz-zle, The tempt-ing sounds I hear: My foes are ev-er near me, A-round me
glo-ry, There shall Thy ser-vant be; And, Je-sus, I have prom-ised To serve Thee

by my side, Nor wan-der from the path-way If Thou wilt be my guide.
and with-in; But, Je-sus, draw Thou near-er, And shield my soul from sin.
to the end; O give me grace to fol-low, My Mas-ter and my Friend.

381   Immortal Love, Forever Full

SERENITY 8.6.8.6.

John G. Whittier, 1807-1892   William V. Wallace, 1814-1865

1. Im-mor-tal Love, for-ev-er full, For-ev-er flow-ing free,
2. We may not climb the heaven-ly steeps To bring the Lord Christ down;
3. But warm, sweet, ten-der, e-ven yet A pres-ent help is He;
4. The heal-ing of His seam-less dress Is by our beds of pain;
5. O Lord and Mas-ter of us all, What-e'er our name or sign,

For - ev - er shared, for - ev - er whole, A nev - er - ebb - ing sea!
In vain we search the low-est deeps, For Him no depths can drown;
And faith has still its Ol - i - vet, And love its Gal - i - lee.
We touch Him in life's throng and press, And we are whole a - gain.
We own Thy sway, we hear Thy call, We test our lives by Thine. A - men.

My Jesus, I Love Thee 382

GORDON 11.11.11.11.

William R. Featherstone, 1842-1878

Adoniram J. Gordon, 1836-1895

1. My Je - sus, I love Thee, I know Thou art mine, For Thee all the
2. I love Thee be - cause Thou hast first lov - ed me, And pur-chased my
3. I will love Thee in life, I will love Thee in death, And praise Thee as
4. In man-sions of glo - ry and end-less de - light, I'll ev - er a -

fol - lies of sin I re - sign; My gra - cious Re - deem - er, my
par - don on Cal - va - ry's tree; I love Thee for wear - ing the
long as Thou lend-est me breath, And say, when the death-dew lies
dore Thee in heav - en so bright; I'll sing with the glit - ter-ing

Sav - iour art Thou; If ev - er I loved Thee, my Je - sus, 'tis now!
thorns on Thy brow; If ev - er I loved Thee, my Je - sus, 'tis now!
cold on my brow: If ev - er I loved Thee, my Je - sus, 'tis now!
crown on my brow: If ev - er I loved Thee, my Je - sus, 'tis now!

383 I Know I Love Thee Better, Lord

8.6.8.6. with Refrain

Frances R. Havergal, 1836-1879 Ralph E.Hudson, 1843-1901

1. I know I love Thee bet-ter, Lord, Than an-y earth-ly joy,
2. I know that Thou art near-er still Than an-y earth-ly throng,
3. Thou hast put glad-ness in my heart, Then well may I be glad;
4. O Sav-iour, pre-cious Sav-iour,mine! What will Thy pres-ence be

For Thou hast giv-en me the peace Which noth-ing can de-stroy.
And sweet-er is the thought of Thee Than an-y love-ly song.
With-out the se-cret of Thy love I could not but be sad.
If such a life of joy can crown Our walk on earth with Thee?

The half has nev-er yet been told, Of love so full and free;

The half has nev-er yet been told, The blood—it cleans-eth me.

Only in Thee, O Saviour Mine

Irregular

Thomas O. Chisholm, 1866- Charles H. Gabriel, 1856-1932

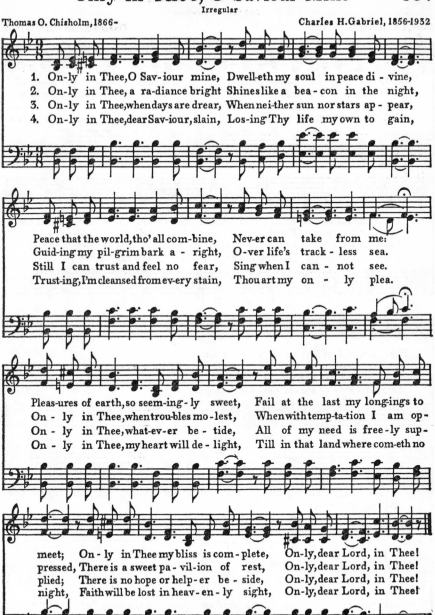

1. On-ly in Thee, O Sav-iour mine, Dwell-eth my soul in peace di-vine,
Peace that the world, tho' all com-bine, Nev-er can take from me:
Pleas-ures of earth, so seem-ing-ly sweet, Fail at the last my long-ings to
meet; On-ly in Thee my bliss is com-plete, On-ly, dear Lord, in Thee!

2. On-ly in Thee, a ra-diance bright Shines like a bea-con in the night,
Guid-ing my pil-grim bark a-right, O-ver life's track-less sea.
On-ly in Thee, when trou-bles mo-lest, When with temp-ta-tion I am op-
pressed, There is a sweet pa-vil-ion of rest, On-ly, dear Lord, in Thee!

3. On-ly in Thee, when days are drear, When nei-ther sun nor stars ap-pear,
Still I can trust and feel no fear, Sing when I can-not see.
On-ly in Thee, what-ev-er be-tide, All of my need is free-ly sup-
plied; There is no hope or help-er be-side, On-ly, dear Lord, in Thee!

4. On-ly in Thee, dear Sav-iour, slain, Los-ing Thy life my own to gain,
Trust-ing, I'm cleansed from ev-ery stain, Thou art my on-ly plea.
On-ly in Thee, my heart will de-light, Till in that land where com-eth no
night, Faith will be lost in heav-en-ly sight, On-ly, dear Lord, in Thee!

385 The Old Rugged Cross

12.8.12.9. with Refrain

George Bennard, 1873-1958

George Bennard, 1873-1958

1. On a hill far a-way stood an old rug-ged cross, The em-blem of
2. O the old rug-ged cross, so de-spised by the world, Has a won-drous at-
3. In the old rug-ged cross, stained with blood so di-vine, A won-drous
4. To the old rug-ged cross I will ev-er be true, Its shame and re-

suf-fering and shame; And I love that old cross, where the dear-est and best
trac-tion for me; For the dear Lamb of God left His glo-ry a-bove
beau-ty I see; For 'twas on that old cross Je-sus suf-fered and died
proach glad-ly bear; Then He'll call me some day to my home far a-way,

For a world of lost sin-ners was slain.
To bear it to dark Cal-va-ry.
To par-don and sanc-ti-fy me.
Where His glo-ry for-ev-er I'll share.

So I'll cher-ish the old rug-ged

cross, _____ Till my tro-phies at last I lay down; I will cling to the
old rug-ged cross,

old rug-ged cross _____ And ex-change it some day for a crown.
cross, the old rug-ged cross,

O the Unsearchable Riches

UNSEARCHABLE RICHES 10.7.10.7. with Refrain

Fanny J. Crosby, 1820-1915

John R. Sweney, 1837-1899

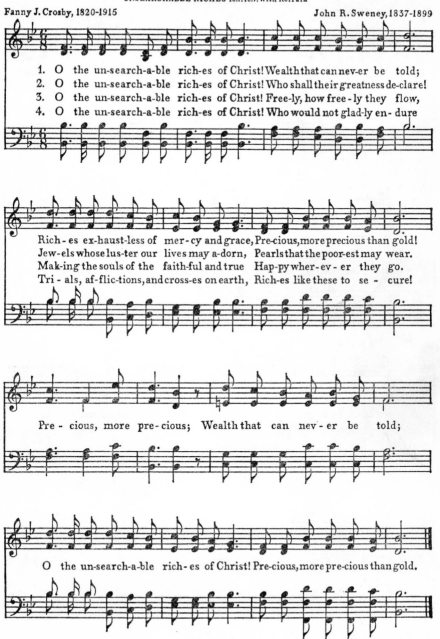

1. O the un-search-a-ble rich-es of Christ! Wealth that can nev-er be told;
2. O the un-search-a-ble rich-es of Christ! Who shall their greatness de-clare!
3. O the un-search-a-ble rich-es of Christ! Free-ly, how free-ly they flow,
4. O the un-search-a-ble rich-es of Christ! Who would not glad-ly en-dure

Rich-es ex-haust-less of mer-cy and grace, Pre-cious, more precious than gold!
Jew-els whose lus-ter our lives may a-dorn, Pearls that the poor-est may wear.
Mak-ing the souls of the faith-ful and true Hap-py wher-ev-er they go.
Tri-als, af-flic-tions, and cross-es on earth, Rich-es like these to se-cure!

Pre-cious, more pre-cious; Wealth that can nev-er be told;

O the un-search-a-ble rich-es of Christ! Pre-cious, more pre-cious than gold.

387 Down from His Splendor in Glory

ROTH 10.6.10.6. with Refrain

Elton M. Roth, 1891-1951   Elton M. Roth, 1891-1951

1. Down from His splen-dor in glo-ry He came, In-to a world of woe;
2. I am un-worth-y to take of His grace, Won-der-ful grace so free;
3. He is the fair-est of thou-sands to me, His love is sweet and true;

Took on Him-self all my guilt and my shame, Why should He love me so?
Yet Je-sus suf-fered and died in my place, E'en for a soul like me.
Won-der-ful beau-ty in Him I now see, More than I ev-er knew.

How can I help but love Him, When He loved me so?

How can I help but love Him, When He loved me so?

Such Love

388

8.10.10.8. with Refrain

C. Bishop

Robert Harkness, 1880-

1. That God should love a sin-ner such as I, Should yearn to change my
2. That Christ should join so free-ly in the scheme, Al - though it meant His
3. That for a wil - ful out-cast such as I The. Fa - ther planned, the
4. And now He takes me to His heart—a son; He asks me not to

sor-row in-to bliss, Nor rest till He had planned to bring me nigh,
death on Cal-va - ry— Did ev - er hu-man tongue find no-bler theme
Sav-iour bled and died, Re - demp-tion for a worth-less slave to buy,
fill a ser-vant's place; The "far - off coun-try" wan-der-ings all are done—

How won - der-ful is love like this!
Than love di - vine that ran-somed me? Such love,_____ such
Who long had law and grace de - fied! Such love,
Wide o - pen are His arms of grace! Such love,

won-drous love! Such love,_____ such won-drous love! That God should
Such love,

love a sin-ner such as I, How won-der-ful is love like this!

389 Master, No Offering Costly and Sweet

LOVE'S OFFERING 6. 4. 6. 4. 6. 6. 4.

Edwin P. Parker, 1836-1925

Edwin P. Parker, 1836-1925

1. Mas-ter, no of-fer-ing Cost-ly and sweet May we, like Mag-da-lene,
2. Dai-ly our lives would show Weak-ness made strong, Toil-some and gloom-y ways
3. Some word of hope for hearts Bur-dened with fears, Some balm of peace for eyes
4. Thus in Thy serv-ice, Lord, Till e-ven-tide Clos-es the day of life,

Lay at Thy feet; Yet may love's in-cense rise, Sweet-er than sac - ri-fice,
Bright-ened with song; Some deeds of kind-ness done, Some souls by pa-tience won,
Blind-ed with tears, Some dews of mer-cy shed, Some way-ward foot-steps led,
May we a - bide. And when earth's la-bors cease, Let us de-part in peace,

Dear Lord, to Thee, Dear Lord, to Thee. A - men.

390 Speak, Lord, in the Stillness

6. 5. 6. 5.

E. May Grimes, 1868-1927

Alfred B. Smith

1. Speak, Lord, in the still - ness, While I wait on Thee;
2. Speak, O bless - ed Mas - ter, In this qui - et hour,
3. For the words Thou speak - est, They are life in - deed;
4. Fill me with the knowl - edge Of Thy glo - rious will;
5. Like a wa - tered gar - den Full of fra - grance rare,

Hushed my heart to lis-ten In ex-pect-an-cy.
Let me see Thy face, Lord, Feel Thy touch of power.
Liv-ing Bread from heav-en, Now my spir-it feed!
All Thine own good pleas-ure In Thy child ful-fill.
Lin-gering in Thy pres-ence, Let my life ap-pear. A-men.

I Sought the Lord

391

PEACE 10.10.10.6.

Unknown, c.1904

George W. Chadwick, 1854-1931

1. I sought the Lord, and af-ter-ward I knew He moved my
2. Thou didst reach forth Thy hand and mine en-fold; I walked and
3. I find, I walk, I love, but O the whole Of love is

soul to seek Him, seek-ing me; It was not I that
sank not on the storm-vexed sea; 'Twas not so much that
but my an-swer, Lord, to Thee! For Thou wert long be-

found, O Sav-iour true: No, I was found of Thee.
I on Thee took hold, As Thou, dear Lord, on me.
fore-hand with my soul: Al-ways Thou lov-edst me. A-men.

392 For What the Saviour Did for Me

PRAISE HIM MORE 8.8.8.6.with Refrain

Blanche Clapper

J. E. Delmarter

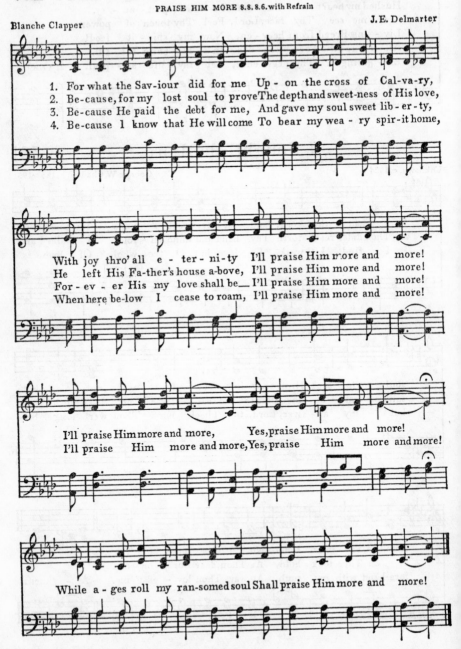

1. For what the Sav-iour did for me Up-on the cross of Cal-va-ry,
2. Be-cause, for my lost soul to prove The depth and sweet-ness of His love,
3. Be-cause He paid the debt for me, And gave my soul sweet lib-er-ty,
4. Be-cause I know that He will come To bear my wea-ry spir-it home,

With joy thro' all e-ter-ni-ty I'll praise Him more and more!
He left His Fa-ther's house a-bove, I'll praise Him more and more!
For-ev-er His my love shall be— I'll praise Him more and more!
When here be-low I cease to roam, I'll praise Him more and more!

I'll praise Him more and more, Yes, praise Him more and more!

While a-ges roll my ran-somed soul Shall praise Him more and more!

He Died for Me

393

ON A TREE 8.6.8.6. with Refrain

John Newton, 1725-1807

Edwin O. Excell, 1851-1921

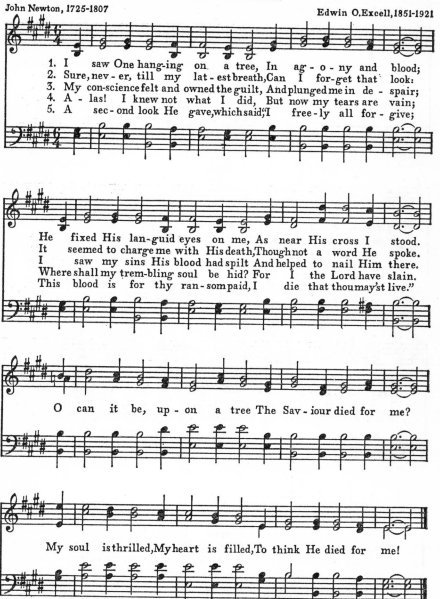

1. I saw One hang-ing on a tree, In ag-o-ny and blood;
2. Sure, nev-er, till my lat-est breath, Can I for-get that look:
3. My con-science felt and owned the guilt, And plunged me in de-spair;
4. A-las! I knew not what I did, But now my tears are vain;
5. A sec-ond look He gave, which said, "I free-ly all for-give;

He fixed His lan-guid eyes on me, As near His cross I stood.
It seemed to charge me with His death, Though not a word He spoke.
I saw my sins His blood had spilt And helped to nail Him there.
Where shall my trem-bling soul be hid? For I the Lord have slain.
This blood is for thy ran-som paid, I die that thou may'st live."

O can it be, up-on a tree The Sav-iour died for me?

My soul is thrilled, My heart is filled, To think He died for me!

394 Loved with Everlasting Love

EVERLASTING LOVE 7.7.7.7.D.

George Wade Robinson, 1838-1877

James Mountain, 1843-1933

1. Loved with ev-er-last-ing love, Led by grace that love to know;
2. Heaven a-bove is soft-er blue, Earth a-round is sweet-er green!
3. Things that once were wild a-larms Can-not now dis-turb my rest;
4. His for-ev-er, on-ly His; Who the Lord and me shall part?

Spir-it, breath-ing from a-bove, Thou hast taught me it is so!
Some-thing lives in ev-ery hue Christ-less eyes have nev-er seen:
Closed in ev-er-last-ing arms, Pil-lowed on the lov-ing breast.
Ah, with what a rest of bliss Christ can fill the lov-ing heart!

O this full and per-fect peace! O this trans-port all di-vine!
Birds with glad-der songs o'er-flow, Flowers with deep-er beau-ties shine,
O to lie for-ev-er here, Doubt, and care, and self re-sign,
Heaven and earth may fade and flee, First-born light in gloom de-cline;

In a love which can-not cease, I am His, and He is mine.
Since I know, as now I know, I am His, and He is mine.
While He whis-pers in my ear, I am His, and He is mine.
But while God and I shall be, I am His, and He is mine.

I Am Not Skilled to Understand 395

8.8.8.7.

Dora Greenwell, 1821-1882

William J. Kirkpatrick, 1838-1921

1. I am not skilled to un-der-stand What God hath willed, what God hath planned,
2. I take Him at His word in-deed: "Christ died for sin-ners," this I read;
3. That He should leave His place on high And come for sin - ful man to die,
4. And O that He ful-filled may see The tra-vail of His soul in me,
5. Yes, liv-ing, dy-ing, let me bring My strength, my sol-ace from this spring;

I on-ly know at His right hand Is one who is my Sav-iour!
For in my heart I find a need Of Him to be my Sav-iour!
You count it strange? so once did I, Be-fore I knew my Sav-iour!
And with His work con-tent-ed be, As I with my dear Sav-iour!
That He who lives to be my King Once died to be my Sav-iour! A-men.

How Gentle God's Commands 396

DENNIS 6.6.8.6.

Philip Doddridge, 1702-1751

Hans G. Nägeli, 1773-1836
Arr. by Lowell Mason, 1792-1872

1. How gen - tle God's com-mands! How kind His pre - cepts are!
2. Be - neath His watch-ful eye His saints se - cure-ly dwell;
3. Why should this anx - ious load Press down your wea - ry mind?
4. His good-ness stands ap-proved, Un - changed from day to day;

Come, cast your bur-dens on the Lord, And trust His con-stant care.
That hand which bears all na-ture up Shall guard His chil-dren well.
Haste to your heaven-ly Fa-ther's throne, And sweet re-fresh-ment find.
I'll drop my bur - den at His feet, And bear a song a-way. A-men.

397 In the Rifted Rock

SWEETLY RESTING 8.7.8.7. with Refrain

Mary D. James

W. Warren Bentley

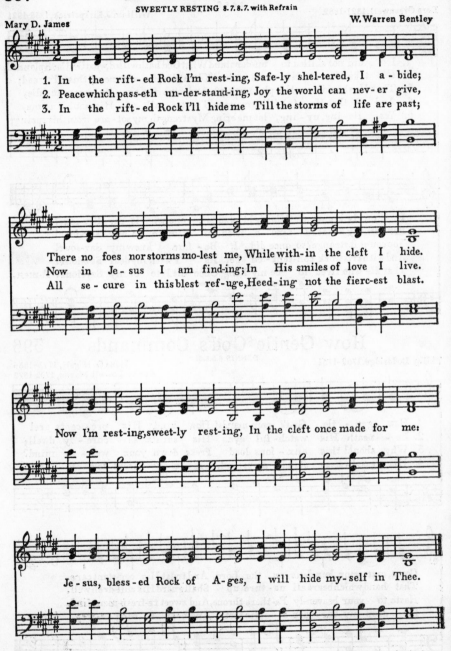

1. In the rift-ed Rock I'm rest-ing, Safe-ly shel-tered, I a-bide;
2. Peace which pass-eth un-der-stand-ing, Joy the world can nev-er give,
3. In the rift-ed Rock I'll hide me Till the storms of life are past;

There no foes nor storms mo-lest me, While with-in the cleft I hide.
Now in Je-sus I am find-ing; In His smiles of love I live.
All se-cure in this blest ref-uge, Heed-ing not the fierc-est blast.

Now I'm rest-ing, sweet-ly rest-ing, In the cleft once made for me:

Je-sus, bless-ed Rock of A-ges, I will hide my-self in Thee.

Dying with Jesus

398

MOMENT 10.10.10.10. with Refrain

Daniel W. Whittle, 1840-1901

May Whittle Moody, b. 1870

1. Dy-ing with Je-sus, by death reck-oned mine, Liv-ing with Je-sus, a
2. Nev-er a tri-al that He is not there, Nev-er a bur-den that
3. Nev-er a weak-ness that He doth not feel, Nev-er a sick-ness that

new life di-vine, Look-ing to Je-sus till glo-ry doth shine, Mo-ment by
He doth not bear, Nev-er a sor-row that He doth not share, Mo-ment by
He can-not heal; Mo-ment by mo-ment, in woe or in weal, Je-sus, my

mo-ment, O Lord, I am Thine.
mo-ment I'm un-der His care. Mo-ment by mo-ment I'm kept in His love;
Sav-iour, a-bides with me still.

Mo-ment by mo-ment I've life from a-bove; Look-ing to Je-sus till

glo-ry doth shine; Mo-ment by mo-ment, O Lord, I am Thine.

399 Anywhere with Jesus

TOWNER 11.11.11.11. with Refrain

Jessie B. Pounds, 1861-1921

Daniel B. Towner, 1850-1919

1. An-y-where with Je-sus I can safe-ly go, An-y-where He
2. An-y-where with Je-sus I am not a-lone: Oth-er friends may
3. An-y-where with Je-sus o-ver land or sea, Tell-ing souls in

leads me in this world be-low; An-y-where with-out Him dear-est
fail me, He is still my own; Though His hand may lead me o-ver
dark-ness of sal-va-tion free; Read-y as He sum-mons me to

joys would fade; An-y-where with Je-sus I am not a-fraid.
drear-y ways, An-y-where with Je-sus is a house of praise.
go or stay, An-y-where with Je-sus when He points the way.

An-y-where! an-y-where! Fear I can-not know;

An-y-where with Je-sus I can safe-ly go.

Simply Trusting Every Day

TRUSTING JESUS 7. 7. 7. 7. with Refrain

Edgar Page Stites, 1836-1921

Ira D. Sankey, 1840-1908

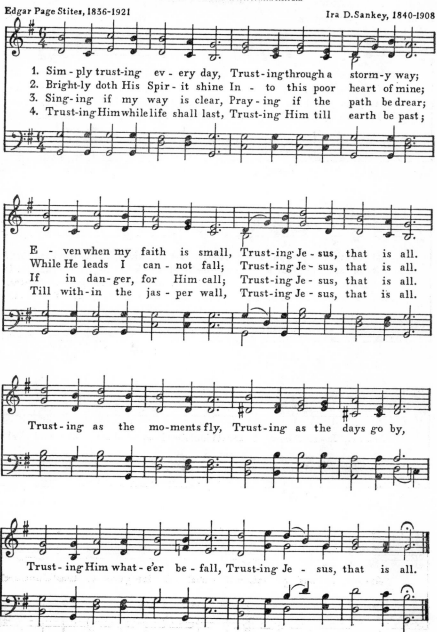

1. Sim - ply trust-ing ev - ery day, Trust-ing through a storm-y way;
2. Bright-ly doth His Spir - it shine In - to this poor heart of mine;
3. Sing-ing if my way is clear, Pray-ing if the path be drear;
4. Trust-ing Him while life shall last, Trust-ing Him till earth be past;

E - ven when my faith is small, Trust-ing Je - sus, that is all.
While He leads I can - not fall; Trust-ing Je - sus, that is all.
If in dan-ger, for Him call; Trust-ing Je - sus, that is all.
Till with-in the jas - per wall, Trust-ing Je - sus, that is all.

Trust-ing as the mo-ments fly, Trust-ing as the days go by,

Trust-ing Him what-e'er be-fall, Trust-ing Je - sus, that is all.

401 'Tis So Sweet to Trust in Jesus

TRUSTING 8.7.8.7. with Refrain

Louisa M.R. Stead, 19th century

William J. Kirkpatrick, 1838-1921

1. 'Tis so sweet to trust in Je-sus, Just to take Him at His word;
2. O how sweet to trust in Je-sus, Just to trust His cleans-ing blood;
3. Yes, 'tis sweet to trust in Je-sus, Just from sin and self to cease;
4. I'm so glad I learned to trust Thee, Pre-cious Je-sus, Sav-iour, Friend;

Just to rest up - on His prom-ise; Just to know, "Thus saith the Lord."
Just in sim - ple faith to plunge me 'Neath the heal - ing, cleans-ing flood!
Just from Je - sus sim-ply tak-ing Life and rest, and joy and peace.
And I know that Thou art with me, Wilt be with me to the end.

Je - sus, Je - sus, how I trust Him! How I've proved Him o'er and o'er!

Je - sus, Je - sus, pre - cious Je - sus! O for grace to trust Him more!

My Jesus, As Thou Wilt

JEWETT 6.6.6.6.D.

Benjamin Schmolck, 1672-1737
Tr. by Jane L. Borthwick, 1813-1897

Carl Maria von Weber, 1786-1826

1. My Je - sus, as Thou wilt! O may Thy will be mine!
2. My Je - sus, as Thou wilt! Though seen through many a tear,
3. My Je - sus, as Thou wilt! All shall be well for me;

In - to Thy hand of love I would my all re - sign;
Let not my star of hope Grow dim or dis - ap - pear;
Each chang-ing fu - ture scene I glad - ly trust with Thee;

Through sor - row or through joy, Con - duct me as Thine own,
Since Thou on earth hast wept And sor - rowed oft a - lone,
Straight to my home a - bove I trav - el calm - ly on,

And help me still to say, "My Lord, Thy will be done."
If I must weep with Thee, My Lord, Thy will be done.
And sing, in life or death, "My Lord, Thy will be done." A-men.

403 I Can Hear My Saviour Calling

NORRIS 8.8.8.9.

E.W. Blandy, 19th century

John S. Norris, 1844-1907

1. I can hear my Sav - iour call - ing, I can
2. Where He leads me I will fol - low, Where He
3. I'll go with Him through the Gar - den, I'll go
4. He will give me grace and glo - ry, He will

hear my Sav - iour call - ing, I can hear my Sav - iour
leads me I will fol - low, Where He leads me I will
with Him through the Gar - den, I'll go with Him through the
give me grace and glo - ry, He will give me grace and

call - ing, "Take thy cross, and fol - low, fol - low me."
fol - low, I'll go with Him, with Him all the way.
Gar - den, I'll go with Him, with Him all the way.
glo - ry, And go with me, with me all the way.

404 Walk in the Light

MANOAH 8.6.8.6.

Bernard Barton, 1784-1849

Henry W. Greatorex's *Collection*, 1851

1. Walk in the light! so shalt Thou know That fel - low-ship of love
2. Walk in the light! and thou shalt find Thy heart made tru - ly His,
3. Walk in the light! and thou shalt own Thy dark-ness passed a - way,
4. Walk in the light! and thine shall be A path, though thorn-y, bright;

His Spir-it on-ly can be-stow, Who reigns in light a-bove.
Who dwells in cloud-less light en-shrined, In whom no dark-ness is.
Be-cause that light hath on Thee shone In which is per-fect day.
For God, by grace, shall dwell in thee, And God Him-self is light. A-men.

My Faith Looks Up to Thee 405

OLIVET 6.6.4.6.6.6.4.

Ray Palmer, 1808-1887

Lowell Mason, 1792-1872

1. My faith looks up to Thee, Thou Lamb of Cal-va-ry, Sav-iour di-
2. May Thy rich grace im-part Strength to my faint-ing heart, My zeal in-
3. While life's dark maze I tread, And griefs a-round me spread, Be Thou my
4. When ends life's transient dream, When death's cold, sul-len stream Shall o'er me

vine! Now hear me while I pray, Take all my guilt a-way,
spire; As Thou hast died for me, O may my love to Thee
guide; Bid dark-ness turn to day, Wipe sor-row's tears a-way,
roll, Blest Sav-iour, then in love, Fear and dis-trust re-move;

O let me from this day Be whol-ly Thine.
Pure, warm, and change-less be, A liv-ing fire.
Nor let me ev-er stray From Thee a-side.
O bear me safe a-bove, A ran-somed soul! A-men.

406 Judge Me, God of My Salvation

AMARA 8.7.8.7. with Refrain

Psalm 43 — William O. Perkins

1. Judge me, God of my sal-va-tion, Plead my cause, for Thee I trust;
2. On Thy strength a-lone re-ly-ing, Why am I cast off by Thee,
3. Light and truth, my way at-tend-ing, Send Thou forth to be my guide,
4. At Thy sa-cred al-tar bend-ing, God, my God, my bound-less joy,

Hear my ear-nest sup-pli-ca-tion, Save me from my foes un-just.
In my help-less sor-row sigh-ing, While the foe op-press-es me?
Till, Thy ho-ly mount as-cend-ing, I with-in Thy house a-bide.
Harp and voice, in wor-ship blending, For Thy praise will I em-ploy.

O my soul, why art thou griev-ing? What dis-qui-ets and dis-mays?

Hope in God; His help re-ceiv-ing, I shall yet my Sav-iour praise.

Teach Me to Be True

407

8.6.8.6. with Refrain

M. Victor Staley

Charles H. Gabriel, 1856-1932

1. Be with me, Lord, each pass - ing hour, And make me pure and true;
2. Thou seest, dear Lord, my path in life; 'Tis Thine to guide the way,
3. I would not ask to look be-yond The pres-ent hour, O Lord,
4. Full well I know Thou canst not err, So I will nev-er fear,

Teach me to ne'er re - fuse Thy call, What-e'er Thou bidd'st me do.
'Tis mine o - be - dience, Lord, to yield, And fol - low day by day.
E - nough for me to hold Thy hand, And take Thee at Thy word.
But, in the dark - est gloom of night, Still feel Thy pres-ence near.

Where - e'er Thou bidd'st me go, dear Lord, What-e'er Thou bidd'st me do,

Make me o - be-dient to Thy will, And teach me to be true.

408 Take the World, but Give Me Jesus

8.7.8.7. with Refrain

Fanny J. Crosby, 1820-1915

John R. Sweney, 1837-1899

1. Take the world, but give me Jesus: All its joys are but a name,
2. Take the world, but give me Jesus, Sweet-est com-fort of my soul:
3. Take the world, but give me Jesus, Let me view His con-stant smile;
4. Take the world, but give me Jesus; In His cross my trust shall be,

But His love a-bid-eth ev-er, Through e-ter-nal years the same.
With my Sav-iour watch-ing o'er me, I can sing though bil-lows roll.
Then throughout my pil-grim jour-ney Light will cheer me all the while.
Till, with clear-er, bright-er vi-sion, Face to face my Lord I see.

O the height and depth of mer-cy! O the length and breadth of love!

O the full-ness of re-demp-tion, Pledge of end-less life a-bove!

Where He May Lead Me, I Will Go   409

I REMEMBER CALVARY 8.8.8.8.with Refrain

W.C. Martin, 19th century

James M. Black, 1856-1938

1. Where He may lead me   I will go,   For I have learned to trust Him so,
2. O   I de-light in His command, Love to be   led by His dear hand;
3. On - ward I   go, no doubt nor fear, Hap-py with Christ, my Sav-iour, near,

And I re-mem-ber 'twas for me, That He was slain   on   Cal-va - ry.
His   di-vine will is sweet to   me, Hal-lowed by blood-stained Cal-va - ry.
Trust-ing that I some day shall see Je - sus, my friend on   Cal-va - ry.

Je-sus shall lead me night and day,   Je-sus shall lead me all the way;

He is the tru-est friend to   me, For I re-mem-ber Cal-va - ry.

410   I Am Trusting Thee, Lord Jesus

BULLINGER 8.5.8.3.

Frances R. Havergal, 1836-1879   Ethelbert W. Bullinger, 1837-1913

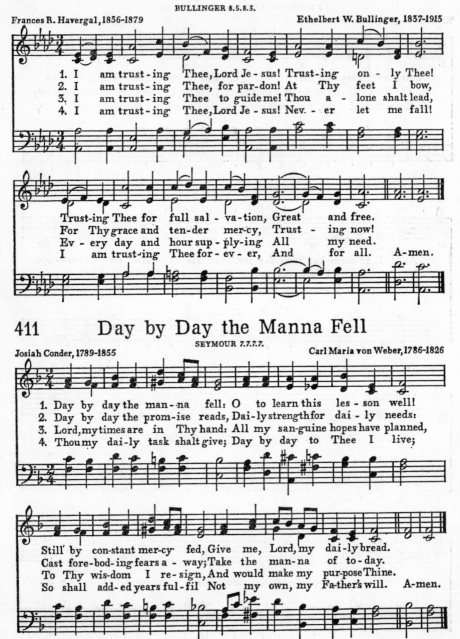

1. I am trust-ing Thee, Lord Je-sus! Trust-ing on-ly Thee!
2. I am trust-ing Thee, for par-don! At Thy feet I bow,
3. I am trust-ing Thee to guide me! Thou a-lone shalt lead,
4. I am trust-ing Thee, Lord Je-sus! Nev-er let me fall!

Trust-ing Thee for full sal-va-tion, Great and free.
For Thy grace and ten-der mer-cy, Trust-ing now!
Ev-ery day and hour sup-ply-ing All my need.
I am trust-ing Thee for-ev-er, And for all. A-men.

411   Day by Day the Manna Fell

SEYMOUR 7.7.7.7.

Josiah Conder, 1789-1855   Carl Maria von Weber, 1786-1826

1. Day by day the man-na fell: O to learn this les-son well!
2. Day by day the prom-ise reads, Dai-ly strength for dai-ly needs:
3. Lord, my times are in Thy hand: All my san-guine hopes have planned,
4. Thou my dai-ly task shalt give; Day by day to Thee I live;

Still' by con-stant mer-cy fed, Give me, Lord, my dai-ly bread.
Cast fore-bod-ing fears a-way; Take the man-na of to-day.
To Thy wis-dom I re-sign, And would make my pur-pose Thine.
So shall add-ed years ful-fil Not my own, my Fa-ther's will. A-men.

I Must Tell Jesus

ORWIGSBURG 10.9.10.9.with Refrain

Elisha A. Hoffman, 1859-1929

Elisha A. Hoffman, 1859-1929

1. I must tell Je-sus all of my tri - als; I can-not bear these bur-dens a-
2. I must tell Je-sus all of my trou-bles, He is a kind, com-pas-sion-ate
3. Tempt-ed and tried, I need a great Sav-iour, One who can help my bur-dens to

lone; In my dis-tress He kind - ly will help me, He ev - er
Friend; If I but ask Him, He will de - liv - er, Make of my
bear; I must tell Je - sus, I must tell Je - sus; He all my

loves and care for His own.
trou-bles quick-ly an end. I must tell Je - sus! I must tell
cares and sor - rows will share.

Je - sus! I can - not bear my bur-dens a - lone; I must tell

Je-sus! I must tell Je-sus! Je-sus can help me, Je-sus a - lone.

413 When We Walk with the Lord

TRUST and OBEY 6.6.9.D. with Refrain

John H. Sammis, 1846-1919

Daniel B. Towner, 1850-1919

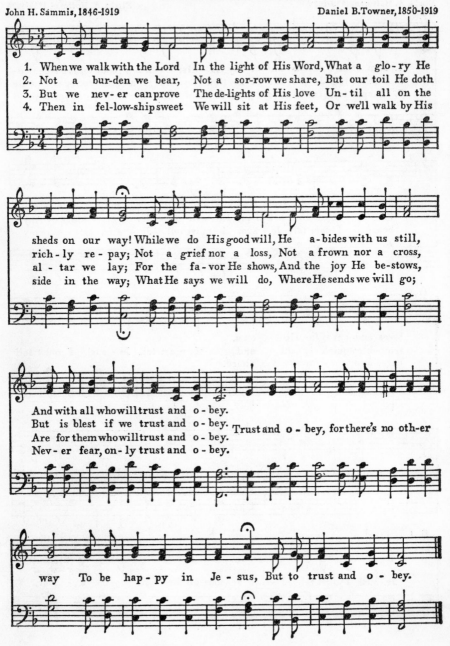

1. When we walk with the Lord In the light of His Word, What a glo-ry He sheds on our way! While we do His good will, He a-bides with us still, And with all who will trust and o-bey.

2. Not a bur-den we bear, Not a sor-row we share, But our toil He doth rich-ly re-pay; Not a grief nor a loss, Not a frown nor a cross, But is blest if we trust and o-bey.

3. But we nev-er can prove The de-lights of His love Un-til all on the al-tar we lay; For the fa-vor He shows, And the joy He be-stows, Are for them who will trust and o-bey.

4. Then in fel-low-ship sweet We will sit at His feet, Or we'll walk by His side in the way; What He says we will do, Where He sends we will go; Nev-er fear, on-ly trust and o-bey.

Trust and o-bey, for there's no oth-er way To be hap-py in Je-sus, But to trust and o-bey.

Dare to Be Brave

COURAGE Irregular with Refrain

W. J. Rooper

Duncan Hume

1. Dare to be brave, dare to be true, Strive for the right, for the
2. Dare to be brave, dare to be true, God is your Fa - ther, He
3. Dare to be brave, dare to be true, God grant you cour - age to

Lord is with you; Fight with sin brave - ly, fight and be strong;
watch - es o'er you; He knows your tri - als; when your heart quails,
car - ry you through; Try to help oth - ers, ev - er be kind,

Christ is your cap - tain, fear on - ly what's wrong.
Call Him to res - cue, His grace nev - er fails. Fight then, good sol - diers,
Let the op - pressed a strong friend in you find.

fight and be brave; Christ is your cap - tain, might - y to save.

415 Stand Up, Stand Up for Jesus

WEBB 7.6.7.6.D.

George Duffield, Jr., 1818-1888

George J. Webb. 1803-1887

1. Stand up, stand up for Je - sus! Ye sol - diers of the cross;
2. Stand up, stand up for Je - sus! The trump-et call o - bey;
3. Stand up, stand up for Je - sus! Stand in His strength a - lone;
4. Stand up, stand up for Je - sus! The strife will not be long;

Lift high His roy - al ban - ner, It must not suf - fer loss;
Forth to the might-y con - flict In this His glo - rious day.
The arm of flesh will fail you: Ye dare not trust your own;
This day the noise of bat - tle, The next the vic - tor's song:

From vic - tory un - to vic - tory His ar - my shall He lead,
Ye that are men now serve Him A - gainst un - num-bered foes;
Put on the gos - pel ar - mor, And, watch-ing un - to prayer,
To him that o - ver - com-eth, A crown of life shall be;

Till ev - ery foe is van-quished, And Christ is Lord in - deed.
Let cour-age rise with dan - ger, And strength to strength op-pose.
Where du - ty calls or dan - ger, Be nev - er want-ing there.
He with the King of glo - ry Shall reign e - ter-nal - ly.

We Rest on Thee

FINLANDIA 11.10.11.10.

416

Edith G. Cherry, d.1897
II Chron. 14:11

Jean Sibelius, 1865-1957
Arr. for *The Hymnal*, 1933

1. "We rest on Thee" our shield and our de - fen-der! We go not forth a-
2. Yea, "in Thy name," O Cap-tain of sal - va - tion! In Thy dear name, all
3. "We go" in faith, our own great weakness feel-ing, And need-ing more each
4. "We rest on Thee" our shield and our de - fen-der! Thine is the bat - tle,

lone a-gainst the foe; Strong in Thy strength, safe in Thy keep-ing ten-der,
oth - er names a - bove; Je - sus our right-eous-ness, our sure foun-da - tion,
day Thy grace to know; Yet from our hearts a song of tri-umph peal-ing:
Thine shall be the praise; When passing through the gates of pearl-y splen-dor,

"We rest on Thee, and in Thy name we go." Strong in Thy strength, safe
Our Prince of glo - ry and our King of love. Je - sus our right - eous-
"We rest on Thee, and in Thy name we go." Yet from our hearts a
Vic - tors we rest with Thee through end-less days. When pass-ing through the

in Thy keep-ing ten - der, "We rest on Thee, and in Thy name we go."
ness, our sure foun-da - tion, Our Prince of glo - ry and our King of love.
song of tri-umph peal-ing: "We rest on Thee, and in Thy name we go."
gates of pearl-y splen-dor, Vic-tors we rest with Thee thro' end-less days. A-men.

417 Faith of Our Fathers

ST. CATHERINE 8.8.8.8.8.8.

Frederick W. Faber, 1814-1863

Henri F. Hemy, 1818-1888
Alt. by James G. Walton, 1821-1905

1. Faith of our fa-thers! liv-ing still In spite of dun-geon, fire, and sword;
2. Our fa-thers, chained in prisons dark, Were still in heart and conscience free;
3. Faith of our fa-thers! we will love Both friend and foe in all our strife,

O how our hearts beat high with joy When-e'er we hear that glo-rious word!
How sweet would be their children's fate, If they, like them, could die for thee!
And preach thee, too, as love knows how By kind-ly words and vir-tuous life:

Faith of our fa-thers! ho-ly faith! We will be true to thee till death! A-men.

418 Rise Up, O Men of God

FESTAL SONG 6.6.8.6.

William Pierson Merrill, 1867-1954

William H. Walter, 1825-1893

1. Rise up, O men of God! Have done with less-er things;
2. Rise up, O men of God! His king-dom tar-ries long;
3. Rise up, O men of God! The church for you doth wait,
4. Lift high the cross of Christ! Tread where His feet have trod;

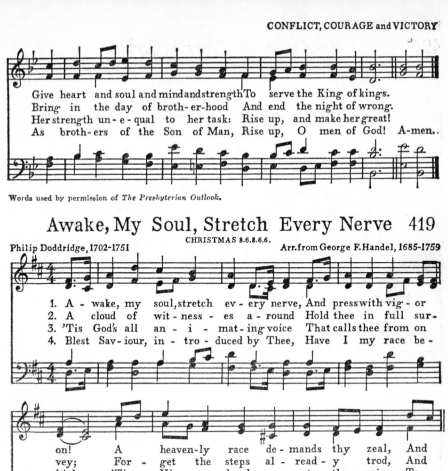

Give heart and soul and mind and strength To serve the King of kings.
Bring in the day of broth-er-hood And end the night of wrong.
Her strength un-e-qual to her task: Rise up, and make her great!
As broth-ers of the Son of Man, Rise up, O men of God! A-men..

Words used by permission of *The Presbyterian Outlook.*

Awake, My Soul, Stretch Every Nerve 419

CHRISTMAS 8.6.8.6.6.

Philip Doddridge, 1702-1751　　　　Arr. from George F. Handel, 1685-1759

1. A - wake, my soul, stretch ev - ery nerve, And press with vig - or
2. A cloud of wit - ness - es a - round Hold thee in full sur -
3. 'Tis God's all an - i - mat-ing voice That calls thee from on
4. Blest Sav-iour, in - tro - duced by Thee, Have I my race be -

on! A heaven-ly race de - mands thy zeal, And
vey; For - get the steps al - read - y trod, And
high; 'Tis His own hand pre - sents the prize To
gun; And, crowned with vic - tory, at Thy feet I'll

an im - mor - tal crown, And an im - mor - tal crown.
on - ward urge thy way, And on - ward urge thy way.
thine as - pir - ing eye, To thine as - pir - ing eye.
lay my hon - ors down, I'll lay my hon - ors down. A-men.

420 Soldiers of Christ, Arise

DIADEMATA 6.6.8.6.D.

Charles Wesley, 1707-1788   George J. Elvery, 1816-1893

1. Sol - diers of Christ, a - rise, And put your ar - mor on,
2. Stand then in His great might, With all His strength en - dued,
3. From strength to strength go on; Wres - tle, and fight, and pray;

Strong in the strength which God sup-plies Through His e - ter-nal Son;
And take, to arm you for the fight, The pan - o - ply of God,
Tread all the powers of dark-ness down, And win the well-fought day:

Strong in the Lord of hosts, And in His might-y power, Who
That, hav - ing all things done, And all your con - flicts past, Ye
Still let the Spir - it cry In all His sol - diers, "Come!" Till

in the strength of Je - sus trusts Is more than con-quer-or.
may o'er-come through Christ a - lone, And stand en - tire at last.
Christ the Lord who reigns on high Shall take the conquerors home. A-men.

Onward, Christian Soldiers

421

ST. GERTRUDE 6.5.6.5. D. with Refrain

Sabine Baring-Gould, 1834-1924

Arthur S. Sullivan, 1842-1900

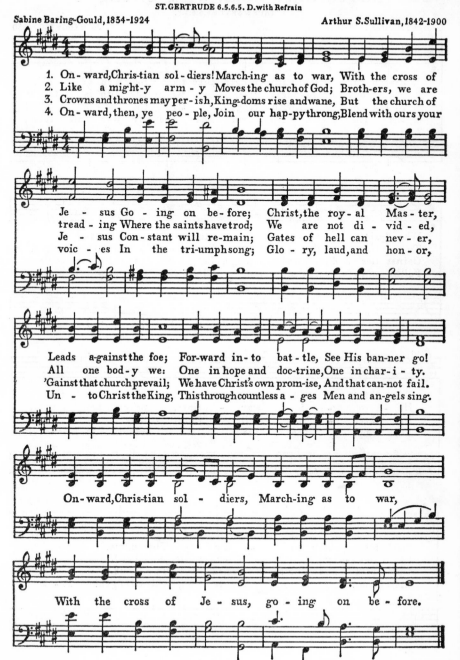

1. On - ward, Chris-tian sol - diers! March-ing as to war, With the cross of
2. Like a might-y arm - y Moves the church of God; Broth-ers, we are
3. Crowns and thrones may per - ish, King-doms rise and wane, But the church of
4. On - ward, then, ye peo - ple, Join our hap-py throng, Blend with ours your

Je - sus Go - ing on be - fore; Christ, the roy - al Mas - ter,
tread - ing Where the saints have trod; We are not di - vid - ed,
Je - sus Con - stant will re - main; Gates of hell can nev - er,
voic - es In the tri-umph song; Glo - ry, laud, and hon - or,

Leads a-gainst the foe; For-ward in - to bat - tle, See His ban-ner go!
All one bod - y we: One in hope and doc-trine, One in char-i - ty.
'Gainst that church prevail; We have Christ's own prom-ise, And that can-not fail.
Un - to Christ the King, This through countless a - ges Men and an-gels sing.

On-ward, Chris-tian sol - diers, March-ing as to war,

With the cross of Je - sus, go - ing on be - fore.

422 March On, O Soul, with Strength

ARTHUR'S SEAT 6.6.6.6.8.8.

George T. Coster, 1835-1912

John Goss, 1800-1880

1. March on, O soul, with strength! Like those strong men of old,
Who, 'gainst en-thron-ed wrong, Stood con-fi-dent and bold;
Who, thrust in prison or cast to flame,
Still made their glo-ry in Thy name.

2. The sons of fa-thers we, By whom our faith is taught
To fear no ill, to fight The ho-ly fight they fought:
He-ro-ic war-riors, ne'er from Christ,
By an-y lure or guile, en-ticed.

3. March on, O soul, with strength, As strong the bat-tle rolls!
'Gainst lies and lusts and wrongs, Let cour-age rule our souls:
In keen-est strife, Lord, may we stand,
Up-held and strength-ened by Thy hand.

4. Not long the con-flict: soon The ho-ly war shall cease,
Faith's war-fare end-ed, won The home of end-less peace!
Look up! the vic-tor's crown at length!
March on, O soul, march on, with strength! A-men.

Lead On, O King Eternal

LANCASHIRE 7.6.7.6.D.

Ernest W. Shurtleff, 1862-1917

Henry Smart, 1813-1879

1. Lead on, O King E - ter - nal, The day of march has come;
2. Lead on, O King E - ter - nal, Till sin's fierce war shall cease,
3. Lead on, O King E - ter - nal, We fol - low, not with fears,

Hence-forth in fields of con - quest Thy tents shall be our home:
And ho - li - ness shall whis-per The sweet a - men of peace;
For glad-ness breaks like morn-ing Wher-e'er Thy face ap - pears;

Through days of prep - a - ra - tion Thy grace has made us strong,
For not with swords loud clash-ing, Nor roll of stir-ring drums:
Thy cross is lift - ed o'er us, We jour-ney in its light;

And now, O King E - ter - nal, We lift our bat - tle song.
With deeds of love and mer - cy, The heaven-ly king-dom comes.
The crown a - waits the con-quest: Lead on, O God of might. A-men.

424 Christians, Arise

10.6.10.6.8.8.8.6.

LeRoy B. Walters, 1915-.

Old English Tune

1. Christ-ians, a-rise and gird your ar-mor on, Cour-age take, ne'er dis-may;
2. Lift up your heads, ye chil-dren of the light, Christ shall come as He said;
3. Go ye and la-bor, 'tis our Lord's command, Great shall be thy re-ward;

E'en though it seems Christ's kingdom tarries long, Strength shall be as thy day.
Soon breaks the dawn, dis-pell-ing shades of night, By His hand thou art led.
Send forth the light and truth to ev-ery land, With thy trust in the Lord.

For Him our long-ing spir-its yearn, Cre-a-tion wait-eth His re-turn;
Give Him thy best, fresh courage take, Our God will not His own for-sake;
Though sor-row, fear, and foe as-sail, The Sav-iour's pres-ence shall not fail;

His glo-rious gos-pel free-ly tell: Christ shall come, All is well!
For soon the trum-pet sound shall tell: Lo, He comes! All is well!
He with His own shall ev-er dwell—Praise the Lord! All is well!

My Soul, Be on Thy Guard 425

LABAN 6.6.8.6.

George Heath, 1750-1822

Lowell Mason, 1792-1872

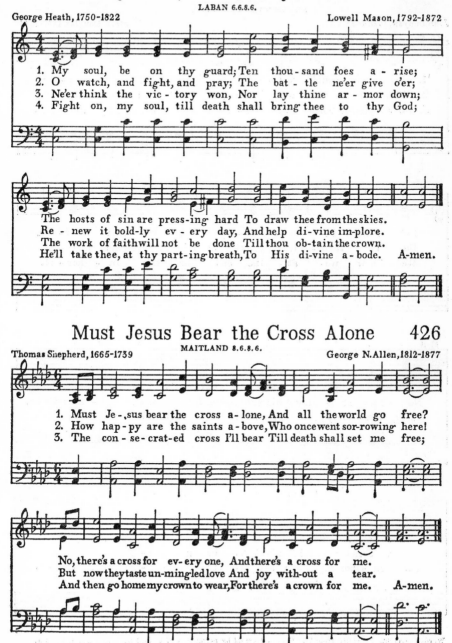

1. My soul, be on thy guard; Ten thou-sand foes a-rise;
2. O watch, and fight, and pray; The bat-tle ne'er give o'er;
3. Ne'er think the vic-tory won, Nor lay thine ar-mor down;
4. Fight on, my soul, till death shall bring thee to thy God;

The hosts of sin are press-ing hard To draw thee from the skies.
Re-new it bold-ly ev-ery day, And help di-vine im-plore.
The work of faith will not be done Till thou ob-tain the crown.
He'll take thee, at thy part-ing breath, To His di-vine a-bode. A-men.

Must Jesus Bear the Cross Alone 426

MAITLAND 8.6.8.6.

Thomas Shepherd, 1665-1739

George N. Allen, 1812-1877

1. Must Je-sus bear the cross a-lone, And all the world go free?
2. How hap-py are the saints a-bove, Who once went sor-rowing here!
3. The con-se-crat-ed cross I'll bear Till death shall set me free;

No, there's a cross for ev-ery one, And there's a cross for me.
But now they taste un-min-gled love And joy with-out a tear.
And then go home my crown to wear, For there's a crown for me. A-men.

427   He Who Would Valiant Be

ST. DUNSTAN'S 6.5.6.5.6.6.6.5.

John Bunyan, 1628-1688, alt.   Winfred Douglas, 1867-1944

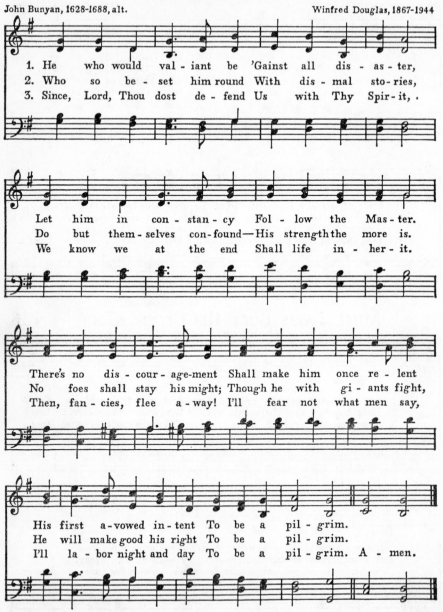

1. He who would val-iant be 'Gainst all dis-as-ter,
2. Who so be-set him round With dis-mal sto-ries,
3. Since, Lord, Thou dost de-fend Us with Thy Spir-it,.

Let him in con-stan-cy Fol-low the Mas-ter.
Do but them-selves con-found—His strength the more is.
We know we at the end Shall life in-her-it.

There's no dis-cour-age-ment Shall make him once re-lent
No foes shall stay his might; Though he with gi-ants fight,
Then, fan-cies, flee a-way! I'll fear not what men say,

His first a-vowed in-tent To be a pil-grim.
He will make good his right To be a pil-grim.
I'll la-bor night and day To be a pil-grim. A-men.

"Are Ye Able," Said the Master

BEACON HILL 8.7.8.7.with Refrain

Earl Marlatt, b.1892

Harry S.Mason, b.1881

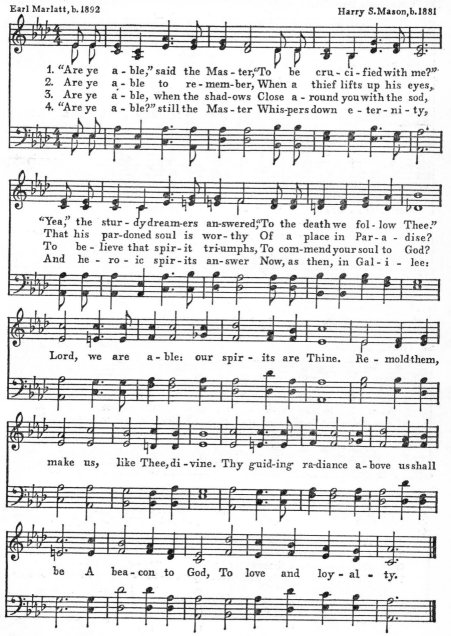

1. "Are ye a - ble," said the Mas - ter, "To be cru - ci - fied with me?"
2. Are ye a - ble to re - mem - ber, When a thief lifts up his eyes,
3. Are ye a - ble, when the shad-ows Close a - round you with the sod,
4. "Are ye a - ble?" still the Mas - ter Whis-pers down e - ter - ni - ty,

"Yea," the stur - dy dream-ers an-swered, "To the death we fol - low Thee."
That his par-doned soul is wor-thy Of a place in Par - a - dise?
To be - lieve that spir-it tri-umphs, To com-mend your soul to God?
And he - ro - ic spir-its an-swer Now, as then, in Gal - i - lee:

Lord, we are a - ble: our spir - its are Thine. Re - mold them,

make us, like Thee, di - vine. Thy guid-ing ra-diance a-bove us shall

be A bea-con to God, To love and loy - al - ty.

429 Fight the Good Fight

PENTECOST 8.8.8.8.

John S.B. Monsell, 1811-1875

William Boyd, 1847-1928

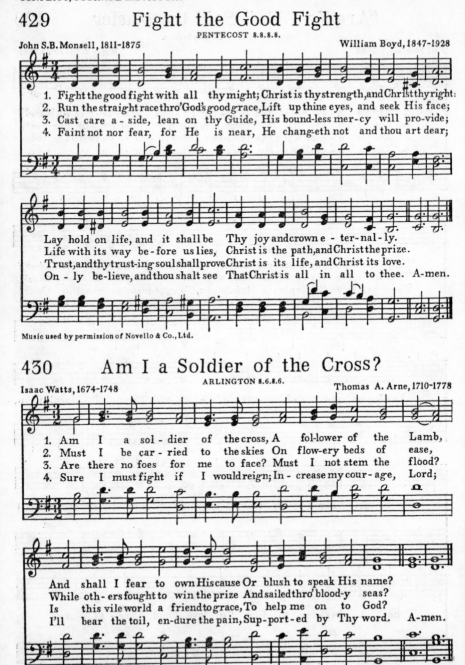

1. Fight the good fight with all thy might; Christ is thy strength, and Christ thy right:
2. Run the straight race thro' God's good grace, Lift up thine eyes, and seek His face;
3. Cast care a-side, lean on thy Guide, His bound-less mer-cy will pro-vide;
4. Faint not nor fear, for He is near, He chang-eth not and thou art dear;

Lay hold on life, and it shall be Thy joy and crown e-ter-nal-ly.
Life with its way be-fore us lies, Christ is the path, and Christ the prize.
Trust, and thy trust-ing soul shall prove Christ is its life, and Christ its love.
On-ly be-lieve, and thou shalt see That Christ is all in all to thee. A-men.

Music used by permission of Novello & Co., Ltd.

430 Am I a Soldier of the Cross?

ARLINGTON 8.6.8.6.

Isaac Watts, 1674-1748

Thomas A. Arne, 1710-1778

1. Am I a sol-dier of the cross, A fol-lower of the Lamb,
2. Must I be car-ried to the skies On flow-ery beds of ease,
3. Are there no foes for me to face? Must I not stem the flood?
4. Sure I must fight if I would reign; In-crease my cour-age, Lord;

And shall I fear to own His cause Or blush to speak His name?
While oth-ers fought to win the prize And sailed thro' blood-y seas?
Is this vile world a friend to grace, To help me on to God?
I'll bear the toil, en-dure the pain, Sup-port-ed by Thy word. A-men.

Brightly Beams Our Father's Mercy 431

LOWER LIGHTS. 8.7.8.7. with Refrain

Philip P. Bliss, 1838-1876

Philip P. Bliss, 1838-1876

1. Bright-ly beams our Fa-ther's mer-cy From His light-house ev-er-more,
2. Dark the night of sin has set-tled, Loud the an-gry bil-lows roar;
3. Trim your fee-ble lamp, my broth-er: Some poor sail-or, tem-pest tossed,

But to us He gives the keep-ing Of the lights a-long the shore.
Ea-ger eyes are watch-ing, long-ing, For the lights a-long the shore.
Try-ing now to make the har-bor, In the dark-ness may be lost.

Let the low-er lights be burn-ing! Send a gleam a-cross the wave!

Some poor faint-ing, strug-gling sea-man You may res-cue, you may save.

432 Rescue the Perishing

RESCUE Irregular with Refrain

Fanny J. Crosby, 1820-1915   William H. Doane, 1832-1915

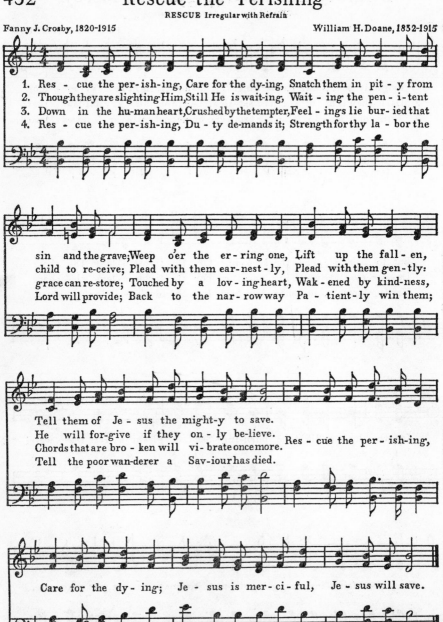

1. Res - cue the per-ish-ing, Care for the dy-ing, Snatch them in pit - y from
2. Though they are slighting Him, Still He is wait-ing, Wait - ing the pen - i-tent
3. Down in the hu-man heart, Crushed by the tempter, Feel - ings lie bur-ied that
4. Res - cue the per-ish-ing, Du - ty de-mands it; Strength for thy la - bor the

sin and the grave; Weep o'er the er - ring one, Lift up the fall - en,
child to re-ceive; Plead with them ear-nest - ly, Plead with them gen-tly:
grace can re-store; Touched by a lov - ing heart, Wak - ened by kind-ness,
Lord will provide; Back to the nar - row way Pa - tient-ly win them;

Tell them of Je - sus the might-y to save.
He will for-give if they on - ly be-lieve.
Chords that are bro - ken will vi - brate once more.   Res - cue the per - ish-ing,
Tell the poor wan-derer a Sav-iour has died.

Care for the dy - ing; Je - sus is mer - ci - ful, Je - sus will save.

I Would Be Like Jesus

BE LIKE JESUS 8.6.8.6.with Refrain

James Rowe, 1865-1933

Bentley D. Ackley, 1872-1958

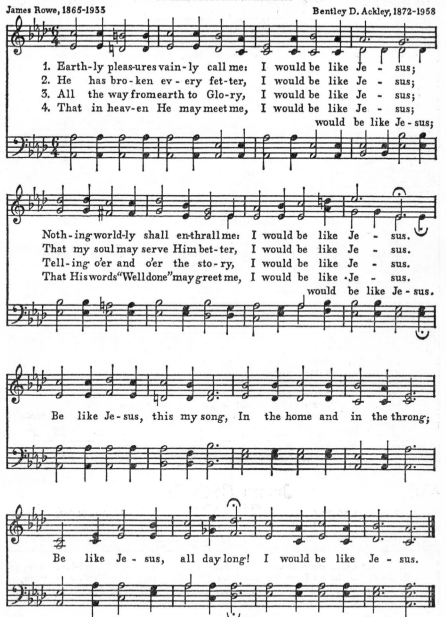

1. Earth-ly pleas-ures vain-ly call me: I would be like Je - sus;
2. He has bro-ken ev-er-y fet-ter, I would be like Je - sus;
3. All the way from earth to Glo-ry, I would be like Je - sus;
4. That in heav-en He may meet me, I would be like Je - sus;
   would be like Je - sus;

Noth-ing world-ly shall en-thrall me: I would be like Je - sus.
That my soul may serve Him bet-ter, I would be like Je - sus.
Tell-ing o'er and o'er the sto-ry, I would be like Je - sus.
That His words "Well done" may greet me, I would be like ·Je - sus.
   would be like Je - sus.

Be like Je-sus, this my song, In the home and in the throng;

Be like Je - sus, all day long! I would be like Je - sus.

434 Where Cross the Crowded Ways of Life

GERMANY 8.8.8.8.

Frank Mason North, 1850-1935   William Gardiner's *Sacred Melodies*, 1815

1. Where cross the crowd-ed ways of life, Where sound the cries of
2. In haunts of wretch-ed - ness and need, On shad-owed thresh-olds
3. From ten-der child-hood's help-less-ness, From wo-man's grief, man's
4. The cup of wa - ter given for Thee Still holds the fresh - ness
5. O Mas-ter, from the moun-tain side, Make haste to heal these
6. Till sons of men shall learn Thy love, And fol-low where Thy

race and clan, A - bove the noise of self - ish
dark with fears, From paths where hide the lures of
bur - dened toil, From fam - ished souls, from sor - row's
of Thy grace; Yet long these mul - ti - tudes to
hearts of pain; A - mong these rest - less throngs a -
feet have trod; Till glo - rious from Thy heaven a -

strife, We hear Thy voice, O Son of Man!
greed, We catch the vi - sion of Thy tears.
stress, Thy heart has nev - er known re - coil.
see The sweet com - pas - sion of Thy face.
bide, O tread the cit - y's streets a - gain,
bove Shall come the Cit - y of our God. A - men.

435   Jesus Calls Us

GALILEE 8.7.8.7.

Cecil F. Alexander, 1823-1895   William H. Jude, 1851-1922

1. Je-sus calls us o'er the tu-mult Of our life's wild, rest-less sea,
2. Je-sus calls us from the wor-ship Of the vain world's gold-en store,
3. In our joys and in our sor-rows, Days of toil and hours of ease,
4. Je-sus calls us: by Thy mer-cies, Sav-iour, may we hear Thy call,

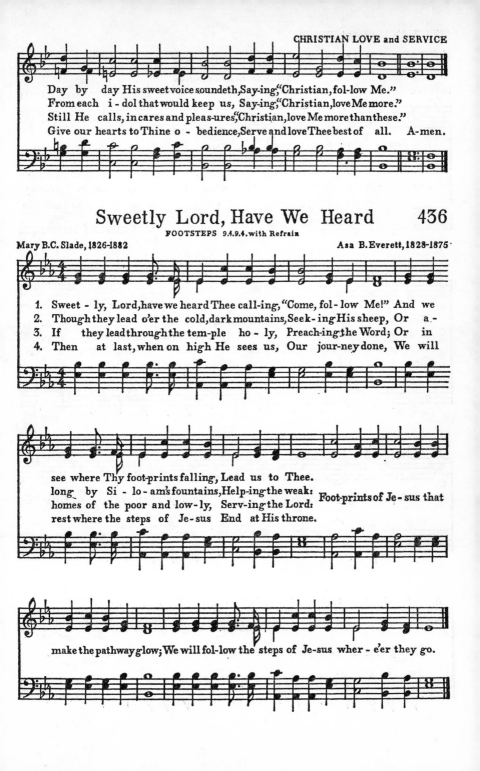

Day by day His sweet voice soundeth, Say-ing, "Christian, fol-low Me."
From each i - dol that would keep us, Say-ing, "Christian, love Me more."
Still He calls, in cares and pleas-ures, "Christian, love Me more than these."
Give our hearts to Thine o - bedience, Serve and love Thee best of all. A-men.

Sweetly Lord, Have We Heard 436

FOOTSTEPS 9.4.9.4. with Refrain

Mary B.C. Slade, 1826-1882   Asa B. Everett, 1828-1875

1. Sweet - ly, Lord, have we heard Thee call-ing, "Come, fol-low Me!" And we
2. Though they lead o'er the cold, dark mountains, Seek-ing His sheep, Or a-
3. If they lead through the tem-ple ho - ly, Preach-ing the Word; Or in
4. Then at last, when on high He sees us, Our jour-ney done, We will

see where Thy foot-prints falling, Lead us to Thee.
long by Si - lo - am's fountains, Help-ing the weak:
homes of the poor and low-ly, Serv-ing the Lord: Foot-prints of Je-sus that
rest where the steps of Je-sus End at His throne.

make the pathway glow; We will fol-low the steps of Je-sus wher-e'er they go.

437 Ready to Suffer Grief or Pain

TILLMAN 8.6.8.6.with Refrain

Unknown

Charles D.Tillman, 1861-1943

1. Read-y to suf-fer grief or pain, Read-y to stand the test;
2. Read-y to go, read-y to bear, Read-y to watch and pray;
3. Read-y to speak, read-y to think, Read-y with heart and brain;
4. Read-y to speak, read-y to warn, Read-y o'er souls to yearn;

Read-y to stay at home and send Oth-ers, if He sees best.
Read-y to stand a-side and give, Till He shall clear the way.
Read-y to stand where He sees fit, Read-y to stand the strain.
Read-y in life, read-y in death, Read-y for His re-turn.

Read-y to go, read-y to stay, Read-y my place to fill;

Read-y for serv-ice, low-ly or great, Read-y to do His will.

Lord, Lay Some Soul upon My Heart 438

LEILA 8.6.8.6. with Refrain

Stanza 1, Leon Tucker
Stanzas 2 and 3, Mack Weaver and B.B. McKinney

B. B. McKinney, 1886-1952

1. Lord, lay some soul up - on my heart, And love that soul through me;
2. Lord, lead me to some soul in sin, And grant that I may be
3. To win that soul for Thee ·a - lone Will be my con - stant prayer;

And may I no - bly do my part To win that soul for. Thee.
En - dued with power and love to win That soul, dear Lord, for Thee.
That when I've reached the great white throne I'll meet that dear one there.

Some. soul. for Thee, some soul for Thee, This is my earn - est plea;

Help me each day, on life's high-way, To win some soul for Thee.

439 Make Me a Blessing

SCHULER 10:7.10.7. with Refrain

Ira B. Wilson, 1880-1950

George S. Schuler, 1882-

1. Out in the highways and by-ways of life, Man-y are wea-ry and sad;
   are wea-ry and sad;
2. Tell the sweet sto-ry of Christ and His love, Tell of His pow'r to for-give;
   His pow'r to for-give;
3. Give as 'twas giv-en to you in your need; Love as the Master loved you:
   the Mas-ter loved you:

Car-ry the sun-shine where darkness is rife, Mak-ing the sor-row-ing glad.
Oth-ers will trust Him if on-ly you prove True, ev-ery mo-ment you live.
Be to the help-less a help-er in-deed; Un-to your mis-sion be true.

Make me a bless-ing, Make me a bless-ing, Out of my

life May Je-sus shine; Make me a bless-ing, O Sav-iour,
out of my life

I pray, Make me a bless-ing to some-one to-day.
I pray Thee, my Saviour,

Channels Only

SUBMISSION 8.7.8.7. with Refrain

440

Mary E. Maxwell

Ada Rose Gibbs

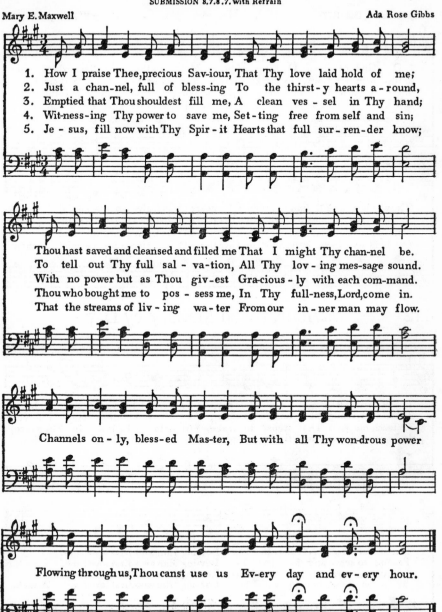

1. How I praise Thee, precious Sav-iour, That Thy love laid hold of me;
2. Just a chan-nel, full of bless-ing To the thirst-y hearts a-round,
3. Emptied that Thou shouldest fill me, A clean ves-sel in Thy hand;
4. Wit-ness-ing Thy power to save me, Set-ting free from self and sin;
5. Je-sus, fill now with Thy Spir-it Hearts that full sur-ren-der know;

Thou hast saved and cleansed and filled me That I might Thy chan-nel be.
To tell out Thy full sal-va-tion, All Thy lov-ing mes-sage sound.
With no power but as Thou giv-est Gra-cious-ly with each com-mand.
Thou who bought me to pos-sess me, In Thy full-ness, Lord, come in.
That the streams of liv-ing wa-ter From our in-ner man may flow.

Channels on-ly, bless-ed Mas-ter, But with all Thy won-drous power

Flowing through us, Thou canst use us Ev-ery day and ev-ery hour.

441 God of Love, O King of Peace

QUEBEC 8.8.8.8.

Henry W. Baker, 1821-1877   Henry W. Baker, 1821-1877

1. O God of love, O King of peace, Make wars throughout the world to cease;
2. Re-mem-ber, Lord, Thy works of old, The won-ders that our fa-thers told;
3. Whom shall we trust but Thee, O Lord? Where rest but on Thy faith-ful word?
4. Where saints and an-gels dwell a-bove, All hearts are knit in ho-ly love;

The wrath of sin-ful man re-strain; Give peace, O God, give peace a-gain!
Re-mem-ber not our sin's dark stain; Give peace, O God, give peace a-gain!
None ev-er called on Thee in vain; Give peace, O God, give peace a-gain!
O bind us in that heavenly chain; Give peace, O God, give peace a-gain! A-men.

442 Saviour, Teach Me, Day by Day

POSEN 7.7.7.7.

Jane E. Leeson, 1807-1882   George C. Strattner, 1650-1705

1. Sav-iour, teach me day by day, Love's sweet les-sons to o-bey;
2. With a child-like heart of love, At Thy bid-ding may I move;
3. Teach me thus Thy steps to trace, Strong to fol-low in Thy grace;
4. Love in lov-ing finds em-ploy, In o-be-dience all her joy;

Sweet-er les-sons can-not be, Lov-ing Him who first loved me.
Prompt to serve and fol-low Thee, Lov-ing Him who first loved me.
Learn-ing how to love from Thee, Lov-ing Him who first loved me.
Ev-er new that joy will be, Lov-ing Him who first loved me. A-men.

O to Be Like Thee

CHRIST LIKE 10.9.10.9.with Refrain

Thomas O. Chisholm, b.1866

William J. Kirkpatrick, 1838-1921

1. O to be like Thee! bless-ed Re-deem - er, This is my con-stant
2. O to be like Thee! full of com-pas-sion, Lov-ing, for - giv - ing,
3. O to be like Thee! while I am plead-ing, Pour out Thy Spir - it,
4. O to be like Thee! Lord, I am com-ing, Now to re - ceive th'a-

long-ing and prayer, Glad-ly I'll for - feit all of earth's treas-ures,
ten-der and kind, Help-ing the help-less, cheer-ing the faint-ing,
fill with Thy love; Make me a tem - ple meet for Thy dwell-ing,
noint-ing di - vine; All that I am and have I am bring-ing,

Je - sus, Thy per - fect like-ness to wear.
Seek-ing the wan-dering sin - ner to find.
Fit me for life and heav-en a - bove.
Lord from this mo - ment all shall be Thine.

O to be like Thee!

O to be like Thee, bless-ed Re-deem - er, pure as Thou art! Come in Thy

sweet-ness, come in Thy full-ness; Stamp Thine own im - age deep on my heart.

444 Christian, Let Your Burning Light

BURNING LIGHT 7.7.7.7. with Refrain

E.G. Coleman, b. 1872

E.G. Coleman, b. 1872

1. Chris-tian, let your burn-ing light Shine on all with lus-ter bright,
2. As you jour-ney here be-low, Shed a ray wher-e'er you go;
3. That your light may guide you through, Bright-ly let it shine a-new,

Let your words and deeds be pure; All for Christ you must en-dure.
Find in this your pure de-light, Let your light shine clear and bright.
Keep up cour-age, nev-er fail, Till you're safe with-in the veil.

Chris-tian, let your light shine, All a-long your way;

You may guide a wan-derer To e-ter-nal day;

You may save from end-less night If you let your lamp burn bright.

Christ of the Upward Way

SURSUM CORDA 6.4.6.4.10.10.

Walter J. Mathams, 1853-1932

George Lomas, 1834-1884

1. Christ of the up-ward way, My guide di-vine,
2. Give me the heart to hear Thy voice and will,
3. Give me the good stout arm To shield the right,
4. Christ of the up-ward way, My guide di-vine,

Where Thou hast set Thy feet May I place mine,
That with-out fault or fear I may ful-fill
And wield Thy sword of truth With all my might,
Where Thou hast set Thy feet May I place mine;

And move and march wher-ev-er Thou hast trod,
Thy pur-pose with a glad and ho-ly zest,
That in the war-fare I must wage for Thee,
And when Thy last call comes se-rene and clear,

Keep-ing face for-ward up the hill of God.
Like one who would not bring less than his best.
More than a vic-tor I may ev-er be.
Calm may my an-swer be: "Lord, I am here." A-men.

446 The Loyalty of Love

LOYALTY 8.7.8.7.D.

Grace Spaulding Petticord, 1910- Myron L. Tweed, 1930-

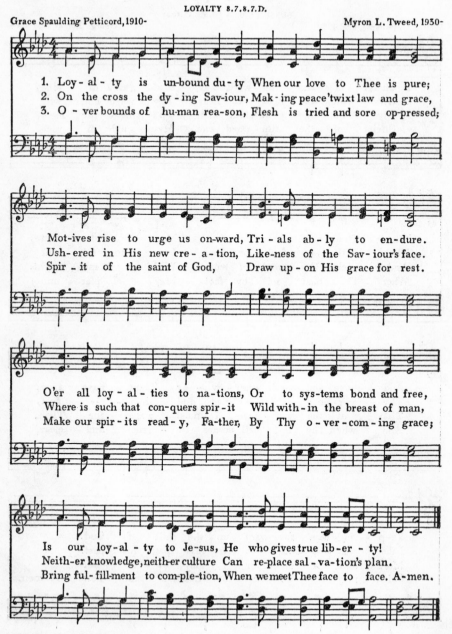

1. Loy-al-ty is un-bound du-ty When our love to Thee is pure;
2. On the cross the dy-ing Sav-iour, Mak-ing peace 'twixt law and grace,
3. O-ver bounds of hu-man rea-son, Flesh is tried and sore op-pressed;

Mot-ives rise to urge us on-ward, Tri-als ab-ly to en-dure.
Ush-ered in His new cre-a-tion, Like-ness of the Sav-iour's face.
Spir-it of the saint of God, Draw up-on His grace for rest.

O'er all loy-al-ties to na-tions, Or to sys-tems bond and free,
Where is such that con-quers spir-it Wild with-in the breast of man,
Make our spir-its read-y, Fa-ther, By Thy o-ver-com-ing grace;

Is our loy-al-ty to Je-sus, He who gives true lib-er-ty!
Neith-er knowledge, neith-er culture Can re-place sal-va-tion's plan.
Bring ful-fill-ment to com-ple-tion, When we meet Thee face to face. A-men.

Jesus, I My Cross Have Taken

ELLESDIE. 8. 7. 8. 7. D.

Henry F. Lyte, 1793-1847

Wolfgang A. Mozart, 1756-1791
Arr. by Hubert P. Main, 1839-1925

1. Je - sus, I my cross have ta - ken, All to leave, and fol - low Thee;
2. Let the world de - spise and leave me, They have left my Sav - iour, too;
3. Haste thee on from grace to glo - ry, Armed by faith, and winged by prayer;

Des - ti - tute, de-spised, for-sa - ken, Thou, from hence, my all shalt be;
Hu - man hearts and looks de-ceive me; Thou art not, like man, un - true;
Heaven's e - ter - nal day's be-fore thee; God's own hand shall guide thee there.

Per - ish ev - ery fond am-bi - tion, All I've sought, and hoped, and known;
And while Thou shalt smile up-on me, God of wis-dom love and might,
Soon shall close thy earth - ly mis-sion, Swift shall pass thy pil - grim days,

Yet how rich is my con-di - tion, God and heav'n are still my own!
Foes may hate, and friends may shun me; Show Thy face, and all is bright.
Hope shall change to glad fru - i - tion, Faith to sight, and prayer to praise. A-men.

448 Give of Your Best to the Master

BARNARD 8,7,8,7,D, with Refrain

Howard B. Grose, 1851-1939

Charlotte A. Barnard, 1830-1869

1. Give of your best to the Mas-ter, Give of the strength of your youth;
2. Give of your best to the Mas-ter, Give Him first place in your heart;
3. Give of your best to the Mas-ter, Naught else is wor-thy His love;

Throw your soul's fresh, glow-ing ar-dor In-to the bat-tle for truth:
Give Him first place in your ser-vice, Con-se-crate ev-ery part:
He gave Him-self for your ran-som, Gave up His glo-ry a-bove;

Je-sus has set the ex-am-ple, Daunt-less was He, young and brave;
Give, and to you shall be giv-en, God His be-lov-ed Son gave;
Laid down His life with-out mur-mur, You from sin's ru-in to save;

Give Him your loy-al de-vo-tion, Give Him the best that you have.
Grate-ful-ly seek-ing to serve Him, Give Him the best that you have.
Give Him your heart's ad-o-ra-tion, Give Him the best that you have.

Give of your best to the Mas-ter, Give of the strength of your youth;

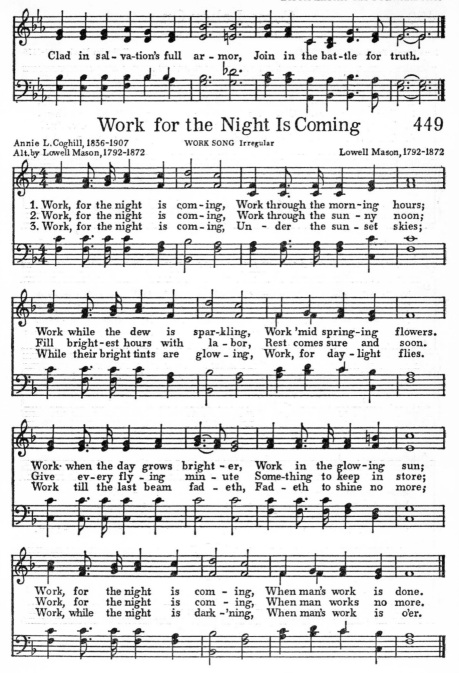

Clad in sal - va-tion's full ar - mor, Join in the bat-tle for truth.

Work for the Night Is Coming 449

Annie L. Coghill, 1836-1907
Alt. by Lowell Mason, 1792-1872

WORK SONG Irregular

Lowell Mason, 1792-1872

1. Work, for the night is com - ing, Work through the morn-ing hours;
2. Work, for the night is com - ing, Work through the sun - ny noon;
3. Work, for the night is com - ing, Un - der the sun - set skies;

Work while the dew is spar-kling, Work 'mid spring-ing flowers.
Fill bright-est hours with la - bor, Rest comes sure and soon.
While their bright tints are glow - ing, Work, for day - light flies.

Work when the day grows bright - er, Work in the glow-ing sun;
Give ev-ery fly - ing min - ute Some-thing to keep in store;
Work till the last beam fad - eth, Fad - eth to shine no more;

Work, for the night is com - ing, When man's work is done.
Work, for the night is com - ing, When man works no more.
Work, while the night is dark -'ning, When man's work is o'er.

450
Come, Labor On

ORA LABORA 4.10.10.10.4.

Jane Laurie Borthwick, 1813-1897, Alt.

T. Tertius Noble, 1867-1953

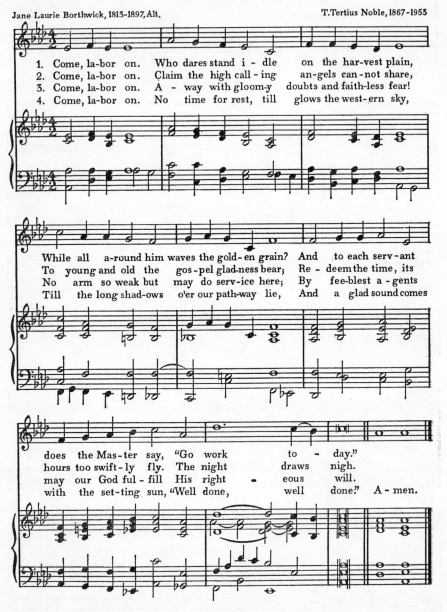

1. Come, la-bor on. Who dares stand i - dle on the har-vest plain,
2. Come, la-bor on. Claim the high call - ing an-gels can - not share,
3. Come, la-bor on. A - way with gloom-y doubts and faith-less fear!
4. Come, la-bor on. No time for rest, till glows the west-ern sky,

While all a-round him waves the gold-en grain? And to each serv-ant
To young and old the gos-pel glad-ness bear; Re - deem the time, its
No arm so weak but may do serv-ice here; By fee-blest a-gents
Till the long shad-ows o'er our path-way lie, And a glad sound comes

does the Mas-ter say, "Go work to - day."
hours too swift-ly fly. The night draws nigh.
may our God ful-fill His right - eous will.
with the set-ting sun, "Well done, well done." A - men.

Sow in the Morn Thy Seed
451

BOYLSTON 6.6.8.6.

James Montgomery, 1771-1854

Lowell Mason, 1792-1872

1. Sow in the morn thy seed, At eve hold not thy hand;
2. Thou know'st not which shall thrive, The late or ear-ly sown;
3. And du-ly shall ap-pear, In ver-dure, beau-ty, strength,
4. Thou canst not toil in vain: Cold, heat, and moist and dry,
5. Then when the glo-rious end, The day of God, shall come,

To doubt and fear give thou no heed, Broad-cast it o'er the land.
Grace keeps the pre-cious germ a-live, When and wher-ev-er strown.
The ten-der blade, the stalk, the ear, And the full corn at length.
Shall fos-ter and ma-ture the grain For gar-ners in the sky.
The an-gel reap-ers shall de-scend, And heaven shout, "Harvest home!" A-men.

We Give Thee but Thine Own
452

SCHUMANN S.M.

William W. How, 1823-1897

Mason and Webb's *Cantica Laudis,* Boston, 1850

1. We give Thee but Thine own, What-e'er the gift may be:
2. May we Thy boun-ties thus As stew-ards true re-ceive,
3. To com-fort and to bless, To find a balm for woe,
4. The cap-tive to re-lease, To God the lost to bring,
5. And we be-lieve Thy word, Though dim our faith may be:

All that we have is Thine a-lone, A trust, O Lord, from Thee.
And glad-ly, as Thou bless-est us, To Thee our first fruits give.
To tend the lone and fa-ther-less, Is an-gels' work be-low.
To teach the way of life and peace-It is a Christ-like thing.
What-e'er for Thine we do, O Lord, We do it un-to Thee. A-men.

453 Who Is on the Lord's Side?

ARMAGEDDON 6.5.6.5.6.5.D.

Frances R. Havergal, 1836-1879

Arr. by John Goss, 1800-1880

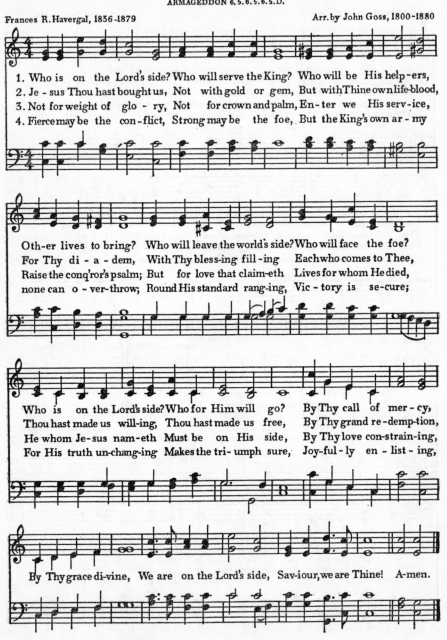

1. Who is on the Lord's side? Who will serve the King? Who will be His help-ers,
2. Je - sus Thou hast bought us, Not with gold or gem, But with Thine own life-blood,
3. Not for weight of glo - ry, Not for crown and palm, En - ter we His serv-ice,
4. Fierce may be the con - flict, Strong may be the foe, But the King's own ar - my

Oth-er lives to bring? Who will leave the world's side? Who will face the foe?
For Thy di - a - dem, With Thy bless-ing fill-ing Each who comes to Thee,
Raise the conq'ror's psalm; But for love that claim-eth Lives for whom He died,
none can o - ver-throw; Round His standard rang-ing, Vic - tory is se-cure;

Who is on the Lord's side? Who for Him will go? By Thy call of mer - cy,
Thou hast made us will-ing, Thou hast made us free, By Thy grand re - demp-tion,
He whom Je-sus nam-eth Must be on His side, By Thy love con-strain-ing,
For His truth un-chang-ing Makes the tri - umph sure, Joy-ful - ly en - list-ing,

By Thy grace di-vine, We are on the Lord's side, Sav-iour, we are Thine! A-men.

If You Love Me

8.7.8.7. with Refrain

E.A.Barnes

John R. Sweney, 1837-1899

1. If you love, as My dis - ci - ples, You will let your love ap - pear;
2. You will shun all sin and e - vil, And will learn to watch and pray;
3. You will love and help each oth - er, And will walk in truth and light;
4. You will be My true dis - ci - ples, And will dwell in peace and love;

You will keep My words and pre-cepts, And will not de - ny Me here.
You will take the cross I give you, And will bear it all the way.
You will look to Me in troub - le, And will know that all is right.
You will watch and be in wait - ing, Till I call you home a - bove.

If you love Me, if you love Me, Keep the pre-cepts that I give;

Thus, in love, the Lord is speak-ing, That the soul may hear and live.
Thus, in love

455   It May Not Be on the Mountain Height

Mary Brown
Charles E. Pryor, 1856-1927, Stanzas 2 and 3.

MANCHESTER Irregular with Refrain

Carrie E. Rounsefell, 1861-1930

1. It   may not be on the mountain height, Or   o - ver the storm-y   sea,
2. Per - haps to-day there are lov-ing words Which Je-sus would have me speak;
3. There's sure-ly some-where a low - ly place In earth's har-vest fields so wide,

It   may not be at the bat-tle's front My Lord will have need of   me;
There may be now in the paths of sin Some wand'rer whom I should seek;
Where I may la-bor through life's short day For Je - sus, the Cru - ci - fied;

But if, by a still, small voice He calls To paths that I do   not know,
O   Sav-iour, if Thou wilt be my guide, Though hard and rug-ged the way,
So, trust-ing my all to Thy ten-der care, And know-ing Thou lov - est me,

I'll an-swer, dear Lord, with my hand in thine, I'll go where You want me to go.
My voice shall ech - o the mes-sage sweet, I'll say what You want me to say.
I'll do Thy will with a heart sin-cere, I'll be what You want me to be.

I'll go where You want me to go, dear Lord, O-ver mountain, or plain, or sea;

I'll say what You want me to say, dear Lord, I'll be what You want me to be.

Take Up Thy Cross

456

GERMANY 8.8.8.8.

Charles W. Everest, 1814-1877

William Gardiner's *Sacred Melodies*, 1815

1. Take up thy cross! the Sav-iour said, If thou wouldst my dis-ci - ple be;
2. Take up thy cross! let not its weight Fill thy weak spir-it with a - larm;
3. Take up thy cross! nor heed the shame, And let thy fool-ish pride be still;
4. Take up thy cross, then, in His strength, And calmly sin's wild del - uge brave;
5. Take up thy cross, and fol - low me, Nor think till death to lay it down;

Take up thy cross with will - ing heart, And hum-bly fol - low aft - er me.
My strength shall bear thy spir - it up, And brace thy heart and nerve thine arm.
Thy Lord did not re-fuse to die Up - on the cross on Cal - v'ry's hill.
'Twill guide thee to a bet - ter home, It points to bliss be-yond the grave.
For on - ly he who bears the cross May hope to wear the glo - rious crown.

457 O Master Workman of the Race

SERAPH (Bethlehem) 8.6.8.6.D.

Jay T. Stocking, 1870-1936   Gottfried W. Fink, 1783-1846

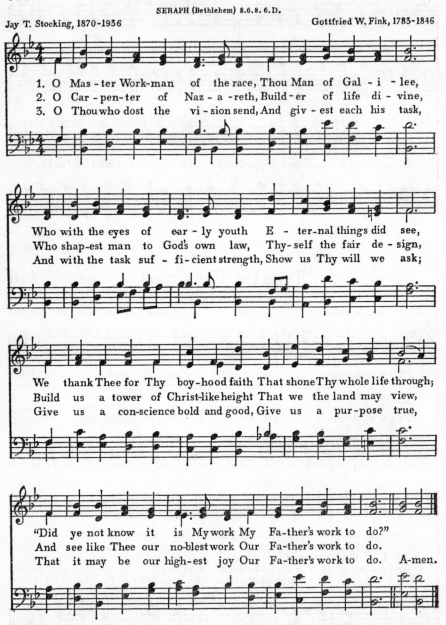

1. O Mas-ter Work-man of the race, Thou Man of Gal-i-lee,
2. O Car-pen-ter of Naz-a-reth, Build-er of life di-vine,
3. O Thou who dost the vi-sion send, And giv-est each his task,

Who with the eyes of ear-ly youth E-ter-nal things did see,
Who shap-est man to God's own law, Thy-self the fair de-sign,
And with the task suf-fi-cient strength, Show us Thy will we ask;

We thank Thee for Thy boy-hood faith That shone Thy whole life through;
Build us a tower of Christ-like height That we the land may view,
Give us a con-science bold and good, Give us a pur-pose true,

"Did ye not know it is My work My Fa-ther's work to do?"
And see like Thee our no-blest work Our Fa-ther's work to do.
That it may be our high-est joy Our Fa-ther's work to do. A-men.

A Charge to Keep I Have   458

BOYLSTON 6.6.8.6.

Charles Wesley, 1707-1788   Lowell Mason, 1792-1872

1. A charge to keep I have, A God to glo - ri - fy,
2. To serve the pres - ent age, My call - ing to ful - fill,
3. Arm me with jeal - ous care, As in Thy sight to live;
4. Help me to watch and pray, And on Thy-self re - ly,

A nev - er - dy-ing soul to save, And fit it for the sky.
O may it all my powers engage, To do my Mas-ter's will.
And O Thy serv-ant, Lord, pre-pare A strict ac-count to give.
As-sured if I my trust be-tray, I shall for - ev - er die. A-men.

Come, Lord and Tarry Not   459

ST. BRIDE 6.6.8.6.

Horatius Bonar, 1808-1889   Samuel Howard, 1710-1782

1. Come, Lord, and tar - ry not; Bring the long-looked-for day;
2. Come, for Thy saints still wait; Dai - ly as-cends their sigh:
3. Come, for cre - a - tion groans, Im - pa - tient of Thy stay,
4. Come, and make all things new; Build up this ru - ined earth;
5. Come, and be - gin Thy reign Of ev - er-last - ing peace;

O why these years of wait-ing here; These a - ges of de - lay?
The Spir-it and the Bride say, "Come." Dost Thou not hear the cry?
Worn out with these long years of ill, These a - ges of de - lay.
Re - store our fad - ed Par - a - dise, Cre - a - tion's sec-ond birth.
Come, take the king-dom to Thy-self, Great King of Right-eous-ness. A-men.

460 There Is a Land of Pure Delight

VARINA 8.6.8.6.D.

Isaac Watts, 1674-1748

George F. Root, 1820-1895

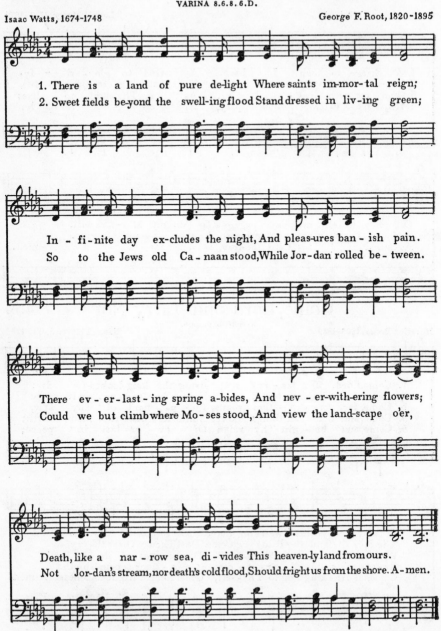

1. There is a land of pure de-light Where saints im-mor-tal reign;
2. Sweet fields be-yond the swell-ing flood Stand dressed in liv-ing green;

In - fi-nite day ex-cludes the night, And pleas-ures ban - ish pain.
So to the Jews old Ca - naan stood, While Jor-dan rolled be - tween.

There ev - er - last - ing spring a-bides, And nev - er-with-ering flowers;
Could we but climb where Mo - ses stood, And view the land-scape o'er,

Death, like a nar - row sea, di - vides This heaven-ly land from ours.
Not Jor-dan's stream, nor death's cold flood, Should fright us from the shore. A-men.

Ten Thousand Times Ten Thousand

461

ALFORD 7.6.8.6.D.

Henry Alford, 1810-1871

John B. Dykes, 1825-1876

1. Ten thou-sand times ten thou-sand In spar-kling rai-ment bright,
2. What rush of al - le - lu - ias Fills all the earth and sky!
3. O then what rap-tured greet-ings On Ca-naan's hap - py shore!
4. Bring near Thy great sal - va-tion, Thou Lamb for sin-ners slain;

The ar-mies of the ran-somed saints Throng up the steeps of light:
What ring-ing of a thou-sand harps Be - speaks the tri-umph nigh!
What knit-ting sev_ered friendships up Where part-ings are no more!
Fill up the roll of Thine e - lect, Then take Thy power and reign!

'Tis fin-ished, all is fin-ished, Their fight with death and sin;
O day for which cre - a - tion And all its tribes were made,
Then eyes with joy shall spar-kle, That brimmed with tears of late,
Ap - pear, De-sire of na-tions, Thine ex - iles long for home;

Fling o-pen wide the gold-en gates And let the vic-tors in!
O joy, for all its for-mer woes A thou-sand fold re-paid!
Or-phans no long-er fa-ther-less, Nor wid-ows des-o-late.
Show in the heav'ns Thy promised sign, Thou Prince and Sav-iour, come! A-men.

462 For All the Saints

SINE NOMINE 10.10.10. with Alleluias

William W. How, 1823-1897

Ralph Vaughn Williams, 1872-1958

Voices in unison

1. For all the saints who from their la-bors rest, Who Thee by faith be-
2. Thou wast their rock, their for-tress, and their might; Thou, Lord, their cap-tain
3. O may Thy sol - diers, faith-ful, true, and bold, Fight as the saints who
4. O blest com-mun - ion, fel-low-ship di - vine! We fee-bly strug-gle,
5. And when the fight is fierce, the war-fare long, Steals on the ear the
6. From earth's wide bound, from o-cean's farthest coast, Through gates of pearl streams

fore the world confessed, Thy Name, O Je - sus, be for-ev - er blest.
in the well-fought fight; Thou, in the dark-ness drear, their one true light.
no-bly fought of old, And win with them the vic-tor's crown of gold.
they in glo-ry shine; Yet all are one in Thee, for all are Thine.
dis-tant tri-umph song, And hearts are brave a-gain, and arms are strong.
in the count-less host, Sing-ing to Fa-ther, Son, and Ho-ly Ghost,

Harmony

Al - le-lu - ia! Al - le-lu - ia! A-men.

Jerusalem the Golden

EWING 7.6.7.6.D.

463

Bernard of Cluny, 12th century
Tr.by John M. Neale, 1818-1866

Alexander Ewing, 1830-1895

1. Je - ru - sa - lem the gold - en With milk and hon - ey blest,
2. They stand, those halls of Zi - on, All ju - bi - lant with song,
3. There is the throne of Da - vid, And there, from care re - leased,
4. O sweet and bless - ed coun - try, The home of God's e - lect!

Be - neath thy con - tem - pla - tion Sink heart and voice op - prest;
And bright with many an an - gel, And all the mar - tyr throng;
The shout of them that tri - umph, The song of them that feast;
O sweet and bless - ed coun - try That ea - ger hearts ex - pect!

I know not, O I know not, What joys a - wait us there,
The Prince is ev - er in them, The day - light is se - rene;
And they, who with their Lead - er, Have con - quered in the fight,
Je - sus, in mer - cy bring us To that dear land of rest,

What ra - dian - cy of glo - ry, What bliss be - yond com - pare!
The pas - tures of the bless - ed Are decked in glo - rious sheen.
For - ev - er and for - ev - er Are clad in robes of white.
Who art, with God the Fa - ther, And Spir - it, ev - er blest. A - men.

464 Hark, Hark, My Soul!

PILGRIMS 11.10.11.10. with Refrain

Frederick W. Faber, 1814-1863

Henry Smart, 1813-1879

1. Hark, hark, my soul! an-gel-ic songs are swell-ing O'er earth's green fields and
2. On-ward we go, for still we hear them sing-ing, "Come, wea-ry souls, for
3. Far, far a-way, like bells at eve-ning peal-ing, The voice of Je-sus

o-ceans wave-beat shore; How sweet the truth those bless-ed strains are tell-ing
Je-sus bids you come;" And through the dark its ech-oes sweet-ly ring-ing,
sounds o'er land and sea, And la-den souls by thousands, meek-ly steal-ing,

Of that new life when sin shall be no more! An-gels of Je-sus,
The mu-sic of the gos-pel leads us home.
Kind Shep-herd, turn their wea-ry steps to Thee.

an-gels of light, Sing-ing to wel-come the pil-grims of the night. A-men.

The Sands of Time Are Sinking

RUTHERFORD 7.6.7.6.7.6.7.5.

Anne Ross Cousin, 1824-1906

Chretien Urhan, 1790-1845
Edward F. Rimbault, 1816-1876

1. The sands of time are sink - ing, The dawn of heav - en breaks;
2. O Christ, He is the foun - tain, The deep, sweet well of love!
3. With mer - cy and with judg - ment My web of time He wove,

The sum-mer morn I've sighed for, The fair, sweet morn a - wakes;
The streams on earth I've tast - ed More deep I'll drink a - bove:
And aye the dews of sor - row Were lus-tered by His love.

Dark, dark hath been the mid - night, But day-spring is at hand,
There to an o - cean full - ness His mer - cy doth ex - pand,
I'll bless the hand that guid - ed, I'll bless the heart that planned,

And glo - ry, glo - ry dwell - eth, In Im - man - uel's land.
And glo - ry, glo - ry dwell - eth In Im - man - uel's land.
When throned where glo - ry dwell - eth In Im - man - uel's land. A - men.

466 Face to Face with Christ

FACE TO FACE 8. 7. 8. 7. with Refrain

Carrie E. Breck, 1855-1934

Grant Colfax Tullar, 1869-1950

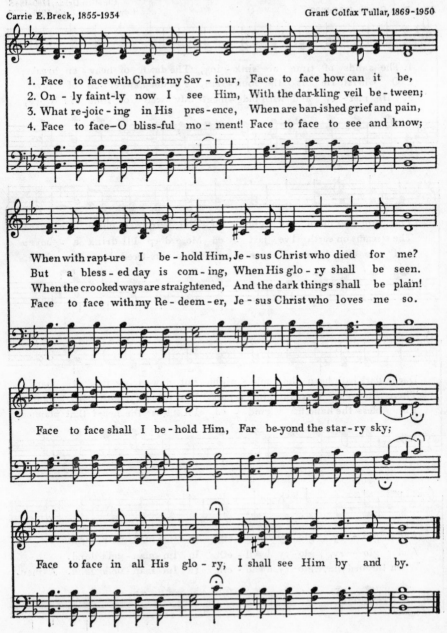

1. Face to face with Christ my Sav - iour, Face to face how can it be,
2. On - ly faint-ly now I see Him, With the dar-kling veil be - tween;
3. What re-joic - ing in His pres - ence, When are ban-ished grief and pain,
4. Face to face—O bliss-ful mo - ment! Face to face to see and know;

When with rapt-ure I be - hold Him, Je - sus Christ who died for me?
But a bless - ed day is com - ing, When His glo - ry shall be seen.
When the crooked ways are straightened, And the dark things shall be plain!
Face to face with my Re - deem - er, Je - sus Christ who loves me so.

Face to face shall I be - hold Him, Far be-yond the star - ry sky;

Face to face in all His glo - ry, I shall see Him by and by.

Some Day the Silver Cord Will Break

8. 8. 8. 8. with Refrain

Fanny J. Crosby 1820-1915

George Stebbins, 1846 - 1945

1. Some day the sil - ver cord will break, And I no more as now shall sing;
2. Some day my earth-ly house will fall, I can-not tell how soon 'twill be,
3. Some day, when fades the gold-en sun Beneath the ros - y-tint - ed west,
4. Some day: till then I'll watch and wait, My lamp all trimmed and burning bright,

But O! the joy when I shall wake With-in the pal - ace of the King!
But this I know, my All - in - all Has now a place in heaven for me.
My bless - ed Lord will say, "Well done!" And I shall en - ter in - to rest.
That when my Lord o-pens the gate, My soul to Him may take its flight.

And I shall see Him face to face, And tell the sto-ry, saved by grace;
shall see to face,

And I shall see Him face to face, And tell the sto-ry, saved by grace.
shall see to face,

468 Sing the Wondrous Love of Jesus

HEAVEN 8. 7. 8. 7. with Refrain

Eliza E. Hewitt, 1851-1920

Emily D. Wilson, 1865-1942

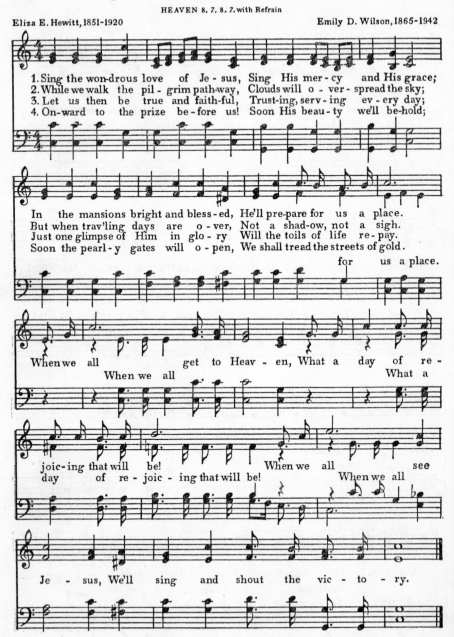

1. Sing the won-drous love of Je - sus, Sing His mer - cy and His grace;
2. While we walk the pil - grim path-way, Clouds will o - ver-spread the sky;
3. Let us then be true and faith-ful, Trust-ing, serv - ing ev - ery day;
4. On-ward to the prize be - fore us! Soon His beau - ty we'll be-hold;

In the mansions bright and bless-ed, He'll pre-pare for us a place.
But when trav'ling days are o - ver, Not a shad-ow, not a sigh.
Just one glimpse of Him in glo - ry Will the toils of life re-pay.
Soon the pearl-y gates will o - pen, We shall tread the streets of gold.

for us a place.

When we all get to Heav - en, What a day of re-
When we all What a

joic-ing that will be! When we all see
day of re - joic - ing that will be! When we all

Je - sus, We'll sing and shout the vic - to - ry.

When My Life-Work Is Ended

14.11.14.11.with Refrain

Fanny J. Crosby, 1820-1915

John R. Sweney, 1837-1899

1. When my life-work is end-ed, and I cross the swell-ing tide, When the
2. O the soul-thrill-ing rap-ture when I view His bless-ed face And the
3. O the dear ones in glo-ry, how they beck-on me to come, And our
4. Through the gates to the cit-y in a robe of spot-less white, He will

bright and glorious morning I shall see;   I shall know my Re-deem-er when I
lus-ter of His kindly beaming eye;   How my full heart will praise Him for the
part-ing at the riv-er I re-call;   To the sweet vales of E-den they will
lead me where no tears will ev-er fall;   In the glad song of a-ges I shall

reach the oth-er side,   And His smile will be the first to wel-come me.
mer-cy, love, and grace,   That pre-pared for me a man-sion in the sky.
sing my wel-come home; But I long to meet my Sav-iour first of all.
min-gle with de-light; But I long to meet my Sav-iour first of all.

I shall know   Him, I shall know Him, And redeemed by His side I shall stand;
I shall know Him,

I shall know   Him, I shall know Him By the print of the nails in His hand.
I shall know Him,

470 There's a Land That Is Fairer Than Day

SWEET BY AND BY 9.9.9.9. with Refrain

Sanford F. Bennett, 1836-1898   Joseph P. Webster, 1819-1875

1. There's a land that is fair-er than day, And by faith we can see it a-far; For the Fa-ther waits o-ver the way To pre-pare us a dwell-ing place there.

2. We shall sing on that beau-ti-ful shore The me-lo-di-ous songs of the blest, And our spir-its shall sor-row no more, Not a sigh for the bless-ing of rest.

3. To our boun-ti-ful Fa-ther a-bove, We will of-fer the trib-ute of praise For the glo-ri-ous gift of His love, And the bless-ings that hal-low our days.

In the sweet by and by, We shall meet on that beau-ti-ful shore; In the sweet by and by, We shall meet on that beau-ti-ful shore.

The Church's One Foundation 471

AURELIA. 7. 6. 7. 6. D.

Samuel John Stone, 1839-1900

Samuel Sebastian Wesley, 1810-1876

1. The Church's one foun-da-tion Is Je-sus Christ her Lord;
2. E - lect from ev - ery na - tion, Yet one o'er all the earth,
3. 'Mid toil and trib-u - la - tion, And tu-mult of her war,
4. Yet she on earth hath un - ion With God the Three in One,

She is His new cre - a - tion By wa - ter and the Word;
Her char - ter of sal - va - tion, One Lord, one faith, one birth;
She waits the con - sum - ma - tion Of peace for - ev - er - more;
And mys - tic sweet com - mun - ion With those whose rest is won;

From heaven He came and sought her To be His ho - ly bride;
One ho - ly name she bless - es, Par - takes one ho - ly food,
Till with the vi - sion glo - rious Her long - ing eyes are blest,
O hap - py ones and ho - ly! Lord, give us grace that we,

With His own blood He bought her, And for her life He died.
And to one hope she press - es, With ev - ery grace en - dued.
And the great church vic - to - rious Shall be the church at rest.
Like them, the meek and low - ly, On high may dwell with Thee. A-men.

472

Rise and Shine

GRANTHAM 7.7.7.7.D.

J.R.Zook, 1857-1919   S.R.Smith, 1853-1916

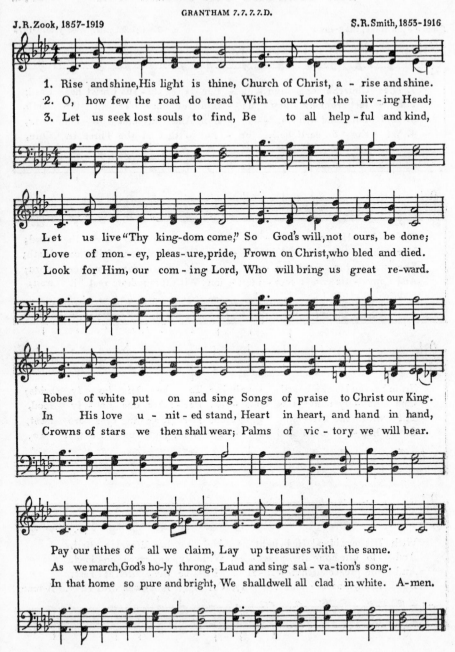

1. Rise and shine, His light is thine, Church of Christ, a - rise and shine.
2. O, how few the road do tread With our Lord the liv-ing Head;
3. Let us seek lost souls to find, Be to all help-ful and kind,

Let us live "Thy king-dom come," So God's will, not ours, be done;
Love of mon-ey, pleas-ure, pride, Frown on Christ, who bled and died.
Look for Him, our com-ing Lord, Who will bring us great re-ward.

Robes of white put on and sing Songs of praise to Christ our King.
In His love u - nit-ed stand, Heart in heart, and hand in hand,
Crowns of stars we then shall wear; Palms of vic - tory we will bear.

Pay our tithes of all we claim, Lay up treasures with the same.
As we march, God's ho-ly throng, Laud and sing sal - va-tion's song.
In that home so pure and bright, We shall dwell all clad in white. A-men.

Glorious Things of Thee Are Spoken 473

AUSTRIAN HYMN 1.7.8.7.D.

John Newton, 1725-1807

Franz Joseph Haydn, 1732-1809

1. Glo - rious things of thee are spo - ken, Zi - on, cit - y of our God;
2. See, the streams of liv - ing wa - ters, Spring-ing from e - ter - nal love,
3. Round each hab - i - ta - tion hov-ering, See the cloud and fire ap - pear,

He whose word can-not be bro - ken, Formed thee for His own a - bode:
Well sup-ply thy sons and daugh-ters, And all fear of want re-move:
For a glo-ry and a cov - ring, Show-ing that the Lord is near:

On the Rock of A - ges found-ed, What can shake thy sure re-pose?
Who can faint while such a riv - er Ev - er flows their thirst t'as-suage?
Thus de - riv - ing from their ban - ner Light by night, and shade by day,

With sal-va-tion's walls sur-round-ed, Thou may'st smile at all thy foes.
Grace which, like the Lord, the giv - er, Nev - er fails from age to age.
Safe they feed up - on the man-na Which He gives them when they pray. Amen.

474 For Christ and the Church

10.12.11.11. with Refrain

Eliza E. Hewitt, 1851-1920

William J. Kirkpatrick, 1858-1921

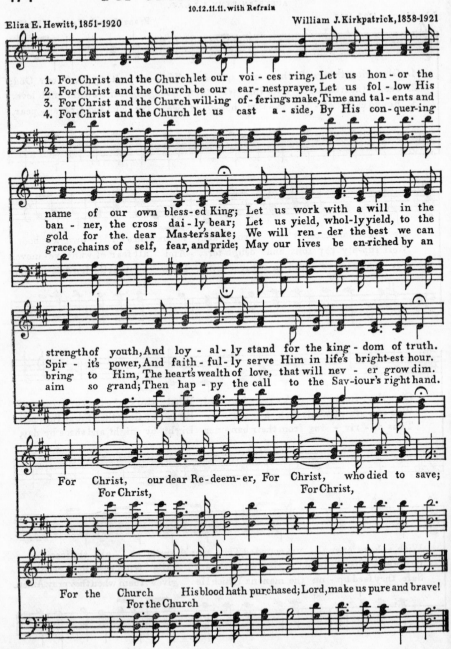

1. For Christ and the Church let our voi - ces ring, Let us hon - or the
2. For Christ and the Church be our ear - nest prayer, Let us fol - low His
3. For Christ and the Church will - ing of - ferings make, Time and tal - ents and
4. For Christ and the Church let us cast a - side, By His con - quer - ing

name of our own bless - ed King; Let us work with a will in the
ban - ner, the cross dai - ly bear; Let us yield, whol - ly yield, to the
gold for the dear Mas - ter's sake; We will ren - der the best we can
grace, chains of self, fear, and pride; May our lives be en - riched by an

strength of youth, And loy - al - ly stand for the king - dom of truth.
Spir - it's power, And faith - ful - ly serve Him in life's bright - est hour.
bring to Him, The heart's wealth of love, that will nev - er grow dim.
aim so grand; Then hap - py the call to the Sav - iour's right hand.

For Christ, our dear Re - deem - er, For Christ, who died to save;
For Christ, For Christ,

For the Church His blood hath purchased; Lord, make us pure and brave!
For the Church

We Join to Worship Thee, O God 475

AZMON 8.6.8.6.

J.N. Hostetter, Jr., 1899—

Carl G.Gläser, 1784-1829
Lowell Mason, 1792-1872

1. We join to wor-ship Thee, O God, With gra-ti-tude and praise;
2. Thy Church,O Lord, Thy pur-chased Bride, Doth coun-sel, wait, and pray:
3. May love di-vine our hearts u-nite As one, O Lord, with Thee;
4. A-noint Thy Church a-new to bear The mes-sage of Thy grace,

Thy mer-cy like an ho-ly cloud Hath cov-ered all our days.
We hum-bly seek Thy will to find; Give wis-dom for to-day.
Il-lume our path, O heaven-ly Light, For we would fol-low Thee.
The suf-fering of Thy cross to share Un-til we see Thy face. A-men.

O Where Are Kings and Empires Now 476

ST. ANNE 8.6.8.6.

A. Cleveland Coxe, 1818-1896

Ascribed to William Croft, 1678-1727

1. O where are kings and em-pires now Of old that went and came?
2. We mark her good-ly bat-tlements, And her foun-da-tions strong;
3. For not like king-doms of the world Thy ho-ly Church, O God!
4. Un-shak-en as e-ter-nal hills, Im-mov-a-ble she stands,

But Lord, Thy Church is pray-ing yet, A thou-sand years the same.
We hear with-in the sol-emn voice Of her un-end-ing song.
Tho' earth-quake shocks are threat-ening her, And tem-pests are a-broad.
A moun-tain that shall fill the earth, A house not made by hands. A-men.

477 Revive Thy Work, O Lord

REVIVE THY WORK 6.6.8.6. with Refrain

Albert Midlane, 1825-1909   James McGranahan, 1840-1907

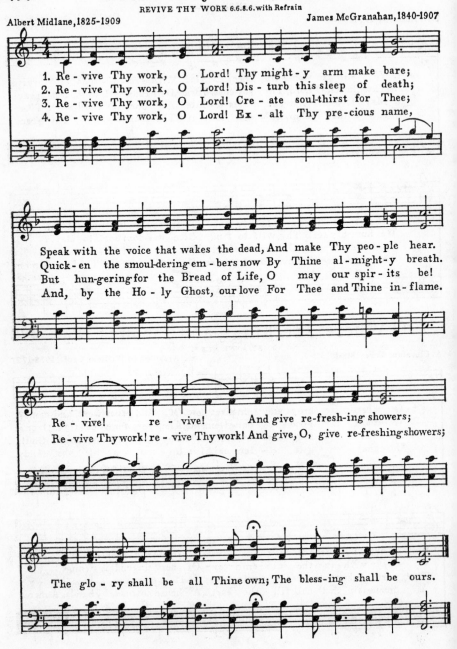

1. Re - vive Thy work, O Lord! Thy might-y arm make bare;
2. Re - vive Thy work, O Lord! Dis - turb this sleep of death;
3. Re - vive Thy work, O Lord! Cre - ate soul-thirst for Thee;
4. Re - vive Thy work, O Lord! Ex - alt Thy pre-cious name,

Speak with the voice that wakes the dead, And make Thy peo - ple hear.
Quick - en the smoul-dering em - bers now By Thine al - might-y breath.
But hun-gering for the Bread of Life, O may our spir - its be!
And, by the Ho - ly Ghost, our love For Thee and Thine in - flame.

Re - vive! re - vive! And give re-fresh-ing showers;
Re - vive Thy work! re - vive Thy work! And give, O, give re-freshing showers;

The glo - ry shall be all Thine own; The bless-ing shall be ours.

A Glorious Church

8.7.8.7. with Refrain

Ralph E. Hudson, 1843-1901   Ralph E. Hudson, 1843-1901

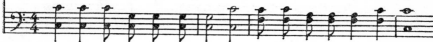

1. Do you hear them com-ing, Christian, Thronging up the steeps of light,
2. Do you hear the stir-ring anthems Fill - ing all the earth and sky?
3. Nev - er fear the clouds of sor-row, Nev - er fear the storms of sin;
4. Wave the ban-ner, shout His prais- es, For our vic - to - ry is nigh!

Clad in glor-ious shin-ing gar-ments, Blood-washed garments pure and white?
'Tis a grand, vic - to - rious arm - y— Lift its ban - ner up on high!
We shall tri-umph on the mor-row, E - ven now our joys be - gin.
We shall join our conquering Sav-iour, We shall reign with Him on high!

'Tis a glo-rious Church, without spot or wrinkle, Washed in the blood of the Lamb;

'Tis a glo-rious Church, with-out spot or wrinkle, Washed in the blood of the Lamb.

479   I Love Thy Kingdom, Lord

ST. THOMAS 6.6.8.6.

Timothy Dwight, 1752-1817   Aaron Williams, 1731-1776

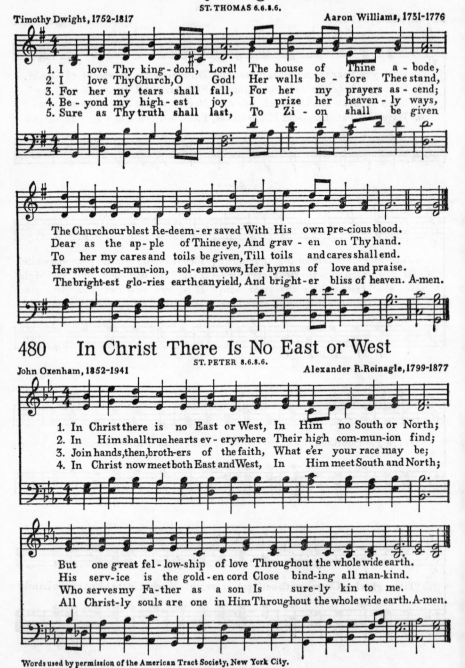

1. I love Thy king-dom, Lord! The house of Thine a-bode,
2. I love Thy Church, O God! Her walls be-fore Thee stand,
3. For her my tears shall fall, For her my prayers as-cend;
4. Be-yond my high-est joy I prize her heaven-ly ways,
5. Sure as Thy truth shall last, To Zi-on shall be given

The Church our blest Re-deem-er saved With His own pre-cious blood.
Dear as the ap-ple of Thine eye, And grav-en on Thy hand.
To her my cares and toils be given, Till toils and cares shall end.
Her sweet com-mun-ion, sol-emn vows, Her hymns of love and praise.
The bright-est glo-ries earth can yield, And bright-er bliss of heaven. A-men.

480   In Christ There Is No East or West

ST. PETER 8.6.8.6.

John Oxenham, 1852-1941   Alexander R. Reinagle, 1799-1877

1. In Christ there is no East or West, In Him no South or North;
2. In Him shall true hearts ev-erywhere Their high com-mun-ion find;
3. Join hands, then, broth-ers of the faith, What e'er your race may be;
4. In Christ now meet both East and West, In Him meet South and North;

But one great fel-low-ship of love Through out the whole wide earth.
His serv-ice is the gold-en cord Close bind-ing all man-kind.
Who serves my Fa-ther as a son Is sure-ly kin to me.
All Christ-ly souls are one in Him Through out the whole wide earth. A-men.

Words used by permission of the American Tract Society, New York City.

Christ Is Made the Sure Foundation 481

REGENT SQUARE 8.7.8.7.8.7.

Latin, 7th century
Tr. by John M. Neale, 1818-1866

Henry Smart, 1813-1879

1. Christ is made the sure foun-da-tion, Christ the head and
2. All that ded-i-ca-ted cit-y, Dear-ly loved of
3. To this tem-ple, where we call Thee, Come, O Lord of
4. Here vouch-safe to all Thy serv-ants What they ask of

cor-ner-stone, Cho-sen of the Lord and pre-cious,
God on high, In ex-ult-ant ju-bi-la-tion
hosts, to-day: With Thy wont-ed lov-ing-kind-ness
Thee to gain, What they gain from Thee for-ev-er

Bind-ing all the Church in one; Ho-ly Zi-on's
Pours per-pet-ual mel-o-dy; God the One in
Hear Thy peo-ple as they pray, And Thy full-est
With the bless-ed to re-tain, And here-aft-er

help for-ev-er, And her con-fi-dence a-lone.
Three a-dor-ing In glad hymns e-ter-nal-ly.
ben-e-dic-tion Shed with-in its walls al-way.
in Thy glo-ry Ev-er-more with Thee to reign. A-men.

482 O Day of Rest and Gladness

MENDEBRAS 7.6.7.6.D.

Christopher Wordsworth, 1807-1885

Old German Melody
Arr. by Lowell Mason, 1792-1872

1. O day of rest and glad-ness, O day of joy and light,
2. On thee, at the cre - a - tion, The light first had its birth;
3. New gra-ces ev - er gain-ing From this our day of rest,

O balm of care and sad-ness, Most beau - ti - ful, most bright:
On thee, for our sal - va-tion, Christ rose from depths of earth;
We reach the rest re - main-ing To spir-its of the blest.

On thee, the high and low - ly, Through a - ges joined in tune,
On thee our Lord, vic - to - rious, The Spir - it sent from heaven,
To Ho - ly Ghost be prais - es, To Fa - ther, and to Son;

Sing, Ho - ly, Ho - ly, Ho - ly, To the great God Tri - une.
And thus on thee, most glo-rious, A tri - ple light was given.
The Church her voice up - rais - es To Thee, blest Three in One. A-men.

Safely Through Another Week 483

SABBATH 7.7.7.7.D.

John Newton, 1725-1807 Lowell Mason, 1792-1872

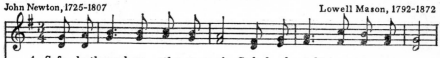

1. Safe - ly through an - oth - er week God has brought us on our way;
2. While we pray for pardoning grace, Through the dear Re - deem - er's name,
3. Here we come Thy name to praise; May we feel Thy pres - ence near:
4. May Thy gos - pel's joy - ful sound Con - quer sin - ners, com - fort saints;

Let us now a bless - ing seek, Wait - ing in His courts to - day:
Show Thy rec - on - cil - ed face, Take a - way our sin and shame;
May Thy glo - ry meet our eyes, While we in Thy house ap - pear;
Make the fruits of grace a - bound, Bring re - lief for all com - plaints:

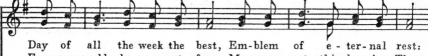

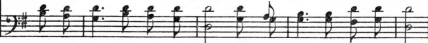

Day of all the week the best, Em - blem of e - ter - nal rest:
From our world - ly cares set free, May we rest this day in Thee:
Here af - ford us, Lord, a taste Of our ev - er - last - ing feast:
Thus may all our Sab - baths prove, Till we join the Church a - bove:

Day of all the week the best, Em - blem of e - ter - nal rest.
From our world - ly cares set free, May we rest this day in Thee.
Here af - ford us, Lord, a taste Of our ev - er - last - ing feast.
Thus may all our Sab - baths prove, Till we join the Church a - bove. A - men.

484 This Is the Day the Lord Hath Made

ARLINGTON 8.6.8.6.

Isaac Watts, 1674-1748

Thomas A. Arne, 1710-1778

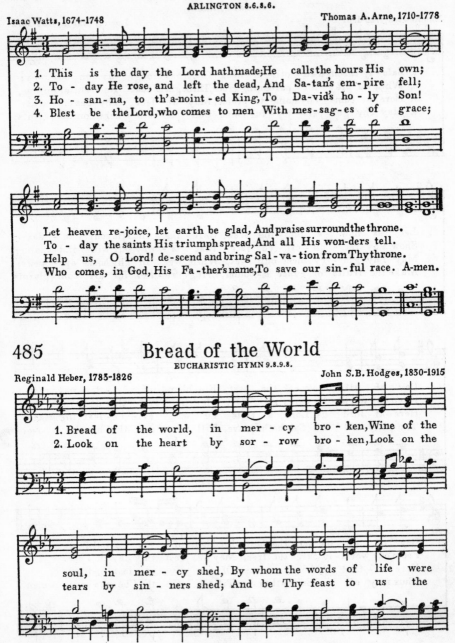

1. This is the day the Lord hath made;He calls the hours His own;
2. To - day He rose, and left the dead, And Sa-tan's em - pire fell;
3. Ho - san-na, to th'a-noint - ed King, To Da-vid's ho - ly Son!
4. Blest be the Lord,who comes to men With mes-sag-es of grace;

Let heaven re-joice, let earth be glad, And praise surround the throne.
To - day the saints His triumph spread,And all His won-ders tell.
Help us, O Lord! de-scend and bring Sal - va - tion from Thy throne.
Who comes, in God, His Fa-ther's name,To save our sin - ful race. A-men.

485 Bread of the World

EUCHARISTIC HYMN 9.8.9.8.

Reginald Heber, 1783-1826

John S.B. Hodges, 1830-1915

1. Bread of the world, in mer - cy bro - ken,Wine of the
2. Look on the heart by sor - row bro - ken,Look on the

soul, in mer - cy shed, By whom the words of life were
tears by sin - ners shed; And be Thy feast to us the

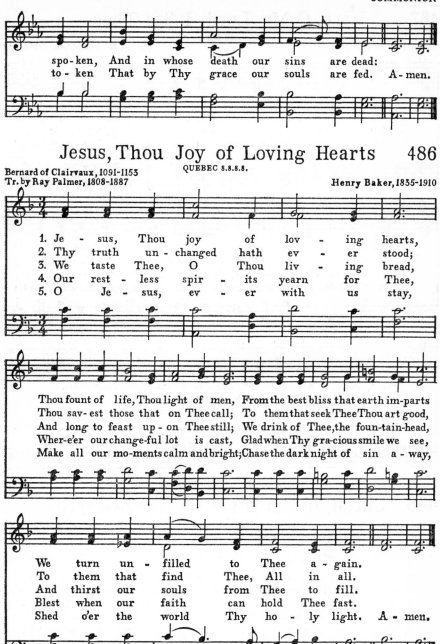

spo-ken, And in whose death our sins are dead:
to-ken That by Thy grace our souls are fed. A-men.

Jesus, Thou Joy of Loving Hearts 486

QUEBEC 8.8.8.8.

Bernard of Clairvaux, 1091-1153
Tr. by Ray Palmer, 1808-1887

Henry Baker, 1835-1910

1. Je - sus, Thou joy of lov - ing hearts,
2. Thy truth un - changed hath ev - er stood;
3. We taste Thee, O Thou liv - ing bread,
4. Our rest - less spir - its yearn for Thee,
5. O Je - sus, ev - er with us stay,

Thou fount of life, Thou light of men, From the best bliss that earth im-parts
Thou sav-est those that on Thee call; To them that seek Thee Thou art good,
And long to feast up-on Thee still; We drink of Thee, the foun-tain-head,
Wher-e'er our change-ful lot is cast, Glad when Thy gra-cious smile we see,
Make all our mo-ments calm and bright; Chase the dark night of sin a-way,

We turn un - filled to Thee a - gain.
To them that find Thee, All in all.
And thirst our souls from Thee to fill.
Blest when our faith can hold Thee fast.
Shed o'er the world Thy ho - ly light. A - men.

487 Here, O My Lord, I See Thee

MORECAMBE 10.10.10.10.

Horatius Bonar, 1808-1889

Frederick Cook Atkinson, 1841-1897

1. Here, O my Lord, I see Thee face to face; Here would I
2. Here would I feed up-on the bread of God, Here drink with
3. This is the hour of ban-quet and of song; This is the
4. Too soon we rise: the sym-bols dis-ap-pear; The feast, though

touch and han-dle things un-seen, Here grasp with firm-er hand e-ter-nal
Thee the roy-al wine of heaven; Here would I lay a-side each earth-ly
heaven-ly ta-ble spread for me; Here let me feast, and, feast-ing, still pro-
not the love, is past and gone; It is e-nough, my Lord, if Thou art

grace, And all my wea-ri-ness up-on Thee lean.
load, Here taste a-fresh the calm of sin for-given.
long The brief, bright hour of fel-low-ship with Thee.
near; My strength is in Thy love, Thy love a-lone. A-men.

488 Christ, in the Night He Was Betrayed

HEBRON 8.8.8.8.

Unknown

Lowell Mason, 1792-1872

1. Christ, in the night He was betrayed, For us a plain ex-am-ple laid;
2. The paschal feast was there prepared, And Lord and serv-ants mu-tual shared;
3. He rose and laid His gar-ments by, When towel and wa-ter were brought nigh;
4. So aft-er He had washed their feet, Re-sumed His gar-ment, took His seat,
5. "Ex-am-ple give I un-to you, As I have done so ye should do,

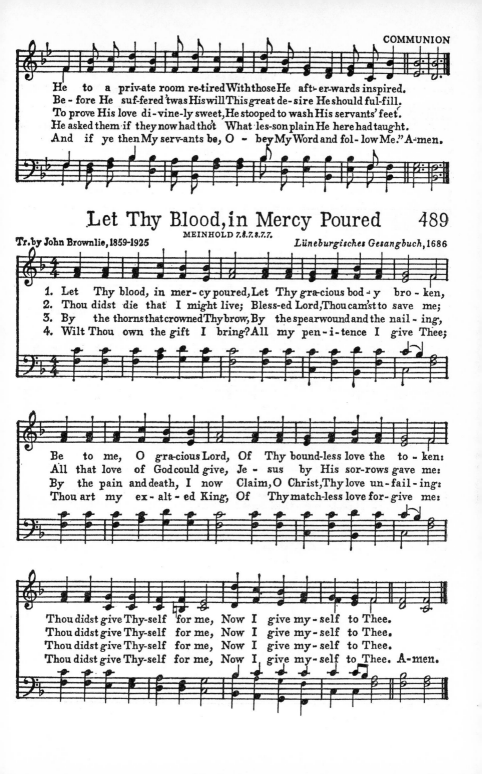

He to a pri-vate room re-tired With those He aft-er-wards inspired.
Be - fore He suf-fered 'twas His will This great de-sire He should ful-fill.
To prove His love di-vine-ly sweet, He stooped to wash His servants' feet.
He asked them if they now had thot What les-son plain He here had taught.
And if ye then My serv-ants be, O - bey My Word and fol-low Me." A-men.

Let Thy Blood, in Mercy Poured 489

MEINHOLD 7.8.7.8.7.7.

Tr. by John Brownlie, 1859-1925

Lüneburgisches Gesangbuch, 1686

1. Let Thy blood, in mer-cy poured, Let Thy gra-cious bod-y bro-ken,
2. Thou didst die that I might live; Bless-ed Lord, Thou cam'st to save me;
3. By the thorns that crowned Thy brow, By the spear wound and the nail-ing,
4. Wilt Thou own the gift I bring? All my pen-i-tence I give Thee;

Be to me, O gra-cious Lord, Of Thy bound-less love the to-ken:
All that love of God could give, Je-sus by His sor-rows gave me:
By the pain and death, I now Claim, O Christ, Thy love un-fail-ing:
Thou art my ex-alt-ed King, Of Thy match-less love for-give me:

Thou didst give Thy-self for me, Now I give my-self to Thee.
Thou didst give Thy-self for me, Now I give my-self to Thee.
Thou didst give Thy-self for me, Now I give my-self to Thee.
Thou didst give Thy-self for me, Now I give my-self to Thee. A-men.

490 Extol the Love of Christ

VARINA 8.6.8.6.D.

Samuel F. Coffman, 1872—   George F. Root, 1820-1895

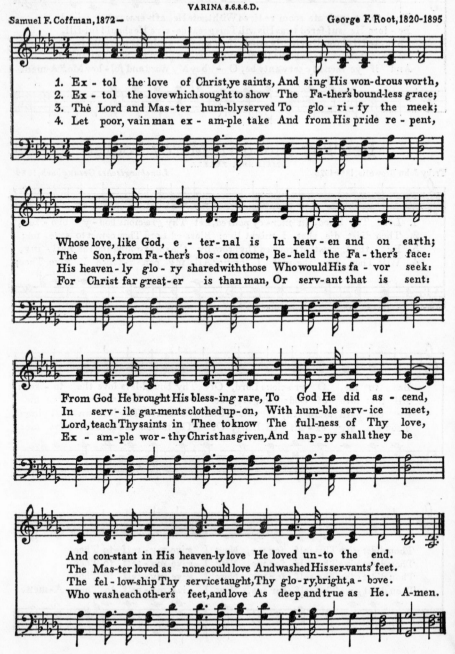

1. Ex - tol the love of Christ, ye saints, And sing His won-drous worth,
2. Ex - tol the love which sought to show The Fa-ther's bound-less grace;
3. The Lord and Mas - ter hum-bly served To glo - ri - fy the meek;
4. Let poor, vain man ex - am-ple take And from His pride re - pent,

Whose love, like God, e - ter-nal is In heav-en and on earth;
The Son, from Fa-ther's bos - om come, Be-held the Fa - ther's face:
His heaven - ly glo - ry shared with those Who would His fa - vor seek:
For Christ far great-er is than man, Or serv-ant that is sent:

From God He brought His bless-ing rare, To God He did as - cend,
In serv - ile gar-ments clothed up-on, With hum-ble serv - ice meet,
Lord, teach Thy saints in Thee to know The full-ness of Thy love,
Ex - am-ple wor - thy Christ has given, And hap-py shall they be

And con-stant in His heaven-ly love He loved un-to the end.
The Mas-ter loved as none could love And washed His ser-vants' feet.
The fel - low-ship Thy service taught, Thy glo - ry, bright, a - bove.
Who wash each oth-er's feet, and love As deep and true as He. A-men.

Come, Holy Spirit, Dove Divine

ERNAN 8.8.8.8.

Adoniram Judson, 1788-1850

Lowell Mason, 1792-1872

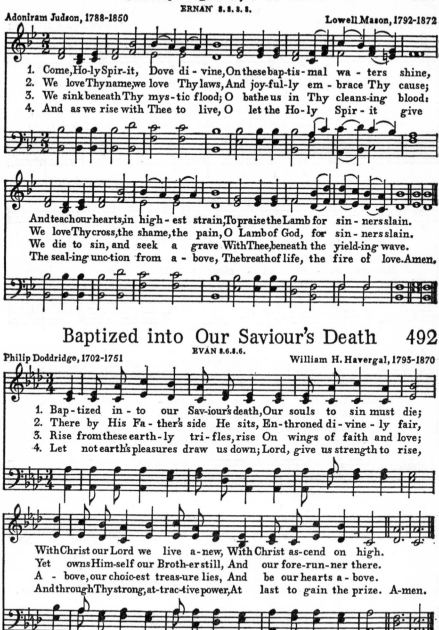

1. Come, Ho-ly Spir-it, Dove di-vine, On these bap-tis-mal wa-ters shine,
2. We love Thy name, we love Thy laws, And joy-ful-ly em-brace Thy cause;
3. We sink beneath Thy mys-tic flood; O bathe us in Thy cleans-ing blood:
4. And as we rise with Thee to live, O let the Ho-ly Spir-it give

And teach our hearts, in high-est strain, To praise the Lamb for sin-ners slain.
We love Thy cross, the shame, the pain, O Lamb of God, for sin-ners slain.
We die to sin, and seek a grave With Thee, beneath the yield-ing wave.
The seal-ing unc-tion from a-bove, The breath of life, the fire of love. Amen.

Baptized into Our Saviour's Death

492

EVAN 8.6.8.6.

Philip Doddridge, 1702-1751

William H. Havergal, 1793-1870

1. Bap-tized in-to our Sav-iour's death, Our souls to sin must die;
2. There by His Fa-ther's side He sits, En-throned di-vine-ly fair,
3. Rise from these earth-ly tri-fles, rise On wings of faith and love;
4. Let not earth's pleasures draw us down; Lord, give us strength to rise,

With Christ our Lord we live a-new, With Christ as-cend on high.
Yet owns Him-self our Broth-er still, And our fore-run-ner there.
A-bove, our choic-est treas-ure lies, And be our hearts a-bove.
And through Thy strong, at-trac-tive power, At last to gain the prize. A-men.

493 Hail to the Brightness

WESLEY 11.10.11.10.

Thomas Hastings, 1784-1872　　　　　　　　　Lowell Mason, 1792-1872

1. Hail to the bright-ness of Zi-on's glad morn-ing,
2. Hail to the bright-ness of Zi-on's glad morn-ing,
3. Lo, in the des-ert rich flow-ers are spring-ing,
4. See, from all lands, from the isles of the o-cean,

Joy to the lands that in dark-ness have lain!
Long by the proph-ets of Is-rael fore-told;
Streams ev-er co-pious are flow-ing a-long;
Praise to the Sav-iour as-cend-ing on high;

Hushed be the ac-cents of sor-row and mourn-ing,
Hail to the mil-lions from bond-age re-turn-ing!
Loud from the moun-tain-tops ech-oes are ring-ing,
Fall-en the wea-pons of war and com-mo-tion,

Zi-on in tri-umph be-gins her mild reign.
Gen-tiles and Jews the blest vi-sion be-hold.
Wastes rise in ver-dure and min-gle in song.
Shouts of sal-va-tion are rend-ing the sky. A-men.

O Zion, Haste

TIDINGS 11.10.11.10.with Refrain

Mary A. Thomson, 1834-1923   James Walch, 1837-1901

1. O Zi - on, haste, thy mis - sion high ful - fill-ing, To tell to all the
2. Pro - claim to ev - ery peo - ple, tongue, and na - tion That God, in whom they
3. Give of thy sons to bear the mes-sage glo - rious; Give of thy wealth to
4. He comes a - gain: O Zi - on, ere Thou meet Him, Make known to ev - ery

world that God is light; That He who made all na - tions is not will - ing
live and move, is love: Tell how He stooped to save His lost cre - a - tion,
speed them on their way; Pour out thy soul for them in prayer vic - to - rious;
heart His sav-ing grace: Let none whom He hath ran-somed fail to greet Him,

One soul should per - ish, lost in shades of night.
And died on earth that man might live a - bove.
And all thou spend-est Je - sus will re - pay.   Pub-lish glad ti-dings,
Through thy neg-lect, un - fit to see His face.

ti - dings of peace, Ti - dings of Je - sus, re - demp-tion and re-lease.

495 Hark! the Voice of Jesus Calling

ELLESDIE 8.7.8.7.D.

Ascribed to Wolfgang A. Mozart, 1756-1791
Arr. by Hubert P. Main, 1839-1925

Daniel March, 1816-1909

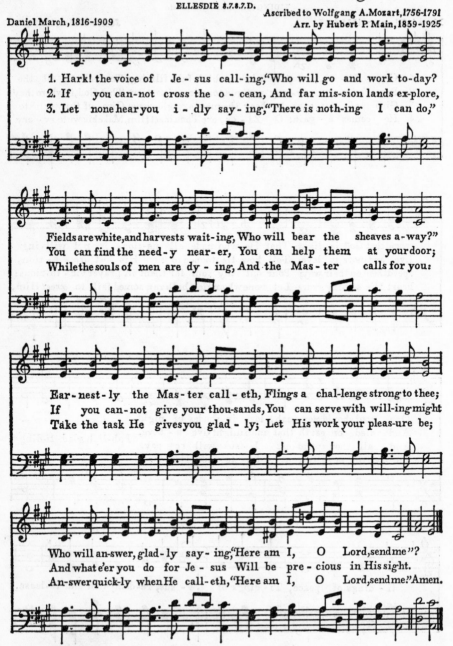

1. Hark! the voice of Je-sus call-ing, "Who will go and work to-day?
2. If you can-not cross the o-cean, And far mis-sion lands ex-plore,
3. Let none hear you i-dly say-ing, "There is noth-ing I can do,"

Fields are white, and harvests wait-ing, Who will bear the sheaves a-way?"
You can find the need-y near-er, You can help them at your door;
While the souls of men are dy-ing, And the Mas-ter calls for you:

Ear-nest-ly the Mas-ter call-eth, Flings a chal-lenge strong to thee;
If you can-not give your thou-sands, You can serve with will-ing might
Take the task He gives you glad-ly; Let His work your pleas-ure be;

Who will an-swer, glad-ly say-ing, "Here am I, O Lord, send me"?
And what e'er you do for Je-sus Will be pre-cious in His sight.
An-swer quick-ly when He call-eth, "Here am I, O Lord, send me." Amen.

Far, Far Away, in Heathen Darkness Dwelling 496

11.10.11.10.with Refrain

James McGranahan, 1840-1907   James McGranahan, 1840-1907

1. Far, far a - way, in hea - then dark - ness dwell - ing;
2. See o'er the world wide - o - pen doors in - vit - ing;
3. "Why will ye die?" the voice of God is call - ing;
4. God speed the day, when those of ev - ery na - tion

Mil - lions of souls for - ev - er may be lost; Who, who will go, sal -
Sol - diers of Christ, a - rise and en - ter in! Chris-tians, a - wake! your
"Why will ye die?" re - ech - o in His name; Je - sus hath died to
"Glo - ry to God!" tri - um-phant-ly shall sing; Ran-somed, re-deemed, re -

va' - tion's sto - ry tell - ing, Look - ing to Je - sus, mind-ing not the cost?
forc - es all u - nit - ing, Send forth the gos-pel, break the chains of sin.
save from death ap - pall - ing, Life and sal-va-tion there-fore go pro-claim.
joic - ing in sal - va - tion, Shout Hal - le lu - jah, for the Lord is King.

"All power is giv - en un - to Me, All power is giv - en un - to Me,

Go ye in-to all the world and preach the gospel, And lo, I am with you al-way."

497 From Greenland's Icy Mountains

MISSIONARY HYMN 7.6.7.6.D.

Reginald Heber, 1783-1826   Lowell Mason, 1792-1872

1. From Green-land's i - cy moun-tains, From In - dia's cor - al strand,
2. What though the spi - cy breez - es Blow soft o'er Cey-lon's isle;
3. Shall we, whose souls are light - ed With wis-dom from on high,
4. Waft, waft, ye winds, His sto - ry, And you, ye wa-ters, roll,

Where A - fric's sun - ny foun-tains Roll down their gold-en sand,
Though ev - ery pros-pect pleas - es, And on - ly man is vile:
Shall we to men be - night - ed The lamp of life de - ny?
Till, like a sea of glo - ry, It spreads from pole to pole;

From many an an - cient riv - er, From many a palm - y plain,
In vain with lav - ish kind-ness The gifts of God are strown;
Sal - va - tion! O sal - va - tion! The joy - ful sound pro - claim,
Till o'er our ransomed na - ture The Lamb for sin - ners slain,

They call us to de - liv - er Their land from er - ror's chain.
The hea-then in his blindness Bows down to wood and stone.
Till earth's re - mot-est na - tion Has learned Mes-si - ah's name.
Re - deem-er, King, Cre - a - tor, In bliss re-turns to reign. A-men.

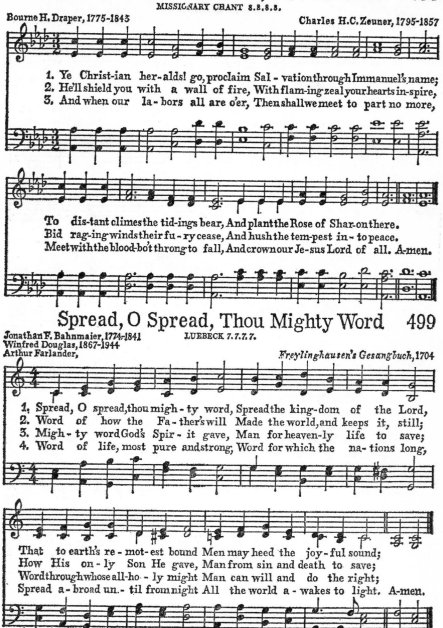

Ye Christian Heralds, Go Proclaim 498

MISSIONARY CHANT 8.8.8.8.

Bourne H. Draper, 1775-1843

Charles H. C. Zeuner, 1795-1857

1. Ye Christ-ian her-alds! go, proclaim Sal - vation through Immanuel's name;
2. He'll shield you with a wall of fire, With flam-ing zeal your hearts in-spire,
3. And when our la-bors all are o'er, Then shall we meet to part no more,

To dis-tant climes the tid-ings bear, And plant the Rose of Shar-on there.
Bid rag-ing winds their fu - ry cease, And hush the tem-pest in - to peace.
Meet with the blood-bo't throng to fall, And crown our Je-sus Lord of all. A-men.

Spread, O Spread, Thou Mighty Word 499

LUEBECK 7.7.7.7.

Jonathan F. Bahnmaier, 1774-1841
Winfred Douglas, 1867-1944
Arthur Farlander,

Freylinghausen's Gesangbuch, 1704

1. Spread, O spread, thou migh - ty word, Spread the king-dom of the Lord,
2. Word of how the Fa - ther's will Made the world, and keeps it, still;
3. Migh - ty word God's Spir - it gave, Man for heaven-ly life to save;
4. Word of life, most pure and strong, Word for which the na - tions long,

That to earth's re - mot-est bound Men may heed the joy-ful sound;
How His on - ly Son He gave, Man from sin and death to save;
Word through whose all-ho - ly might Man can will and do the right;
Spread a-broad un - til from night All the world a - wakes to light. A-men.

500 We've a Story to Tell to the Nations

MESSAGE 10.8.8.7.7.with Refrain

H. Ernest Nichol, 1862-1928

H. Ernest Nichol, 1862-1928

1. We've a sto-ry to tell to the na-tions That shall turn their hearts to the right, A sto-ry of truth and mer-cy, A sto-ry of peace and light, A sto-ry of peace and light.

2. We've a song to be sung to the na-tions That shall lift their hearts to the Lord, A song that shall con-quer e-vil And shat-ter the spear and sword, And shat-ter the spear and sword.

3. We've a mes-sage to give to the na-tions That the Lord who reign-eth a-bove Hath sent us His Son to save us And show us that God is love, And show us that God is love.

4. We've a Sav-iour to show to the na-tions, Who the path of sor-row has trod, That all of the world's great peo-ples Might come to the truth of God, Might come to the truth of God.

For the darkness shall turn to dawn-ing, And the dawn-ing to noon-day bright,

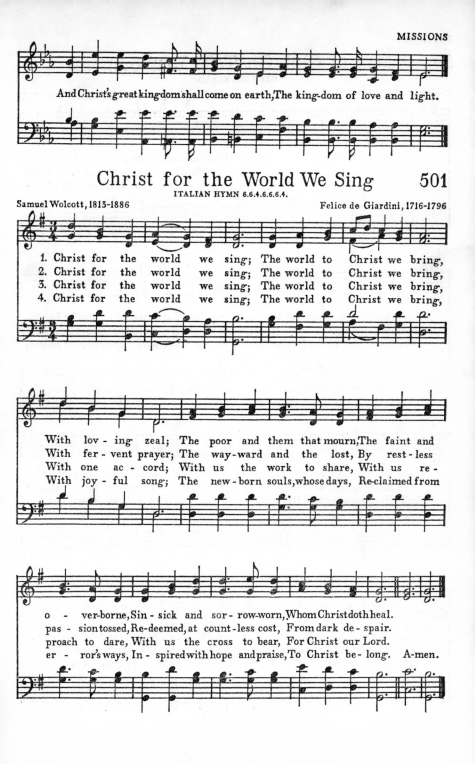

And Christ's great kingdom shall come on earth, The kingdom of love and light.

Christ for the World We Sing 501

ITALIAN HYMN 6.6.4.6.6.6.4.

Samuel Wolcott, 1813-1886

Felice de Giardini, 1716-1796

1. Christ for the world we sing; The world to Christ we bring,
2. Christ for the world we sing; The world to Christ we bring,
3. Christ for the world we sing; The world to Christ we bring,
4. Christ for the world we sing; The world to Christ we bring,

With lov - ing zeal; The poor and them that mourn, The faint and
With fer - vent prayer; The way-ward and the lost, By rest-less
With one ac - cord; With us the work to share, With us re-
With joy - ful song; The new-born souls, whose days, Re-claimed from

o - ver-borne, Sin - sick and sor - row-worn, Whom Christ doth heal.
pas - sion tossed, Re-deemed, at count-less cost, From dark de - spair.
proach to dare, With us the cross to bear, For Christ our Lord.
er - ror's ways, In - spired with hope and praise, To Christ be - long. A-men.

502 Men of God, Go Take Your Stations

HARWELL 8.7.8.7.D.

Thomas Kelly, 1769-1854   Lowell Mason, 1792-1872

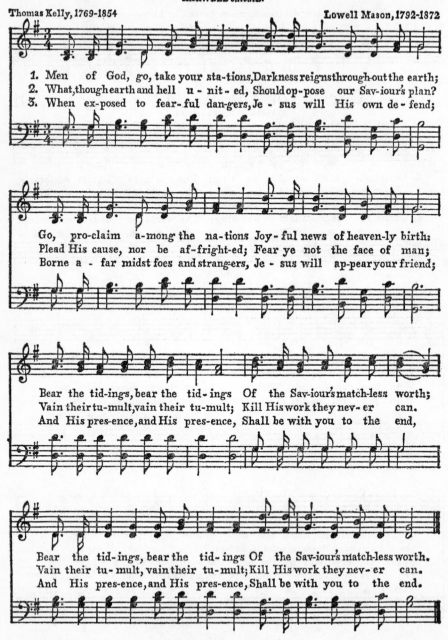

1. Men of God, go, take your sta-tions, Darkness reigns through-out the earth;
2. What, though earth and hell u - nit - ed, Should op-pose our Sav-iour's plan?
3. When ex-posed to fear-ful dan-gers, Je - sus will His own de - fend;

Go, pro-claim a-mong the na-tions Joy-ful news of heaven-ly birth:
Plead His cause, nor be af-fright-ed; Fear ye not the face of man;
Borne a - far midst foes and strangers, Je - sus will ap-pear your friend;

Bear the tid-ings, bear the tid-ings Of the Sav-iour's match-less worth;
Vain their tu-mult, vain their tu-mult; Kill His work they nev- er can.
And His pres-ence, and His pres-ence, Shall be with you to the end,

Bear the tid-ings, bear the tid-ings Of the Sav-iour's match-less worth.
Vain their tu - mult, vain their tu-mult; Kill His work they nev- er can.
And His pres-ence, and His pres-ence, Shall be with you to the end.

Go and Seek the Lost

ZION 8.7.8.7.4.7. with Repeat

Henry B. Hartzler, 1840-1920

Thomas Hastings, 1784-1872

1. Go and seek the lost and dy-ing; Preach the world's glad ju-bi-lee;
2. Go and tell the bless-ed sto-ry Of the ho-ly Lamb of God;
3. May the peace of God at-tend you, As you gath-er pre-cious spoil;
4. Fare you well! what-e'er. be-tide you, Look to Je-sus for His grace;

Like the her-ald an-gels, fly-ing, Bear God's mes-sage o'er the sea;
Show the poor. His grace and glo-ry; Lead the dy-ing to His blood,
May His arms of love de-fend you, All as-saults of e-vil foil.
He will com-fort, cheer, and guide you, Till at last, in His em-brace,

Toil for Je-sus, Till the blind His glo-ry see,
Ev-er cry-ing, O be-hold the Lamb of God!
May His pres-ence Cheer you on the field of toil,
Safe for-ev-er, You shall see Him. face to face,

Toil for Je-sus, Till the blind His glo-ry see.
Ev-er cry-ing, O be-hold the Lamb of God!
May His pres-ence Cheer you on the field of toil.
Safe for-ev-er, You shall see Him face to face. A-men.

504 The Call for Reapers

HARVEST-TIME 8.7.8.7. with Refrain

John O. Thompson, 1782-1818   J.B.O.Clemm, 19th century

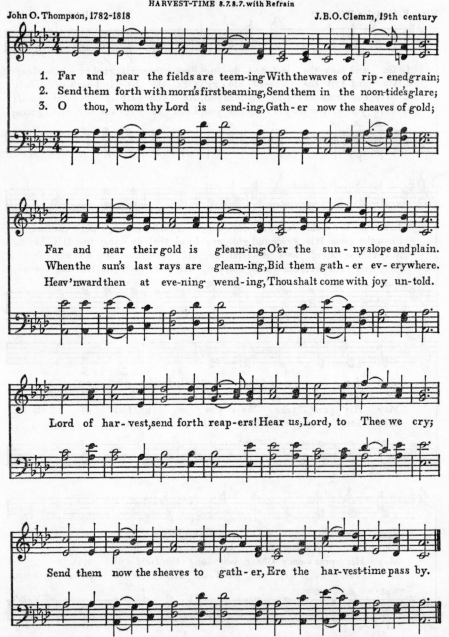

1. Far and near the fields are teem-ing With the waves of rip - ened grain;
2. Send them forth with morn's first beaming, Send them in the noon-tide's glare;
3. O thou, whom thy Lord is send-ing, Gath - er now the sheaves of gold;

Far and near their gold is gleam-ing O'er the sun - ny slope and plain.
When the sun's last rays are gleam-ing, Bid them gath - er ev - erywhere.
Heav'nward then at eve-ning wend-ing, Thou shalt come with joy un-told.

Lord of har - vest, send forth reap-ers! Hear us, Lord, to Thee we cry;

Send them now the sheaves to gath - er, Ere the har-vest-time pass by.

Heralds of Christ

NATIONAL HYMN 10.10.10.10.

Laura S. Copenhaver, 1868-1940

George William Warren 1828-1902

Repeated before stanzas 2,3,4

1. Her - alds of Christ, who bear the King's com-mands,
2. Thro' des-ert ways, dark fen, and deep mo - rass,
3. Where once the twist - ing trail in dark-ness wound
4. Lord, give us faith and strength the road to build,

Im - mor - tal ti - dings in your mor - tal hands,
Thro' jun - gles, ra - ging seas, and moun-tain pass,
Let march - ing feet and joy - ous song re - sound,
To see the prom - ise of the day ful - filled,

Pass on and car - ry swift the news ye bring;
Build ye the road, and fal - ter not nor stay;
Where burned the fu - neral pyres, let chil - dren sing;
When war shall be no more and strife shall cease

Make straight, make straight the high - way of the King.
In ev - ery land pre - pare the King's high - way.
Make straight, make straight the high - way of the King.
Up - on the high - way of the Prince of Peace. A-men.

506 We Have Heard the Joyful Sound

JESUS SAVES 7.6.7.6.7.7.7.6.

Priscilla J. Owens, 1829-1907   William J. Kirkpatrick, 1838-1921

1. We have heard the joy - ful sound: Je - sus saves! Je - sus saves!
2. Waft it on the roll - ing tide; Je - sus saves! Je - sus saves!
3. Sing a - bove the bat - tle strife, Je - sus saves! Je - sus saves!
4. Give the winds a might - y voice, Je - sus saves! Je - sus saves!

Spread the ti - dings all a - round: Je - sus saves! Je - sus saves!
Tell to sin - ners far and wide: Je - sus saves! Je - sus saves!
By His death and end - less life, Je - sus saves! Je - sus saves!
Let the na - tions now re - joice, Je - sus saves! Je - sus saves!

Bear the news to ev - ery land, Climb the steeps and cross the waves;
Sing, ye is - lands of the sea; Ech - o back, ye o - cean caves;
Sing it soft - ly through the gloom, When the heart for mer - cy craves;
Shout sal - va - tion full and free, High-est hills and deep - est caves;

On - ward! 'tis our Lord's com - mand: Je - sus saves! Je - sus saves!
Earth shall keep her ju - bi - lee: Je - sus saves! Je - sus saves!
Sing in tri - umph o'er the tomb, Je - sus saves! Je - sus saves!
This our song of vic - to - ry: Je - sus saves! Je - sus saves!

Hear the Voice of Jesus Say

7.7.7.7.with Refrain

Charles E. Clouse, 1891—   Charles E. Clouse, 1891-

1. Hear the voice of Je-sus say, "Who will go and work to-day?"
2. Fields are white, but work-ers few, Lord of har-vest calls for you;
3. Like the proph-et years a-go, Fire di-vine set lips a-glow,
4. Je-sus has a work for all, For the great and for the small;

Who will glad-ly an-swer aye? Here am I, send me!
An-swer Him with heart so true, Here am I, send me!
An-swer Him who asks "Who will go?" Here am I, send me!
Now re-ply to His earn-est call, Here am I, send me!

Here am I, O Lord, send me! O-ver plain or o-ver sea,

An-y-where it pleas-eth Thee, Here am I, send me!

So Send I You

11.10.11.10.with Refrain

E. Margaret Clarkson, 1915—

John W. Peterson, 1921—

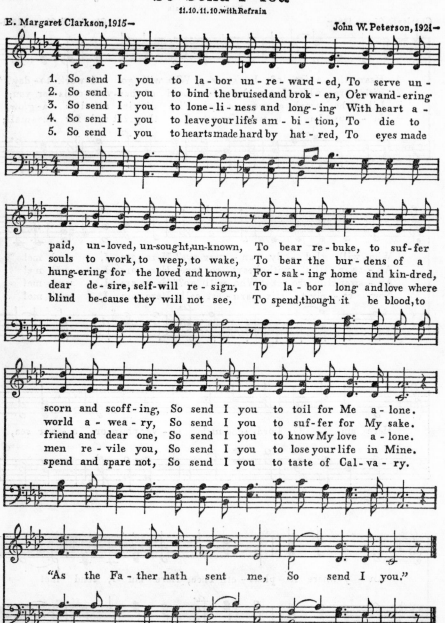

1. So send I you to la-bor un-re-ward-ed, To serve un-
2. So send I you to bind the bruised and brok-en, O'er wand-ering
3. So send I you to lone-li-ness and long-ing With heart a-
4. So send I you to leave your life's am-bi-tion, To die to
5. So send I you to hearts made hard by hat-red, To eyes made

paid, un-loved, un-sought,un-known, To bear re-buke, to suf-fer
souls to work, to weep, to wake, To bear the bur-dens of a
hung-ering for the loved and known, For-sak-ing home and kin-dred,
dear de-sire, self-will re-sign, To la-bor long and love where
blind be-cause they will not see, To spend, though it be blood, to

scorn and scoff-ing, So send I you to toil for Me a-lone.
world a-wea-ry, So send I you to suf-fer for My sake.
friend and dear one, So send I you to know My love a-lone.
men re-vile you, So send I you to lose your life in Mine.
spend and spare not, So send I you to taste of Cal-va-ry.

"As the Fa-ther hath sent me, So send I you."

Go, Labor On! Spend and Be Spent 509

PENTECOST 8.8.8.8.

Horatius Bonar, 1808-1889

William Boyd, 1847-1928

1. Go, la-bor on! spend, and be spent, Thy joy to do the Fa-ther's will:
2. Go, la-bor on; 'tis not for naught; Thy earthly loss is heaven-ly gain:
3. Go, la-bor on while it is day: The world's dark night is hastening on;
4. Toil on, faint not, keep watch, and pray, Be wise the err-ing soul to win;

It is the way the Mas-ter went; Should not the ser-vant tread it still?
Men heed thee, love thee, praise thee not; The Mas-ter prais-es: what are men?
Speed, speed thy work, cast sloth a-way; It is not thus that souls are won.
Go forth in - to the world's highway; Com-pel the wanderer to come in. A-men.

Music used by permission of Novello & Co., Ltd.

Fling Out the Banner 510

WALTHAM 8.8.8.8.

George W. Doane, 1799-1859

John B. Calkin, 1827-1905

1. Fling out the ban-ner! let it float Sky-ward and sea-ward, high and wide;
2. Fling out the ban-ner! heath-en lands Shall see from far the glo-rious sight,
3. Fling out the ban-ner! sin-sick souls That sink and per-ish in the strife,
4. Fling out the ban-ner! let it float Sky-ward and sea-ward, high and wide,

The sun that lights its shin-ing folds, The cross on which the Sav-iour died.
And na-tions, crowding to be born, Bap-tize their spir-its in its light.
Shall touch in faith its ra-diant hem, And spring immortal in - to life.
Our glo-ry on - ly in the cross, Our on-ly hope, the Cru-ci-fied. A-men.

511 God of the Prophets

TOULON 10.10.10.10.

Denis Wortman, 1835-1922

Genevan Psalter, 1543
Louis Bourgeois, 1510-1561

1. God of the proph - ets, Bless the proph - ets' sons;
2. A - noint them proph - ets! Make their ears at - tent
3. Make them e - van - gels, Her - alds of Thy cross,

E - li - jah's man - tle o'er E - li - sha cast;
To Thy di - vin - est speech; their hearts a - wake
Forth may they go to tell all realms Thy grace;

Each age its sol - emn task may claim but once;
To hu - man need; their lips make el - o - quent
In - spired of Thee, may they count all but loss,

Make each one no - bler, strong - er than the last.
To gird the right and ev - er - y e - vil break.
And stand at last with joy be - fore Thy face. A - men.

Pour Out Thy Spirit from on High

HOLLEY 8.8.8.8.

James Montgomery, 1771-1854

George Hews, 1806-1873

1. Pour out Thy Spir-it from on high; Lord, Thine or-dain-ed serv-ants bless;
2. With-in Thy tem-ple when they stand To teach the truth as taught by Thee,
3. Wis-dom and zeal and faith im-part, Firmness with meek-ness from a-bove,
4. To watch and pray, and nev-er faint; By day and night strict guard to keep;
5. Then, when their work is fin-ished here, In hum-ble hope their charge re-sign,

Grac-es and gifts to each sup-ply, And clothe them with Thy righteousness.
Sav-iour, like stars in Thy right hand The an-gels of the church-es be.
To bear Thy peo-ple on their heart, And love the souls whom Thou dost love.
To warn the sin-ner, cheer the saint, Nour-ish Thy lambs and feed Thy sheep.
When the Chief Shepherd shall appear, O God, may they and we be Thine. A-men.

Behold the Sure Foundation Stone

ST. AGNES 8.6.8.6.

513

Isaac Watts, 1674-1748

John B. Dykes, 1823-1876

1. Be-hold the sure foun-da-tion stone Which God in Zi-on lays,
2. Cho-sen of God, to sin-ners dear, We now a-dore Thy name;
3. The fool-ish build-ers, scribe and priest, Re-ject it with dis-dain;
4. What though the gates of hell with-stood? Yet must this build-ing rise;

To build our heaven-ly hopes up-on, And His e-ter-nal praise.
We trust our whole sal-va-tion here, Nor can we suf-fer shame.
Yet on this Rock the church shall rest, And en-vy rage in vain.
'Tis Thine own work, al-might-y God, And wondrous in our eyes. A-men.

514 The Lord Our God Alone Is Strong

TRURO 8.8.8.8.

Caleb T. Winchester, 1847-1920

T. Williams, *Psalmodia Evangelica*, 1789

1. The Lord our God a-lone is strong; His hands built not for one brief day;
2. His mountains lift their sol-emn forms To watch in si-lence o'er the land;
3. Thou sovereign God, re-ceive the praise Thy will-ing ser-vants of-fer Thee;
4. And let those learn, who here shall meet, True wis-dom is with rev'rence crowned,

His wondrous works, through ages long, His wisdom and His power display.
The roll-ing o-cean, rocked with storms, Sleeps in the hollow of His hand.
Ac-cept the prayer that thousands raise, And let these halls Thy temple be.
And sci-ence walks with hum-ble feet To seek the God that faith hath found. Amen.

515 Thou, Whose Unmeasured Temple Stands

DUNDEE 8.6.8.6.

William Cullen Bryant, 1794-1878

The Scottish Psalter, 1615

1. Thou, whose un-meas-ured tem-ple stands, Built o-ver earth and sea,
2. And let the Com-fort-er and Friend, Thy Ho-ly Spir-it, meet
3. May they who err be guid-ed here To find the bet-ter way;
4. May faith grow firm, and love grow warm, And pure de-vo-tion rise,

Ac-cept the walls that hu-man hands Have raised, O God, to Thee.
With those who here in wor-ship bend Be-fore Thy mer-cy-seat.
And they who mourn, and they who fear, Be strength-ened as they pray.
While round these hallowed walls the storm Of earth-born pas-sion dies. A-men.

Almighty Lord, with One Accord 516

AZMON 8.6.8.6.

M. Woolsey Stryker, 1851-1929

Carl G. Gläser, 1784-1829
Arr. by Lowell Mason, 1792-1872

1. Al-might-y Lord with one ac-cord We of-fer Thee our youth,
2. Thy cause doth claim our souls by name, Be-cause that we are strong;
3. Let fall on ev-ery col-lege hall The lus-ter of Thy cross,
4. Our hearts be ruled, our spir-its schooled A-lone Thy will to seek,

And pray that Thou would'st give us now The war-fare of the truth.
In all the land, one stead-fast band, May we to Christ be-long.
That love may dare Thy work to share And count all else as loss.
And when we find Thy bless-ed mind, In-struct our lips to speak. A-men.

Lord and Saviour, True and Kind 517

POSEN 7.7.7.7.

Handley C.G. Moule, 1841-1920

George C. Strattner, 1650-1705

1. Lord and Sav-iour, true and kind, Be the mas-ter of my mind;
2. Here I train for life's swift race; Let me do it in Thy grace:
3. Thou hast made me mind and soul; I for Thee would use the whole:
4. Striv-ing, think-ing, learn-ing still, Let me fol-low thus Thy will,

Bless, and guide, and strengthen still All my powers of thought and will.
Here I arm me for life's fight; Let me do it in Thy might.
Thou hast died that I might live; All my powers to Thee I give.
Till my whole glad na-ture be Trained for du-ty and for Thee. A-men.

518 O Perfect Love

PERFECT LOVE 11.10.11.10.

Dorothy B. Gurney, 1858-1932

Joseph Barnby, 1838-1896

1. O per-fect Love, all hu-man thought tran-scend-ing,
2. O per-fect Life, be Thou their full as-sur-ance
3. Grant them the joy which bright-ens earth-ly sor-row;

Low-ly we kneel in prayer be-fore Thy throne,
Of ten-der char-i-ty and stead-fast faith,
Grant them the peace which calms all earth-ly strife,

That theirs may be the love that knows no end-ing,
Of pa-tient hope, and qui-et, brave en-dur-ance,
And to life's day the glo-rious un-known mor-row

Whom Thou for-ev-er-more dost join in one.
With child-like trust that fears nor pain nor death.
That dawns up-on e-ter-nal love and life. A-men.

The Voice That Breathed o'er Eden

LLANFYLLIN 7.6.7.6. D.

John Keble, 1792-1866   Welsh Melody, 1865

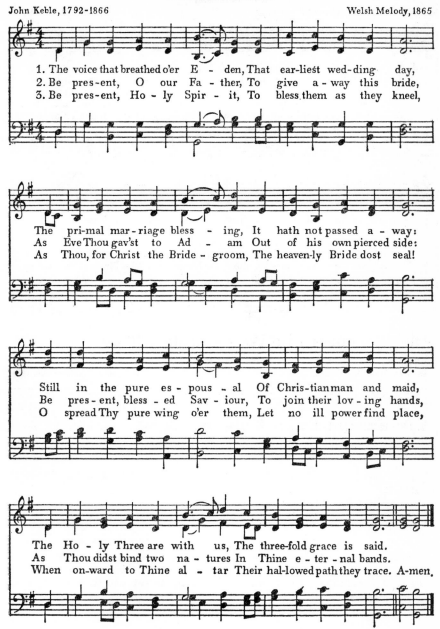

1. The voice that breathed o'er E - den, That ear-liest wed-ding day,
2. Be pres-ent, O our Fa - ther, To give a-way this bride,
3. Be pres-ent, Ho - ly Spir - it, To bless them as they kneel,

The pri-mal mar-riage bless - ing, It hath not passed a - way:
As Eve Thou gav'st to Ad - am Out of his own pierced side:
As Thou, for Christ the Bride - groom, The heaven-ly Bride dost seal!

Still in the pure es - pous - al Of Chris-tian man and maid,
Be pres - ent, bless - ed Sav - iour, To join their lov - ing hands,
O spread Thy pure wing o'er them, Let no ill power find place,

The Ho - ly Three are with us, The three-fold grace is said.
As Thou didst bind two na - tures In Thine e - ter - nal bands.
When on-ward to Thine al - tar Their hal-lowed path they trace. A-men.

520   O God of Wisdom

AMAMUS 8.6.8.6.

Menno M. Brubacher, 1874-1956   Walter E. Yoder, 1889-

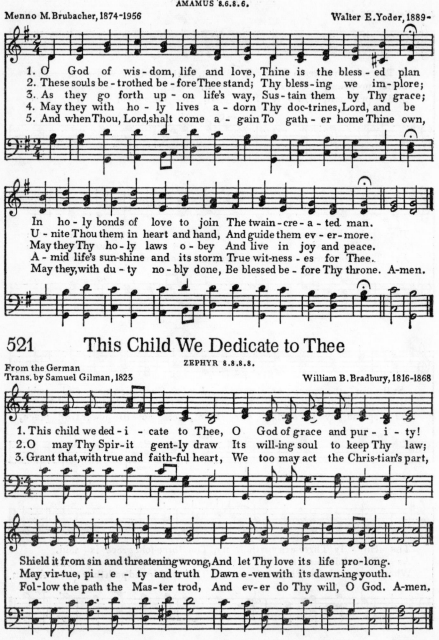

1. O God of wis-dom, life and love, Thine is the bless-ed plan
2. These souls be-trothed be-fore Thee stand; Thy bless-ing we im-plore;
3. As they go forth up-on life's way, Sus-tain them by Thy grace;
4. May they with ho-ly lives a-dorn Thy doc-trines, Lord, and be
5. And when Thou, Lord, shalt come a-gain To gath-er home Thine own,

In ho-ly bonds of love to join The twain-cre-a-ted man.
U-nite Thou them in heart and hand, And guide them ev-er-more.
May they Thy ho-ly laws o-bey And live in joy and peace.
A-mid life's sun-shine and its storm True wit-ness-es for Thee.
May they, with du-ty no-bly done, Be blessed be-fore Thy throne. A-men.

521   This Child We Dedicate to Thee

ZEPHYR 8.8.8.8.

From the German
Trans. by Samuel Gilman, 1823   William B. Bradbury, 1816-1868

1. This child we ded-i-cate to Thee, O God of grace and pur-i-ty!
2. O may Thy Spir-it gent-ly draw Its will-ing soul to keep Thy law;
3. Grant that, with true and faith-ful heart, We too may act the Chris-tian's part,

Shield it from sin and threatening wrong, And let Thy love its life pro-long.
May vir-tue, pi-e-ty and truth Dawn e-ven with its dawn-ing youth.
Fol-low the path the Mas-ter trod, And ev-er do Thy will, O God. A-men.

Friend of the Home 522

ELLERS 10.10.10.10.

Howell Elvet Lewis, 1860-1953   Edward J. Hopkins, 1818-1901

1. Friend of the home, as when, in Gal - i - lee,
The moth-ers brought their lit - tle ones to Thee,
So we, dear Lord, would now the chil - dren bring,
And seek for them the shel-ter of Thy wing.

2. Lord, may Thy church, as with a moth-er's care,
For Thee the lambs with - in her bos - om bear;
And grant, as morn - ing grows to noon, that they
Still in her love and ho - ly serv-ice stay.

3. Draw, through the child, the par - ents near - er Thee,
En - due their home with grow-ing sanc - ti - ty;
And gath - er all, by earth - ly homes made one,
In heaven, O Christ, when earth-ly days are done. A - men.

Words used by permission of Mrs. Mary Elvet Lewis.

523 O Thou Whose Gracious Presence Blest

WHITTIER (REST). 8.6.8.8.6.

Louis F. Benson, 1855-1930

Frederick C. Maker, 1844-1927

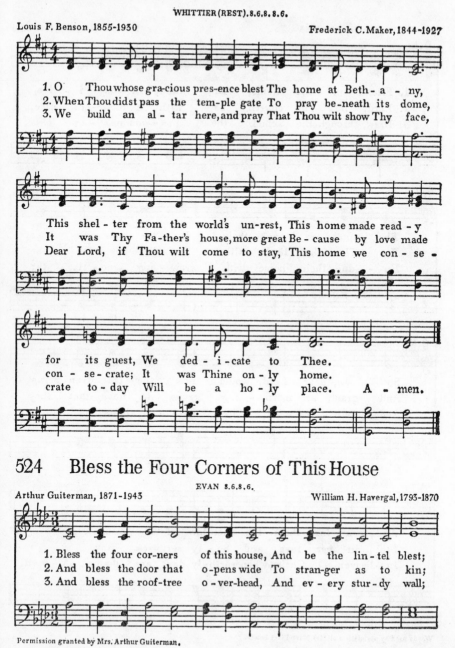

1. O Thou whose gra-cious pres-ence blest The home at Beth-a-ny,
2. When Thou didst pass the tem-ple gate To pray be-neath its dome,
3. We build an al-tar here, and pray That Thou wilt show Thy face,

This shel-ter from the world's un-rest, This home made read-y
It was Thy Fa-ther's house, more great Be-cause by love made
Dear Lord, if Thou wilt come to stay, This home we con-se-

for its guest, We ded-i-cate to Thee.
con-se-crate; It was Thine on-ly home.
crate to-day Will be a ho-ly place. A-men.

524 Bless the Four Corners of This House

EVAN 8.6.8.6.

Arthur Guiterman, 1871-1943

William H. Havergal, 1793-1870

1. Bless the four cor-ners of this house, And be the lin-tel blest;
2. And bless the door that o-pens wide To stran-ger as to kin;
3. And bless the roof-tree o-ver-head, And ev-ery stur-dy wall;

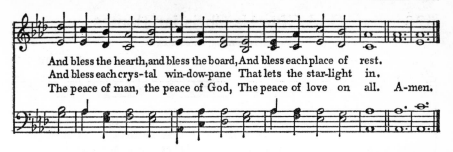

And bless the hearth, and bless the board, And bless each place of rest.
And bless each crys-tal win-dow-pane That lets the star-light in.
The peace of man, the peace of God, The peace of love on all. A-men.

Gracious Saviour, Who Didst Honor   525

MOTHERHOOD 8.7.8. 7. 7. 7.

Emily L. Shirreff, 1814-1897   L. Meadows White, 1860-1950

1. Gra-cious Sav-iour, who didst hon-or Wom-an-kind as wom-an's son;
2. Je - sus, Son of hu-man moth-er, Bless our moth-er-hood, we pray;
3. Thou who didst with Jo-seph la - bor, Nor didst hum-ble work dis-dain,
4. Thou who didst go forth in sor - row Toil - ing for the souls of men,

Ver - y Man though God-be-got-ten, And with God the Fa-ther one;
Give us grace to lead our chil-dren, Draw them to Thee day by day;
Grant we may Thy foot-steps fol-low Pa - tient - ly through toil or pain;
Thou who shalt draw all men to Thee, Though de-spised, re - ject-ed then,

Grant our wom-an - hood may be Con - se- crat-ed, Lord, to Thee.
May our sons and daugh-ters be Ded - i - cat-ed, Lord, to Thee.
May our qui - et home life be Lived, O Lord, in Thee, to Thee.
Hum-ble though our in-fluence be, Use it in the world for Thee. A-men.

526 God, Give Us Christian Homes

CHRISTIAN HOME. IRREGULAR

B. B. McKinney, 1886-1952

B. B. McKinney, 1886-1952

1. God, give us Chris-tian homes! Homes where the Bi-ble is loved and taught, Homes where the Mas-ter's will is sought, Homes crowned with beau-ty Thy love hath wrought; God, give us Chris-tian homes; God, give us Chris-tian homes!

2. God, give us Chris-tian homes! Homes where the fa-ther is true and strong, Homes that are free from the blight of wrong, Homes that are joy-ous with love and song; God, give us Chris-tian homes; God, give us Chris-tian homes!

3. God, give us Chris-tian homes! Homes where the moth-er, in queen-ly quest, Strives to show oth-ers Thy way is best, Homes where the Lord is an hon-ored guest; God, give us Chris-tian homes; God, give us Chris-tian homes!

4. God, give us Chris-tian homes! Homes where the chil-dren are led to know Christ in His beau-ty Who loves them so, Homes where the al-tar fires burn and glow; God, give us Chris-tian homes; God, give us Chris-tian homes! A-men.

Lord of Life and King of Glory

SICILIAN MARINERS' HYMN 8.7.8.7.8.7.

Christian Burke, 1859-c.1915

Arr. from a Sicilian Melody, 1794

1. Lord of life and King of glo - ry, Who didst deign a
2. Grant us then pure hearts and pa - tient, That in all we
3. May we keep our ho - ly call - ing Stain-less in its

child to be, Cra - dled on a moth-er's bo - som,
do or say Lit - tle ones our deeds may cop - y
fair re - nown, That when all the work is o - ver

Throned up - on a moth - er's knee: For the chil - dren
And be nev - er led a - stray, Lit - tle feet our
And we lay the bur - den down, Then the chil - dren

Thou hast giv - en We must an - swer un - to Thee.
steps may fol - low In a safe and nar-row way.
Thou hast giv - en Still may be our joy and crown. A - men.

528 O Happy Home

SANDRINGHAM 11.10.11.10.

Carl J.P.Spitta, 1801-1859
Trans.by Sarah B.Findlater, 1823-1907

Joseph Barnby, 1838-1896

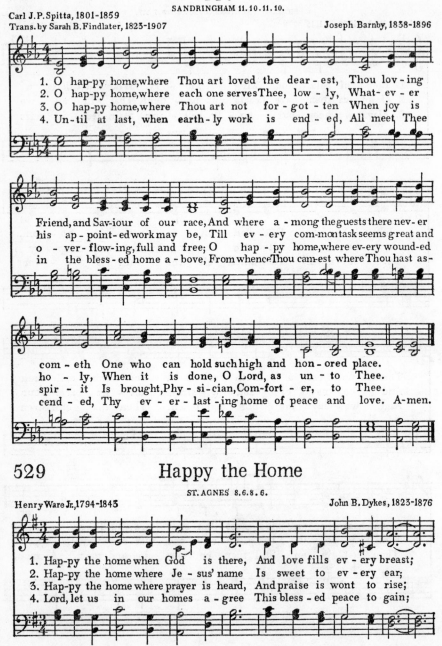

1. O hap-py home, where Thou art loved the dear-est, Thou lov-ing
2. O hap-py home, where each one serves Thee, low-ly, What-ev-er
3. O hap-py home, where Thou art not for-got-ten When joy is
4. Un-til at last, when earth-ly work is end-ed, All meet Thee

Friend, and Sav-iour of our race, And where a-mong the guests there nev-er
his ap-point-ed work may be, Till ev-ery com-mon task seems great and
o-ver-flow-ing, full and free; O hap-py home, where ev-ery wound-ed
in the bless-ed home a-bove, From whence Thou cam-est where Thou hast as-

com-eth One who can hold such high and hon-ored place.
ho-ly, When it is done, O Lord, as un-to Thee.
spir-it Is brought, Phy-si-cian, Com-fort-er, to Thee.
cend-ed, Thy ev-er-last-ing home of peace and love. A-men.

529 Happy the Home

ST.AGNES 8.6.8.6.

Henry Ware Jr.,1794-1843

John B.Dykes, 1823-1876

1. Hap-py the home when God is there, And love fills ev-ery breast;
2. Hap-py the home where Je-sus' name Is sweet to ev-ery ear;
3. Hap-py the home where prayer is heard, And praise is wont to rise;
4. Lord, let us in our homes a-gree This bless-ed peace to gain;

When one their wish and one their prayer, And one their heavenly rest.
Where children ear - ly speak His fame, And par-ents hold Him dear.
Where par-ents love the sa - cred Word And all its wis - dom prize.
U - nite our hearts in love to Thee, And love to all will reign. A-men.

Be Present at Our Table, Lord   530

OLD HUNDREDTH 8.8.8.8.

John Cennick, 1718 -1755

Louis Bourgeois, 1510-1561

1. Be pres - ent at our ta - ble, Lord, Be
2. We thank Thee, Lord, for this our food, For

here and ev - ery-where a - dored; These mer-cies bless, and
life, and health, and ev - ery good: Let man - na to our

grant that we May live and work to - day with Thee.
souls be given—The Bread of Life sent down from heaven. A - men.

531 # When He Cometh

JEWELS 8:6.8.5. with Refrain

William O. Cushing, 1823-1902

George F. Root, 1820-1895

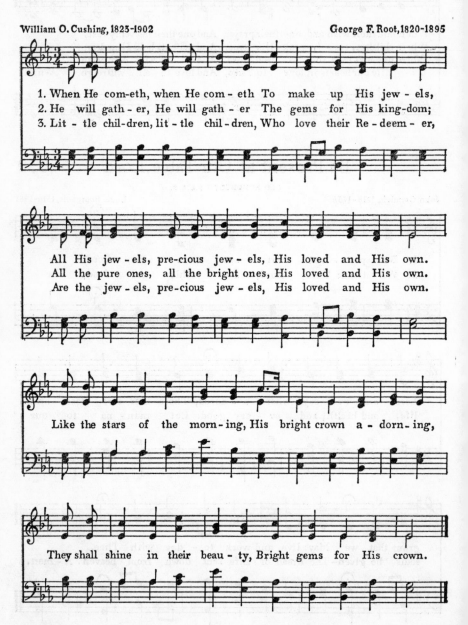

1. When He com-eth, when He com-eth To make up His jew-els,
2. He will gath-er, He will gath-er The gems for His king-dom;
3. Lit-tle chil-dren, lit-tle chil-dren, Who love their Re-deem-er,

All His jew-els, precious jew-els, His loved and His own.
All the pure ones, all the bright ones, His loved and His own.
Are the jew-els, pre-cious jew-els, His loved and His own.

Like the stars of the morn-ing, His bright crown a-dorn-ing,

They shall shine in their beau-ty, Bright gems for His crown.

All Things Bright and Beautiful   532

GREYSTONE 7.6.7.6.D. with Refrain

Cecil Frances Alexander, 1823-1895
Stanza 1 to be repeated as refrain after stanzas 2-5.

W.R.Waghorne 1881-1942

1. All things bright and beau-ti-ful, All crea-tures great and small,

All things wise and won-der-ful, The Lord God made them all.

2. Each lit-tle flower that o-pens, Each lit-tle bird that sings,
3. The cold wind in the win-ter, The pleas-ant sum-mer sun,
4. The tall trees in the green-wood, The mead-ows where we play,
5. He gave us eyes to see them, And lips that we might tell

He made their glow-ing col-ors, He made their ti-ny wings.
The ripe fruits in the gar-den—He made them ev-ery one.
The rush-es by the wa-ter We gath-er ev-ery day;
How great is God Al-might-y, Who has made all things well.

533 I Think When I Read That Sweet Story

SWEET STORY. IRREGULAR

Greek Melody

Jemima T. Luke, 1813-1906

Arr. by William B. Bradbury, 1816-1868

1. I think when I read that sweet sto-ry of old,
2. I wish that His hands had been placed on my head,
3. Yet still to His foot-stool in prayer I may go,
4. I long for the joy of that glo-ri-ous time,

When Je-sus was here a-mong men,
That His arm had been thrown a-round me,
And ask for a share in His love;
The sweet-est and bright-est and best,

How He called lit-tle chil-dren as lambs to His fold,
And that I might have seen His kind look when He said,
And if I now earn-est-ly seek Him be-low,
When chil-dren who come from each coun-try and clime

I should like to have been with them then.
"Let the lit-tle ones come un-to Me."
I shall see Him and know Him a-bove.
Shall crowd to His arms and be blest.

I Am So Glad That Our Father in Heaven   534

JESUS LOVES EVEN ME 10.10. 10.10. with Refrain

Philip P. Bliss, 1838-1876   Philip P. Bliss, 1838-1876

1. I am so glad that our Fa-ther in heaven Tells of His love in the
2. Though I for-get Him and wan-der a-way, Kind-ly He fol-lows wher-
3. O if there's on-ly one song I can sing, When in His beau-ty I

Book He has given; Won-der-ful things in the Bi-ble I see;
ev-er I stray; Back to His dear lov-ing arms would I flee
see the great King, This shall my song in e-ter-ni-ty be:

This is the dear-est that Je-sus loves me.
When I re-mem-ber that Je-sus loves me.   I am so glad that
O what a won-der that Je-sus loves me.

Je-sus loves me, Je-sus loves me, Je-sus loves me; I am so

glad that Je-sus loves me, Je-sus loves ev-en me.

535   Father, Lead Me Day by Day

POSEN 7. 7. 7. 7.

John P. Hopps, 1834-1912   George C. Strattner, 1650-1705

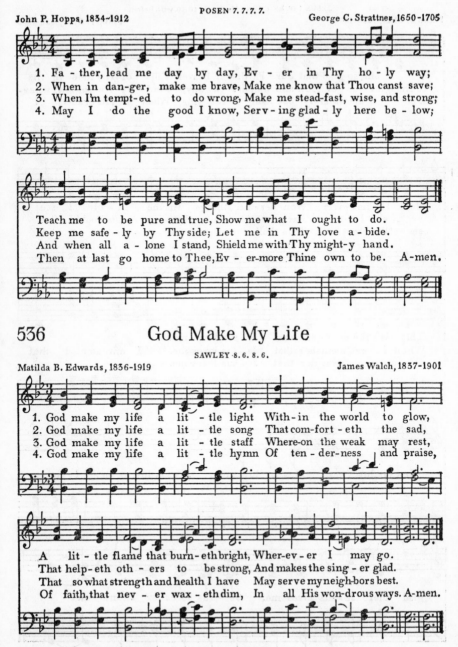

1. Fa - ther, lead me day by day, Ev - er in Thy ho - ly way;
2. When in dan-ger, make me brave, Make me know that Thou canst save;
3. When I'm tempt-ed to do wrong, Make me stead-fast, wise, and strong;
4. May I do the good I know, Serv - ing glad - ly here be - low;

Teach me to be pure and true, Show me what I ought to do.
Keep me safe - ly by Thy side; Let me in Thy love a - bide.
And when all a - lone I stand, Shield me with Thy might - y hand.
Then at last go home to Thee, Ev - er-more Thine own to be. A-men.

536   God Make My Life

SAWLEY 8. 6. 8. 6.

Matilda B. Edwards, 1836-1919   James Walch, 1837-1901

1. God make my life a lit - tle light With - in the world to glow,
2. God make my life a lit - tle song That com-fort - eth the sad,
3. God make my life a lit - tle staff Where-on the weak may rest,
4. God make my life a lit - tle hymn Of ten - der-ness and praise,

A lit - tle flame that burn-eth bright, Wher-ev - er I may go.
That help-eth oth - ers to be strong, And makes the sing - er glad.
That so what strength and health I have May serve my neigh-bors best.
Of faith, that nev - er wax-eth dim, In all His won-drous ways. A-men.

Words copyright. Used by permission of Miss C. Morely Holder.

I Love Thee

LOVE TO CHRIST 11.11.11.11.

Unknown

Ingall's *Christian Harmony*, 1805

1. I love Thee, my Jesus, I love Thee, my Lord;
2. O Jesus, my Saviour, with Thee I am blest,
3. O who's like my Saviour? He's my friend and king;

I love Thee, my Saviour, I love Thee, my God:
My life and salvation, my joy and my rest:
He smiles, and He loves me and helps me to sing:

I love Thee, I love Thee, and that Thou dost know;
Thy name be my theme, and Thy love be my song;
I'll praise Him, I'll praise Him with notes loud and clear,

But how much I love Thee my actions will show.
Thy grace shall inspire me and keep my heart strong.
And make Him my treasure while serving Him here. A-men.

538   Tell Me the Stories of Jesus.

STORIES OF JESUS 8.4.8.4.5.4.5.4.

William H. Parker, 1845-1929   Frederick Challinor, 1866-1952

1. Tell me the sto-ries of Je-sus I love to hear; Things I would
2. First let me hear how the chil-dren Stood round His knee, And I shall
3. In - to the cit-y I'd fol-low The chil-dren's band, Wav - ing a

ask Him to tell me If He were here: Scenes by the way-side,
fan - cy His bless-ing Rest-ing on me: Words full of kind-ness,
branch of the palm tree High in my hand; One of His her-alds,

Tales of the sea, Sto-ries of Je-sus, Tell them to me.
Deeds full of grace, All in the love-light Of Je-sus' face.
Yes, I would sing Loud-est ho-san-nas! Je - sus is King!

539   Father, We Thank Thee for the Night

ONSLOW 8.8.8.8.

Rebecca J. Weston   Daniel Batchellor, 1845-1934

1. Fa-ther, we thank Thee for the night, And for the pleas-ant morn-ing light;
2. Help us to do the things we should, To be to oth-ers kind and good;

From *Songs and Games for Little Ones*, by G. Walker and Harriet Jenks.
Copyright 1911 by Oliver Ditson Company. Used by permission.

For rest and food and lov-ing care, And all that makes the world so fair.
In all we do, in work or play, To love Thee bet-ter day by day. A-men.

Saviour, Bless a Little Child 540

DEAR JESUS HEAR ME 7.7.7.7. with Refrain

Fanny J. Crosby, 1820-1915   William B. Bradbury, 1816-1868

1. Sav-iour, bless a lit-tle child; Teach my heart the way to Thee; Make it
2. I am young, but Thou hast said, All who will may come to Thee; Feed my
3. Je-sus, help me, I am weak; Let me put my trust in Thee; Teach me
4. I would nev-er go a-stray, Nev-er turn a-side from Thee; Keep me

gen-tle good and mild;   Lov-ing Sav-iour, care for me.
soul with liv-ing bread;   Lov-ing Sav-iour, care for me.   Dear Je-sus, hear me,
how and what to speak;   Lov-ing Sav-iour, care for me.
in the heaven-ly way;   Lov-ing Sav-iour, care for me.

Hear Thy lit-tle child to-day; Hear, O hear me, Hear me when I pray. A-men.

541 In Our Work and in Our Play

ROSSLYN 7.7.7.7.7.7.

Whitfield G. Wills, 1841-1891

English Melody

1. In our work and in our play, Je - sus, ev - er
2. May we in Thy strength sub - due E - vil tem - pers,
3. Chil - dren of the King are we! May we loy - al

with us stay; May we al - ways strive to be
words un - true, Thoughts im - pure, and deeds un - kind,
to Him be; Try to please Him ev - ery day,

True and faith - ful un - to Thee. Then we truth - ful -
All things hate - ful to Thy mind. Then we truth - ful -
In our work and in our play. Then we truth - ful -

ly can sing, We are chil - dren of the King.
ly can sing, We are chil - dren of the King.
ly can sing, We are chil - dren of the King.

Jesus, Tender Shepherd, Hear Me 542

EVENING PRAYER (STAINER) 8.7.8.7.

Mary L. Duncan, 1814-1840

John Stainer, 1840-1901

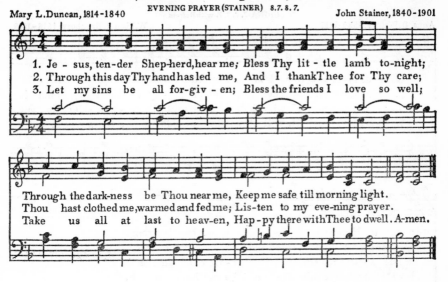

1. Je - sus, ten-der Shep-herd, hear me; Bless Thy lit - tle lamb to-night;
2. Through this day Thy hand has led me, And I thank Thee for Thy care;
3. Let my sins be all for-giv - en; Bless the friends I love so well;

Through the dark-ness be Thou near me, Keep me safe till morning light.
Thou hast clothed me, warmed and fed me; Lis-ten to my eve-ning prayer.
Take us all at last to heav-en, Hap-py there with Thee to dwell. A-men.

Just As I Am, Thine Own to Be 543

JUST AS I AM 8.8.8.6.

Marianne Hearn, 1834-1909

Joseph Barnby, 1838-1896

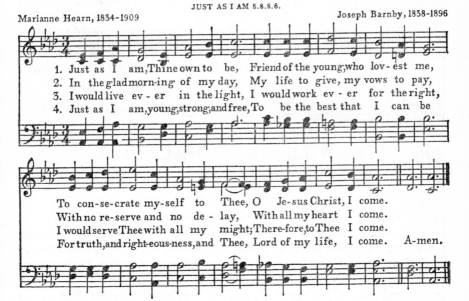

1. Just as I am, Thine own to be, Friend of the young, who lov-est me,
2. In the glad morn-ing of my day, My life to give, my vows to pay,
3. I would live ev - er in the light, I would work ev - er for the right,
4. Just as I am, young, strong, and free, To be the best that I can be

To con-se-crate my-self to Thee, O Je-sus Christ, I come.
With no re-serve and no de - lay, With all my heart I come.
I would serve Thee with all my might; There-fore, to Thee I come.
For truth, and right-eous-ness, and Thee, Lord of my life, I come. A-men.

544 ## Jesus Loves Me, This I Know

CHINA 7.7.7:7. with Refrain

Anna B. Warner, 1820-1915

William B. Bradbury, 1816-1868

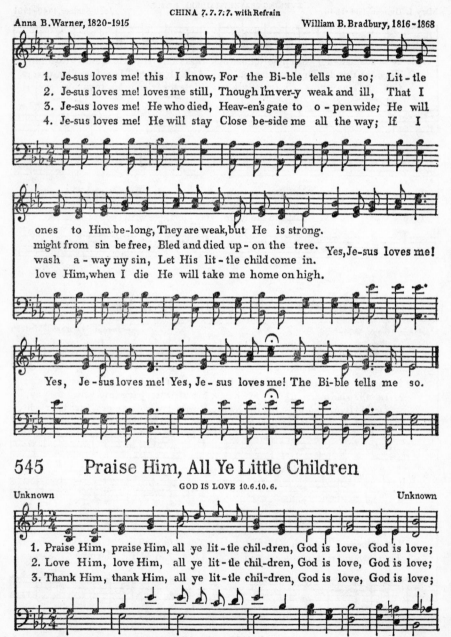

1. Je-sus loves me! this I know, For the Bi-ble tells me so; Lit-tle
2. Je-sus loves me! loves me still, Though I'm ver-y weak and ill, That I
3. Je-sus loves me! He who died, Heav-en's gate to o-pen wide; He will
4. Je-sus loves me! He will stay Close be-side me all the way; If I

ones to Him be-long, They are weak, but He is strong.
might from sin be free, Bled and died up-on the tree. Yes, Je-sus loves me!
wash a-way my sin, Let His lit-tle child come in.
love Him, when I die He will take me home on high.

Yes, Je-sus loves me! Yes, Je-sus loves me! The Bi-ble tells me so.

545 ## Praise Him, All Ye Little Children

GOD IS LOVE 10.6.10.6.

Unknown

Unknown

1. Praise Him, praise Him, all ye lit-tle chil-dren, God is love, God is love;
2. Love Him, love Him, all ye lit-tle chil-dren, God is love, God is love;
3. Thank Him, thank Him, all ye lit-tle chil-dren, God is love, God is love;

Praise Him, praise Him, all ye lit-tle chil-dren, God is love, God is love.
Love Him, love Him, all ye lit-tle chil-dren, God is love, God is love.
Thank Him, thank Him, all ye lit-tle chil-dren, God is love, God is love.

Hushed Was the Evening Hymn 546

SAMUEL 6.6.6.6.8.8.

James D. Burns, 1823-1864   Arthur S. Sullivan, 1842-1900

1. Hushed was the eve-ning hymn, The tem-ple courts were dark, The
2. The old man, meek and mild, The priest of Is-rael, slept; His
3. O give me Sam-uel's heart: A low-ly heart, that waits Where
4. O give me Sam-uel's mind: A sweet, un-mur-muring faith, O -

lamp was burn-ing dim Be-fore the sa-cred ark, When sud-den-ly a
watch the tem-ple-child, The lit-tle Le-vite, kept; And what from E - li's
in Thy house Thou art, Or watch-es at Thy gates! By day and night, a
be-dient and re-signed To Thee in life and death! That I may read with

Voice di-vine Rang through the si-lence of the shrine.
sense was sealed, The Lord to Han-nah's son re-vealed.
heart that still Moves at the breath-ing of Thy will.
child-like eyes Truths that are hid-den from the wise. A-men.

547 The Wise May Bring Their Learning

Unknown
The Book of Praise for Children, 1881

ELLON 7. 6. 7. 6. D.

George F. Root, 1820-1895

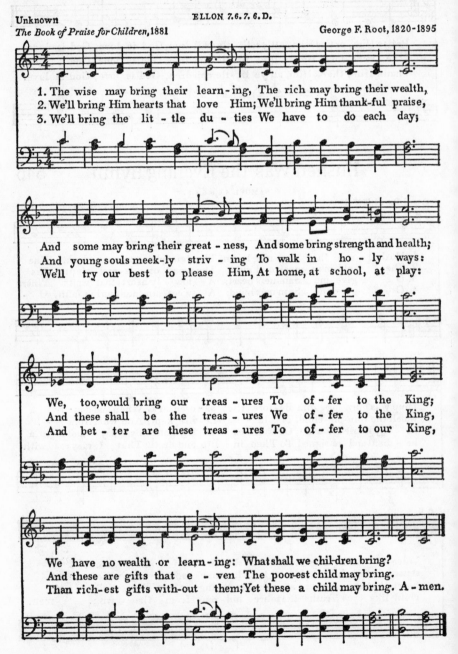

1. The wise may bring their learn-ing, The rich may bring their wealth,
2. We'll bring Him hearts that love Him; We'll bring Him thank-ful praise,
3. We'll bring the lit-tle du-ties We have to do each day;

And some may bring their great-ness, And some bring strength and health;
And young souls meek-ly striv-ing To walk in ho-ly ways:
We'll try our best to please Him, At home, at school, at play:

We, too, would bring our treas-ures To of-fer to the King;
And these shall be the treas-ures We of-fer to the King,
And bet-ter are these treas-ures To of-fer to our King,

We have no wealth or learn-ing: What shall we chil-dren bring?
And these are gifts that e-ven The poor-est child may bring.
Than rich-est gifts with-out them; Yet these a child may bring. A-men.

Lord, Teach a Little Child to Pray 548

INNOCENCE 8.6.8.5.

Unknown

Jeanne Miller, 1941-

1. Lord, teach a lit-tle child to pray, And O, ac-cept my prayer!
2. A lit-tle spar-row can-not fall, Un-no-ticed, Lord, by Thee;
3. Teach me to do what-e'er is right, And when I sin, for-give;

Thou hear-est ev-ery word I say, For Thou art ev-ery-where.
And though I am so young and small, Thou dost take care of me.
And make it still my chief de-light To love Thee while I live. A-men.

Copyright 1962 by Jeanne Miller Hostetler.

Jesus, Friend of Little Children 549

DARYL 8.5.8.3.

Walter J. Matthams, 1853-1932

J. H. Maunder, 1858-1920

1. Je-sus, Friend of lit-tle chil-dren, Be a friend to me,
2. Show me what my love should cher-ish, What, too, it should shun,
3. Step by step, O lead me on-ward, Up-ward in-to youth,
4. Nev-er leave me nor for-sake me, Ev-er be my friend,

Take my hand and ev-er keep me Close to Thee.
Lest my feet in paths of ev-il Swift should run.
Wis-er, strong-er still, be-com-ing In Thy truth.
For I need Thee from life's dawn-ing To life's end. A-men.

550   Saviour, While My Heart Is Tender

EVENING PRAYER (STEBBINS) 8.7.8.7.

John Burton, 1803-1877   George C. Stebbins, 1846-1945

1. Sav-iour, while my heart is ten-der I would yield that heart to Thee;
2. Take me now, Lord Je-sus, take me, Let my youth-ful heart be Thine;
3. Send me, Lord, where Thou wilt send me On-ly do Thou guide my way;
4. Thine I am, O Lord, for-ev-er, To Thy serv-ice set a-part;

All my powers to Thee sur-ren-der, Thine and on-ly Thine to be.
Thy de-vo-ted ser-vant make me; Fill my soul with love di-vine.
May Thy grace through life at-tend me, Glad-ly then shall I o-bey.
Suf-fer me to leave Thee nev-er; Seal Thine im-age on my heart. A-men.

551   Great God, We Sing That Mighty Hand

WAREHAM 8.8. 8. 8.

Philip Doddridge, 1702-1751   William Knapp, 1698-1768

1. Great God, we sing that might-y hand By which sup-port-ed still we stand;
2. By day, by night, at home, a-broad, Still are we guard-ed by our God,
3. With grate-ful hearts the past we own; The fu-ture, all to us un-known,
4. In scenes ex-alt-ed or de-pressed, Thou art our joy, and Thou our rest;

The ope-ning year Thy mer-cy shows: That mercy crowns it till it close.
By His in-ces-sant boun-ty fed, By His un-er-ring coun-sel led.
We to Thy guard-ian care com-mit, And peaceful leave be-fore Thy feet.
Thy good-ness all our hopes shall raise, Adored through all our changing days. A-men.

Another Year Is Dawning

552

SALVATORI 7.6.7.6.D.

Frances R. Havergal, 1836-1879   J. Michael Haydn, 1737-1806

1. An - oth - er year is dawn - ing! Dear Fa - ther, let it be,
2. An - oth - er year of mer - cies, Of faith-ful - ness and grace;
3. An - oth - er year of serv - ice, Of wit - ness for Thy love;

In work-ing or in wait - ing, An - oth - er year with Thee;
An - oth - er year of glad-ness In the shin - ing of Thy face;
An - oth - er year of train-ing For ho - lier work a - bove;

An - oth - er year of lean - ing Up - on Thy lov - ing breast,
An - oth - er year of prog - ress, An - oth - er year of praise,
An - oth - er year is dawn - ing! Dear Fa - ther, let it be;

An - oth - er year of trust-ing, Of qui - et, hap-py rest.
An - oth - er year of prov-ing Thy pres-ence all the days.
On earth, or else in heav - en, An - oth - er year for Thee. A-men.

553 We Plow the Fields and Scatter

Matthias Claudius, 1740-1815
Trans. by Jane M. Campbell, 1817-1878

WIR PFLÜGEN. 7. 6. 7. 6. D. with Refrain

Johann A.P. Schulz, 1747-1800

1. We plow the fields and scat-ter The good seed on the land,
2. He on-ly is the Ma-ker Of all things near and far;
3. We thank Thee, then, O Fa-ther, For all things bright and good,

But it is fed and wa-tered By God's al-might-y hand;
He paints the way-side flow-er, He lights the eve-ning star;
The seed-time and the har-vest, Our life, our health, our food:

He sends the snow in win-ter, The warmth to swell the grain,
The winds and waves o-bey Him, By Him the birds are fed;
Ac-cept the gifts we of-fer For all Thy love im-parts,

The breez-es and the sun-shine, And soft re-fresh-ing rain.
Much more to us, His chil-dren, He gives our dai-ly bread.
And, what Thou most de-sir-est, Our hum-ble, thank-ful hearts.

All good gifts a-round us Are sent from heaven a-bove;

Then thank the Lord, O thank the Lord For all His love. A-men.

For the Beauty of the Earth 554

DIX 7.7.7.7.7.7.

Folliott S. Pierpoint, 1835-1917   Abridged from a Chorale by Conrad Kocher, 1786-1872

1. For the beau-ty of the earth, For the beau-ty of the skies,
2. For the won-der of each hour Of the day and of the night,
3. For the joy of hu-man love, Broth-er, sis-ter, par-ent, child,
4. For Thy Church, that ev-er-more Lift-eth ho-ly hands a-bove,
5. For Thy-self, best gift di-vine, For our sin so free-ly given;

For the love which from our birth O-ver and a-round us lies,
Hill and vale, and tree and flower, Sun and moon, and stars of light,
Friends on earth, and friends a-bove; For all gen-tle thoughts and mild,
Of-fering up on ev-ery shore Its pure sac-ri-fice of love,
For that great, great love of Thine, Peace on earth and joy in heaven,

Christ our God, to Thee we raise This our hymn of grate-ful praise. A-men.

555 Sing to the Lord of Harvest

GREENLAND. 7.6.7.6.D.

John S. B. Monsell, 1811-1875

J. Michael Haydn, 1737-1806
Arr. in B. Jachob, *National Psalmody*, 1819

1. Sing to the Lord of har-vest, Sing songs of love and praise;
2. By Him the clouds drop fat-ness, The des-erts bloom and spring,
3. Heap on His sa-cred al-tar The gifts His good-ness gave,
4. To God, the gra-cious Fa-ther, Who made us "ver-y good,"

With joy-ful hearts and voic-es Your al-le-lu-ias raise;
The hills leap up in glad-ness, The val-leys laugh and sing.
The gold-en sheaves of har-vest, The souls He died to save.
To Christ Who, when we wan-dered, Re-stored us with His blood,

By Him the roll-ing sea-sons In fruit-ful or-der move;
He fill-eth with His full-ness All things with large in-crease;
Your hearts lay down be-fore Him, When at His feet ye fall,
And to the Ho-ly Spir-it, Who doth up-on us pour

Sing to the Lord of har-vest A song of hap-py love.
He crowns the year with good-ness, With plen-ty and with peace.
And with your lives a-dore Him, Who gave His life for all.
His bless-ed dews and sun-shine, Be praise for-ev-er-more. A-men.

Come, Ye Thankful People, Come 556

ST. GEORGE'S, WINDSOR 7.7.7.7.D.

Henry Alford, 1810-1871 George J. Elvey, 1816-1893

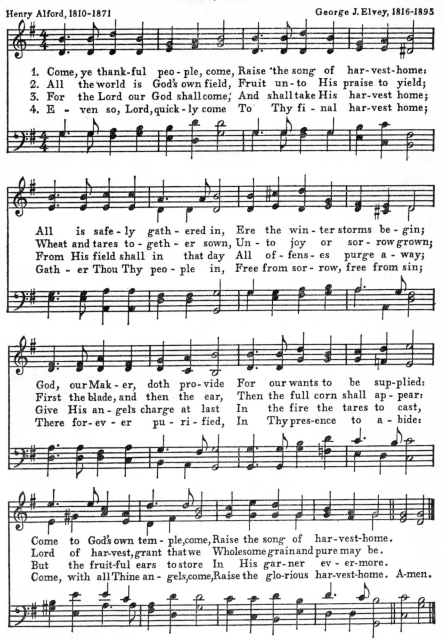

1. Come, ye thank-ful peo - ple, come, Raise the song of har-vest-home:
2. All the world is God's own field, Fruit un - to His praise to yield;
3. For the Lord our God shall come, And shall take His har-vest home;
4. E - ven so, Lord, quick - ly come To Thy fi - nal har-vest home;

All is safe - ly gath - ered in, Ere the win - ter storms be - gin;
Wheat and tares to - geth - er sown, Un - to joy or sor - row grown;
From His field shall in that day All of - fens - es purge a - way;
Gath - er Thou Thy peo - ple in, Free from sor - row, free from sin;

God, our Mak - er, doth pro - vide For our wants to be sup-plied:
First the blade, and then the ear, Then the full corn shall ap - pear:
Give His an - gels charge at last In the fire the tares to cast,
There for - ev - er pu - ri - fied, In Thy pres-ence to a - bide:

Come to God's own tem - ple, come, Raise the song of har-vest-home.
Lord of har-vest, grant that we Wholesome grain and pure may be.
But the fruit-ful ears to store In His gar-ner ev - er-more.
Come, with all Thine an - gels, come, Raise the glo-rious har-vest-home. A-men.

557 Praise to God, Immortal Praise

ABBOTT 7.7.7.7.

Anna L. Barbauld, 1745-1825

Asahel Abbott

1. Praise to God, im-mor-tal praise, For the love that crowns our days;
2. For the bless-ings of the field, For the stores the gar-dens yield,
3. Clouds that drop re-fresh-ing dews, Suns that ge-nial heat dif-fuse,
4. All that Spring with boun-teous hand, Scat-ters o'er the smil-ing land;
5. These, great God, to Thee we owe, Source whence all our bless-ings flow,

Boun-teous source of ev-ery joy, Let Thy praise our tongues employ.
For the joy which har-vest brings, Grate-ful prais-es now we sing.
Flocks that whit-en all the plain, Yel-low sheaves of rip-ened grain;
All that lib-eral Au-tumn pours From her o-ver-flow-ing stores;
And for these our souls shall raise Grate-ful vows and sol-emn praise. Amen.

558 When Thy Heart, with Joy O'erflowing

BULLINGER 8.5.8.5.

Theodore C. Williams, 1855-1913

Ethelbert W. Bullinger, 1837-1913

1. When thy heart, with joy o'er-flow-ing, Sings a thank-ful prayer,
2. When the har-vest sheaves in-gath-ered Fill thy barns with store,
3. If thy soul, with power up-lift-ed, Yearns for glo-rious deed,
4. Share with him thy bread of bless-ing, Sor-row's bur-den share;

In thy joy, O let thy broth-er With thee share.
To thy God and to thy broth-er Give the more.
Give thy strength to serve thy broth-er In his need.
When thy heart en-folds a broth-er, God is there.

God of Our Fathers, Whose Almighty Hand 559

NATIONAL HYMN 10.10.10.10.

Daniel C. Roberts, 1841-1907　　　　　　　George W. Warren, 1828-1902

Trumpets, before each stanza.

1. God of our fa-thers, whose al-might-y hand
2. Thy love di-vine hath led us in the past,
3. From war's a-larms, from dead-ly pes-ti-lence,
4. Re - fresh Thy peo - ple on their toil-some way,

Leads forth in beau - ty all the star - ry band
In this free land by Thee our lot is cast;
Be Thy strong arm our ev - er - sure de - fense;
Lead us from night to nev - er - end - ing day;

Of shin - ing worlds, in splen-dor through the skies,
Be Thou our rul - er, guard-ian, guide and stay,
Thy true re - lig - ion in our hearts in - crease,
Fill all our lives with love and grace di - vine,

Our grate - ful songs be - fore Thy throne a - rise.
Thy word our law, Thy paths our cho - sen way.
Thy boun - teous good - ness nour - ish us in peace.
And glo - ry, laud, and praise be ev - er Thine. A-men.

560 My Country, 'Tis of Thee

AMERICA 6.6.4.6.6.6.4.

Samuel F. Smith, 1808-1895

Ascribed to Henry Carey, 1690-1745

1. My coun-try, 'tis of thee, Sweet land of
2. My na-tive coun-try thee, Land of the
3. Let mu-sic swell the breeze, And ring from
4. Our fa-thers' God, to Thee, Auth-or of

lib-er-ty, Of thee I sing; Land where my
no-ble free, Thy name I love; I love thy
all the trees Sweet free-dom's song: Let mor-tal
lib-er-ty, To Thee we sing: Long may our

fa-thers died, Land of the pil-grim's pride,
rocks and rills, Thy woods and tem-pled hills;
tongues a-wake; Let all that breathe par-take;
land be bright With free-dom's ho-ly light;

From ev-ery moun-tain-side Let free-dom ring.
My heart with rap-ture thrills Like that a-bove.
Let rocks their si-lence break, The sound pro-long.
Pro-tect us by Thy might, Great God, our King.

God Bless Our Native Land
561

DORT 6.6.4.6.6.6.4.

Stanzas 1 and 2, Siegfried A. Mahlmann, 1771-1826
Stanza 3, William E. Hickson, 1803-1870

Lowell Mason, 1792-1872

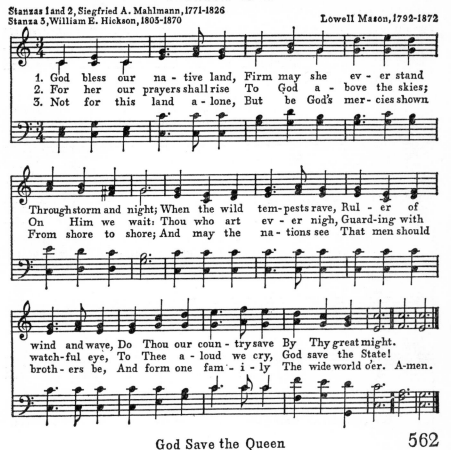

1. God bless our na - tive land, Firm may she ev - er stand
2. For her our prayers shall rise To God a - bove the skies;
3. Not for this land a - lone, But be God's mer - cies shown

Through storm and night; When the wild tem-pests rave, Rul - er of
On Him we wait: Thou who art ev - er nigh, Guard-ing with
From shore to shore; And may the na - tions see That men should

wind and wave, Do Thou our coun - try save By Thy great might.
watch-ful eye, To Thee a - loud we cry, God save the State!
broth - ers be, And form one fam - i - ly The wide world o'er. A-men.

God Save the Queen
562

May be sung to tune on opposite page.

God save our gracious Queen! Long live our noble Queen!
God save the Queen!
Send her victorious, happy and glorious,
Long to live over us:
God save the Queen!

Thy choicest gifts in store, on her be pleased to pour;
Long may she reign.
May she defend our laws and ever give us cause
To sing with heart and voice:
"God save the Queen!"

563 God the Omnipotent!

RUSSIAN HYMN 11.10.11.9.

Henry F. Chorley, 1808-1872; v. 1,3
John Ellerton, 1826-1893; v. 2,4.

Alexis F. Lwoff, c.1798-1870

1. God the Om-nip-o-tent! King, who or-dain-est
2. God the All-mer-ci-ful! earth hath for-sak-en
3. God the All-right-eous One! man hath de-fied Thee;
4. So shall Thy chil-dren in thank-ful de-vo-tion

Thun-der Thy clar-ion, the light-ning Thy sword;
Meek-ness and mer-cy and slight-ed Thy word;
Yet to e-ter-ni-ty stand-eth Thy word;
Laud Him who saved them from per-il and sword;

Show forth Thy pit-y on high where Thou reign-est;
Bid not Thy wrath in its ter-rors a-wak-en;
False-hood and wrong shall not tar-ry be-side Thee;
Sing-ing in cho-rus from o-cean to o-cean,

Give to us peace in our time, O Lord!
Give to us peace in our time, O Lord!
Give to us peace in our time, O Lord!
Peace to the na-tions and praise to the Lord. A-men.

O Beautiful for Spacious Skies 564

MATERNA 8.6.8.6.D.

Katharine Lee Bates, 1859-1929　　　　　　　　Samuel A. Ward, 1847-1903

1. O beau-ti-ful for spa-cious skies For am-ber waves of grain,
2. O beau-ti-ful for pil-grim feet, Whose stern, im-pas-sioned stress
3. O beau-ti-ful for he-roes proved In lib-er-at-ing strife,
4. O beau-ti-ful for pa-triot dream That sees, be-yond the years,

For pur-ple moun-tain maj - es-ties A-bove the fruit-ed plain!
A thor-ough-fare for free-dom beat A-cross the wil-der-ness!
Who more than self their coun-try loved, And mer-cy more than life!
Thine al-a-bas-ter cit-ies gleam, Un-dimmed by hu-man tears!

A-mer-i-ca! A-mer-i-ca! God shed His grace on thee,
A-mer-i-ca! A-mer-i-ca! God mend thine ev-ery flaw,
A-mer-i-ca! A-mer-i-ca! May God thy gold re-fine,
A-mer-i-ca! A-mer-i-ca! God shed His grace on thee,

And crown thy good with broth-er-hood From sea to shin-ing sea.
Con-firm thy soul in self-con-trol, Thy lib-er-ty in law.
Till all suc-cess be no-ble-ness, And ev-ery gain di-vine.
And crown thy good with broth-er-hood From sea to shin-ing sea. A-men.

Were You There?

WERE YOU THERE Irregular

Negro spiritual

Arr. by Donald Frederick, 1917—

1. Were you there when they cru-ci-fied my Lord? (Were you there?)
2. Were you there when they nailed Him to the tree? (Were you there?)
3. Were you there when they laid Him in the tomb? (Were you there?)
4. Were you there when He rose up from the dead? (Were you there?)

Were you there when they cru-ci-fied my Lord? (Were you there?)
Were you there when they nailed Him to the tree? (Were you there?)
Were you there when they laid Him in the tomb? (Were you there?)
Were you there when He rose up from the dead? (Were you there?)

Oh, some-times it caus-es me to trem-ble, trem-ble,
Oh, some-times it caus-es me to trem-ble, trem-ble,
Oh, some-times it caus-es me to trem-ble, trem-ble,
Oh, some-times it caus-es me to trem-ble, trem-ble,

trem-ble, Were you there when they cru-ci-fied my Lord? (Were you there?)
trem-ble, Were you there when they nailed Him to the tree? (Were you there?)
trem-ble, Were you there when they laid Him in the tomb? (Were you there?)
trem-ble, Were you there when He rose up from the dead? (Were you there?)

Let Us Break Bread Together

COMMUNION SPIRITUAL Irregular

Negro spiritual

Arr. by Donald Frederick, 1917—

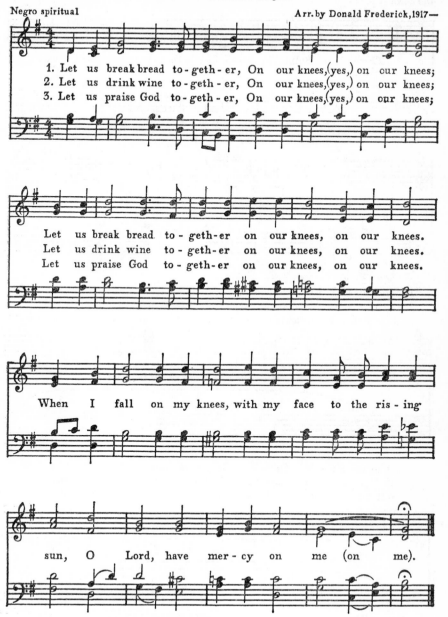

1. Let us break bread to-geth-er, On our knees,(yes,) on our knees;
2. Let us drink wine to-geth-er, On our knees,(yes,) on our knees;
3. Let us praise God to-geth-er, On our knees,(yes,) on our knees;

Let us break bread to-geth-er on our knees, on our knees.
Let us drink wine to-geth-er on our knees, on our knees.
Let us praise God to-geth-er on our knees, on our knees.

When I fall on my knees, with my face to the ris-ing

sun, O Lord, have mer-cy on me (on me).

567 Balm in Gilead

Unknown

Spiritual

There is a Balm in Gil-e-ad To make the wound-ed whole,

Fine

There is a Balm in Gil-e-ad To heal the sin-sick soul.

1. Some-times I feel dis-cour-aged, And think my work's in vain, But
2. Don't ev-er feel dis-cour-aged, For Je-sus is your friend, And
3. If you cannot preach like Pe-ter, If you cannot pray like Paul, You can

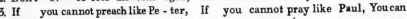

Hum

then the Ho-ly Spir-it Re-vives my soul a-gain.
if you lack for know-ledge, He'll not re-fuse to lend.
tell the love of Je-sus And say, "He died for all."

D.C.

Lord, I Want to Be a Christian 568

I WANT TO BE A CHRISTIAN 8.6.8.3. with Refrain

Negro Melody
Arr. by Donald Frederick, 1917 —

Negro spiritual

1. Lord, I want to be a Chris-tian, In-a my heart, in-a my
2. Lord, I want to be more lov-ing, In-a my heart, in-a my
3. Lord, I want to be more ho-ly, In-a my heart, in-a my
4. I don't want to be like Ju-das, In-a my heart, in-a my

heart; Lord, I want to be a Chris-tian, In-a my heart.
heart; Lord, I want to be more lov-ing, In-a my heart.
heart; Lord, I want to be more ho-ly, In-a my heart.
heart; But I want to be like Je-sus, In-a my heart.

In-a my heart (In-a my heart), In-a my heart (In-a my heart);

Lord, I want to be a Chris-tian, In-a my heart.
Lord, I want to be more lov-ing, In-a my heart.
Lord, I want to be more ho-ly, In-a my heart.
Lord, I want to be like Je-sus, In-a my heart.

569 Praise God, from Whom All Blessings Flow

OLD HUNDREDTH 8.8.8.8.

Thomas Ken, 1637-1711

Genevan Psalter, 1551

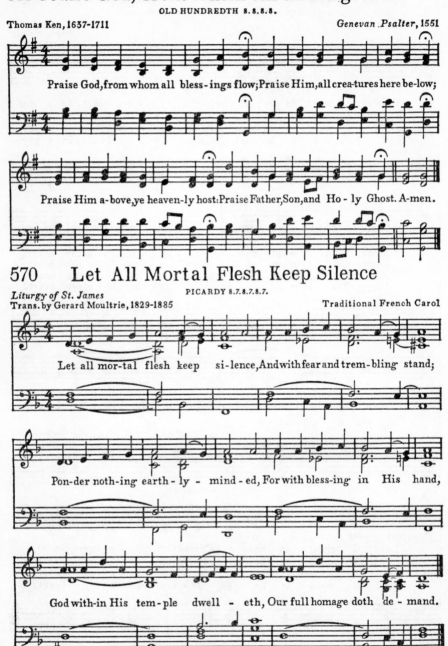

Praise God, from whom all bless-ings flow; Praise Him, all crea-tures here be-low;

Praise Him a-bove, ye heaven-ly host: Praise Father, Son, and Ho-ly Ghost. A-men.

570   Let All Mortal Flesh Keep Silence

PICARDY 8.7.8.7.8.7.

Liturgy of St. James
Trans. by Gerard Moultrie, 1829-1885

Traditional French Carol

Let all mor-tal flesh keep si-lence, And with fear and trem-bling stand;

Pon-der noth-ing earth-ly - mind-ed, For with bless-ing in His hand,

God with-in His tem-ple dwell - eth, Our full homage doth de - mand.

Jesus, Stand Among Us
BEMERTON 6.5.6.5.

571

William Pennefather, 1816-1873

Friedrich Filitz, 1804-1876

Je - sus, stand a - mong us In Thy ris - en power;

Let this time of wor - ship Be a hal-lowed hour. A - men.

O Worship the Lord
PORTER Irregular

572

Psalm 96:9

Robert G. McCutchan, 1877-1958

O wor - ship the Lord in the beau - ty of ho - li - ness;

Serve Him with glad - ness, all the earth. A - men.

573 Send Out Thy Light

LUX FIAT

Psalm 43:3

Charles F. Gounod, 1818-1895

Send out Thy light and Thy truth, let them lead me; O let them bring me to Thy ho - ly hill. Send out Thy light and Thy truth, let them lead me; O let them bring me to Thy ho - ly hill. O let them lead me, O let them lead me; O let them bring me to Thy ho - ly hill. A - men.

Glory Be to the Father

GLORIA PATRI

Source Unknown, 2nd century

Henry W. Greatorex, 1813-1858

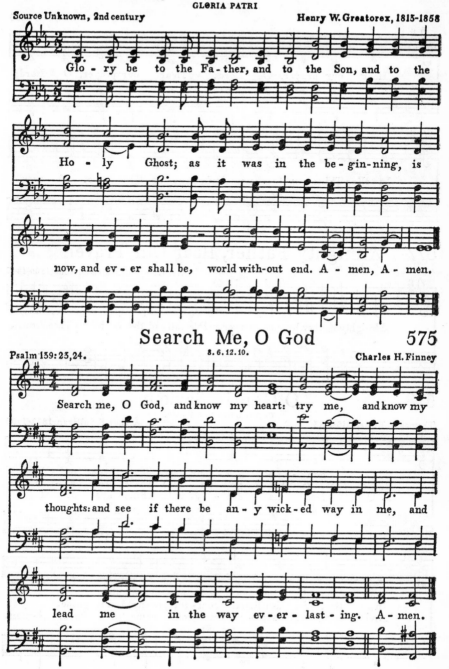

Glo - ry be to the Fa - ther, and to the Son, and to the

Ho - ly Ghost; as it was in the be - gin - ning, is

now, and ev - er shall be, world with-out end. A - men, A - men.

Search Me, O God

8. 6. 12. 10.

575

Psalm 159: 23, 24.

Charles H. Finney

Search me, O God, and know my heart: try me, and know my

thoughts: and see if there be an - y wick - ed way in me, and

lead me in the way ev - er - last - ing. A - men.

576 Hear Our Prayer, O Lord

5.5.6.5.

George Whelpton, 1847-1950

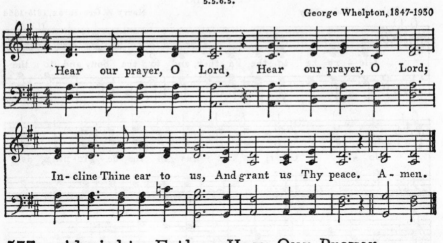

Hear our prayer, O Lord, Hear our prayer, O Lord;

In-cline Thine ear to us, And grant us Thy peace. A-men.

577 Almighty Father, Hear Our Prayer

Arr. from Felix Mendelssohn, 1809-1847

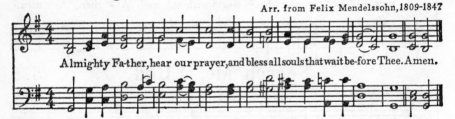

Almighty Fa-ther, hear our prayer, and bless all souls that wait be-fore Thee. Amen.

578 O Gentle Saviour

CHORAL RESPONSE 10.10.

Thomas R. Birks, 1810-1883

Arthur S. Sullivan, 1842-1900

1. O gen - tle Sav - iour, from Thy throne on high,
2. Go where we go, a - bide where we a - bide,
3. O lead us dai - ly with Thine eye of love,

Look down in love and hear our hum - ble cry.
In life, in death, our com - fort, strength and guide.
And bring us safe - ly to our home a - bove. A-men.

579 Twofold Amen
GREEK LITURGY

580 Threefold Amen
DANISH

A - men, A - men.

A-men, A-men, A - men.

Sevenfold Amen   581
John Stainer, 1840-1901

A - men, A - men,
A-men, A-men, A - men, A -
A - men,

- men,   A - men,
men,   A - men, A - men.
A - men,

Lord, Let Us Now Depart in Peace   582
DISMISSAL 8.8.8.6.   George Whelpton, 1847-1930

Lord, let us now de-part in peace, Who in Thy name are gath-ered here;

Dis-close the bright-ness of Thy face, And be for-ev-er near. A-men.

583 The Lord Bless You and Keep You

Numbers 6:24-26

Peter C. Lutkin, 1858-1931

THE SCRIPTURE READINGS

Public worship is greatly enriched and the service made more meaningful as the worshippers participate both in congregational song and the reading of the Scriptures. This section of the hymnal provides selected scriptural passages for both unison and responsive readings.

The scriptural readings are taken from the King James Version. Slight changes have been made by substituting words of current meaning and usage instead of archaic or obsolete terms and the addition or removal of a preposition or conjunction to aid in the readability and continuity of thought.

The unison readings are in consecutive scriptural order with relation to the beginning passage of each reading. The responsive readings are divided into four categories; each category follows a plan of selection as indicated by the table of contents.

The public reading of scripture should and can be a moving experience. Hebrew poetry, and psalmody in particular, was written with antiphonal reading and singing in mind. In preparing these responsive readings this has been taken into consideration and a number of the readings arranged with the parallel thought as the response rather than alternate verses. It is our desire and hope that the use of these scriptural readings will give a new dimension to the service of public worship.

The Lord's Prayer

Our Father, which art in heaven; hallowed be thy name. Thy kingdom come. Thy will be done in earth, as it is in heaven. Give us this day our daily bread. And forgive us our debts, as we forgive our debtors. And lead us not into temptation, but deliver us from evil; for thine is the kingdom, and the power, and the glory, for ever. Amen.

Matthew 6:9-13.

UNISON READINGS

584   Ten Commandments

God spake all these words, saying,
I am the Lord thy God, which
brought thee out of the land of Egypt,
out of the house of bondage.

I. Thou shalt have no other gods
before me.

II. Thou shalt not make unto thee
any graven image, or any likeness of
any thing that is in heaven above, or
that is in the earth beneath, or that is
in the water under the earth: thou
shalt not bow down thyself to them,
nor serve them: for I, the Lord thy
God, am a jealous God, visiting the
iniquity of the fathers upon the chil-
dren unto the third and fourth generation of them that hate me; and
showing mercy unto thousands of
them that love me, and keep my
commandments.

III. Thou shalt not take the name
of the Lord thy God in vain; for the
Lord will not hold him guiltless that
taketh his name in vain.

IV. Remember the Sabbath-day, to
keep it holy. Six days shalt thou
labor, and do all thy work; but the
seventh day is the Sabbath of the
Lord thy God; in it thou shalt not do
any work, thou, nor thy son, nor thy
daughter, thy man-servant, nor thy
maid-servant, nor thy cattle, nor thy
stranger that is within thy gates: for
in six days the Lord made heaven and
earth, the sea, and all that in them is,
and rested the seventh day; wherefore the Lord blessed the Sabbath-
day and hallowed it.

V. Honor thy father and thy
mother; that thy days may be long
upon the land which the Lord thy
God giveth thee.

VI. Thou shalt not kill.

VII. Thou shalt not commit adultery.

VIII. Thou shalt not steal.

IX. Thou shalt not bear false wit-
ness against thy neighbor.

X. Thou shalt not covet thy neighbor's house, thou shalt not covet thy
neighbor's wife, nor his man-servant,
nor his maid-servant, nor his ox, nor
his ass, nor anything that is thy
neighbor's.
                            —Exodus 20:1-17.

585   The Two Ways

Blessed is the man that walketh not
in the counsel of the ungodly, nor
standeth in the way of sinners, nor
sitteth in the seat of the scornful.

But his delight is in the law of the
Lord; and in his law doth he meditate day and night.

And he shall be like a tree planted
by the rivers of water, that bringeth
forth his fruit in his season; his leaf
also shall not wither; and whatsoever
he doeth shall prosper.

The ungodly are not so: but are
like the chaff which the wind driveth
away.

Therefore the ungodly shall not
stand in the judgment, nor sinners
in the congregation of the righteous.

For the Lord knoweth the way of
the righteous: but the way of the
ungodly shall perish.   —Psalm 1.

586   The Shepherd's Care

The Lord is my shepherd; I shall
not want.

He maketh me to lie down in green
pastures: he leadeth me beside the
still waters.

He restoreth my soul: he leadeth
me in the paths of righteousness for
his name's sake.

Yea, though I walk through the val-
ley of the shadow of death, I will fear

no evil: for thou art with me; thy rod and thy staff they comfort me.

Thou preparest a table before me in the presence of mine enemies: thou anointest my head with oil; my cup runneth over.

Surely goodness and mercy shall follow me all the days of my life: and I will dwell in the house of the Lord for ever. —Psalm 23.

587 The Joy of Worship

How amiable are thy tabernacles, O Lord of hosts!

My soul longeth, yea, even fainteth for the courts of the Lord:

My heart and my flesh crieth out for the living God.

Yea, the sparrow hath found an house, and the swallow a nest for herself,

Where she may lay her young, even thine altars, O Lord of Hosts, my King, and my God.

Blessed are they that dwell in thy house: they will be still praising thee.

Blessed is the man whose strength is in thee; in whose heart are the ways of them.

Who passing through the valley of weeping make it a well; the rain also filleth the pools.

They go from strength to strength, every one of them in Zion appeareth before God.

O Lord God of hosts, hear my prayer: give ear, O God of Jacob.

Behold, O God, our shield, and look upon the face of thine anointed.

For a day in thy courts is better than a thousand.

I had rather be a doorkeeper in the house of my God, than to dwell in the tents of wickedness.

For the Lord God is a sun and shield: the Lord will give grace and glory:

No good thing will he withhold from them that walk uprightly.

O Lord of hosts, blessed is the man that trusteth in thee. —Psalm 84.

588 A Call to Praise

Make a joyful noise unto the Lord, all ye lands.

Serve the Lord with gladness: come before his presence with singing.

Know ye that the Lord he is God: it is he that hath made us, and not we ourselves:

We are his people, and the sheep of his pasture.

Enter into his gates with thanksgiving, and into his courts with praise: be thankful unto him, and bless his name.

For the Lord is good: his mercy is everlasting; and his truth endureth to all generations. —Psalm 100.

589 The Comforting Hope

Let not your heart be troubled: ye believe in God, believe also in me.

In my Father's house are many mansions: if it were not so, I would have told you. I go to prepare a place for you.

And if I go and prepare a place for you, I will come again, and receive you unto myself; that where I am, there ye may be also.

And whither I go ye know, and the way ye know.

Thomas saith unto him, Lord, we know not whither thou goest; and how can we know the way?

Jesus saith unto him, I am the way, the truth, and the life: no man cometh unto the Father, but by me.

If ye had known me, ye should have known my Father also: and from henceforth ye know him, and have seen him.

Philip saith unto him, Lord, show us the Father, and it sufficeth us.

Jesus saith unto him, Have I been so long time with you, and yet hast thou not known me, Philip? he that hath seen me hath seen the Father; and how sayest thou then, Show us the Father?

Believest thou not that I am in the Father, and the Father in me? the words that I speak unto you I speak not of myself: but the Father that dwelleth in me, he doeth the works.

Believe me that I am in the Father, and the Father in me: or else believe me for the very works' sake.

Verily, verily, I say unto you, He that believeth on me, the works that I do shall he do also; and greater works than these shall he do; because I go unto my Father.

And whatsoever ye shall ask in my name, that will I do, that the Father may be glorified in the Son.

—John 14:1-13.

590　A More Excellent Way

Though I speak with the tongues of men and of angels, and have not love, I am become as sounding brass, or a tinkling cymbal.

And though I have the gift of prophecy, and understand all mysteries, and all knowledge; and though I have all faith, so that I could remove mountains, and have not love, I am nothing.

And though I bestow all my goods to feed the poor, and though I give my body to be burned, and have not love, it profiteth me nothing.

Love suffereth long, and is kind; love envieth not; love vaunteth not itself, is not puffed up.

Doth not behave itself unseemly, seeketh not her own, is not easily provoked, thinketh no evil;

Rejoiceth not in iniquity, but rejoiceth in the truth;

Beareth all things, believeth all things, hopeth all things, endureth all things.

Love never faileth; but whether there be prophecies, they shall fail; whether there be tongues, they shall cease; whether there be knowledge, it shall vanish away.

For we know in part, and we prophesy in part.

But when that which is perfect is come, then that which is in part shall be done away.

When I was a child, I spake as a child, I understood as a child, I thought as a child; but when I became a man, I put away childish things.

For now we see through a glass, darkly; but then face to face; now I know in part; but then shall I know even as also I am known.

And now abideth faith, hope, love, these three; but the greatest of these is love.　　　—I Corinthians 13.

591　The Mind of Christ

Let this mind be in you, which was also in Christ Jesus:

Who, being in the form of God, thought it not robbery to be equal with God:

But made himself of no reputation, and took upon him the form of a servant, and was made in the likeness of men:

And being found in fashion as a man, he humbled himself, and became obedient unto death, even the death of the cross.

Wherefore God also hath highly exalted him, and given him a name which is above every name.

That at the name of Jesus every knee should bow, of things in heaven, and things in earth, and things under the earth;

And that every tongue should confess that Jesus Christ is Lord, to the glory of God the Father.

And Jesus said, Ye know that the princes of the Gentiles exercise dominion over them, and they that are great exercise authority upon them.

But it shall not be so among you: but whosoever will be great among you, let him be your minister;

And whosoever will be chief among you, let him be your servant:

Even as the Son of man came not to be ministered unto, but to minister, and to give his life a ransom for many.

—Philippians 2:5-11; Matthew 20:25-28.

RESPONSIVE READINGS

592   Christ in Prophecy

Therefore the Lord himself shall give you a sign; Behold, a virgin shall conceive, and bear a son, and shall call his name Immanuel.

And there shall come forth a rod out of the stem of Jesse, and a Branch shall grow out of his roots:

And the spirit of the Lord shall rest upon him, the spirit of wisdom and understanding, the spirit of counsel and might, the spirit of knowledge and of the fear of the Lord;

And shall make him of quick understanding in the fear of the Lord: and he shall not judge after the sight of his eyes, neither reprove after the hearing of his ears:

But with righteousness shall he judge the poor, and reprove with equity for the meek of the earth: and he shall smite the earth with the rod of his mouth, and with the breath of his lips shall he slay the wicked.

And righteousness shall be the girdle of his loins, and faithfulness the girdle of his reins.

Behold my servant, whom I uphold; mine elect, in whom my soul delighteth; I have put my spirit upon him: he shall bring forth judgment to the Gentiles.

He shall not cry, nor lift up, nor cause his voice to be heard in the street.

A bruised reed shall he not break, and the smoking flax shall he not quench:

He shall bring forth judgment unto truth.

He shall not fail nor be discouraged, till he have set judgment in the earth:

And the isles shall wait for his law.

Go through, go through the gates; prepare ye the way of the people; cast up, cast up the highway; gather out the stones; lift up a standard for the people.

Behold, the Lord hath proclaimed unto the end of the world, Say ye to the daughter of Zion, Behold, thy salvation cometh; behold, his reward is with him, and his work before him.

—Isaiah 7:14; 11:1-5; 42:1-4; 62:10, 11.

593   Songs of the Nativity

And Mary said, My soul doth magnify the Lord,

And my spirit hath rejoiced in God my Saviour.

For he hath regarded the low estate of his handmaiden:

For, behold, from henceforth all generations shall call me blessed.

For he that is mighty hath done to me great things;

And holy is his name. And his mercy is on them that fear him from generation to generation.

He hath showed strength with his arm;

He hath scattered the proud in the imagination of their hearts.

He hath put down the mighty from their seats,

And exalted them of low degree.

He hath filled the hungry with good things;

And the rich he hath sent empty away.

And Zacharias prophesied saying, Blessed be the Lord God of Israel; for he hath visited and redeemed his people,

And hath raised up an horn of salvation for us in the house of his servant David;

As he spake by the mouth of his holy prophets, which have been since the world began: That we should be saved from our enemies,

And from the hand of all that hate us;

To perform the mercy promised to our fathers,

And to remember his holy covenant; The oath which he sware to our father Abraham, That he would grant unto us, that we being delivered out of the hand of our enemies might serve him without fear, In holiness and righteousness before him, all the days of our life.

Then Simeon took the child up in his arms, and blessed God, and said,

Lord, now lettest thou thy servant depart in peace, according to thy word:

For mine eyes have seen thy salvation, Which thou hast prepared before the face of all people;

A light to lighten the Gentiles, and the glory of thy people Israel.
—Luke 1:46-53, 68-75; 2:28-32.

594   Birth of Christ

And there were in the same country shepherds abiding in the field, keeping watch over their flock by night.

And, lo, the angel of the Lord came upon them, and the glory of the Lord shone round about them: and they were sore afraid.

And the angel said unto them, Fear not: for, behold, I bring you good tidings of great joy, which shall be to all people.

For unto you is born this day in the city of David a Saviour, which is Christ the Lord.

And this shall be a sign unto you; Ye shall find the babe wrapped in swaddling clothes, lying in a manger.

And suddenly there was with the angel a multitude of the heavenly host praising God, and saying,

Glory to God in the highest, and on earth peace, good will toward men.

And it came to pass, as the angels were gone away from them into heaven, the shepherds said one to another,

Let us now go even unto Bethlehem, and see this thing which is come to pass, which the Lord hath made known unto us.

And they came with haste, and found Mary, and Joseph, and the babe lying in a manger.

And when they had seen it, they made known abroad the saying which was told them concerning this child.

And all they that heard it wondered at those things which were told them by the shepherds.

But Mary kept all these things, and pondered them in her heart.

And the shepherds returned, glorifying and praising God for all the things that they had heard and seen, as it was told unto them.
—Luke 2:8-20.

595 The Triumphal Entry

And when they came nigh to Jerusalem, unto Bethphage and Bethany, at the mount of Olives, he sendeth forth two of his disciples, and saith unto them,

Go your way into the village over against you: and as soon as ye be entered into it, ye shall find a colt tied, whereon never man sat; loose him, and bring him. And if any man say unto you, Why do ye this? say ye that the Lord hath need of him; and straightway he will send him hither.

And they went their way, and found the colt tied by the door without in a place where two ways met; and they loose him. And certain of them that stood there said unto them, What do ye, loosing the colt?

And they said unto them even as Jesus had commanded; and they let them go.

And they brought the colt to Jesus, and cast their garments on him; and he sat upon him.

And many spread their garments in the way; and others cut down branches off the trees, and strawed them in the way.

And they that went before, and they that followed, cried,

Saying, Hosanna; Blessed is he that cometh in the name of the Lord: Blessed be the kingdom of our father David, that cometh in the name of the Lord: Hosanna in the highest. And Jesus entered into Jerusalem, and into the temple:

And when he was come into Jerusalem, all the city was moved, saying, Who is this?

And the multitude said, This is Jesus the prophet of Nazareth of Galilee.
—Mark 11:1-11; Matthew 21:10, 11.

596 The Suffering Saviour

UNISON

Who hath believed our report? and to whom is the arm of the Lord revealed? For he shall grow up before him as a tender plant, and as a root out of a dry ground: He hath no form nor comeliness; and when we shall see him, there is no beauty that we should desire him.

He is despised and rejected of men:

A man of sorrows and acquainted with grief:

And we hid as it were our faces from him:

He was despised, and we esteemed him not.

Surely he hath borne our griefs, and carried our sorrows:

Yet we did esteem him stricken, smitten of God, and afflicted.

But he was wounded for our transgressions,

He was bruised for our iniquities:

The chastisement of our peace was upon him;

And with his stripes we are healed.

All we like sheep have gone astray;

We have turned every one to his own way;

And the Lord hath laid on him the iniquity of us all.

UNISON

He was oppressed, and he was afflicted, yet he opened not his mouth: He is brought as a lamb to the slaughter, and as a sheep before its shearers is dumb, so he openeth not his mouth.

He was taken from prison and from judgment:

And who shall declare his generation?

For he was cut off out of the land of the living:

For the transgression of my people was he stricken.

And they made his grave with the wicked,

And with the rich in his death;

Because he had done no violence,

Neither was any deceit in his mouth.

Yet it pleased the Lord to bruise him;

Unison

He hath put him to grief: When thou shalt make his soul an offering for sin, he shall see his seed, He shall prolong his days, and the pleasure of the Lord shall prosper in his hand. He shall see of the travail of his soul, and shall be satisfied: By his knowledge shall my righteous servant justify many; for he shall bear their iniquities. Therefore will I divide him a portion with the great, and he shall divide the spoil with the strong; Because he hath poured out his soul unto death: And he was numbered with the transgressors, And he bare the sin of many, and made intercession for the transgressors.

—Isaiah 53.

597 Christ on the Cross

And Jesus bearing his cross went forth into a place called the place of a skull, which is called in the Hebrew, Golgotha:

Where they crucified him, and two other with him, on either side one, and Jesus in the midst.

And Pilate wrote a title, and put it on the cross. And the writing was, JESUS OF NAZARETH THE KING OF THE JEWS.

This title then read many of the Jews: for the place where Jesus was crucified was nigh to the city: and it was written in Hebrew, and Greek, and Latin.

Then said the chief priests of the Jews to Pilate, Write not, The King of the Jews; but that he said, I am King of the Jews.

Pilate answered, What I have written I have written.

Then the soldiers, when they had crucified Jesus, took his garments, and made four parts, to every soldier a part; and also his coat: now the coat was without seam, woven from the top throughout.

They said therefore among themselves, Let us not rend it, but cast lots for it, whose it shall be:

That the scripture might be fulfilled, which saith, They parted my raiment among them, and for my vesture they did cast lots.

These things therefore the soldiers did.

Now there stood by the cross of Jesus his mother, and his mother's sister, Mary the wife of Cleophas, and Mary Magdalene.

When Jesus therefore saw his mother, and the disciple standing by, whom he loved, he saith unto his mother, Woman, behold thy son! Then saith he to the disciple, Behold thy mother!

And from that hour that disciple took her unto his own home.

After this, Jesus knowing that all things were now accomplished, that the scripture might be fulfilled, saith, I thirst.

Now there was set a vessel full of vinegar: and they filled a spunge with vinegar, and put it upon hyssop, and put it to his mouth.

When Jesus therefore had received the vinegar, he said, It is finished: and he bowed his head, and gave up the ghost.

—John 19:17-30.

598   The Risen Lord

In the end of the sabbath, as it began to dawn toward the first day of the week, came Mary Magdalene and the other Mary to see the sepulchre.

And, behold, there was a great earthquake: for the angel of the Lord descended from heaven, and came and rolled back the stone from the door, and sat upon it. His countenance was like lightning, and his raiment white as snow: And for fear of him the keepers did shake, and became as dead men.

And the angel answered and said unto the women, Fear not ye: for I know that ye seek Jesus, which was crucified. He is not here: for he is risen as he said. Come, see the place where the Lord lay. And go quickly, and tell his disciples that he is risen from the dead; and, behold, he goeth before you into Galilee; there shall ye see him: lo, I have told you.

And they departed quickly from the sepulchre with fear and great joy; and did run to bring his disciples word.

And as they went to tell his disciples, behold, Jesus met them, saying, All hail. And they came and held him by the feet, and worshipped him.

Then said Jesus unto them, Be not afraid: go tell my brethren that they go into Galilee, and there shall they see me.

Then the same day at evening, being the first day of the week, when the doors were shut where the disciples were assembled for fear of the Jews, came Jesus and stood in the midst, and saith unto them, Peace be unto you. And when he had so said, he shewed unto them his hands and his side.

Then were the disciples glad, when they saw the Lord.

And after eight days again his disciples were within, and Thomas with them: then came Jesus, the doors being shut, and stood in the midst, and said, Peace be unto you.

Then saith he to Thomas, Reach hither thy finger, and behold my hands; and reach hither thy hand, and thrust it into my side: and be not faithless, but believing.

And Thomas answered and said unto him, My Lord and my God.

Jesus saith unto him, Thomas, because thou hast seen me, thou hast believed: blessed are they that have not seen, and yet have believed.

—Matthew 28:1-10; John 20:19, 20, 26-29.

599   Christ and Immortality

Now is Christ risen from the dead, and become the firstfruits of them that slept. For since by man came death,

By man came also the resurrection of the dead.

For as in Adam all die,

Even so in Christ shall all be made alive.

But every man in his own order: Christ the firstfruits;

Afterward they that are Christ's at his coming.

Then cometh the end, when he shall have delivered up the kingdom to God, even the Father; when he shall have put down all rule and all authority and power. For he must reign, till he hath put all enemies under his feet.

The last enemy that shall be destroyed is death.

There is one glory of the sun, and another glory of the moon, and another glory of the stars:

For one star differeth from another star in glory.

So also is the resurrection of the dead. It is sown in corruption;

It is raised in incorruption:

It is sown in dishonor;

It is raised in glory:

It is sown in weakness;

It is raised in power;

It is sown a natural body;

It is raised a spiritual body.

There is a natural body, and there is a spiritual body. And so it is written, The first man Adam was made a living soul;

The last Adam was made a quickening spirit.

The first man is of the earth, earthy:

The second man is the Lord from heaven.

And as we have borne the image of the earthy,

We shall also bear the image of the heavenly.

For this corruptible must put on incorruption,

And this mortal must put on immortality.

So when this corruptible shall have put on incorruption, and this mortal shall have put on immortality, then shall be brought to pass the saying that is written, Death is swallowed up in victory.

O death, where is thy sting? O grave, where is thy victory?

The sting of death is sin; and the strength of sin is the law.

But thanks be to God, which giveth us the victory through our Lord Jesus Christ.

—I Corinthians 15:20-26, 41-45, 47, 49, 53-57.

600 Ascension and Intercession

And Jesus led them out as far as to Bethany, and he lifted up his hands, and blessed them.

And it came to pass, while he blessed them, he was parted from them, and carried up into heaven.

Wherefore God also hath highly exalted him, and given him a name which is above every name:

That at the name of Jesus every knee should bow, of things in heaven, and things in earth, and things under the earth: And that every tongue should confess that Jesus Christ is Lord, to the glory of God the Father.

Seeing then that we have a great high priest, that is passed into the heavens, Jesus the Son of God, let us hold fast our profession.

For we have not an high priest which cannot be touched with the feeling of our infirmities; but was in all points tempted like as we are, yet without sin.

Let us therefore come boldly unto the throne of grace, that we may obtain mercy, and find grace to help in time of need.

For Christ is not entered into the holy places made with hands, which are the figures of the true; but into heaven itself, now to appear in the presence of God for us:

Wherefore he is able also to save them to the uttermost that come unto God by him, seeing he ever liveth to make intercession for them.

For such an high priest became us, who is holy, harmless, undefiled, separate from sinners, and made higher than the heavens;

Having therefore, brethren, boldness to enter into the holiest by the blood of Jesus, Let us draw near with a true heart in full assurance of faith, having our hearts sprinkled from an evil conscience, and our bodies washed with pure water.

Let us hold fast the profession of our faith without wavering; (for he is faithful that promised).

—Luke 24:50, 51; Philippians 2:9-11; Hebrews 4:14-16; 9:24; 7:25, 26; 10:19, 22, 23.

601   Return of Christ

But I would not have you to be ignorant, brethren, concerning them which are asleep, that ye sorrow not, even as others which have no hope.

For if we believe that Jesus died and rose again, even so them also which sleep in Jesus will God bring with him.

For this we say unto you by the word of the Lord, that we which are alive and remain unto the coming of the Lord shall not precede them which are asleep.

For the Lord himself shall descend from heaven with a shout, with the voice of the archangel, and with the trump of God: and the dead in Christ shall rise first.

Then we which are alive and remain shall be caught up together with them in the clouds, to meet the Lord in the air: And so shall we ever be with the Lord.

Wherefore comfort one another with these words.

But of the times and the seasons, brethren, ye have no need that I write unto you. For yourselves know perfectly that the day of the Lord so cometh as a thief in the night.

For when they shall say, Peace and safety; then sudden destruction cometh upon them, as travail upon a woman with child; and they shall not escape.

But ye, brethren, are not in darkness, that that day should overtake you as a thief. Ye are all the children of light, and the children of the day:

We are not of the night, nor of darkness. Therefore let us not sleep, as do others; but let us watch and be sober.

For they that sleep sleep in the night; and they that be drunken are drunken in the night.

But let us, who are of the day, be sober, putting on the breastplate of faith and love; and for an helmet, the hope of salvation.

For God hath not appointed us to wrath, but to obtain salvation by our Lord Jesus Christ,

Who died for us, that, whether we wake or sleep, we should live together with him.

—I Thessalonians 4:13-18; 5:1-10.

602   God's Invitation

Ho, everyone that thirsteth, come ye to the waters, and he that hath no money; come ye, buy and eat;

Yea, come, buy wine and milk without money and without price.

Wherefore do ye spend money for that which is not bread?

And your labor for that which satisfieth not?

Hearken diligently unto me, and eat ye that which is good,

And let your soul delight itself in fatness.

Seek ye the Lord while he may be found;

Call ye upon him while he is near;

Let the wicked forsake his way,

And the unrighteous man his thoughts;

Let him return unto the Lord, and he will have mercy upon him;

And to our God, for he will abundantly pardon.

For my thoughts are not your thoughts,

Neither are your ways my ways, saith the Lord.

For as the heavens are higher than the earth,

So are my ways higher than your ways, and my thoughts than your thoughts.

For as the rain cometh down and the snow from heaven, And returneth not thither, but watereth the earth, And maketh it bring forth and bud, that it may give seed to the sower and bread to the eater;

So shall my word be that goeth forth out of my mouth; It shall not return unto me void, but it shall accomplish that which I please, And it shall prosper in the thing whereto I sent it.

For ye shall go out with joy, and be led forth with peace; The mountains and the hills shall break forth before you into singing;

And all the trees of the field shall clap their hands.

Instead of the thorn shall come up the fir-tree.

Instead of the brier shall come up the myrtle-tree:

And it shall be to the Lord for a name,

For an everlasting sign that shall not be cut off.

—Isaiah 55.

603   Christian Baptism

Then cometh Jesus from Galilee to Jordan unto John, to be baptized of him.

But John forbad him, saying, I have need to be baptized of thee, and comest thou to me?

And Jesus answering said unto him, Suffer it to be so now: for thus it becometh us to fulfill all righteousness.

Then he suffered him.

And Jesus, when he was baptized, went up straightway out of the water: and, lo, the heavens were opened unto him, and he saw the Spirit of God descending like a dove, and lighting upon him:

And lo a voice from heaven, saying, This is my beloved Son, in whom I am well pleased.

And Jesus came and spake unto them, saying, All power is given unto me in heaven and in earth.

Go ye therefore, and teach all nations, baptizing them in the name of the Father, and of the Son, and of the Holy Ghost:

Then Peter said unto them, Repent, and be baptized every one of you in the name of Jesus Christ for the remission of sins, and ye shall receive the gift of the Holy Ghost.

For the promise is unto you, and to your children, and to all that are afar off, even as many as the Lord our God shall call.

Then they that gladly received his word were baptized.

Know ye not, that so many of us as were baptized into Jesus Christ were baptized into his death?

Therefore we are buried with him by baptism into death: that like as Christ was raised up from the dead by the glory of the Father, even so we also should walk in newness of life.

For if we have been planted together in the likeness of his death, we shall be also in the likeness of his resurrection:

Knowing this, that our old man is crucified with him, that the body of sin might be destroyed, that henceforth we should not serve sin.

Likewise reckon ye also yourselves to be dead indeed unto sin, but alive unto God through Jesus Christ our Lord.

—Matthew 3:13-17; 28:18, 19; Acts 2:38, 39, 41; Romans 6:3-6, 11.

604 Seeking the Lost

What man of you, having an hundred sheep, if he lose one of them, doth not leave the ninety and nine in the wilderness, and go after that which is lost, until he find it?

And when he hath found it, he layeth it on his shoulders, rejoicing. And when he cometh home, he calleth together his friends and neighbors, saying unto them, Rejoice with me; for I have found my sheep which was lost.

I say unto you, that likewise joy shall be in heaven over one sinner that repenteth, more than over ninety and nine just persons, which need no repentance.

Either what woman having ten pieces of silver, if she lose one piece, doth not light a candle, and sweep the house, and seek diligently till she find it?

And when she hath found it, she calleth her friends and her neighbors together, saying, Rejoice with me; for I have found the piece which I had lost.

Likewise, I say unto you, there is joy in the presence of the angels of God over one sinner that repenteth.

And he said, A certain man had two sons: And the younger of them said to his father, Father, give me the portion of goods that falleth to me. And he divided unto them his living.

And not many days after the younger son gathered all together, and took his journey into a far country, and there wasted his substance with riotous living.

And when he came to himself, he said, How many hired servants of my father's have bread enough and to spare, and I perish with hunger! And he arose, and came to his father.

But when he was yet a great way off, his father saw him, and had compassion, and ran, and fell on his neck, and kissed him.

And the son said unto him, Father, I have sinned against heaven, and in thy sight, and am no more worthy to be called thy son.

UNISON

But the father said to his servants, Bring forth the best robe, and put it on him; and put a ring on his hand, and shoes on his feet: And bring hither the fatted calf, and kill it; and let us eat, and be merry: For this my son was dead, and is alive again; he was lost, and is found.

—Luke 15:4-13, 17, 20-24.

605 The Saviour Speaks

Come unto me, all ye that labor and are heavy laden,

And I will give you rest.

Take my yoke upon you, and learn of me; for I am meek and lowly in heart:

And ye shall find rest unto your souls.

For my yoke is easy,

And my burden is light.

Enter ye in at the strait gate: for
wide is the gate, and broad is the way,
that leadeth to destruction, and many
there be which go in thereat:

**Because strait is the gate, and nar-
row is the way, which leadeth unto
life, and few there be that find it.**

Not every one that saith unto me
Lord, Lord, shall enter into the king-
dom of heaven; but he that doeth the
will of my Father which is in heaven.

**Many will say to me in that day,
Lord, Lord, have we not prophesied
in thy name? and in thy name have
cast out devils? and in thy name
done many wonderful works?**

And then will I profess unto them, I
never knew you: depart from me, ye
that work iniquity.

**Therefore whosoever heareth these
sayings of mine, and doeth them, I
will liken him unto a wise man,
which built his house upon a rock:**

And the rain descended, and the
floods came, and the winds blew, and
beat upon that house; and it fell not:
for it was founded upon a rock.

**And everyone that heareth these
sayings of mine, and doeth them
not, shall be likened unto a foolish
man, which built his house upon the
sand:**

And the rain descended, and the
floods came, and the winds blew, and
beat upon that house; and it fell: and
great was the fall of it.

**And it came to pass, when Jesus
had ended these sayings, the peo-
ple were astonished at his doctrine:
For he taught them as one having
authority, and not as the scribes.**

—Matthew 11:28-30; 7:13, 14, 21-29.

606 The House of Worship

I was glad when they said unto me,
Let us go into the house of the Lord.

**Our feet shall stand within thy
gates, O Jerusalem.**

Lord, I have loved the habitation of
thy house, and the place where
thine honor dwelleth.

**Come, and let us go up to the
mountain of the Lord, and to the
house of the God of Jacob;**

And he will teach us of his ways,
and we will walk in his paths.

**And Jesus came to Nazareth, where
he had been brought up; and as
his custom was, he went into the
synagogue on the Sabbath day,
and stood up for to read.**

And there was delivered unto him
the book of the prophet Isaiah.

**And when he had opened the book,
he found the place where it was
written,**

The Spirit of the Lord is upon me,
because he hath anointed me to
preach the gospel to the poor;

**He hath sent me to heal the broken-
hearted,**

To preach deliverance to the cap-
tives, and recovering of sight to the
blind,

**To set at liberty them that are
bruised, to preach the acceptable
year of the Lord.**

Behold, bless ye the Lord, all ye serv-
ants of the Lord, which by night
stand in the house of the Lord.

**The Lord that made heaven and
earth bless thee out of Zion.**

—Psalm 122:1, 2; 26:8; Micah 4:2; Luke
4:16-19; Psalm 134:1, 3.

Now the first day of the feast of unleavened bread the disciples came to Jesus,

> **Saying unto him, Where wilt thou that we prepare for thee to eat the passover?**

And he said, Go into the city to such a man, and say unto him, The Master saith, My time is at hand; I will keep the passover at thy house with my disciples.

> **And the disciples did as Jesus had appointed them; and they made ready the passover.**

Now when the even was come, he sat down with the twelve.

> **And as they did eat, he said, Verily I say unto you, that one of you shall betray me.**

And they were exceeding sorrowful, and began every one of them to say unto him, Lord, is it I?

> **And he answered and said, He that dippeth his hand with me in the dish, the same shall betray me.**

The Son of man goeth as it is written of him: but woe unto that man by whom the Son of man is betrayed! it had been good for that man if he had not been born.

> **Then Judas, which betrayed him, answered and said, Master, is it I?**

He said unto him, Thou hast said.

> **And as they were eating, Jesus took bread, and blessed it, and brake it, and gave it to the disciples, and said, Take, eat; this is my body.**

And he took the cup, and gave thanks, and gave it to them, saying, Drink ye all of it; For this is my blood of the new testament, which is shed for many for the remission of sins.

> **But I say unto you, I will not drink henceforth of this fruit of the vine, until that day when I drink it new with you in my Father's kingdom.**

The cup of blessing which we bless, is it not the communion of the blood of Christ?

> **The bread which we break, is it not the communion of the body of Christ?**

For I have received of the Lord that which also I delivered unto you, That the Lord Jesus the same night in which he was betrayed took bread:

> **And when he had given thanks, he brake it, and said,**

Take, eat: this is my body, which is broken for you: this do in remembrance of me.

> **After the same manner also he took the cup, when he had supped, saying,**

This cup is the new testament in my blood: this do ye, as oft as ye drink it, in remembrance of me.

> **For as often as ye eat this bread, and drink this cup, ye do shew the Lord's death till he come.**

—Matthew 26:17-29; I Corinthians 10:16; 11:23-26.

608   A Missionary Melody

O sing unto the Lord a new song;

> **Sing unto the Lord, all the earth.**

Sing unto the Lord, bless his name;

> **Shew forth his salvation from day to day.**

Declare his glory among the heathen,

> **His wonders among all people.**

For the Lord is great, and greatly to be praised:

> **He is to be feared above all gods.**

For all the gods of the nations are idols:

But the Lord made the heavens.

Honor and majesty are before him:

Strength and beauty are in his sanctuary.

Give unto the Lord, O ye kindreds of the people, give unto the Lord glory and strength.

Give unto the Lord the glory due unto his name: bring an offering, and come into his courts.

O worship the Lord in the beauty of holiness: fear before him, all the earth.

Say among the heathen, that the Lord reigneth: The world also shall be established that it shall not be moved: he shall judge the people righteously.

Let the heavens rejoice, and let the earth be glad;

Let the sea roar, and the fulness thereof.

Let the field be joyful, and all that is therein:

Then shall all the trees of the wood rejoice before the Lord: for he cometh, for he cometh to judge the earth: he shall judge the world with righteousness, and the people with his truth.

—Psalm 96.

609   The Whitened Harvest

And Jesus went about all the cities and villages, teaching in their synagogues, and preaching the gospel of the kingdom, and healing every sickness and every disease among the people.

But when he saw the multitudes, he was moved with compassion on them, because they fainted, and

were scattered abroad, as sheep having no shepherd.

Then saith he unto his disciples, The harvest truly is plenteous, but the laborers are few; Pray ye therefore the Lord of the harvest, that he will send forth laborers into his harvest.

For there is no difference between the Jew and the Greek: for the same Lord over all is rich unto all that call upon him. For whosoever shall call upon the name of the Lord shall be saved.

How then shall they call on him in whom they have not believed?

How shall they believe in him of whom they have not heard?

How shall they hear without a preacher?

And how shall they preach, except they be sent?

As it is written, How beautiful are the feet of them that preach the gospel of peace, and bring glad tidings of good things!

Say not ye, There are yet four months, and then cometh harvest?

Behold, I say unto you, Lift up your eyes, and look on the fields; for they are white already to harvest.

UNISON
He that goeth forth and weepeth, bearing precious seed, shall doubtless come again with rejoicing, bringing his sheaves with him.

—Matthew 9:35-38; Romans 10:12-15; John 4:35; Psalm 126:6.

610   The Great Commission

Then the eleven disciples went away into Galilee, into a mountain where Jesus had appointed them.

And when they saw him, they worshipped him: but some doubted.

514

And Jesus came and spake unto them, saying, All power is given unto me in heaven and in earth.

Go ye therefore, and teach all nations, baptizing them in the name of the Father, and of the Son, and of the Holy Ghost: Teaching them to observe all things whatsoever I have commanded you: and, lo, I am with you alway, even unto the end of the world.

Jesus said unto them, Thus it is written, and thus it behoved Christ to suffer, and to rise from the dead the third day:

And that repentance and remission of sins should be preached in his name among all nations, beginning at Jerusalem.

And ye are witnesses of these things.

And, behold, I send the promise of my Father upon you: but tarry ye in the city of Jerusalem, until ye be endued with power from on high.

They asked of him, saying, Lord, wilt thou at this time restore again the kingdom to Israel?

And he said unto them, It is not for you to know the times or the seasons, which the Father hath put in his own power.

But ye shall receive power, after that the Holy Ghost is come upon you: And ye shall be witnesses unto me both in Jerusalem, and in all Judaea, and in Samaria, and unto the uttermost part of the earth.

And when he had spoken these things, while they beheld, he was taken up; and a cloud received him out of their sight.

—Matthew 28:16-20; Luke 24:46-49; Acts 1:6-9.

611 Prayer of the Penitent

Have mercy upon me, O God, according to thy lovingkindness;

According unto the multitude of thy tender mercies blot out my transgressions.

Wash me thoroughly from mine iniquity,

And cleanse me from my sin.

For I acknowledge my transgressions;

And my sin is ever before me.

Against thee, thee only, have I sinned, and done this evil in thy sight:

That thou mightest be justified when thou speakest, and be clear when thou judgest.

Behold, I was shapen in iniquity;

And in sin did my mother conceive me.

Behold, thou desirest truth in the inward parts;

And in the hidden part thou shalt make me to know wisdom.

Purge me with hyssop, and I shall be clean:

Wash me, and I shall be whiter than snow.

Make me to hear joy and gladness; that the bones which thou hast broken may rejoice. Hide thy face from my sins,

And blot out all mine iniquities.

Create in me a clean heart, O God;

And renew a right spirit within me.

Cast me not away from thy presence;

And take not thy holy Spirit from me.

Restore unto me the joy of thy salvation;

And uphold me with thy free Spirit:

Then will I teach transgressors thy ways;

And sinners shall be converted unto thee.

Deliver me from bloodguiltiness, O God, thou God of my salvation:

And my tongue shall sing aloud of thy righteousness.

O Lord, open thou my lips;

And my mouth shall show forth thy praise.

For thou desirest not sacrifice; else would I give it:

Thou delightest not in burnt offerings.

The sacrifices of God are a broken spirit;

A broken and a contrite heart, O God, thou wilt not despise.

—Psalm 51:1-17.

612   The New Birth

There was a man of the Pharisees, named Nicodemus, a ruler of the Jews:

The same came to Jesus by night, and said unto him, Rabbi, we know that thou art a teacher come from God: for no man can do these miracles that thou doest, except God be with him.

Jesus answered and said unto him, Verily, verily, I say unto thee, Except a man be born again, he cannot see the kingdom of God.

Nicodemus saith unto him, How can a man be born when he is old? can he enter a second time into his mother's womb, and be born?

Jesus answered, Verily, verily, I say unto thee, Except a man be born of water and of the Spirit, he cannot enter into the kingdom of God.

That which is born of the flesh is flesh; and that which is born of the Spirit is spirit. Marvel not that I said unto thee, Ye must be born again.

The wind bloweth where it listeth, and thou hearest the sound thereof, but canst not tell whence it cometh, and whither it goeth:

So is every one that is born of the Spirit.

And as Moses lifted up the serpent in the wilderness, even so must the Son of man be lifted up:

That whosoever believeth in him should not perish, but have eternal life. For God so loved the world, that he gave his only begotten Son, that whosoever believeth in him should not perish, but have everlasting life.

—John 3:1-8, 14-16.

613   The Joy of Forgiveness

Blessed is he whose transgression is forgiven, whose sin is covered.

Blessed is the man unto whom the Lord imputeth not iniquity, and in whose spirit there is no guile.

When I kept silence, my bones waxed old through my roaring all the day long.

For day and night thy hand was heavy upon me: my moisture is turned into the drought of summer.

I acknowledged my sin unto thee,

And mine iniquity have I not hid.

I said, I will confess my transgressions unto the Lord;

And thou forgavest the iniquity of my sin.

For this shall every one that is godly pray unto thee in a time when thou mayest be found:

Surely in the floods of great waters they shall not come nigh unto him.

Thou art my hiding place; thou shalt preserve me from trouble;

Thou shalt compass me about with songs of deliverance.

I will instruct thee and teach thee in the way which thou shalt go:

I will guide thee with mine eye.

Be ye not as the horse, or as the mule, which have no understanding:

Whose mouth must be held in with bit and bridle, lest they come near unto thee.

Many sorrows shall be to the wicked:

But he that trusteth in the Lord, mercy shall compass him about.

Be glad in the Lord, and rejoice, ye righteous:

And shout for joy, all ye that are upright in heart.

—Psalm 32.

614   Christian Assurance

And this is the record, that God hath given to us eternal life, and this life is in his Son.

He that hath the Son hath life; and he that hath not the Son of God hath not life.

These things have I written unto you that believe on the name of the Son of God; that ye may know that ye have eternal life, and that ye may believe on the name of the Son of God.

And this is the confidence that we have in him, that, if we ask any thing according to his will, he heareth us:

And if we know that he hear us, whatsoever we ask, we know that we have the petitions that we desired of him.

Hereby know we that we dwell in him, and he in us, because he hath given us of his Spirit.

We know that we have passed from death unto life, because we love the brethren.

For the which cause I also suffer these things: nevertheless I am not ashamed: for I know whom I have believed, and am persuaded that he is able to keep that which I have committed unto him against that day.

And we know that all things work together for good to them that love God, to them who are the called according to his purpose.

For we know that if our earthly house of this tabernacle were dissolved, we have a building of God, an house not made with hands, eternal in the heavens.

—I John 5:11-15; 4:13; 3:14; II Timothy 1:12; Romans 8:28; II Corinthians 5:1.

615   The Indwelling Spirit

There is therefore now no condemnation to them which are in Christ Jesus, who walk not after the flesh, but after the Spirit.

For the law of the Spirit of life in Christ Jesus hath made me free from the law of sin and death.

For what the law could not do, in that it was weak through the flesh, God, sending his own Son in the likeness of sinful flesh, and for sin, condemned sin in the flesh:

That the righteousness of the law might be fulfilled in us, who walk not after the flesh, but after the Spirit.

For they that are after the flesh do mind the things of the flesh;

But they that are after the Spirit, the things of the Spirit.

For to be carnally minded is death;

But to be spiritually minded is life and peace:

Because the carnal mind is enmity against God:

For it is not subject to the law of God, neither indeed can be.

So then they that are in the flesh cannot please God.

But ye are not in the flesh, but in the Spirit if so be that the Spirit of God dwell in you.

Now if any man have not the Spirit of Christ, he is none of his.

And if Christ be in you, the body is dead because of sin: but the Spirit is life because of righteousness.

But if the Spirit of him that raised up Jesus from the dead dwell in you, he that raised up Christ from the dead shall also quicken your mortal bodies by his Spirit that dwelleth in you.

UNISON

Therefore, brethren, we are debtors, not to the flesh, to live after the flesh. For if ye live after the flesh, ye shall die: but if ye through the Spirit do mortify the deeds of the body, ye shall live. For as many as are led by the Spirit of God, they are the sons of God.

—Romans 8:1-14.

616   Victory over Sin

What shall we say then? Shall we continue in sin, that grace may abound?

God forbid. How shall we, that are dead to sin, live any longer therein?

Know ye not, that so many of us as were baptized into Jesus Christ were baptized unto his death?

Therefore we are buried with him by baptism into death: that like as Christ was raised up from the dead by the glory of the Father, even so we also should walk in newness of life.

For if we have been planted together in the likeness of his death, we shall be also in the likeness of his resurrection:

Knowing this, that our old man is crucified with him, that the body of sin might be destroyed, that henceforth we should not serve sin. For he that is dead is freed from sin.

Now if we be dead with Christ we believe that we shall also live with him:

Knowing that Christ being raised from the dead dieth no more; death hath no more dominion over him.

For in that he died, he died unto sin once: but in that he liveth, he liveth unto God.

Likewise reckon ye also yourselves to be dead indeed unto sin, but alive unto God through Jesus Christ our Lord.

Let not sin therefore reign in your mortal body, that ye should obey it in the lusts thereof. Neither yield ye your members as instruments of unrighteousness unto sin.

But yield yourselves unto God, as those that are alive from the dead, and your members as instruments of righteousness unto God.

For sin shall not have dominion over you: for ye are not under the law, but under grace.

For the wages of sin is death; but the gift of God is eternal life through Jesus Christ our Lord.

—Romans 6:1-14, 23.

617 The Way of Holiness

The wilderness and the solitary place shall be glad; and the desert shall rejoice, and blossom as the rose.

It shall blossom abundantly, and rejoice even with joy and singing:

The glory of Lebanon shall be given unto it,

The excellency of Carmel and Sharon;

They shall see the glory of the Lord,

The excellency of our God.

Strengthen ye the weak hands, and confirm the feeble knees.

Say to them that are of a fearful heart, Be strong, fear not:

Behold your God will come with vengeance,

Even God with a recompense; he will save you.

Then the eyes of the blind shall be opened, and the ears of the deaf shall be unstopped.

Then shall the lame man leap as an hart, and the tongue of the dumb shall sing:

For in the wilderness shall waters break out, and streams in the desert.

And the parched ground shall become a pool, and the thirsty ground springs of water:

In the habitation of dragons, where each lay, shall be grass with reeds and rushes.

And an highway shall be there, and a way, and it shall be called the way of holiness;

The unclean shall not pass over it; but it shall be for the redeemed;

The wayfaring men, though fools, shall not err therein.

No lion shall be there, nor any ravenous beast shall go up thereon,

They shall not be found there; but the redeemed shall walk there:

And the ransomed of the Lord shall return, and come to Zion with songs and everlasting joy upon their heads:

They shall obtain joy and gladness, and sorrow and sighing shall flee away.

—Isaiah 35.

618 Obedience unto God

Blessed are the undefiled in the way, who walk in the law of the Lord.

Blessed are they that keep his testimonies and that seek him with the whole heart.

They also do no iniquity: they walk in his ways.

Thou hast commanded us to keep thy precepts diligently.

O that my ways were directed to keep thy statutes!

Then shall I not be ashamed, when I have respect unto all thy commandments.

I will praise thee with uprightness of heart, when I shall have learned thy righteous judgments.

I will keep thy statutes: O forsake me not utterly.

Wherewithal shall a young man cleanse his way?

By taking heed thereto according to thy word.

With my whole heart have I sought thee:

O let me not wander from thy commandments.

Thy word have I hid in mine heart, that I might not sin against thee.

Blessed art thou, O Lord: teach me thy statutes.

With my lips have I declared all the judgments of thy mouth.

I have rejoiced in the way of thy testimonies, as much as in all riches.

I will meditate in thy precepts, and have respect unto thy ways.

I will delight myself in thy statutes: I will not forget thy word.
—Psalm 119:1-16.

619 The Way of Happiness

And seeing the multitudes, he went up into a mountain: and when he was set, his disciples came unto him: And he opened his mouth, and taught them saying, Blessed are the poor in spirit:

For theirs is the kingdom of heaven.

Blessed are they that mourn:

For they shall be comforted.

Blessed are the meek:

For they shall inherit the earth.

Blessed are they which do hunger and thirst after righteousness:

For they shall be filled.

Blessed are the merciful:

For they shall obtain mercy.

Blessed are the pure in heart:

For they shall see God.

Blessed are the peacemakers:

For they shall be called the children of God.

Blessed are they which are persecuted for righteousness' sake:

For theirs is the kingdom of heaven.

Blessed are ye, when men shall revile you, and persecute you, and shall say all manner of evil against you falsely, for my sake.

Rejoice, and be exceeding glad: for great is your reward in heaven: for so persecuted they the prophets which were before you.
—Matthew 5:1-12.

620 Temperance

Wine is a mocker, strong drink is raging:

And whosoever is deceived thereby is not wise.

Who hath woe?

Who hath sorrow?

Who hath contentions?

Who hath babbling?

Who hath wounds without cause?

Who hath redness of eyes?

They that tarry long at the wine; they that go to seek mixed wine.

At the last it biteth like a serpent, and stingeth like an adder.

Woe unto them that rise up early in the morning, that they may follow strong drink;

That continue until night, till wine inflame them!

Woe unto them that are mighty to drink wine, and men of strength to mingle strong drink:

Which justify the wicked for reward, and take away the righteousness of the righteous from him!

Woe unto him that giveth his neighbor drink,

That puttest thy bottle to him, and makest him drunken.

Know ye not that ye are the temple of God, and that the Spirit of God dwelleth in you?

If any man defile the temple of God, him shall God destroy; for the temple of God is holy, which temple ye are.

This I say then, Walk in the Spirit, and ye shall not fulfil the lust of the flesh.

For the flesh lusteth against the Spirit, and the Spirit against the flesh: and these are contrary the one to the other: so that ye cannot do the things that ye would. But if ye be led of the Spirit, ye are not under the law.

Now the works of the flesh are manifest, which are these; Adultery, fornication, uncleanness, lasciviousness, Idolatry, witchcraft, hatred, variance, emulations, wrath, strife, seditions, heresies, Envyings, murders, drunkenness, revellings, and such like:

Of the which I tell you before, as I have also told you in time past, that they which do such things shall not inherit the kingdom of God.

—Proverbs 20:1; 23:29, 30, 32; Isaiah 5:11, 22, 23; Habakkuk 2:15; I Corinthians 3:16, 17; Galatians 5:16-21.

621   Sowing and Reaping

The fruit of the Spirit is love, joy, peace, longsuffering, gentleness, goodness, faith, meekness, temperance: against such there is no law.

And they that are Christ's have crucified the flesh with the affections and lusts.

If we live in the Spirit, let us also walk in the Spirit.

Let us not be desirous of vainglory, provoking one another, envying one another.

Brethren, if a man be overtaken in a fault, ye which are spiritual, restore such an one in the spirit of meekness; considering thyself, lest thou also be tempted.

Bear ye one another's burdens, and so fulfill the law of Christ.

For if a man think himself to be something, when he is nothing, he deceiveth himself.

But let every man prove his own work, and then shall he have rejoicing in himself alone, and not in another: for every man shall bear his own burden.

Let him that is taught in the word communicate unto him that teacheth in all good things.

Be not deceived; God is not mocked: for whatsoever a man soweth, that shall he also reap.

For he that soweth to his flesh shall of the flesh reap corruption;

But he that soweth to the Spirit shall of the Spirit reap life everlasting.

And let us not be weary in well doing: for in due season we shall reap, if we faint not.

As we have therefore opportunity, let us do good unto all men, especially unto them who are of the household of faith.

As many as walk according to this rule, peace be on them, and mercy, and upon the Israel of God.

UNISON

The grace of our Lord Jesus Christ be with your spirit. Amen.

—Galatians 5:22-26; 6:1-10, 16, 18.

622   The Cost of Discipleship

And there went great multitudes with him: and he turned, and said unto them,

If any man come to me, and hate not his father, and mother, and wife, and children, and brethren, and sisters, yea, and his own life also, he cannot be my disciple.

And whosoever doth not bear his cross, and come after me, cannot be my disciple.

For which of you, intending to build a tower, sitteth not down first, and counteth the cost, whether he have sufficient to finish it?

Lest haply, after he hath laid the foundation, and is not able to finish it, all that behold it begin to mock him,

Saying, This man began to build, and was not able to finish.

Or what king, going to make war against another king, sitteth not down first, and consulteth whether he be able with ten thousand to meet him that cometh against him with twenty thousand?

Or else, while the other is yet a great way off, he sendeth an ambassage and desireth conditions of peace.

So likewise, whosoever he be of you that forsaketh not all that he hath, he cannot be my disciple.

For whosoever will save his life shall lose it: but whosoever will lose his life for my sake, the same shall save it.

—Luke 14:25-33; 9:24.

623   Suffering for Christ

This is thankworthy, if a man for conscience toward God endure grief, suffering wrongfully.

For what glory is it, if, when ye be buffeted for your faults, ye shall take it patiently?

But if, when ye do well, and suffer for it, ye take it patiently, this is acceptable with God.

For even hereunto were ye called: because Christ also suffered for you, leaving you an example, that ye should follow his steps.

Beloved, think it not strange concerning the fiery trial which is to try you, as though some strange thing happened unto you:

But rejoice, inasmuch as ye are partakers of Christ's sufferings; that, when his glory shall be revealed, ye may be glad also with exceeding joy.

If ye be reproached for the name of Christ, happy are ye; for the spirit of glory and of God resteth upon you:

On their part he is evil spoken of, but on your part he is glorified.

But let none of you suffer as a murderer, or as a thief, or as an evil doer, or as a busybody in other men's matters.

Yet if any man suffer as a Christian, let him not be ashamed; but let him glorify God on this behalf.

For even Christ pleased not himself;

But, as it is written, The reproaches of them that reproached thee fell on me.

For whatsoever things were written aforetime were written for our learning,

That we through patience and comfort of the scriptures might have hope.

Now the God of patience and consolation grant you to be like-minded one toward another according to Christ Jesus:

That ye may with one mind and one mouth glorify God, even the Father of our Lord Jesus Christ.

—I Peter 2:19-21; 4:12-16; Romans 15:3-6.

624   The New Commandment

Jesus said, A new commandment I give unto you, That ye love one another; as I have loved you, that ye also love one another.

By this shall all men know that ye are my disciples, if ye have love one to another.

My little children, these things write I unto you, that ye sin not.

And if any man sin, we have an advocate with the Father, Jesus Christ the righteous:

And he is the propitiation for our sins: and not for ours only, but also for the sins of the whole world.

And hereby we do know that we know him, if we keep his commandments.

He that saith, I know him, and keepeth not his commandments, is a liar, and the truth is not in him.

But whoso keepeth his word, in him verily is the love of God perfected: hereby know we that we are in him.

He that saith he abideth in him ought himself also so to walk, even as he walked.

He that saith he is in the light, and hateth his brother, is in darkness even until now.

He that loveth his brother abideth in the light, and there is none occasion of stumbling in him.

But he that hateth his brother is in darkness, and walketh in darkness, and knoweth not whither he goeth, because that darkness hath blinded his eyes.

Beloved, let us love one another: for love is of God; and every one that loveth, is born of God, and knoweth God.

He that loveth not, knoweth not God; for God is love. In this was manifested the love of God toward us, because that God sent his only begotten Son into the world, that we might live through him.

Herein is love, not that we loved God, but that he loved us, and sent his Son to be the propitiation for our sins.

Beloved, if God so loved us, we ought also to love one another.

—John 13:34, 35; I John 2:1-6, 9-11; 4:7-11.

625 The Second Mile

Ye have heard that it was said to them of old time, Thou shalt not kill; And whosoever shall kill shall be in danger of the judgment.

But I say unto you, That whosoever is angry with his brother without a cause shall be in danger of the judgment:

And whosoever shall say to his brother, Raca, shall be in danger of the council:

But whosoever shall say, Thou fool, shall be in danger of hell fire.

Ye have heard that it hath been said, An eye for an eye, and a tooth for a tooth:

But I say unto you, Resist not evil: But whosoever shall smite thee on thy right cheek, turn to him the other also.

And if any man will sue thee at the law, and take away thy coat,

Let him have thy cloak also.

And whosoever shall compel thee to go a mile,

Go with him twain.

Give to him that asketh thee,

And from him that would borrow of thee turn not thou away.

Ye have heard that it hath been said, Thou shalt love thy neighbor, and hate thine enemy.

But I say unto you, Love your enemies, bless them that curse you, do good to them that hate you, and pray for them that despitefully use you, and persecute you; that ye may be the children of your Father who is in heaven: For he maketh his sun to rise on the evil and on the good, and sendeth rain on the just and on the unjust.

For if ye love them that love you, what reward have ye? do not even the publicans the same? And if ye salute your brethren only, what do ye more than others? do not even the publicans so?

Be ye therefore perfect, even as your Father which is in heaven is perfect.

—Matt. 5:21, 22, 38-48.

626   Peace among Men

Blessed are the peacemakers: for they shall be called the children of God.

Follow peace with all men, and holiness, without which no man shall see the Lord:

If it be possible, as much as lieth in you, live peaceably with all men.

Jesus said unto them: Peace I leave with you, my peace I give unto you: Not as the world giveth, give I unto you. Let not your heart be troubled, neither let it be afraid.

These things I have spoken unto you, that in me ye might have peace.

In the world ye shall have tribulation: but be of good cheer; I have overcome the world.

Come, behold the works of the Lord, what desolations he hath made in the earth.

He maketh wars to cease unto the end of the earth; he breaketh the bow, and cutteth the spear in sunder; he burneth the chariot in the fire.

Be still, and know that I am God:

I will be exalted among the nations, I will be exalted in the earth.

And he shall judge among many people, and rebuke strong nations afar off;

And they shall beat their swords into plowshares, and their spears into pruninghooks: Nation shall not lift up a sword against nation, neither shall they learn war any more.

But they shall sit every man under his vine and under his fig tree; and none shall make them afraid: for the mouth of the Lord of hosts hath spoken it.

For all people will walk every one in the name of his god, and we will walk in the name of the Lord our God for ever and ever.

—Matthew 5:9; Hebrews 12:14; Romans 12:18; John 14:27; 16:33; Psalm 46:8-10; Micah 4:3-5.

627   Jesus Teaches Prayer

And it came to pass, that, as he was praying in a certain place, when he ceased, one of his disciples said unto him, Lord, teach us to pray, as John also taught his disciples. And he said unto them, When ye pray, say,

UNISON

Our Father which art in heaven, Hallowed be thy name. Thy kingdom come. Thy will be done in earth, as it is in heaven. Give us this day our daily bread. And forgive us our debts, as we forgive our debtors. And lead us not into temptation, but deliver us from evil: For thine is the kingdom, and the power, and the glory, for ever. Amen.

And he said unto them, Which of you shall have a friend, and shall go unto him at midnight, and say unto him, Friend, lend me three loaves;

For a friend of mine in his journey is come to me, and I have nothing to set before him?

And he from within shall answer and say, Trouble me not: the door is now shut, and my children are with me in bed; I cannot rise and give thee.

I say unto you, Though he will not rise and give him, because he is his friend, yet because of his importunity he will rise and give him as many as he needeth.

And I say unto you, Ask, and it shall be given you; seek and ye shall find; knock, and it shall be opened unto you.

For every one that asketh receiveth; and he that seeketh findeth; and to him that knocketh it shall be opened.

If a son shall ask bread of any of you that is a father, will he give him a stone? or if he ask a fish, will he for a fish give him a serpent? Or if he shall ask an egg, will he offer him a scorpion?

If ye then, being evil, know how to give good gifts unto your children: how much more shall your heavenly Father give the Holy Spirit to them that ask him?

—Luke 11:1-13.

628   Thirsting for God

As the hart panteth after the water brooks,

So panteth my soul after thee, O God.

My soul thirsteth for God, for the living God:

When shall I come and appear before God?

My tears have been my meat day and night,

While they continually say unto me, Where is thy God?

Why art thou cast down, O my soul?

And why art thou disquieted in me?

Hope thou in God:

For I shall yet praise him for the help of his countenance.

Deep calleth unto deep at the noise of thy waterspouts:

All thy waves and thy billows are gone over me.

Yet the Lord will command his lovingkindness in the daytime,

And in the night his song shall be with me, and my prayer unto the God of my life.

Judge me, O God, and plead my cause against an ungodly nation:

O deliver me from the deceitful and unjust man.

O send out thy light and thy truth: let them lead me;

Let them bring me unto thy holy hill, and to thy tabernacles.

Then will I go unto the altar of God, unto God my exceeding joy;

Yea, upon the harp will I praise thee, O God my God.

Why art thou cast down, O my soul? and why art thou disquieted within me?

Hope in God: for I shall yet praise him, who is the help of my countenance, and my God.

—Psalm 42:1-3, 5, 7-9; 43:1, 3-5.

629   Blessings from God

Bless the Lord, O my soul;

And all that is within me, bless his holy name.

Bless the Lord, O my soul,

And forget not all his benefits:

Who forgiveth all thine iniquities;

Who healeth all thy diseases;

Who redeemeth thy life from destruction;

Who crowneth thee with lovingkindness and tender mercies;

Who satisfieth thy mouth with good things;

So that thy youth is renewed like the eagle's.

The Lord executeth righteousness and judgment for all that are oppressed.

He made known his ways unto Moses, his acts unto the children of Israel.

The Lord is merciful and gracious, slow to anger, and plenteous in mercy.

He will not always chide: neither will he keep his anger for ever.

He hath not dealt with us after our sins;

Nor rewarded us according to our iniquities.

For as the heaven is high above the earth,

So great is his mercy toward them that fear him.

As far as the east is from the west,

So far hath he removed our transgressions from us.

Like as a father pitieth his children,

So the Lord pitieth them that fear him.

For he knoweth our frame; he remembereth that we are dust.

As for man, his days are as grass: as a flower of the field, so he flourisheth. For the wind passeth over it, and it is gone; And the place thereof shall know it no more.

But the mercy of the Lord is from everlasting to everlasting upon them that fear him, and his righteousness unto children's children;

To such as keep his covenant, and to those that remember his commandments to do them.

The Lord hath prepared his throne in the heavens; and his kingdom ruleth over all.

Bless the Lord, ye his angels, that excel in strength, that do his commandments, hearkening unto the voice of his word.

Bless ye the Lord, all ye his hosts:

Ye ministers of his, that do his pleasure.

Bless the Lord, all his works in all places of his dominion:

Bless the Lord, O my soul.
—Psalm 103.

630   Gratitude to God

I love the Lord, because he hath heard my voice and my supplications.

Because he hath inclined his ear unto me, therefore will I call upon him as long as I live.

The sorrows of death compassed me, and the pains of hell got hold upon me: I found trouble and sorrow.

Then called I upon the name of the Lord; O Lord, I beseech thee, deliver my soul.

Gracious is the Lord, and righteous; yea, our God is merciful.

The Lord preserveth the simple: I was brought low, and he helped me.

Return unto thy rest, O my soul; for the Lord hath dealt bountifully with thee.

For thou hast delivered my soul from death, mine eyes from tears, and my feet from falling.

What shall I render unto the Lord for all his benefits toward me?

I will take the cup of salvation, and call upon the name of the Lord. I will pay my vows unto the Lord now in the presence of all his people. I will walk before the Lord in the land of the living.

O Lord, truly I am thy servant; I am thy servant, and the son of thine handmaid: thou hast loosed my bonds.

I will offer to thee the sacrifice of thanksgiving, and will call upon the name of the Lord. I will pay my vows unto the Lord now in the presence of all his people.

—Psalm 116:1-8, 12-14, 9, 16-18.

631 The Goodness of God

I will extol thee, my God, O king; and I will bless thy name for ever and ever.

Every day will I bless thee; and I will praise thy name for ever and ever.

Great is the Lord, and greatly to be praised;

And his greatness is unsearchable.

One generation shall praise thy works to another, and shall declare thy mighty acts.

I will speak of the glorious honor of thy majesty, and of thy wondrous works.

And men shall speak of the might of thy terrible acts: and I will declare thy greatness.

They shall abundantly utter the memory of thy great goodness, and shall sing of thy righteousness.

The Lord is gracious and full of compassion;

Slow to anger, and of great mercy.

The Lord is good to all:

And his tender mercies are over all his works.

All thy works shall praise thee, O Lord;

And thy saints shall bless thee.

They shall speak of the glory of thy kingdom, and talk of thy power;

To make known to the sons of men his mighty acts, and the glorious majesty of his kingdom.

Thy kingdom is an everlasting kingdom,

And thy dominion endureth throughout all generations.

The Lord upholdeth all that fall,

And raiseth up all those that be bowed down.

The eyes of all wait upon thee; and thou givest them their meat in due season.

Thou openest thine hand, and satisfiest the desire of every living thing.

The Lord is righteous in all his ways,

And holy in all his works.

The Lord is nigh unto all them that call upon him,

To all that call upon him in truth.

He will fulfill the desire of them that fear him:

He also will hear their cry, and will save them.

The Lord preserveth all them that love him:

But all the wicked will he destroy.

My mouth shall speak the praise of the Lord:

And let all flesh bless his holy name for ever and ever.

—Psalm 145.

I am the true vine, and my Father is the husbandman.

Every branch in me that beareth not fruit he taketh away:

And every branch that beareth fruit, he purgeth it, that it may bring forth more fruit.

Now ye are clean through the word which I have spoken unto you.

Abide in me, and I in you.

As the branch cannot bear fruit of itself, except it abide in the vine; no more can ye, except ye abide in me.

I am the vine, ye are the branches:

He that abideth in me, and I in him, the same bringeth forth much fruit: for without me ye can do nothing.

If a man abide not in me, he is cast forth as a branch, and is withered:

And men gather them, and cast them into the fire, and they are burned.

If ye abide in me, and my words abide in you, ye shall ask what ye will, and it shall be done unto you.

Herein is my Father glorified, that ye bear much fruit; and so shall ye be my disciples.

Even as the Father hath loved me, so have I loved you: abide ye in my love.

If ye keep my commandments, ye shall abide in my love; even as I have kept my Father's commandments, and abide in his love.

These things have I spoken unto you, that my joy may be in you, and that your joy may be made full.

This is my commandment, that ye love one another, even as I have loved you.

Ye have not chosen me, but I have chosen you and ordained you, that ye should go and bring forth fruit, and that your fruit should remain.

That whatsoever ye shall ask of the Father in my name, he may give it you.

—John 15:1-12, 16.

633   Consecration

I beseech you therefore, brethren, by the mercies of God, that ye present your bodies a living sacrifice, holy, acceptable unto God, which is your reasonable service.

And be not conformed to this world: but be ye transformed by the renewing of your mind, that ye may prove what is that good, and acceptable, and perfect will of God.

For I say, through the grace given unto me, to every man that is among you, not to think of himself more highly than he ought to think;

But to think soberly, according as God hath dealt to every man the measure of faith.

For as we have many members in one body, and all members have not the same office;

So we, being many, are one body in Christ, and every one members one of another.

Having then gifts differing according to the grace that is given to us,

Whether prophecy, let us prophesy according to the proportion of faith;

Or ministry, let us wait on our ministering:

Or he that teacheth, on teaching;

Or he that exhorteth, on exhortation:

He that giveth, let him do it with simplicity;

He that ruleth, with diligence;

He that sheweth mercy, with cheerfulness.

Let love be without hypocrisy.

Abhor that which is evil; cleave to that which is good.

Be kindly affectioned one to another with brotherly love; in honor preferring one another;

Not slothful in business; fervent in spirit; serving the Lord;

Rejoicing in hope; patient in tribulation; continuing instant in prayer;

Distributing to the necessity of saints; given to hospitality.

Bless them which persecute you: bless, and curse not.

Rejoice with them that do rejoice, and weep with them that weep.

Be of the same mind one toward another.

Mind not high things, but condescend to men of low estate.

Be not wise in your own conceits.

Recompense to no man evil for evil.

Provide things honest in the sight of all men.

If it be possible, as much as lieth in you, live peaceably with all men.

Dearly beloved, avenge not yourselves, but rather give place unto wrath: for it is written, Vengeance is mine; I will repay, saith the Lord.

UNISON
Therefore if thine enemy hunger, feed him; if he thirst, give him drink: for in so doing thou shalt heap coals of fire on his head.
Be not overcome of evil but overcome evil with good.
—Romans 12.

634 Trust and Confidence

The Lord is my light and my salvation; whom shall I fear?

The Lord is the strength of my life; of whom shall I be afraid?

When the wicked, even mine enemies and my foes, came upon me to eat up my flesh,

They stumbled and fell.

Though a host should encamp against me,

My heart shall not fear;

Though war should rise against me,

Even then will I be confident.

One thing have I asked of the Lord, that will I seek after;

That I may dwell in the house of the Lord all the days of my life, to behold the beauty of the Lord, and to inquire in his temple.

For in the time of trouble he will hide me in his pavilion;

In the secret of his tabernacle will he hide me; he will set me up upon a rock.

And now shall mine head be lifted up above mine enemies round about me;

Therefore will I offer in his tabernacle sacrifices of joy; I will sing, yea, I will sing praises unto the Lord.

Hear, O Lord, when I cry with my voice;

Have mercy also upon me, and answer me.

When thou saidst, Seek ye my face;

My heart said unto thee, Thy face, Lord, will I seek.

Hide not thy face from me; put not thy servant away in anger:

Thou hast been my help; leave me not, neither forsake me, O God of my salvation.

When my father and my mother forsake me,

Then the Lord will take me up.

Teach me thy way, O Lord, and lead me in a plain path, because of mine enemies.

Deliver me not over unto the will of mine enemies, for false witnesses are risen up against me, and such as breathe out cruelty.

I had fainted, unless I had believed to see the goodness of the Lord in the land of the living.

Wait on the Lord:

Be of good courage, and he will strengthen thine heart:

Wait, I say, on the Lord.

—Psalm 27.

635 God Our Strength

God is our refuge and strength, a very present help in trouble.

Therefore will we not fear, though the earth be removed, and though the mountains be carried into the midst of the sea;

Though the waters thereof roar and be troubled,

Though the mountains shake with the swelling thereof.

There is a river, the streams whereof shall make glad the city of God,

The holy place of the tabernacles of the Most High.

God is in the midst of her; she shall not be moved:

God shall help her, and that right early.

The nations raged, the kingdoms were moved:

He uttered his voice, the earth melted.

The Lord of hosts is with us;

The God of Jacob is our refuge.

He maketh wars to cease unto the end of the earth;

He breaketh the bow, and cutteth the spear in sunder; he burneth the chariot in fire.

Be still, and know that I am God: I will be exalted among the nations, I will be exalted in the earth.

The Lord of hosts is with us; the God of Jacob is our refuge.

—Psalm 46.

636 Security in God

He that dwelleth in the secret place of the most High shall abide under the shadow of the Almighty.

I will say of the Lord, He is my refuge and my fortress: my God; in him will I trust.

Surely he shall deliver thee from the snare of the fowler, and from the harmful pestilence.

He shall cover thee with his feathers, and under his wings shalt thou trust: his truth shall be thy shield and buckler.

Thou shalt not be afraid for the terror by night,

Nor for the arrow that flieth by day;

For the pestilence that walketh in darkness,

Nor for the destruction that wasteth at noonday.

A thousand shall fall at thy side,

And ten thousand at thy right hand;

But it shall not come nigh thee. Only with thine eyes shalt thou behold and see the reward of the wicked.

Because thou hast made the Lord, which is my refuge, even the Most High, thy habitation; There shall no evil befall thee, neither shall any plague come nigh thy dwelling.

For he shall give his angels charge over thee, to keep thee in all thy ways.

They shall bear thee up in their hands, lest thou dash thy foot against a stone.

Thou shalt tread upon the lion and the adder:

The young lion and the dragon shalt thou trample under feet.

Because he hath set his love upon me, therefore will I deliver him;

I will set him on high, because he hath known my name.

He shall call upon me, and I will answer him;

I will be with him in trouble;

I will deliver him and honor him.

With long life will I satisfy him, and shew him my salvation.
—Psalm 91.

637   The Father's Care

Lay not up for yourselves treasures upon earth, where moth and rust doth corrupt, and where thieves break through and steal:

But lay up for yourselves treasures in heaven, where neither moth nor rust doth corrupt, and where thieves do not break through nor steal:

For where your treasure is, there will your heart be also.

No man can serve two masters: for either he will hate the one, and love the other; or else he will hold to the one and despise the other. Ye cannot serve God and mammon.

Therefore I say unto you, Take no thought for your life, what ye shall eat, or what ye shall drink; nor yet for your body, what ye shall put on. Is not the life more than meat, and the body than raiment?

Behold the fowls of the air: for they sow not, neither do they reap, nor gather into barns; yet your heavenly Father feedeth them.

Are ye not much better than they?

Which of you by taking thought can add one cubit unto his stature? And why take ye thought for raiment? Consider the lilies of the field, how they grow; they toil not, neither do they spin:

And yet I say unto you, That even Solomon in all his glory was not arrayed like one of these.

Wherefore, if God so clothe the grass of the field, which today is, and tomorrow is cast into the oven, shall he not much more clothe you, O ye of little faith?

Therefore take no thought, saying, What shall we eat? or, What shall we drink? or, Wherewithal shall we be clothed? For after all these things do the Gentiles seek: for your heavenly Father knoweth that ye have need of all these things.

UNISON

But seek ye first the kingdom of God, and his righteousness; and all these things shall be added unto you. Take therefore no thought for the morrow: for the morrow shall take thought for the things of itself. Sufficient unto the day is the evil thereof.
—Matthew 6:19-21, 24-34.

Now faith is the substance of things hoped for, the evidence of things not seen.

For by it the elders obtained a good report.

Through faith we understand that the worlds were framed by the word of God, so that things which are seen were not made of things which do appear.

By faith Abel offered unto God a more excellent sacrifice than Cain, by which he obtained witness that he was righteous, God testifying of his gifts: and by it he being dead yet speaketh.

By faith Enoch was translated that he should not see death; and was not found, because God had translated him:

For before his translation he had this testimony, that he pleased God.

But without faith it is impossible to please him: for he that cometh to God must believe that he is, and that he is a rewarder of them that diligently seek him.

By faith Noah being warned of God of things not seen as yet, moved with fear, prepared an ark to the saving of his house;

By the which he condemned the world, and became heir of the righteousness which is by faith.

By faith Abraham, when he was called to go out into a place which he should after receive for an inheritance, obeyed; and he went out, not knowing whither he went.

By faith Abraham, when he was tried, offered up Isaac: and he that had received the promises offered up his only begotten son,

Of whom it was said, That in Isaac shall thy seed be called:

Accounting that God was able to raise him up, even from the dead; from whence also he received him in a figure.

By faith Isaac blessed Jacob and Esau concerning things to come.

By faith Jacob, when he was a dying, blessed both the sons of Joseph: and worshipped, leaning upon the top of his staff.

By faith Joseph, when he died, made mention of the departing of the children of Israel; and gave commandment concerning his bones.

By faith Moses, when he was born, was hid three months of his parents, because they saw he was a proper child; and they were not afraid of the king's commandment.

By faith Moses, when he was come to years, refused to be called the son of Pharaoh's daughter:

Choosing rather to suffer affliction with the people of God, than to enjoy the pleasures of sin for a season;

Esteeming the reproach of Christ greater riches than the treasures in Egypt: for he had respect unto the recompense of the reward.

—Hebrews 11:1-8, 17-26.

639   Stewardship

The earth is the Lord's, and the fulness thereof;

The world, and they that dwell therein.

Honor the Lord with thy substance,

And with the firstfruits of all thine increase:

All the tithe of the land, whether of the seed of the land, or of the fruit of the tree, is the Lord's:

It is holy unto the Lord.

Will a man rob God?

Yet ye have robbed me.

Wherein have we robbed thee?

In tithes and offerings.

Bring ye all the tithes into the storehouse, that there may be meat in mine house, and prove me now herewith, saith the Lord of Hosts, if I will not open you the windows of heaven, and pour you out a blessing that there shall not be room enough to receive it.

This I say, He which soweth sparingly shall reap also sparingly; And he which soweth bountifully shall reap also bountifully.

Every man according as he purposeth in his heart, so let him give;

Not grudgingly, or of necessity: for God loveth a cheerful giver.

And God is able to make all grace abound toward you; that ye, always having all sufficiency in all things, may abound to every good work.

As every man hath received the gift, even so minister the same one to another, as good stewards of the manifold grace of God.

Upon the first day of the week let every one of you lay by him in store, as God hath prospered him, that there be no gatherings when I come.

Render therefore unto Caesar the things which are Caesar's; and unto God the things that are God's.

—Psalm 24:1; Proverbs 3:9; Leviticus 27:30; Malachi 3:8, 10; II Corinthians 9:6-8; I Peter 4:10; I Corinthians 16:2; Matthew 22:21.

640   The Heavenly Home

And I saw a new heaven and a new earth: for the first heaven and the first earth were passed away; and there was no more sea.

And I John saw the holy city, new Jerusalem, coming down from God out of heaven, prepared as a bride adorned for her husband.

And I heard a great voice out of heaven saying, Behold, the tabernacle of God is with men, and he will dwell with them, and they shall be his people, and God himself shall be with them, and be their God.

And God shall wipe away all tears from their eyes; and there shall be no more death, neither sorrow, nor crying, neither shall there be any more pain: for the former things are passed away.

And he that sat upon the throne said, Behold, I make all things new. And he said unto me, Write: for these words are true and faithful.

And he said unto me, It is done. I am Alpha and Omega, the beginning and the end. I will give unto him that is athirst of the fountain of the water of life freely.
He that overcometh shall inherit all things; and I will be his God, and he shall be my son.

And there came unto me one of the seven angels which had the seven vials full of the seven last plagues, and talked with me, saying, Come hither, I will show thee the bride, the Lamb's wife.

And he carried me away in the spirit to a great and high mountain, and showed me that great city, the holy Jerusalem, descending out of heaven from God,

Having the glory of God: and her light was like unto a stone most precious, even like a jasper stone, clear as crystal.

And I saw no temple therein: for the Lord God Almighty and the Lamb are the temple of it.

And the city had no need of the sun, neither of the moon, to shine in it: for the glory of God did lighten it, and the Lamb is the light thereof.

And he showed me a pure river of water of life, clear as crystal, proceeding out of the throne of God and of the Lamb.

In the midst of the street of it, and on either side of the river, was there the tree of life, which bare twelve manner of fruits, and yielded her fruit every month: and the leaves of the tree were for the healing of the nations.

And there shall be no more curse: but the throne of God and of the Lamb shall be in it; and his servants shall serve him:

And they shall see his face; and his name shall be in their foreheads.

And there shall be no night there; and they need no candle, neither light of the sun; for the Lord God giveth them light: and they shall reign for ever and ever.

—Revelation 21:1-7, 9-11, 22, 23; 22:1-5.

641   God in Nature

The heavens declare the glory of God;

And the firmament sheweth his handywork.

Day unto day uttereth speech,

And night unto night sheweth knowledge.

There is no speech nor language, where their voice is not heard.

Their line is gone out through all the earth, and their words to the end of the world.

In them hath he set a tabernacle for the sun, Which is as a bridegroom coming out of his chamber, and rejoiceth as a strong man to run a race.

His going forth is from the end of the heaven, and his circuit unto the ends of it: and there is nothing hid from the heat thereof.

He sendeth the springs into the valleys, which run among the hills.

They give drink to every beast of the field: the wild asses quench their thirst.

By them shall the fowls of the heaven have their habitation, which sing among the branches.

He appointed the moon for seasons: the sun knoweth his going down.

Thou makest darkness, and it is night: wherein all the beasts of the forest do creep forth.

The young lions roar after their prey, and seek their meat from God.

The sun ariseth, they gather themselves together, and lay them down in their dens.

Man goeth forth unto his work and to his labor until the evening.

O Lord, how manifold are thy works! in wisdom hast thou made them all: the earth is full of thy riches.

O Lord our Lord, how excellent is thy name in all the earth!

—Psalm 19:1-6; 104:10-12, 19-24; 8:1.

642   God and the Nation

All the commandments which I command thee this day shall ye observe to do, that ye may live,

> **And thou shalt remember all the way which the Lord thy God led thee.**

For the Lord thy God bringeth thee into a good land, a land of brooks of water, of fountains and depths that spring out of valleys and hills;

> **A land of wheat, and barley, and vines, and fig trees, and pomegranates; a land of olive trees and honey;**

A land wherein thou shalt eat bread without scarceness, thou shalt not lack any thing in it; a land whose stones are iron, and out of whose hills thou mayest dig brass.

> **When thou hast eaten and art full, then thou shalt bless the Lord thy God for the good land which he hath given thee.**

Beware that thou forget not the Lord thy God, in not keeping his commandments, and his judgments, and his statutes, which I command thee this day:

> **Lest when thou hast eaten and art full, and hast built goodly houses, and dwelt therein;**

And when thy herds and thy flocks multiply, and thy silver and thy gold is multiplied, and all that thou hast is multiplied;

> **Then thine heart be lifted up, and thou forget the Lord thy God,**

And thou say in thine heart, My power and the might of mine hand hath gotten me this wealth.

> **But thou shalt remember the Lord thy God: for it is he that giveth thee power to get wealth that he**

may establish his covenant which he sware unto thy fathers, as it is this day.

And it shall be, if thou do at all forget the Lord thy God, and walk after other gods, and serve them, and worship them, I testify against you this day that ye shall surely perish.

> **As the nations which the Lord destroyeth before your face, so shall ye perish; because ye would not be obedient unto the voice of the Lord your God.**
> —Deuteronomy 8:1, 2, 7-14, 17-20.

643   God and the Family

Now these are the commandments, the statutes, and the judgments, which the Lord your God commanded to teach you, that ye might do them in the land whither ye go to possess it:

> **That thou mightest fear the Lord thy God, to keep all his statutes and his commandments, which I command thee, thou, and thy son, and thy son's son, all the days of thy life; and that thy days may be prolonged.**

And thou shalt love the Lord thy God with all thine heart, and with all thy soul, and with all thy might.

UNISON
> **And these words, which I command thee this day, shall be in thine heart:**
> **And thou shalt teach them diligently unto thy children, and shalt talk of them when thou sittest in thine house, and when thou walkest by the way, and when thou liest down, and when thou risest up.**
> **And thou shalt bind them for a sign upon thine hand, and they shall be as frontlets between thine eyes. And thou shalt write them upon the posts of thy house, and on thy gates.**

The fear of the Lord is the beginning of knowledge:

But fools despise wisdom and instruction.

My son, hear the instruction of thy father.

And forsake not the law of thy mother:

For they shall be an ornament of grace unto thy head, and chains about thy neck.

Train up a child in the way he should go: and when he is old, he will not depart from it.

Children, obey your parents in the Lord: for this is right.

Honor thy father and mother; which is the first commandment with promise;

That it may be well with thee, and thou mayest live long on the earth.

And, ye fathers, provoke not your children to wrath: but bring them up in the nurture and admonition of the Lord.

—Deuteronomy 6:1, 2, 5-9; Proverbs 1:7-9; 22:6; Ephesians 6:1-4.

644   Counsel for Youth

My son, forget not my law; but let thine heart keep my commandments:

For length of days, and long life, and peace, shall they add to thee.

Let not mercy and truth forsake thee, bind them about thy neck; write them upon the table of thine heart:

So shalt thou find favor and good understanding in the sight of God and man.

Trust in the Lord with all thine heart;

And lean not unto thine own understanding.

In all thy ways acknowledge Him,

And he shall direct thy paths.

Be not wise in thine own eyes:

Fear the Lord, and depart from evil.

Honor the Lord with thy substance, and with the first-fruits of all thine increase:

So shall thy barns be filled with plenty.

My son, if thine heart be wise, my heart shall rejoice, even mine.

Yea, my heart shall rejoice, when thy lips speak right things.

My son, give me thine heart,

And let thine eyes observe my ways.

Rejoice, O young man, in thy youth; and let thy heart cheer thee in the days of thy youth, and walk in the ways of thine heart; and in the sight of thine eyes: but know thou, that for all these things God will bring thee into judgment.

UNISON
Remember now thy Creator in the days of thy youth, while the evil days come not, nor the years draw nigh, when thou shalt say, I have no pleasure in them.

—Proverbs 3:1-7, 9, 10; 23:15, 16, 26; Ecclesiastes 11:9, 12:1.

645   God the Incarnate Son

In the beginning was the Word, and the Word was with God, and the Word was God.

The same was in the beginning with God.

All things were made by him; and without him was not anything made that was made.

In him was life; and the life was the light of men.

And the light shineth in darkness; and the darkness comprehended it not.

There was a man sent from God, whose name was John.

The same came for a witness, to bear witness of the Light, that all men through him might believe.

He was not that Light, but was sent to bear witness of that Light.

That was the true Light, which lighteth every man that cometh into the world.

He was in the world, and the world was made by him, and the world knew him not.

He came unto his own, and his own received him not.

But as many as received him, to them gave he power to become the sons of God, even to them that believe on his name:

Which were born, not of blood, nor of the will of the flesh, nor of the will of man, but of God.

And the Word was made flesh, and dwelt among us, and we beheld his glory, the glory as of the only begotten of the Father, full of grace and truth.

—John 1:1-14.

646 The Holy Spirit's Work

If ye love me, keep my commandments.

And I will pray the Father, and he shall give you another Comforter, that he may abide with you for ever;

Even the Spirit of truth; whom the world cannot receive, because it seeth him not, neither knoweth him:

But ye know him; for he dwelleth with you, and shall be in you.

I will not leave you comfortless: I will come to you.

Yet a little while, and the world seeth me no more; but ye see me: because I live, ye shall live also.

At that day ye shall know that I am in my Father, and ye in me, and I in you.

But now I go my way to him that sent me; and none of you asketh me, Whither goest thou?

But because I have said these things unto you, sorrow hath filled your heart.

Nevertheless I tell you the truth: It is expedient for you that I go away:

For if I go not away, the Comforter will not come unto you; but if I depart, I will send him unto you.

And when he is come he will reprove the world of sin, and of righteousness, and of judgment:

Of sin, because they believe not on me;

Of righteousness, because I go to my Father, and ye see me no more;

Of judgment, because the prince of this world is judged.

I have yet many things to say unto you, but ye cannot bear them now.

Howbeit when he, the Spirit of truth, is come, he will guide you into all truth:

For he shall not speak of himself; but whatsoever he shall hear, that shall he speak: and he will show you things to come.

He shall glorify me: for he shall receive of mine, and shall show it unto you.

These things I have spoken unto you, that in me ye might have peace. In the world ye shall have tribulation: but be of good cheer; I have overcome the world.

—John 14:15-20; 16:5-14, 33.

Knowing this first, that no prophecy of the scripture is of any private interpretation.

For the prophecy came not in old time by the will of man: but holy men of God spake as they were moved by the Holy Ghost.

All scripture is given by inspiration of God, and is profitable for doctrine, for reproof, for correction, for instruction in righteousness:

That the man of God may be perfect, thoroughly furnished unto all good works.

Study to show thyself approved unto God, a workman that needeth not to be ashamed, rightly dividing the word of truth.

For the word of God is quick, and powerful, and sharper than any two-edged sword, piercing even to the dividing asunder of soul and spirit, and of the joints and marrow, and is a discerner of the thoughts and intents of the heart.

But these are written, that ye might believe that Jesus is the Christ, the Son of God; and that believing ye might have life through his name.

For whatsoever things were written aforetime were written for our learning, that we through patience and comfort of the scriptures might have hope.

Teach me, O Lord, the way of thy statutes; and I shall keep it unto the end.

Give me understanding, and I shall keep thy law; yea, I shall observe it with my whole heart.

For ever, O Lord, thy word is settled in heaven.

Thy word is a lamp unto my feet, and a light unto my path.

The entrance of thy words giveth light; it giveth understanding unto the simple.

Great peace have they which love thy law: and nothing shall offend them.

—II Peter 1:20, 21; II Timothy 3:16, 17; 2:15; Hebrews 4:12; John 20:31; Romans 15:4; Psalm 119:33, 34, 89, 105, 130, 165.

648   The Lord's Day

Remember the sabbath day, to keep it holy.

UNISON

Six days shalt thou labor, and do all thy work:
But the seventh day is the sabbath of the Lord thy God: in it thou shalt not do any work.
For in six days the Lord made heaven and earth, the sea, and all that in them is, and rested the seventh day: wherefore the Lord blessed the sabbath day, and hallowed it.

And Jesus said unto them, The sabbath was made for man, and not man for the sabbath:

Therefore the Son of man is Lord also of the sabbath.

And when the sabbath was past, very early in the morning the first day of the week, the women came unto the sepulchre at the rising of the sun.

And entering into the sepulchre, they saw a young man sitting on the right side, clothed in a long white garment; and they were affrighted.

And he saith unto them, Be not affrighted: Ye seek Jesus of Nazareth, which was crucified: he is risen; he is not here: behold the place where they laid him.

Then the same day at evening, being the first day of the week, when the doors were shut where the disciples were assembled for fear of the Jews, came Jesus and stood in the midst, and saith unto them, Peace be unto you.

Unto him that loved us, and washed us from our sins in his own blood,

And hath made us kings and priests unto God and his Father; to him be glory and dominion for ever and ever. Amen.

—Exodus 20:8-11; Mark 2:27, 28; 16:1, 2, 5, 6; John 20:19; Revelation 1:5, 6.

649   Thanksgiving Day

O give thanks unto the Lord for he is good;

For his mercy endureth for ever.

Let the redeemed of the Lord say so, whom he hath redeemed from the hand of the enemy;

And gathered them out of the lands, from the east, and from the west, from the north, and from the south.

They wandered in the wilderness in a solitary way; they found no city to dwell in.

Hungry and thirsty, their soul fainted in them.

Then they cried unto the Lord in their trouble, and he delivered them out of their distresses.

And he led them forth by the right way, that they might go to a city of habitation.

Oh that men would praise the Lord for his goodness, and for his wonderful works to the children of men!

For he satisfieth the longing soul, and filleth the hungry soul with goodness.

Such as sit in darkness and in the shadow of death, being bound in affliction and iron;

Because they rebelled against the words of God, and contemned the counsel of the Most High:

Therefore he brought down their heart with labor; they fell down, and there was none to help.

Then they cried unto the Lord in their trouble, and he saved them out of their distresses.

He brought them out of darkness and the shadow of death,

And brake their bands in sunder.

Oh that men would praise the Lord for his goodness, and for his wonderful works to the children of men!

For he hath broken the gates of brass, and cut the bars of iron in sunder.

Fools because of their transgression, and because of their iniquities, are afflicted.

Their soul abhorreth all manner of meat; and they draw near unto the gates of death.

Then they cry unto the Lord in their trouble, and he saveth them out of their distresses.

He sent his word, and healed them, and delivered them from their destructions.

Oh that men would praise the Lord for his goodness, and for his wonderful works to the children of men!

And let them sacrifice the sacrifices of thanksgiving, and declare his works with rejoicing.

—Psalm 107:1-22.

650 Watchnight and New Year

I will praise thee, O Lord, with my whole heart;

I will shew forth all thy marvellous works.

I will be glad and rejoice in thee:

I will sing praise to thy name, O thou most high.

The Lord also will be a refuge for the oppressed,

A refuge in times of trouble.

But thou, O Lord, shalt endure for ever; and thy remembrance unto all generations.

I said, O my God, take me not away in the midst of my days: thy years are throughout all generations.

Of old hast thou laid the foundation of the earth:

And the heavens are the work of thy hands.

They shall perish, but thou shalt endure: yea, all of them shall wax old like a garment; as a vesture shalt thou change them, and they shall be changed:

But thou art the same, and thy years shall have no end.

O Lord, thou hast searched me, and known me.

Thou knowest my downsitting and mine uprising, thou understandest my thought afar off.

For there is not a word in my tongue, but, lo, O Lord, thou knowest it altogether.

Thou hast beset me behind and before, and laid thine hand upon me.

Such knowledge is too wonderful for me; it is high, I cannot attain unto it.

Yea, the darkness hideth not from thee; but the night shineth as the day: the darkness and the light are both alike to thee.

How precious also are thy thoughts unto me, O God! how great is the sum of them!

If I should count them, they are more in number than the sand: when I awake, I am still with thee.

Search me, O God, and know my heart:

Try me, and know my thoughts: And see if there be any wicked way in me, and lead me in the way everlasting.

—Psalm 9:1, 2, 9; 102:12, 24-27; 139:1, 2, 4-6, 12, 17, 18, 23, 24.

651   God the Creator

In the beginning God created the heaven and the earth.

And the earth was without form, and void; and darkness was upon the face of the deep.

And the Spirit of God moved upon the face of the waters. And God said, Let there be light: and there was light.

And God saw the light, that it was good: and God divided the light from the darkness.

And God called the light Day, and the darkness he called Night.

And the evening and the morning were the first day.

By the word of the Lord were the heavens made;

And all the host of them by the breath of his mouth.

He gathereth the waters of the sea together as an heap:

He layeth up the depth in storehouses.

Let all the earth fear the Lord:

Let all the inhabitants of the world stand in awe of him.

For he spake, and it was done;

He commanded, and it stood fast.

Let us come before his presence with thanksgiving,

And make a joyful noise unto him with psalms.

For the Lord is a great God,

And a great King above all gods.

In his hand are the deep places of the earth:

The strength of the hills is his also.

The sea is his, and he made it:

And his hands formed the dry land.

O come, let us worship and bow down:

Let us kneel before the Lord our maker. For he is our God; and we are the people of his pasture, and the sheep of his hand.

—Genesis 1:1-5; Psalm 33:6-9; 95:2-7.

652   The Prayer of Our Lord

These words spake Jesus, and lifted up his eyes to heaven, and said,

Father, the hour is come; glorify thy Son, that thy Son also may glorify thee:

I have glorified thee on the earth: I have finished the work which thou gavest me to do.

And now, O Father, glorify thou me with thine own self, with the glory which I had with thee before the world was.

I pray for them: I pray not for the world, but for them which thou hast given me; for they are thine.

And all mine are thine, and thine are mine; and I am glorified in them.

And now I am no more in the world, but these are in the world, and I come to thee.

Holy Father, keep through thine own name those whom thou hast given me, that they may be one, as we are.

While I was with them in the world, I kept them in thy name: those that thou gavest me I have kept, and none of them is lost, but the son of perdition; that the scripture might be fulfilled.

And now come I to thee; and these things I speak in the world, that they might have my joy fulfilled in themselves.

I have given them thy word; and the world hath hated them, because they are not of the world, even as I am not of the world.

I pray not that thou shouldest take them out of the world, but that thou shouldest keep them from the evil.

They are not of the world, even as I am not of the world.

Sanctify them through thy truth: thy word is truth.

As thou hast sent me into the world, even so have I also sent them into the world.

And for their sakes I sanctify myself, that they also might be sanctified through the truth.

Neither pray I for these alone, but for them also which shall believe on me through their word;

That they all may be one; as thou, Father, art in me, and I in thee, that they also may be one in us:

That the world may believe that thou hast sent me.

I in them, and thou in me, that they may be made perfect in one; and that the world may know that thou hast sent me, and hast loved them, as thou hast loved me.

—John 17:1, 4, 5, 9-21, 23.

541

Table of Contents
Unison and Responsive Readings

Scriptural Index

Unison and Responsive Readings

Genesis		Psalms (cont.)		Luke		II Corinthians	
1:1-5	651	119:1-16	618	1:46-53	593	5:1	614
		119:33, 34, 89,		1:68-75	593	9:6-8	639
Exodus		105, 130, 165	647	2:8-20	594		
20:1-17	584	122:1, 2	606	2:28-32	593	**Galatians**	
20:8-11	648	126:6	609	4:16-19	606	5:16-21	620
		134:1, 3	606	9:24	622	5:22-26	621
Leviticus		139:1, 2, 4-6,		11:1-13	627	6:1-10, 16, 18	621
27:30	639	12, 17, 18,		14:25-33	622	6:1-4	643
		23, 24	650	15:4-13, 17,			
Deuteronomy		145	631	20-24	604	**Ephesians**	
6:1, 2, 5-9	643			24:46-49	610	6:1-14	643
8:1, 2, 7-14,		**Isaiah**		24:50, 51	600		
17-20	642	5:11, 22, 23	620			**Philippians**	
		7:14	592	**John**		2:5-11	591
Proverbs		11	592	1:1-14	645	2:9-11	600
1:7-9	643	11:1-5	592	3:1-8, 14-16	612		
3:1-7, 9, 10	644	35	617	4:35	609	**I Thessalonians**	
3:9	639	42:1-4	592	13:34, 35	624	4:13-18	601
20:1	620	53	596	14:1-13	589	5:1-10	601
22:6	643	55	602	14:15-20	646		
23:15, 16, 26	644	62:10	592	14:27	626	**II Timothy**	
23:29, 30, 32	620			15:1-12, 16	632	1:12	614
		Micah		16:5-14, 33	646	2:15	647
Ecclesiastes		4:2	606	16:33	626	3:16, 17	647
11:9	644	4:3-5	626	17:1, 4, 5,			
12:1	644			9-21, 23	652	**Hebrews**	
		Habakkuk		19:17-30	597	4:12	647
Psalms		2:15	620	20:19	648	4:14-16	600
1	585			20:19, 20	598	7:25, 26	600
8:1	641	**Malachi**		20:26-29	598	9:24	600
9:1, 2, 9	650	3:8, 10	639	20:31	647	10:19, 22, 23	600
19:1-6	641					11:1-8, 17-26	638
23	586	**Matthew**		**Acts**		12:14	626
24:1	639	3:13-17	603	1:6-9	610		
26:8	606	5:1-12	619	2:38, 39, 41	603	**I Peter**	
27	634	5:9	626			2:19-21	623
32	613	5:21, 22,		**Romans**		4:10	639
33:6-9	651	38-48	625	6:1-14, 23	616	4:12-16	623
42:1-3, 5, 7, 8	628	6:19-21, 24-34	636	6:3-6, 11	603		
43:1, 3-5	628	7:13, 14, 21-29	605	8:1-14	615	**II Peter**	
46	635	9:35-38	609	8:28	614	1:20, 21	647
46:8-10	626	11:28-30	605	10:12-15	609		
51:1-17	611	20:25-28	591	12	633	**I John**	
84	587	21:10, 11	595	12:18	626	2:1-6, 9-11	624
91	636	22:21	639	15:3-6	623	3:14	614
95:2-7	651	26:17-29	607	15:4	647	4:7-11	624
96	608	28:16-20	610			4:13	614
100	588	28:18, 19	603	**I Corinthians**		5:11-15	614
102:12, 24-27	650	28:1-10	598	3:16, 17	620		
103	629			10:16	607	**Revelation**	
104:10-12,		**Mark**		11:23-26	607	1:5, 6	648
19-24	641	2:27, 28	648	13	590	21:1-7, 9-11,	
107:1-22	649	11:1-11	595	15:20-26, 41-45,		22, 23	640
116:1-8, 9,		16:1, 2, 5, 6	648	47, 49, 53-57	599	22:1-5	640
12-14, 16-18	630			16:2	638		

Index of Scriptural Allusions

Index of Authors, Translators, and Sources

Index of Composers, Arrangers, and Sources

Metrical Index

Index of Tunes

Topical Index

565

Index of First Lines and Titles

Titles are in small capitals.

First lines are in lower case type.